Knowledge Studies in Higher Education

Volume 13

Scope of the Series
Even though knowledge is the main content of teaching and universities are key knowledge producers, scholars have only recently begun to actively explore research on knowledge studies in higher education. As this field of study has grown, it has increasingly overlapped with the research focus of other fields, namely research and science policy, and information studies. However, these three fields have developed independently with little interaction between them, causing our understanding of knowledge to be limited, compartmented, and lacking a multidimensional perspective. This book series is designed to improve knowledge studies in higher education by stimulating interactions between these different approaches.

Coverage in this series includes:

- University and knowledge production
- R & D funding systems
- Education reforms
- Innovation systems for emerging regions
- School curriculum and knowledge
- Social utility of knowledge production
- University research and in-house research
- Research collaborations.

With its comprehensive overview and multidisciplinary perspective, this series provides scholars and policymakers with the theory and data they need to make more informed decisions regarding knowledge research in higher education.

Jill Dickinson • Teri-Lisa Griffiths

Editors

Professional Development for Practitioners in Academia

Pracademia

note the series — knowledge studies
in HE

🐎 Springer

Editors
Jill Dickinson ⓘ
School of Law
University of Leeds
Leeds, UK

Teri-Lisa Griffiths ⓘ
Department of Law and Criminology
Sheffield Hallam University
Sheffield, UK

ISSN 2566-7106   ISSN 2566-8315   (electronic)
Knowledge Studies in Higher Education
ISBN 978-3-031-33745-1   ISBN 978-3-031-33746-8   (eBook)
https://doi.org/10.1007/978-3-031-33746-8

This Springer imprint is published by the registered company Springer Nature Switzerland AG
The registered company address is: Gewerbestrasse 11, 6330 Cham, Switzerland

Acknowledgment

In the spirit of this collection, the editors would like to acknowledge and thank all of their collaborators, contributors, and everyone in their network who has supported their professional and career journeys as pracademics to date.

Acknowledgment

Contents

Chapter 1
Introduction

Jill Dickinson ⓘ and Teri-Lisa Griffiths ⓘ

[handwritten: definition(s).!]

Who or What Are 'Pracademics'?

A pracademic is a professional with dual identities, those of practitioner and academic. Since the term was first coined by Volpe and Chandler (1999), the concept of the pracademic has developed to describe "those who have occupied significant positions as both academics and practitioners" (Posner, 2009, p. 16). Although the term was initially explored within specific fields, Dickinson et al. (2020) examined the phenomena of pracademics using a case study approach, and discovered that pracademics from multi-disciplinary backgrounds shared experiences, distinctive to their pracademic identities. In our view, this finding necessitates further exploration of the pracademic and their influence within the higher education (HE) environment. Although we have provided a working definition here, it is important to highlight that you will find contributors' own definitions of the concept within each chapter. For us, this underlines the diversity and fluidity associated with the term. The scope of this collection will continue the work of investigating multi-disciplinary manifestations of pracademics and pracademia with the aim of elucidating both the features of this distinct group and the cohesions with the rest of the academy.

J. Dickinson
School of Law, University of Leeds, Leeds, UK
e-mail: j.dickinson1@leeds.ac.uk

T.-L. Griffiths (✉)
Department of Law & Criminology, Sheffield Hallam University, Sheffield, UK
e-mail: teri-lisa.griffiths@shu.ac.uk

© The Author(s), under exclusive license to Springer Nature
Switzerland AG 2023
J. Dickinson, T.-L. Griffiths (eds.), *Professional Development for Practitioners in Academia*, Knowledge Studies in Higher Education 13,
https://doi.org/10.1007/978-3-031-33746-8_1

The Emergence and Growth of the Pracademic in Higher Education

In this section, we will explore the emergence of pracademics within the setting of the United Kingdom (UK). It is important to note here that the discourse around pracademia is predominantly focussed on the Western context, although this is changing, for example Chaaban et al. (2021) explore pracademics within Arabia. While this collection brings together contributions from an international perspective, we believe that the UK provides a useful example for understanding the significance of the increasing numbers of pracademics in relation to policy development within HE. Since the late 1980s, the growth of HE within the UK has been driven by policy that focusses on the need for a skilled workforce to meet industry demand. The shift from "elite to mass higher education" (Shattock, 1999, p. 9) resulted in a surge in HE applicants; from 405,000 in 1994 to 750,000 in 2021/22 (Bolton, 2022). This was underpinned by the expansion of the HE sector as a result of the Further and Higher Education Act 1992, which conferred university status on those polytechnic colleges and institutions that offered higher qualifications with a focus on professional vocational degrees, for example engineering and teacher training (Pratt, 1997).

Despite one of the motivations for the Further and Higher Education Act 1992 being to remove the binary organisation of HE within the UK, there are undoubtedly remaining distinctions between post and pre-1992 higher education institutions (HEIs). This can be attributed to the increased marketisation of the sector which was accelerated by the introduction, and increase, of student tuition fees following the recommendations of the Dearing Report (Greenaway & Haynes, 2003) and the Browne Review (Tomlinson, 2017). As a result, HEIs must be able to articulate their distinctive offer to prospective students. Naturally, older HEIs highlighted their research expertise and newer, post-1992 institutions focussed on the quality of their teaching and offer of applied learning. It is for this reason that pracademics were more likely to be employed within post-1992 institutions, although this is changing.

With an increasing and diversifying student body, it is perhaps expected that faculty and professional services would also experience diversification as a result. Examples include academics moving into, and between, managerial roles (Mercer, 2009); professional services staff engaging with research and 'quasi academic' activity (Whitchurch, 2008); and of course, pracademics. The reasons why distinctions between HEIs, and staff roles within them, are more nebulous cannot be separated from wider policy. The introduction of the Research Excellence Framework (REF)[1] and, later, the Teaching Excellence Framework (TEF)[2] require HEIs to categorise the work of their academics in contributing to an overall ranking. There are many criticisms of these grading exercises, including negative impacts on

---

[1] The REF is the UK's system for assessing the quality of research in UK higher education institutions (REF, 2022).

[2] The TEF is a scheme run by the Office for Students that aims to encourage Higher Education providers to deliver excellence in teaching, learning and student outcomes (OfS, 2022).

innovative teaching approaches (Kneale, 2018) and the impulse for HEIs to 'game' the system (Kinsey, 2019). Nevertheless, the outcomes impact funding for every HEI in the UK. Whilst the REF has been in place for some time, the TEF is more recent, meaning that we can expect to see an impact on faculty composition over the next few years. Considering that one of the aspects of quality assessed by the TEF is 'student outcomes and learning gain' (Department for Education, 2017), this increased focus on student skill acquisition may result in pracademics becoming more prevalent across a range of universities, beyond those post-1992 HEIs where applied learning is exalted. This leads us to an exploration of our current understanding of pracademic identities for this burgeoning group.

? much potential for pracademia —o pre 1992's

Pracademic Identities: Professional Values and Esteem

If we consider that professional identity is an ongoing project, influenced by both past experiences and the current context, we can posit that pracademics, and the concept of pracademia, are both evolving alongside the changing HE landscape. Our current understanding of pracademic identities, suggests that professional values and esteem are at the fore. Though we caution against considering this diverse group as a homogeneous class, there are commonalities in experiences which merit exploration.

commonalities exist but ≠ homogeneous grp

Professional Values

Pracademics report that they hold on to professional values from their previous practice, even when they transition full-time into academic roles (Dickinson et al., 2020). This can have implications for their teaching practice and research endeavours, as they navigate their changing practitioner status and their new role as educators and researchers. When pracademics are considering their responsibilities to students as the future professionals, it is reflection, rather than replication, that they hope to foster.

There are some reports of 'accidental academics' who started out as visiting guest lecturers, predicated on their professional experience, subsequently discovering determination to teach full-time. Yet, many pracademics make deliberate transitions from practice to academia, or to a dual role. A common motivation is to influence the future of their previous professions by encouraging students to consider how they might reform practice through a critical exploration of current procedure. Pracademics also tend to report how they wish to foster a closeness to practice, both through maintaining their knowledge of external professional environments and by encouraging students to consider the 'real world' implications of theoretical knowledge. The negotiation of professional identity which can occur within this liminal space may have implications on pracademics' professional esteem.

*practitioners —o educators) identity.
researchers —o educators ? commonalities
                            • (my thoughts)*

Professional Esteem

Newer pracademics occupy an unusual position as both highly experienced professionals and novice academics; it is this unique position which can create both insecurity and assurance for pracademics seeking professional esteem.

Within the marketised HE sector, pracademics recognise their value as 'boundary spanners' (Posner, 2009) between students and the 'real world'. Reports of engaging with students through sharing stories of practice, enabling links with external contacts, and communicating industry concerns, demonstrate how pracademics conceive their contribution to the sector. Pracademics also tend to feel confident that their sector knowledge is a 'selling point' for prospective students, which reflects the policy direction in HE. It is no surprise that pracademics tend to consider problem-based and applied learning as their preferred approach, with team working, autonomy, and relationship-building as specific attributes that pracademics report fostering with their students. However, there is evidence of insecurity and feelings of imposter syndrome related to this asset. By way of illustration, pracademics are aware that their practitioner experience will eventually become dated, particularly if they made a full transition into academia and struggle to maintain links with practice due to the pressures of their new roles. There are also continued reports of pracademics feeling invisible, lonely, and undervalued (Mynott & Zimmatore, 2021) which can similarly impact their sense of self.

In terms of professional identity, our previous research demonstrated how some participants rejected the label of pracademic as 'elitist' or because there was a risk of creating a false dichotomy between different types of academics (Dickinson et al., 2020). Similar misgivings are reported by others (Chaaban et al., 2021; Eacott, 2022). We acknowledge these concerns and have no desire to create divisions between academics. Therefore, before we go any further, we wish to clarify that the intention of this edited collection is not to propose a dichotomy between 'career' academics (namely, those who have followed a more traditional path to academia) and pracademics. We are not suggesting that pracademics are a panacea, for example to the development of university-industry relationships or student employability. Conversely, many career academics also play important roles in responding to these challenges and pracademics are often engaged with research. We believe that pracademics can contribute to a diverse faculty for the benefit of all.

Organisation of This Book

This book will appeal to a broad audience of those interested in the HE sector and its development. The book also includes detailed reflections from experienced professionals, providing a wealth of career management advice for a range of professionals including, pre-transition, novice, and established pracademics. The content is divided into three parts. Although these sections are designed to cover the major concerns around this distinct academic group of pracademics, each chapter can also be explored as a standalone contribution, owing to the multidisciplinary nature of the assembled contributors. Although most of the chapters are situated within a specific disciplinary context, they have a wider application to a range of subjects where there is potential alignment with the same themes. Each chapter opens with an 'At a glance' section, which summarises the content, and ends with some 'Points for Reflection', which the editors hope will provide a framework for further discussion. In Part I, Pracademic Identities, contributors explore the distinctive features of practitioners' transitions into academia and consider future developmental opportunities for pracademics. In Part II, Professional Development, pracademic contributors share their experiences of progressing their careers and professional identities within HE. In Part III, Teaching Practice, the impact of practitioner and pracademic perspectives on pedagogy is considered.

Pracademic Identities

In Chap. 2, Mary Kitchener explores the acculturation of pracademics, presenting ways within which pracademics can manage the tacit practices of academia, and how induction processes might be reconsidered with pracademics in mind. Mary recognises pracademics' contribution to knowledge and advocates for a diverse HE sector.

In Chap. 3, Suzanne Hodgson reflects on her own journey from healthcare practitioner to academic in a discipline where practice is predominant and essential. She recommends peer networking and tailored institutional support to remove barriers to scholarship for new nurse academics.

Moving onto Chap. 4, Michelle Stirk uses the accountancy context to reflect on how pracademics can draw on the skills, knowledge, and experience that they bring with them from practice into academia. Situating her reflections within the broader context, she also considers the future direction of HE, and subsequently, the pracademic.

In Chap. 5, Catherine Wilkinson and Samantha Wilkinson consider the experiences of career academics within disciplines which have a strong practice-focussed culture. They consider how imposter syndrome can manifest within the academy and how varied expertise is valued.

Chapter 6 provides a multi-national perspective as Paul Campbell, Trista Hollweck, and Deborah Netolicky draw on their own narrative accounts to critically examine the concept of pracademia, the knowledge mobilisation of pracademics, and the community spaces within which they operate.

In the last chapter in this section, Chap. 7, Helen Taylor examines how external networks can play a key role in developing multi-faceted professional identity as an early career pracademic, drawing on her own involvement in the Housing Studies Association.

Professional Development

In Chap. 8, Funmi Obembe focuses on the transition between practice and academia, drawing on empirical data and reflecting on her own experiences from the field of technology. She makes recommendations for the consideration of HEIs and individuals.

In Chap. 9, the book's editors report on findings from their research with pracademics and consider how objects may support professional reflection through an exploration of sociomateriality in the context of pracademic career transitions.

Next, in Chap. 10, Caroline Hunter and Helen Carr report on findings from their empirical study into pracademics' perspectives of law school requirements for a PhD and experiences of doctoral studies. Their chapter reflects on the changing landscape of HE and the risks associated with devaluing practitioner experience.

In Chap. 11, Jan Gurung reflects on the challenges of being a research-active colleague whilst balancing a professional services role, highlighting the emergence of hybrid professionals within HE. Jan's chapter provides a challenge to current research practice through the application of her knowledge and insights as a psychotherapist.

In the last chapter of this section, Chap. 12, Steve Johnson and Mark Ellis reflect on their own experiences as pracademics within business schools to explore how the increasing numbers of pracademics presents a valuable opportunity for developing research with impact.

Teaching Practice

In Chap. 13, Sally Skea reflects on her experience of dual practitioner and academic roles and considers how pracademics can influence employability delivery in HE. This contribution encourages the reader to reflect on their positionality when it comes to the purpose of HEIs and HE.

Next, in Chap. 14, Nichola Cadet foregrounds practitioner perspectives of the benefits and challenges of teaching a simulation module within the discipline of criminology.

Within Chap. 15, Alan Forster, Nick Pilcher, Stuart Tennant, Nigel Craig, and Laurent Galbrun chart the key role of pracademics in the field of construction and engineering.

In Chap. 16, Emily Walsh explores pracademia from the perspective of a former commercial property lawyer who joined an interdisciplinary academic team to teach law to real estate students.

In Chap. 17, Omar Madhloom and Laura Bradley explore how pracademics can support clinical legal practice and argue for the importance of encouraging students to develop their autonomy for future practice. Whilst their contribution focusses on the legal context, there are reflections for those interested in experiential learning more broadly.

Finally, Chap. 18, Abinash Panda explores the concept of the 'boundary spanner' in detail, through a consideration of how pracademics within business schools can work towards developing business leadership competences with their students.

Each of the chapters in these three parts includes an 'At a glance' section at the outset and all contributions close with some editorial prompts to support readers' reflections on the content.

In the concluding chapter, the editors draw together the main contributions made by the chapters and identify cross-cutting themes. In doing so, they reflect on the opportunities presented by the increasing attention being paid to pracademics and the future potential for the development of the pracademic role as an integral and important part of the HE context. The conclusion ends with a call from the editors for continuing, meaningful dialogue around the value of pracademia to HE stakeholders, with the aim of suggesting potential directions for the development of future research and evidence-informed intervention.

References

Bolton, P. (2022). *Higher education student numbers* (House of Commons Library research briefing 7857). https://researchbriefings.files.parliament.uk/documents/CBP-7857/CBP-7857.pdf

Chaaban, Y., Sellami, A., Sawalhi, R., & Elkhouly, M. (2021). Exploring perceptions of pracademics in an Arab context. *Journal of Professional Capital and Community, 7*(1), 83–97.

Department for Education. (2017). *Teaching excellence and student outcomes framework specification*. Department for Education. https://assets.publishing.service.gov.uk/government/uploads/system/uploads/attachment_data/file/658490/Teaching_Excellence_and_Student_Outcomes_Framework_Specification.pdf

Dickinson, J., Fowler, A., & Griffiths, T. L. (2020). Pracademics? Exploring transitions and professional identities in higher education. *Studies in Higher Education, 47*(2), 290–304. https://doi.org/10.1080/03075079.2020.1744123

Eacott, S. (2022). Pracademia: An answer but not the answer to an enduring question. *Journal of Professional Capital and Community, 7*(1), 57–70.

Greenaway, D., & Haynes, M. (2003). Funding higher education in the UK: The role of fees and loans. *The Economic Journal, 113*(485), 150–166.

Kinsey, D. (2019). Understanding the REF and TEF, and what they mean for postgraduate students. *A Guide for Psychology Postgraduates, 96*, 96–101.

Kneale, P. E. (2018). Where might pedagogic research focus to support students' education in a REF-TEF world. *Journal of Geography in Higher Education, 42*(4), 487–497.

Mercer, J. (2009). Junior academic-manager in higher education: An untold story? *International Journal of Educational Management., 23*, 348–359.

Mynott, J. P., & Zimmatore, M. (2021). Pracademic productive friction: Boundary crossing and pressure points. *Journal of Professional Capital and Community, 7*(1), 45–56.

Office for Students (OfS). (2022, October 7). *About the TEF.* https://www.officeforstudents.org.uk/advice-and-guidance/teaching/about-the-tef/

Posner, P. L. (2009). The pracademic: An agenda for re-engaging practitioners and academics. *Public Budgeting & Finance, 29*(1), 12–26.

Pratt, J. (1997). *The polytechnic experiment: 1965–1992.* Society for Research into Higher Education & The Open University Press.

Research Excellence Framework (REF). (2022). *About the REF.* https://www.ref.ac.uk/about-the-ref/

Shattock, M. L. (1999). The impact of the Dearing report on UK higher education. *Higher Education Management, 11*(1), 7–18.

Tomlinson, M. (2017). Student perceptions of themselves as 'consumers' of higher education. *British Journal of Sociology of Education, 38*(4), 450–467.

Volpe, M. R., & Chandler, D. (1999). Resolving conflicts in institutions of higher education: Challenges for pracademics. *CNCR-Hewlett Foundation Seed Grant White Papers, 8.* https://readingroom.law.gsu.edu/seedgrant/8

Whitchurch, C. (2008). Shifting identities and blurring boundaries: The emergence of third space professionals in UK higher education. *Higher Education Quarterly, 62*(4), 377–396.

Dr Jill Dickinson is an Associate Professor in Law at the University of Leeds. A former Solicitor specialising in Real Estate, Jill's research interests encompass place-making, learning landscapes, and professional development. As an SFHEA, Jill was selected to review the Advance HE Global Teaching Excellence Awards and her approach to research has been recognized through the Emerald Literati Awards.

Teri-Lisa Griffiths is a Senior Lecturer in Criminology at Sheffield Hallam University. Her teaching is focused on the development of student employability and academic skills, working with external partners to provide relevant and high-quality experiences for students. Her research interests are student engagement and professional development. As a former careers adviser, Teri-Lisa is interested in how education and professional identity can influence career and development choices. She is a co-founder of the pracademia community of practice.

Part I
Pracademic Identities

Chapter 2
'Don't Take Your Briefcase': Navigating a Career Change from Professional Practice to the Academic Role

Mary Kitchener

Abstract This chapter will feature key considerations for prospective and recently transitioned pracademics to understand the regularities of working in higher education (HE) as an academic. Recognising that plenty of educational practices and procedures in HE are understood tacitly, the day to day working patterns, including the type, pace, freedom and flexibility of work, will be brought into focus. Moreover, the paradox between gaining employment predicated on professional knowledge and skills – and how this is not comparably recognised as valuable once in HE – will be highlighted. Accentuating what type of expertise is valued, pracademics can set to reposition professional knowledge into explicit universal understanding. These are unique challenges, associated with transitioning from a diverse range of professional backgrounds to an academic role, that may not be considered in induction support. Yet the rising value of pracademics in HE, not just for their ability to ensure that graduates continue to meet employers' requirements, but also a familiarity with working in a market economy, can have clear benefits to HE. Therefore, recommendations on approaches to aid a successful transition from profession to academic will be outlined.

Keywords Pracademic transitions · Pracademic experiences · Professional knowledge · Professional development · Induction · Induction support · Induction handbook · Mentoring · Mentors · Higher education sector · Academic literacy · Teaching experience · Teacher training

M. Kitchener (✉)
Oxford Centre for Academic Enhancement and Development, Oxford Brookes University, Wheatley Campus, Oxford, UK
e-mail: m.kitchener@brookes.ac.uk

© The Author(s), under exclusive license to Springer Nature
Switzerland AG 2023
J. Dickinson, T.-L. Griffiths (eds.), *Professional Development for Practitioners in Academia*, Knowledge Studies in Higher Education 13,
https://doi.org/10.1007/978-3-031-33746-8_2

11

At a Glance
- Reports participant experiences of their transition into an academic role from practice
- Considers some of the challenges of working as an academic
- Highlights the increasing recognition and value of pracademic knowledge
- Makes recommendations to aid a successful transition, which includes more bespoke support for pracademics to ensure positive and enriching transitions to an academic career.

Introduction

The transition from professional practice to academia should be seen as an entire career change. It involves: the move into a different role (academic); a different set of skills (teaching, research and service); a different sector; and a different organisational culture (a culture that, arguably, has "many different quirks" (Simendinger et al., 2000)).

Kamler and Thompson (2006) contend that a new academic will, traditionally, prepare through the process of writing and defending a piece of original academic work to gain a Doctor of Philosophy (PhD), while situated within the scholarly community. This apprenticeship position involves socialisation into the academic role and thus can be viewed as a career academic pathway (Barnacle & Mewburn, 2010).

However, a pracademic is unlikely to get an apprenticeship to be an academic. Instead, the equivalent socialisation would have been in a profession-vocation. Thus, it is unsurprising that the transition from professional practice to academia is viewed as challenging (see, for example, Simendinger et al. (2000), Diekelmann (2004), and Blenkinsopp and Stalker (2004)). Wilson et al. (2014) identified culture shock as a signature experience for those crossing from professional practice to a career as an academic. Citing the first six months to a year as being the most challenging period of transition, they identified career change challenges such as workload, stress, and pace of work as explicit examples of transitioning from industry to Higher Education (HE). Equally, van Lankveld et al. (2017) found that even new lecturers from a teaching background had widespread anxiety, self-doubt, and feelings of inadequacy during the early years in the post.

Myers (2017) likened the transition to the switching of identifying with one tribe to another – the respective tribes being professional practice and academia. These feelings can foster a strong sense of "belonging" to the tribe, but the opposite can also be true. It is possible that a feeling of alienation will be experienced. Identifying with the professional practice tribe can create a feeling of *"otherness"* when new to HE (Myers, 2017, p. 42). Furthermore, Shreeve (2011) argued that when new to the academic role, the lack of understanding around how professional experience was valued in HE diminished pracademics' status and security. This was further undermined by new and unfamiliar academic practices, and widespread presumed knowledge related to the systems and processes in HE, suggesting that many practices in HE are tacit.

Additionally, there may be a sense of loss for previous professional status and recognition as Gourlay (2011a, b), Shreeve (2011), and Smith and Boyd (2012) identified. However, Simendinger et al. (2000, p. 106) highlighted how the change from professional status to that of an early career academic, possibly on a decreased salary band, can cause tensions as well as loss of power and prestige, as the transitioning professionals come to recognise that they will need to prove themselves again in a new cultural environment. Thus, it is not surprising that van Lankveld et al. (2017) found that lecturers felt compelled to cite their professional status for credibility within teaching.

What is cumulatively evident in these studies is the gap between experienced practice-rich professionals entering into a relatively unknown pracademic role with feasibly inadequate consideration to the transfer of knowledge and skills. What is required is for pracademics to have an awareness of the nature and expectations of an academic role and, equally, effective support to help guide successful transitions into HE.

Methodology

Practices and Procedures of Working in an Academic Role

Academic work is the creating and sharing of knowledge by individuals or teams with a prominent level of expertise or skills (Coates & Goedegebuure, 2010). The academic role involves several key duties – namely planning, designing, and delivery of teaching and/or research (Higher Education Statistics Agency, 2014) – overlapping with other roles, such as managing, writing, and networking which shapes the role over time (Blaxter et al., 1998). The accepted normalised practice, assumptions, and behaviours that represent the academic working culture may be embodied and unobserved by career academics but are likely to be novel to pracademics.

The following points highlight findings from my doctoral research (Kitchener, 2021) on how pracademics experienced the change from their professional practice to the role of a full-time academic. The research adopted an ethnographic, narrative, interpretivist approach to capture the voices of 16 neophyte and established pracademics from multiple higher education institutions (HEIs) across the United Kingdom (UK). Through conversational-expository methods – blog posts and comments, semi-structured interviews, and conversations on the model of the BBC's Listening Project (BBC, 2017) – the narrative accounts illuminated the following themes.

Findings

Academic First Impressions: Comparisons to Previous Role

> … a very different working environment that I had ever experienced before. (Dave[1])

As the quote from Dave illustrates, the workplace patterns of an academic role may be distinctive in comparison to a former professional career. The findings highlighted several first impressions that participants remarked on involving the working patterns of being an academic.

> I love the freedoms and sometimes have to check that I'm not dreaming! (Dave)

It was highlighted that interactions with other colleagues were limited. In fact, one participant stated that they could spend a whole week at work and not see some colleagues, particularly if they did not work in shared offices. This, for some, was a challenge, as they had experience of working in a team environment. Yet, the limited interactions may relate to the flexibility of work. Freedom regarding where to work as an academic was emphasised and declared as diametrically different from previous working practices. For example, in a clinical setting of a hospital:

> I didn't need to put my 'out of office' on detailing which room I'm in each session of the day. I didn't need to tell people if I was off to use the facilities either! Very different from clinical practice there. (Richard)

This extreme change in day-to-day working practices was referred to by one participant as "…in the Twilight Zone" (Ayden). While some relished the freedom and flexibility of working patterns, others required a period of readjustment. What was clear was the nature of the role held a different rhythm and pace to that of many professions whose pace was governed by being reactive and directed by the immediate needs of their service users.

> Planning work commitments is done months in advance, difficult when you've been living for the next 10 minutes and what emergency will fly through the door for the last 12 years. (Richard)

What was emphasised was the change to the *pace of work* that reflected HEIs having a slower pace of work than the participants had experienced in their professional background:

> [I was] told to slow down. (Sandra)

The change in pace was often viewed positively as an opportunity to pursue passions and specialisms. However, the new pace required gaining a different set of competencies:

> Having the change [chance] to read research again was exciting, but getting focused and finding a starting point took time. (Simeon)

---

[1] Pseudonyms have been allocated throughout to protect participant confidentiality.

Reading research papers requires a high cognitive load to concentrate and comprehend. Significantly, the pace of work reflects the practices that are valued in HE and the sector has created the environment for this to flourish, for example providing quiet spaces to work.

These experiences resonate with that of *Sophie* (Gourlay, 2011b). Moving from practice within clinical nursing to an academic career, *Sophie* considered that she had "landed on the moon" and paradoxically she felt "lucky to be here, but at the same time unworthy...I am in mourning for my previous clinical life" (Gourlay, 2011b, p. 598). *Sophie* felt a sense of "loss" with the change in her status from that of an experienced clinician to an academic who lacked experience and was unfamiliar with postgraduate study and research. She compared her skills and experiences to having different "tools of the trade" in that she felt that she spoke in practical, clinical terms whilst her colleagues spoke in theoretical, abstract terms (Gourlay, 2011b, p. 598).

Academic First Impressions: The Role of an Academic

One point of interest was regarding self-identification as an academic. Although pracademics held the title, the role, the responsibilities, and, in most cases, a combination of HE qualifications and professional practice experience, somehow on the journey from practice to academia, pracademics had recognised that they were not a "traditional academic". Potentially this could illustrate the transitions around identifying with one tribe, then another. As indicated earlier, it is possible that a feeling of not belonging, or "otherness", when new to an academic role could be experienced (Myers, 2017, p. 42). This uncertainty in self-identification suggested that pracademics had not completely transitioned to the role yet.

One notable contention in transitioning to the role that was raised by the participants was the seeming lack of value placed on professional knowledge.

Professional and Academic Knowledge

The Knowledge Paradox

One of the significant challenges that pracademics face when arriving at academic employment is the paradox between gaining employment predicated on professional knowledge and skills – and how this is not comparably recognised as valuable once in HE (Kitchener, 2021). This can come as a surprise as the academic posts were often offered based on industrial experience. Yet some participants perceived that once they began in an HEI, their professional experience seemed to be no longer valued.

Moreover, this suggests a paradox. Arguably it is a practitioners' professional knowledge that has enabled them to be employed in HE, yet it seems that once in an academic post, the value of this knowledge rapidly decreases. Compounding this loss is the fact that, as full-time academics, pracademics are no longer holding a substantive position that reinforces and updates their professional knowledge, which can result in a rapid loss of industry credentials. Yet, Wilson et al. (2014) assert that professional practice is equal to that of academic knowledge, as it is a vital part of the curriculum for students entering the world of work. However, the value of such knowledge seems not to be fully realised, even in post-1992 HEIs[2] that have a history of provisioning professional qualifications.

> I suppose I had felt that I had gone from being a really highly competent, experienced, knowledgeable common senior member of the profession into a team of people… but perhaps not seeing me for the knowledge and expertise that I had. (Amanda)

Recognising the nature and value of knowledge in HE can help aid the transition from professional practice to the academic role. However, as Sandra warns us, it necessitates a period of time to adapt professional knowledge to gain recognition:

> Get over being an accountant, learn to be an academic…It is okay not to feel you do not know anything as industry knowledge transfers – just not right away. (Sandra)

Accentuating what type of expertise is valued, pracademics can set to reposition professional knowledge as explicit universal understanding. Furthermore, gaining qualifications such as a master's or a doctoral degree can help the pracademic with this transition by providing opportunities to engage in academic practices.

Yet, a dualism between professions and academia is a misconception. The sector and industry have a porous boundary and have always been interdependent. What needs to be questioned is the type of expertise that is valued and whether this knowledge reflects the prevailing current position of the academic world.

The Rise of the Pracademic?

Shapin (2012) reflected that academics were usually associated with working in a so-called "ivory tower". Yet this phrase seemed an incongruent description to reflect the current socio-political context of HE as, arguably, the academic role has been affected by the systematic move to a mass system from an elite model (see, for example, Trow, 1973; Gordon & Whitchurch, 2010; Collini, 2012). Thus, the UK economy is the significant influencer of the prevailing socio-political climate within HE. This has shifted the dominant discourse of government interventions towards a free-market ideology (Delucchi & Korgen, 2002) with an economic agenda (Collini, 2012), resulting in the marketisation of HE (Fox, 2002). The consequence is the dominance of neo-liberal ideology operationalised through new public managerialism (Archer, 2008).

---

[2] Former polytechnics or Higher Education colleges that were granted university status in the United Kingdom with the Further and Higher Education Act, 1992.

The impact has been to transform the academic role into one within which academics are measured by both teaching performance, and retention and employment outcomes of students, with an additional need to gain recognition for high-impact research (University and College Union, 2009). Such UK government interventions, such as the Teaching Excellence and Student Outcomes Framework (TEF), have increasingly positioned the student as a customer with countervailing pressure to provide a consistent student experience. Consequently, there has been a change in the self-understanding of academics (Billot, 2010) and, significantly, a suggestion that HEIs are situated within the tensions of the current socio-political context and the role of the sector in society.

A significant tension seems to be that many institutions, particularly since the Higher Education Act 2004, have been transformed into quasi-autonomous organisations, regulated by market conditions. The trend seems directed towards combining academic and vocational pathways and more vocational progression into HE (UK Commission for Employment and Skills, 2016) as success data is measured by high-level employment outcomes. Returning to my research, the participants were mostly drawn from post-1992 HEIs which hints that such institutions may have never left their vocational traditions. Yet, this seems to contradict why pracademics recognised the tension between their experiences of working in an academic post and this broader neo-liberal ideology.

> HE is badly managed and does not understand students...we all need to be student-centred. (Sandra)

> I was part of the – project which involved a pitch, I was trying to build my research profile as an academic which again is something you do as an academic, and we got encouraged to put in for, for this pitch and we had the first meeting I looked at the package of work which had been assigned to us and in the meeting, I said 'Well okay that looks like, like three month's work' or thereabouts. One of the other people said 'You better be kidding, it's at least four years', (laughter) and I said 'Well it is only really three months' work, this isn't a huge amount of work' yes, yes but his point was it was going to take four years because we've got four years funding, right, and that was a real kind of wow moment for me because in business you'd never do this. (Jane)

The polytechnic association with professional and vocational provision (Whitburn et al., 1980; Robinson, 1968) seems to accord with the dominant rhetoric of this agenda. Now that HE in the UK is a mixture of polytechnic and older university traditions, with a neoliberal ideology operationalised through new public managerialism (Archer, 2008), it is now focused on measuring employability impact. Thus, post-1992 universities have competed heavily for students in relation to both academic and vocational programmes. This seems to suggest that HE providers are increasingly conflicted as to where they situate themselves within the 'market'. This may well challenge the dominance of vocationally relevant programmes being offered in the post-1992 sector as the pre-1992 sector and Russell Group[3] procure

---

[3] The Russell Group is a 24 member collective of UK universities described as "world-class, research-intensive universities" who "produce more than two-thirds of the world leading research produced in UK universities." (Russell Group, n.d.)

market share. This contrasts with how professional education was previously viewed by society as the potentially inferior to traditional academic programmes (Faskhoodi et al., 2016).

Significantly, this recognises the need for pracademics. Practical, work-based knowledge and skills will intensify across the sector (Andalo, 2011). Moreover, HE is also recognised as fundamental in the credentialing process for entry into certain professions (Collini, 2012; GuildHE, 2019). This ideological direction is fuelled by the rise in the number of professions (Macdonald, 1999), particularly in industrial, capitalist nations (Yee, 2001), and an increase in the number of people anticipated to hold higher qualifications between 2014 and 2024 (UK Commission for Employment and Skills, 2016). Finally, the introduction of a new regulator for the sector – the Office for Students (OfS) – by the Higher Education and Research Act 2017 has set one of the critical metrics for success as being improved employability (Universities UK, 2016).

This may be illustrating a disconnection between the current academic culture and the prevailing socio-political climate. While it is plausible to suggest that the two distinctive types of knowledge – intellectual and practical – potentially hold different values in HE, market conditions seem to place value on professional experience, knowledge, skills, and expertise. Myers (2017, p. 45) suggests that, with the introduction of the REF and TEF as measures of impact and reach across HE in the UK, an "intellectual cross-training" between practitioners and academics should "strengthen all composite parts", necessarily leading to better outcomes for all. For example, Dickinson et al. (2020) noted how pracademics put significant value on highlighting the connection between theory and practice to their students.

To strengthen these parts, the current support mechanisms for early-career academics must recognise this diversity and the value that pracademics bring to an academic role. Worryingly, since the Dearing Report (National Committee of Inquiry into Higher Education, 1997) emphasised the need for induction support for academics, particularly formal induction, processes have tended not to recognise the diversity of backgrounds on entry to an academic role (Scott, 1995; Bandow et al., 2007; Kitchener, 2021). Yet, most academic staff inflow had come from a professional background (Higher Education Statistics Agency, 2020). This *one-size-fits-all approach* to induction, alongside assumptions made by institutions around pracademics' understanding of academic working practices illustrated earlier, (Kitchener, 2021) indicate adaptations of induction processes are required.

The following recommendations are made to enhance the unique transition from professional background to the demands of an academic role.

Conclusion

The following support strategies can enhance the transition to an academic role. These support strategies comprise drawing upon established pracademics as mentors; developing a dynamic academic handbook to help pracademics in their new field; and emphasising the practical craft of teaching within threshold lecturer preparation programmes. These interventions may serve to better acknowledge the diversity of backgrounds of those making the transition into an academic role and to recognise possible assumptions embedded within the prevailing practices.

Established Pracademics as Mentors

Used frequently within HE, initial professional development often involves the formal support of a mentor (Baume & Kahn, 2004). A mentor is often seen as a role model. However, the approach for allocating a mentor can be indiscriminate, as well as confusing, for both mentor and mentee, which consequently leads to anxiety (Baume & Kahn, 2004).

Yet the value of a mentor lies in not only being able to familiarise pracademics with the academic role but also working as a role model to aid in shaping their provisional academic self (Ibarra, 1999). However, mentor support can be haphazard and, when it is good, it can often be attributed to luck (Kitchener, 2021). Having in place systematic support for all pracademics, particularly with a mentor from a similar background, offers the opportunity to discuss the academic role and responsibilities. This would help in comprehending the number of quirks that Simendinger et al. (2000) identified which professionals entering an academic role within HE found. Furthermore, as Martensson (2000) recognised, conversations could be utilised to deconstruct the tacit knowledge that pracademics were assumed to already know.

Dynamic Academic Handbook

Social interactions can act as a means to draw out organisational tacit knowledge so that it becomes explicit knowledge (Nonaka, 1994). By unpacking tacit knowledge with an experienced mentor, pracademics could then make this knowledge explicit and share this through a dynamic academic handbook. Similar to induction guides that are often utilised to onboard new staff members, this dynamic handbook would be issued by each department. The ownership of the document would be held by the department for both established and neophyte pracademics, as well as career academics, to add contributions. Care must be taken to ensure that the handbook does not become too subjective. One way to overcome this is to have the handbook as a standing item for discussion during team meetings to foster a sense of collegiality and highlight the value that new and existing academics jointly bring to HE.

This could be a substantial active guide to aid pracademics in unpacking the role as well as contributing to the continual development of the department by drawing on prior experiences that have developed through non-traditional academic routes. This handbook, as an asynchronous tool, could offer clarity as an ongoing recorded conversation for new and existing pracademics who may be unclear as to the expectations of the university systems, faculty, and the academic role. Furthermore, the handbook would further assist what Bandow et al. (2007) and Simendinger et al. (2000) recommended for finding the benchmarks of expectations in each institution.

Adaptations to Threshold Lecturer Preparation Programmes

Threshold lecturer preparation programmes, such as the Postgraduate Certificate in Teaching in Higher Education qualification, are a frequent probationary requirement for gaining credibility as a lecturer. These programmes can be helpful as they offer an informal meeting place for discussing the processes and procedures involved in an academic role and the context of HE (Harland, 2012). However, Trowler and Cooper (2002) highlighted a mismatch between what was promoted on the threshold lecturer preparation programmes and the experiences of neophyte academic teaching staff, suggesting a disconnect between the immediate needs of lecturers' practice and the programme content. Furthermore, some concerns were raised as to the knowledge that the facilitators assumed that pracademics had on arrival to the programme; for example, the assumption that all participants were already familiar with pedagogical terms (Kitchener, 2021). These observations by pracademics who have not had a background in HE, like post-doctoral academics have, seem justifiable.

However, this assumption that theoretical knowledge is not as valued as practical strategies for facilitating teaching seems unwise. While it would be good to increase the quotient of craft knowledge training in threshold lecturer preparation programmes. it is also crucial that new lecturers develop rich conceptions of teaching, along with an understanding of HE pedagogy and language and, particularly, skills for challenging didactic models and notions of knowledge transmission. As Prosser and Trigwell (1999) argue, good teaching involves lecturers commanding a well-articulated view of the rationale for their teaching practices, an understanding of the variation in how students learn, and how they can guide and shape the teaching context to ensure effective learning.

These findings highlight the disparity in perception of the value of such programmes. For example, it seems that such programmes are applying a deep approach to teaching, the "what works" and "why it works" rationale proffered by Prosser and Trigwell (1999) requiring a deep approach to neophyte academics' learning (Marton & Säljö, 1976). However, it could be seen that this was meeting a surface approach to learning (Biggs, 1999), reflecting the time pressure that some might be experiencing. There is a case for being mindful when developing the curriculum to ensure that basic 'HE teaching skills' are developed at the start of threshold lecturer preparation programmes. Adapting the curriculum towards practical skills, such as using classroom technology, the methods of teaching in lectures and seminars, provision of effective academic advising, and use of questioning techniques to facilitate learning, for example, could be considered. However, it needs to be highlighted that this would be the pedagogical equivalent of fast food; it will cure an immediate need, but it will not sustain.

Academic Literacy Support

Some pracademics may not have had experiences of being an HE student and thus, assumptions cannot be made about the knowledge of academic literacy that they gained through previous qualifications. For example, two participants in my research completed their professional qualifications in their industry and had not attended an HEI. Thus, there is a need for support mechanisms to make space available for developing and enhancing specific academic skills, such as academic writing conventions, critical thinking, and digital competence. The use of online platforms, similar to study skill sites, often available for students in HE, could be made available as information portals to encourage pracademics towards self-directed, 'pick and mix' engagement or, if permissible, one-to-one bespoke support sessions.

Conversations About the Academic Role

While the earlier recommendations have focused on engaging in supportive activities within a pracademic's institution, a useful strategy advocated by Dickinson et al. (2020) could be to connect pracademics into a wider community. This could be to a national field of HE through a network of notably new pracademics who are experiencing, or who have experienced, a transition from practice into HE such as the Pracademics HE Advance Connect Network (see: https://connect.advance-he. ac.uk/topics/16122/feed), or similar.

Recommendation to Enhance HE from Pracademics

Another aspect is to recognise what pracademics bring into HE through encouraging learning from each other as part of a community of practice to help foster a sense of legitimacy to their skills and knowledge. Pracademics, with this distinctive, interstitial position between public and professional practice spheres, could act as a resource for harmonising discourses and practices.

Pracademics have experience in working for clients in a manner that recognises the demands of a market economy. In parallel, pracademics also have an extensive experience of working within a profession and, are characterised by being situated to act, and advise, on behalf of others (Parsons, 1954) as well as demonstrating allegiance to ethics and the societal commonweal. Yet, some pracademics may have entered an academic role due to the frustrations of working within a market economy. So, pracademics may not have placed all-embracing value on this economic ideology recognising, through their professional experiences, possible moral and political consequences. Thus, pracademics could offer guidance and lessons learned to inform and enhance HE practices.

Pracademics should be valued and supported in HE through induction practices that recognise and cherish the diversity of backgrounds. Symbiotically, pracademics can support HE through the changing nature of the sector to ensure student learning and outcomes are met and, notably, the distinctive value of HE as a place for debate and dialogue is not lost.

Points for Reflection
- Kitchener demonstrates how pracademics experience a complete career change and asserts that the university sector should not assume that pracademics have prior knowledge of the conventions of HE and an academic role. Is this your experience, or not?
- The chapter examines how employment as an academic is predicated on professional knowledge and skills, yet once pracademics commence their role, the value of this knowledge decreases. How can we ensure that pracademics can maintain their professional knowledge? Is this necessary, or not?
- The author suggests that pracademics are well placed to support the changing HE sector. Do you see any advantages or disadvantages to this proposition?

References

Andalo, D. (2011, March 21). The rise of the dual professional lecturers. *The Guardian.* Available: https://www.theguardian.com/higher-education-network/2011/mar/21/part-time-lecturers-dual-profession

Archer, L. (2008). Younger academics' construction of 'authenticity', 'success' and professional identity. *Studies in Higher Education, 33*(4), 385–403.

Bandow, D., Minsky, B., & Voss, R. (2007). Reinventing the future: Investigating career transitions from industry to Academia. *Journal of Human Resource Education, 1*, 23–37.

Barnacle, R., & Mewburn, I. (2010). Learning networks and the journey of 'becoming a Doctor'. *Studies in Higher Education, 35*, 433–444.

Baume, D., & Kahn, P. (Eds.). (2004). *Enhancing staff and educational development.* RoutledgeFalmer.

BBC (2017) *Listening Projects.* Available: https://www.bbc.co.uk/sounds/brand/b01cqx3b. Accessed 29 Sep 2017.

Biggs, J. (1999). *Teaching for quality learning in university*. Society for Research into Higher Education.

Billot, J. (2010). The imagined and the real: Identifying the tensions for academic identity. *Higher Education Research & Development, 29*(6), 709–721. https://doi.org/10.1080/0729436 0.2010.487201

Blaxter, L., Hughes, C., & Tight, M. (1998). Writing on academic careers. *Studies in Higher Education, 23*(3), 281–295. https://doi.org/10.1080/03075079812331380256

Blenkinsopp, J., & Stalker, B. (2004). Identity work in the transition from manager to management academic. *Management Decision, 42*(3/4), 418–429.

Coates, H., & Goedegebuure, L. (2010). *Research briefing changing academic profession*. https:// melbourne-cshe.unimelb.edu.au/__data/assets/pdf_file/0007/2565070/Why-we-need-to-reconceptualise-Australias-future-academic-workforce.pdf

Collini, S. (2012). *What are universities for?* Penguin.

Delucchi, M., & Korgen, K. (2002). "We're the customer – We pay the tuition". Student consumerism among undergraduate sociology majors. *Teaching Sociology, 30*(January), 100–107.

Dickinson, J., Fowler, A., & Griffiths, T. (2020). Pracademics? Exploring transitions and professional identities in higher education. *Studies in Higher Education*. https://doi.org/10.108 0/03075079.2020.1744123

Diekelmann, N. (2004). New pedagogies for nursing: Experienced practitioners as new faculty: New pedagogies and new possibilities. *Journal of Nursing Education, 43*(3), 101–103.

Faskhoodi, B., Zarghami, S., Ghaedi, Y., & Barkhordari, R. (2016). The relation of vocational training to academic education. *Journal of Family and Research, 13*(33), 77–95.

Fox, C. (2002). The massification of higher education. In D. Hayes & R. Wynyard (Eds.), *The McDonaldization of higher education*. Bergin & Garvey.

Gordon, G., & Whitchurch, C. (2010). *Academic professional identities in higher education*. Routledge.

Gourlay, L. (2011a). New lecturers and the myth of 'communities of practice'. *Studies in Continuing Education, 33*(1), 67–77.

Gourlay, L. (2011b). "I'd landed on the Moon': A new lecturer leaves the academy. *Teaching in Higher Education, 16*(5), 591–601. https://doi.org/10.1080/13562517.2011.605548

GuildHE. (2019). *Our policy position*. https://guildhe.ac.uk/

Harland, T. (2012). *University teaching. An introductory guide*. Routledge.

Higher Education Statistics Agency. (2014). *Staff in Higher Education Institutions 2008/09; 2009/10; 2010/11; 2011/12; 2012/13*. Higher Education Statistics Agency. https://www.hesa. ac.uk/data-and-analysis/staff/working-in-he

Higher Education Statistics Agency. (2020). *Inflow and outflow of academic staff*. www.hesa. ac.uk/data-and-analysis/staff/location

Ibarra, H. (1999). Provisional selves: Experimenting with image and identity in professional adaptation. *Administrative Science Quarterly, 44*, 764–791.

Kamler, B., & Thompson, P. (2006). *Helping doctoral students write. Pedagogies for supervision*. Routledge.

Kitchener, M. (2021). *Supporting academics' full-time transition from professional practice to university. A qualitative study*. Unpublished EdD thesis, Oxford Brookes University.

Macdonald, K. (1999). *The sociology of professions*. Sage.

Martensson, M. (2000). A critical review of knowledge management as a tool. *Journal of Knowledge Management, 4*(3), 204–216.

Marton, F., & Säljö, R. (1976). On qualitative differences in learning – I: Outcome and process. *British Journal of Educational Psychology, 46*, 4–11.

Myers, P. (2017). From creative practitioner to academic: Navigation, transformation and identity. *New Vistas, 3*(1), 40–45.

National Committee of Inquiry into Higher Education. (1997). *Higher education in the learning society. Report of the national inquiry into higher education* (The Dearing Report). HMSO.

Nonaka, I. (1994). A dynamic theory of organizational knowledge creation. *Organization Science, 5*(1), 14–37.

Parsons, T. (1954). The professions and social structure. In T. Parsons (Ed.), *Essays in sociological theory* (pp. 34–49). The Free Press.

Prosser, M., & Trigwell, K. (1999). *Understanding learning and teaching: The experience in higher education*. Society for Research into Higher Education and Open University Press.

Robinson, E. (1968). *The new polytechnics*. Penguin.

Russell Group. (n.d.). *Our universities*. Russell Group. https://russellgroup.ac.uk/about/our-universities

Scott, P. (1995). *The meanings of mass higher education*. Open University Press.

Shapin, S. (2012). The Ivory tower: The history of a figure of speech and its cultural uses. *British Society for the History of Science, 45*(1), 1–27. https://doi.org/10.1017/S0007087412000011845

Shreeve, A. (2011). Being in two camps: Conflicting experiences for practice-based academics. *Studies in Continuing Education, 33*(1), 79–91.

Simendinger, E., Puia, G., Kraft, K., & Jasperson, M. (2000). The career transition from practitioner to academic. *Career Development International, 5*(2), 106–111.

Smith, C., & Boyd, P. (2012). Becoming an academic: The reconstruction of identity by recently appointed lecturers in Nursing, Midwifery, and the Allied Health professions. *Innovations in Education and Teaching International, 49*(1), 63–72. https://doi.org/10.1080/1470329 7.2012.647784

Trow, M. (1973). *Problems in the transition from Elite to mass higher education*. Carnegie Commission on Higher Education.

Trowler, P., & Cooper, A. (2002). Teaching and learning regimes: Implicit theories and recurrent practices in the enhancement of teaching and learning through educational development programmes. *Higher Education Research & Development., 21*(3), 221–240.

UK Commission for Employment and Skills. (2016, April). *Working futures 2014–2024*. https://dera.ioe.ac.uk/26069/1/Working_Futures_final_evidence_report.pdf

Universities UK. (2016, September). *Higher education in England: Provision, skills and graduates*. https://www.universitiesuk.ac.uk/policy-and-analysis/reports/Documents/2016/higher-education-in-england-provision-skills-and-graduates.pdf

University and College Union. (2009, January 25). *UCU statement on academic freedom*. https://www.ucu.org.uk/academicfreedom

van Lankveld, T., Schoonenboom, J., Volman, M., Croiset, G., & Beishuizen, J. (2017). Developing a teacher identity in the university context: A systematic review of the literature. *Higher Education Research and Development, 36*(2), 325–342.

Whitburn, J., Mealing, M., & Cox, C. (1980). *People in polytechnics: A survey of polytechnic staff and students, 1972–1973*. [data collection]. UK Data Service. SN:832. https://doi.org/10.5255/UKDA-SN-832-1.

Wilson, M. J., Wood, L., Solomonides, I., Dixon, P., & Goos, M. (2014). Navigating the career transition from industry to Academia. *Industry and Higher Education, 28*(1), 5–13. https://pdfs.semanticscholar.org/ef7c/d023b0cc8b92534973541f658e034866dc73.pdf

Yee, H. (2001). *The concept of profession: A historical perspective based on the accounting profession in China*. https://pdfs.semanticscholar.org/b4fa/e45dccc1113d13bb878f7b00f3a9f fb991e3.pdf

Dr Mary Kitchener works as a senior lecturer in educational development at Oxford Brookes. She is the Programme leader for the EXPLORE programme; an integrated and holistic approach to role-specific professional development. Moving into teaching in Higher Education in 2016 was the catalyst for her doctoral thesis on professional academics and she gained her EdD in 2021. Mary's research and publications also include a handbook for creating a gender-sensitive curriculum, and British Values. Her external work involves being an independent end point assessor for Advance HE, CATE reviewer, as well as an external examiner at the University of Suffolk for their UKPSF provision.

Chapter 3
From Expert to Novice: A Lecturer's Tale

Suzanne Hodgson

Abstract This chapter offers a lived and critically reflective account of the transition from clinical practice to academia. This will be framed by extant knowledge gained from published reflective accounts and empirical research exploring this phenomenon. Evidence-based suggestions for how faculty can support new nurse academics and how new nurse academics can perhaps help themselves are included. It is hoped that by reading this chapter, those in the early stages of transition to academia might identify with some of the challenges, trials, and tribulations, and not feel quite so isolated. Readers who may be contemplating such a move will gain realistic expectations of this career change. Finally, those employing and supporting novice nursing academics will gain insight into their needs and experiences to support their transition, improve their working lives and reduce attrition.

Keywords Nurse academics · Novice pracademics · Transition support · Scholarly activity · Mentoring · Professional networks · Pracademic researchers · Researcher development

At a Glance
- Critically reflects on the lived experience of the transition from clinical practice to academia.
- Framed by extant knowledge gained from published reflective accounts and empirical research exploring this phenomenon.
- Makes evidence-based suggestions for how faculty can support new nurse academics and how new nurse academics can facilitate their own professional development.

(continued)

S. Hodgson (✉)
Department of Nursing, UNITEC, Auckland, New Zealand
e-mail: suzyhodgsonnz@gmail.com

© The Author(s), under exclusive license to Springer Nature
Switzerland AG 2023
J. Dickinson, T.-L. Griffiths (eds.), *Professional Development for Practitioners in Academia*, Knowledge Studies in Higher Education 13,
https://doi.org/10.1007/978-3-031-33746-8_3

- Inspires those in the early stages of transition to academia to identify some of the challenges, trials and tribulations, so they may not feel quite so isolated.

Introduction

This chapter has its foundations in my own experiences of, and reflections on, the transition from clinical practice to academia. The literature contained within this chapter is reflective of my own, and some of my former colleagues', experiences and more widely indicates deep flaws in the way in which many new nurse lecturers are supported in the transition from clinical practice to academia. The experiences of nurses moving into academic roles is explored in a range of academic literature (see, for example, Korkosz et al., 2020; Miner, 2019; Ruiz & Gonzales, 2021; Power & Warren, 2021) and overall, this evidence does not make for comfortable reading.

International research highlights a global staffing crisis in nursing faculties, (Miner, 2019; Stamps et al., 2021) from the USA (Stanley & Martin, 2021) to Australia (McDermid et al., 2013), with the United Kingdom (UK) reflecting the same results (Hunter & Hayter, 2019). In some contexts, vacancies in nursing faculties have forced a reduction in the number of nursing students admitted to courses (Glover et al., 2021; Stamps et al., 2021). This of course has implications for the numbers entering an already depleted qualified nursing workforce.

Nursing departments vary considerably in the emphasis they place on research, scholarly activity, publishing, and teaching (Korkosz et al., 2020). Novice academics may experience different pressures depending on the international context in which they are working. Some faculties hold PhDs in high esteem and require nurse academics to have them on appointment (Geraghty & Oliver, 2018). Many nursing faculties in the UK will employ academics without any postgraduate qualifications, often favouring those with recent and/or significant clinical experience. Internationally, because of faculty vacancies, universities have been forced to employ novice nurse lecturers who lack significant preparation for the teaching requirements of the role (Summers, 2017). Kenny et al. (2004) propose that traditional nurse education in the UK may be frozen in the past, and the school of nursing model is still relatively commonplace in the UK. Unfortunately, this culture has the potential to impede the scholarly development of nurse academics, creating an environment where they may find it difficult to be competitive from a research perspective on an international stage.

In some contexts, bid writing, research, and publication outputs are immediate requirements for new nurse academics (Viveiros et al., 2021). In other institutions, nurse academics struggle to take research or scholarly time due to high teaching volumes, support of students in practice, and pastoral support workloads (Singh et al., 2021). Irrespective of the nature of these pressures, the challenges and stress encountered in transitioning to the role of new nursing academic has similarities across multi-national contexts (Boyd & Lawley, 2009; Wenner et al., 2020).

Benner's (1982) work, *From Novice to Expert*, is frequently applied throughout this body of literature (see, for example, Brown & Sorrell, 2017; Ruiz & Gonzales, 2021) alongside both identity theory (Murray et al., 2014) and role transition theory (McDermid et al., 2018; Murray et al., 2014; Stanley & Martin, 2021). Benner's (1982) text, a constant presence in nurse education for 40 years, outlines a model of transition from novice nurse to expert practitioner, with stages of progress outlined within.

In academia, the novice educator is identified as one with fewer than three to five years of teaching experience (Specht, 2013) yet, in some institutions, retaining lecturers for this length of time appears to be increasingly difficult (Singh et al., 2021). This creates a situation where there is a perpetual cycle of recruitment, with new lecturers being employed but, with fewer experienced faculty members available to provide the kind of mentorship, highlighted in the literature, to be fundamental to their retention (Glover et al., 2021; Jeffers & Mariani, 2017; Stanley & Martin, 2021). Equally, the burden on these experienced academics to provide such mentorship may be accentuated by the ongoing issue of attrition, thus leaving them with limited time, energy, and emotional capacity for mentorship (Singh et al., 2021). In turn, this leaves new nursing academics flailing, feeling overworked, and stressed, resulting in many returning to practice or pursuing different career opportunities (Summers, 2017). And so, the cycle of recruitment and attrition continues. The next section will outline some key themes from my professional reflections. These will be analysed in the context of extant literature, before I make some recommendations for those considering an academic career, new pracademics, and the higher education managers responsible for supporting them.

Key Themes

Personal Journey

> *I was never meant to be a nurse …*

I was hesitant about starting this chapter with this particular sentence as I wanted to avoid giving the impression that I hadn't valued the time in what I consider to be my previous profession. Then I read a paper by Susie Cartledge who starts her narrative with "I never intended on being a nurse…" (Cartledge, 2019, p. 1), and I realised that the pathways, or indeed 'falls', into nursing, just like academia, are diverse.

I was never meant to be a nurse, or at least, I never set out to be one. I fell into nursing because of poor A-level results and the desire to 'just go to university'. In retrospect, I was always going to *be* in healthcare. As a young carer for most of my formative years, I was around hospitals a lot. I have always had a passion for health and understanding people's health choices, and the ways in which social and psychological factors influence health and wellbeing.

My journey into academia began with a conversation on a beach, where my husband suggested that I should teach. At this point, we had travelled extensively, and I had worked in the UK and overseas as a nurse in a variety of different roles. I had never quite found my niche, and in fact my frequent role changes were a source of much amusement to my friends and family. I now know I should probably have entered academia much earlier on in my career. I trained as a children's nurse from 1993 to 1997, 'did my time' on a very busy general children's ward in London, and then moved into child and adolescent mental health.

In the following years, I worked in a number of different roles, eventually undertaking further training to become a health visitor. In 2012, I finally decided to start the journey into academia that we had discussed on that beach a few years before.

With more motivation than ever to pursue an academic role, I decided to study for a master's degree in Psychology. At this point, I was relatively ambivalent about being a nurse and felt the need to expand my knowledge and educational repertoire. My master's degree was transformational in many ways, and it was here where I found a passion for academia.

My research education was phenomenal during this time, and I became confident with both quantitative and qualitative research approaches. I thoroughly enjoyed the primary research I undertook and received excellent supervision. During my master's degree, the notion of undertaking a PhD became part of my psyche; something that a first-generation university graduate from a lower socio-economic background would most likely not have even been aware of, never mind considered, a few years before. However, at this stage, we once again travelled overseas, and I secured my first teaching role.

This first role was in a private tertiary college. It was in this role where I started to understand that, whilst my clinical background enabled me to get the job, I was now entering both a new profession and career which I had not fully anticipated. I took over from my predecessor with immediate effect and was handed a USB drive containing their teaching materials. I thought I was ready and prepared, and naively turned up for my first teaching session, having read through the slides, impatient to get started. I stumbled through the four hours of teaching and by the end of it, I was distraught. I had not anticipated how difficult it would be to use someone else's materials, to understand how teaching should be delivered, or how to properly engage with the students. I had observed a few sessions with the previous tutor and as a result, thought that taking over was going to be straightforward; it wasn't. However, over time and with more practice and self-directed learning, I started to feel more comfortable in my teaching 'skin' and decided to take the plunge and commence my PhD.

Finding My Collegial Buddies

After a year, I transferred my PhD back to the UK and this is where I found my collegial family, my PhD buddies, and my lecturing team. It is not an exaggeration to say that I would have not only struggled to complete my PhD without these two groups of people, but I would also have found the first few years of teaching in a university more challenging. My PhD buddies have accompanied me on this journey, and the stars aligned to bring us together. Not everyone is lucky enough to find their people early on and for some nurses transitioning from practice to academia, the road can be isolating, and sometimes treacherous. However, finding a collegial family may prove to be fundamental to the transition to the role (Brown & Sorrell, 2017; McDermid et al., 2016) and as Jeffers and Mariani (2017) report, these informal relationships with academic peers may be the lifeline needed to stay in academia. These might be people who start an academic role concurrently, those who perhaps share a practice or research interest, or individuals who just naturally show an affinity for one another. Irrespective of how these people come together, it is often not until years later that their value and worth may be understood.

These will be the people who, during lonely and isolating moments, a new academic can call on to offload, to ask silly questions, and to generally bolster their confidence when it is needed the most. They are the ones who celebrate a particularly positive teaching session together and who share the absolute mess of a session without judgement. Not everything will go right and if these people are authentic, they will share their mess-ups too.

Do You Need a PhD?

Research has shown that whilst the number of nurses undertaking PhDs continues to rise, the rates of successful completion are low (Gerraghty & Oliver, 2018). Nursing is different in relation to recruitment for academic positions. In other disciplines, I saw young doctoral candidates commence their, often funded, PhD journeys straight from full-time undergraduate or postgraduate studies, often with the aim of gaining a position as a lecturer. Many of these doctoral researchers achieved this by the time they were in their late twenties, reflecting a more traditional route into academia when compared to nursing (Hunter & Hayter, 2019). Because of the emphasis on research in other disciplines, for example psychology, the requirement for lecturing positions tends to be either achievement, or close to completion, of a PhD. In the UK, the nursing academic workforce traditionally tends to be older because there is a requirement to have significant clinical experience for the role of the nursing academic (Hunter & Hayter, 2019). Research activity is often perceived by both lecturers and faculty as secondary to teaching and, in many examples, there has been no requirement to have a PhD or even master's qualification for entry level lecturing positions.

Academics with PhDs in nursing departments in the UK are becoming more common but finding the time and opportunity to complete a PhD whilst working in a full-time role can be very challenging (Geraghty & Oliver, 2018). The benefits of having a PhD in a nursing department are many and whilst it shouldn't necessarily be a requirement to have a PhD to work as an entry level nursing lecturer, an increase in the number of research active nursing lecturers may help to improve the research agenda in nursing departments. Supporting pre-registration and post-registration research-focussed masters' dissertations is far more credible and effective when the supervisor has completed independent primary research themselves, either via a master's or PhD. Furthermore, the outputs from these supervisory relationships may contribute to Research Excellence Framework (REF)[1] funding.

My PhD has also been fundamental in facilitating autonomy in my academic role. I have a niche area of research, and because of the networks I have created via my research dissemination, I have been empowered by my mentors and managers to pursue projects and activities which benefit my career progression but also showcase the university. Kenny et al. (2004) discuss the socialisation process in the move from healthcare roles into academic roles. They suggest that workplace cultures which promote autonomy, individual progression, and development are of most benefit and value to new nursing academics (Kenny et al., 2004).

Making a Successful Transition

Having confidence in one's existing clinical identity and associated knowledge can be an initial lifeline when commencing an academic role but might be best used as a transitional coping strategy or tool (Murray et al., 2014). It is easy to become overwhelmed in academic institutions. At this time, when the university environment is unfamiliar, where processes appear convoluted, and established academics appear to be unattainably more experienced and knowledgeable, relying on existing knowledge is important.

Students benefit from, and appreciate, real life stories, authentic practitioners, and those who have extensive and exciting experiences in practice. For the novice nurse educator, these experiences and stories may act as a safety net in the turbulence of role transition. Anderson (2009) uses a "mermaid entering the sea of academia" metaphor to emphasise the need to adopt a holistic approach to orientate new nurse academics to the role. Concepts such as drowning, treading water, and beginning strokes (Anderson, 2009) are identifiable metaphors for new nursing academics and provide a potential sense of relief and solidarity. As academics become more experienced, there will be a requirement to take on leadership roles, develop curricula, and engage in increasing levels of research and scholarly activity. However, this will happen in due course, and returning to the foundations of core nursing knowledge can be bolstering in times of self-doubt and low confidence.

Novice nurse lecturers are employed because of their extensive clinical specialist skills but are frequently required to teach a multitude of different topics, with which they may not be familiar (Korkosz et al., 2020). Whilst their knowledge of a topic might be vague, and the nuances of assessment policies and procedures might be complex, what new nurse academics do know is how to be a nurse. Boyd and Lawley

---

[1] The Research Excellence Framework is a 'process of expert review' that aims to 'secure the continuation of a world-class, dynamic and responsive research base across the full academic spectrum within UK higher education'. (REF, 2022).

(2009) suggest that this knowledge can be a coping mechanism when a new environment causes novice academic lecturers to feel out of their depth. However, whilst it can be a lifeline when making the transition to academia it shouldn't prevent novice academics from embracing their new career.

Being Authentic

There is a somewhat misguided self-expectation as a new educator to have all the answers. After all, many nurses enter academia from the position of expert practitioner (Benner, 1982) where stakeholders and patients expect a high level of knowledge. Entering academia can create tensions between these two contexts and Grassley et al. (2020) found that novice nurse academics can frequently miss being regarded as an expert in their new role.

Being authentic is held in high regard by students and being humble enough to say, 'I don't know, but I'll find out' engenders respect and encourages students to become aware that lecturers are partners in their learning. When I started my nursing career, I was in awe of experienced colleagues and the same happened when I entered academia. I perceived these learned colleagues to be at the peak of their careers, that they were all-knowing, and they were my role models and the focus of my career ambition. It has taken me a while to realise that these academics are also people with lives, insecurities, and anxieties, and whilst they might have a very specialist skill set and be experts in their fields, they too are fallible, vulnerable, and require empathy and support as much as the rest of us.

Realistic Expectations and Preparation

Realistic expectations when moving from a clinical to a faculty role are necessary to prepare those contemplating this move (Stanley & Martin, 2021). Frequently, nurses enter academia to take a break from clinical practice (Ruiz & Gonzales, 2021) or view it as a somewhat easier alternative. It is often not well understood by nurses that commencing an academic role is in fact starting a new career, which requires further study and has the potential to expose them to a multitude of different pressures. There is also a lack of awareness that this new role will require a different skill set to that which they have been using, often expertly, in their clinical practice (Cleary et al., 2011). An expert practitioner does not always translate into being an effective academic or teacher (Smith et al., 2019).

Many nurses enter academia with limited research and scholarly experience and may find this to be a significant challenge in supervising research-based dissertations, which is often a key component of their new role. Whilst their previous clinical experience provides them with clinical currency (Fisher, 2005) to trade with their learners, the literature demonstrates how the lack of knowledge and understanding around pedagogy, classroom management, processes, curriculum, and assessment are frequent causes of anxiety and frustration (Anderson, 2009; Boyd & Lawley, 2009; Cleary et al., 2011; Murray et al., 2014; Power & Warren, 2021).

Nursing patients obviously differs considerably from teaching student nurses (Glover et al., 2021), but I have seen colleagues become overly invested in their students' personal lives and trying to solve problems for which they are not responsible. Universities tend to have extensive student support services, and the job is to refer on, not to fix. Perhaps colleagues are tempted to get involved with this aspect of students' lives as it is a familiar and comfortable role. However, this can be time-consuming, and can contribute to a perceived lack of other time to undertake essential aspects of the academic role, such as research and scholarly activity.

Connecting the Dots Between Clinical Practice and Academia

Recruitment

Realistic job adverts and a better assessment of both the desire to teach and an understanding of the academic environment would be beneficial parts of the recruitment process (Smith et al., 2019). At interview, it would be valuable to assess the candidate's desire to teach, understanding of pedagogical approaches, and insight into the academic environment (McDermid et al., 2018). Understanding the research and scholarly activity requirements of a role is essential as departments move forward in an increasingly competitive research landscape and where, in the UK, REF funding will become increasingly important. Senior clinical nursing roles require significant experience as a pre-requisite and there is an expectation of a deep and comprehensive understanding of the role.

Universities, however, frequently ask for this level of clinical experience for what is essentially a junior role in a different profession, and which often results in a drop in salary for these experienced nurses. Salary may be a prohibitive factor in recruiting experienced nurses to faculty roles, an issue which warrants further attention but is beyond the scope of this chapter.

Testing the Water

A more structured approach to the transition from clinical practice to academia could also form a part of an academic career progression framework for nurses. Secondment opportunities are available each year for clinicians to work in nurse academia part-time to gain experience of the academic environment whilst remaining in their current clinical role.

Many secondees subsequently transition to full-time academic roles whilst some quickly return to practice. Irrespective of the outcome, this seems like a sensible way to 'try on' the role of academic. Anecdotally, it seems that there are few nurses who join universities because of a specified career aim to teach but for a multitude of other reasons, such as clinical burn-out. Some new lecturers are surprised to find that they thrive in the teaching environment, but others may stay because they cannot face the return to clinical practice. This latter group require significant mentorship and support to ensure that they remain focussed on the student experience and quality teaching, and are empowered to find a sense of purpose and passion within the academic environment.

Lecturer practitioners or sessional lecturers are employed by some universities. These roles allow such academics the opportunity to continue with their specialist clinical practice roles alongside making their transition into academia (Wenner et al., 2020). I have seen colleagues who came into the institution as part-time academics still working in specialist clinical practice, and who, for the first few years, sought solace in the academic environment and even considered a full-time move into academia. However, as they have become more experienced in the academic environment, the unique pressures in academia have meant that they would now never contemplate this as a permanent move. This hybrid role may, however, provide a useful compromise for those who want to join academia but are not ready or prepared to give up their identities as clinical practitioners. Boyd and Lawley (2009) suggest that new nurse academics seek credibility through knowledge of current practice, rather than via research or scholarly activity, as they see this as important to students. If they maintain this part-time academic role, this is entirely feasible.

Structured and Well-Planned Inductions

New nurse lecturers need time and a structured and well-planned orientation, accompanied by ongoing mentorship or buddying. This approach has been positively received according to the findings of a number of studies concerning this role transition (Glover et al., 2021; Laari et al., 2021; Ruiz & Gonzalez, 2021; Stamps et al., 2021). Immediately overwhelming new lecturers with leadership roles and full days of teaching, with little opportunity to shadow others, is likely to result in a high attrition rate for new academics (Boyd & Lawley, 2009). Exploiting their time and talents as soon as they arrive may be a short-term solution to staffing crises but in the long-term it will be counterproductive. Planning for the long-term requires a structured, on-campus, and face-to-face induction, particularly in the current climate where increasingly, new academics are not necessarily provided with a dedicated onsite workspace. As previously mentioned, new nurse academics need to be supported to find their people, many of whom will be fundamental to a lasting career in academia.

Realistic expectations and protected time for both scholarly activity and continuous professional development are also needed (McDermid et al., 2018). There is often a concern from new and experienced nurse lecturers that there is little time for either of these activities. However, Boyd and Lawley (2009) suggest that new nursing academics may immerse themselves in supporting students in clinical practice and liaising with clinical practice colleagues to mitigate being out of clinical practice themselves. Immersion in this environment may be a reason for a lack of scholarly output, whilst at the same time providing a sense of being in a safe and familiar space. However, academics in the UK are allocated research and scholarly activity hours as part of academic work planning and therefore support is needed to facilitate and prioritise this.

Buddies and Formal Mentorship

Where new academics have been provided with structured mentorship, the challenges that they may face in their role transition may be mitigated by having a peer to talk to and to guide them through the first few months and years in their new role (Grassley et al., 2020; McDermid et al., 2018; Miner, 2019). My personal experience of participating in a buddy system for new staff, especially for those new to academia, is that it has been well received. Unfortunately, because of the COVID-19 pandemic, new academics' recent experiences of transitioning into academia has been negatively affected by the introduction of hybrid working, frequent lockdowns, and a reduction of time on campus, impacting upon even the most cohesive and positive teams. In the US context, Power and Warren (2021) reflect on their transition to academia during the COVID-19 pandemic, indicating that the usual challenges faced in this transition were accentuated due to the requirement to work from home. Using Bandura's (2002) social learning theory to frame their reflections, they indicate the lack of socialisation to their new roles being a significant barrier to their ability to adapt and cope with the challenges presented by teaching remotely during the global pandemic (Power & Warren, 2021).

The COVID-19 pandemic has forced many academics from traditional, often collegial, office space to spend more time working from home, which has increased isolation from peers. The informal mentorship 'in the nursing corridor', referred to in Boyd and Lawley (2009, p. 298), has not been available to new colleagues during the pandemic. Many new nursing academics have commenced their roles without either allocated office space or the mentorship and informal support mechanisms, provided by default, in a busy, vibrant, traditional collegiate campus setting (Power & Warren, 2021). In Miner (2019), positive transition experiences were reflected in the atmosphere and environment of the faculty and in the time spent with colleagues through informal or extra-curricular activities. Miner (2019) and Grassley et al. (2020) further found that mentors, both formal and informal, can make a significant difference to the experiences of new nurse academics. Similarly, Laari et al. (2021) found that novice nurse lecturers in Ghana had similar experiences to those described above and were self-reliant on finding informal supportive relationships in their transition to academia. Prior teaching experience is not necessarily a panacea either; McDermid et al. (2013) highlight the challenges faced by experienced sessional teachers when they transition to full-time academic positions. It is likely that sessional lecturers have more finite roles in teaching and assessing and the move to permanent roles may present significant challenges in relation to their broader scope. In fact, navigating processes has been shown to be one of the most stressful and isolating experience on entry into academia (Boyd & Lawley, 2009). Therefore, supportive transitions are also necessary for those who already have significant teaching experience (McDermid et al., 2013).

The infrastructure which supports university processes can be opaque and therefore hard to navigate. This can be disconcerting for new academics who, on commencement, may initially be unable to gain access to learning materials, and to find where for example, teaching spaces are located. A buddy system or formal mentorship can mitigate much of the initial frustration and stress experienced by new nurse academics (Glover et al., 2021). However approachable an individual line manager is, junior academics can often feel like a burden and are reluctant to ask for help. Whilst many of these new academics have been leaders and specialist practitioners in their fields, they may have joined academia with unrealistic expectations and can begin to struggle quite early on (Dempsey, 2007). The sense of incompetence can be difficult to manage considering their previous autonomous and expert roles and the reticence to ask for help can be hugely challenging in developing new role identity. Having a buddy can often offer a safe space for information exchange and the offloading of anxieties.

Ideally, teaching should provide a nurse lecturer with a high level of job satisfaction, gained from what I perceive to be the privilege of training the new generation of nurses and nurse leaders. This requires the supporting and nurturing of new academics by experienced ones. Being thrown in to giving lectures and supporting seminars with minimal experience is just as unacceptable as expecting a newly qualified nurse to run a ward, albeit with less risk to human life in the classroom (hopefully). The quality of academic programmes is fuelled by the integrity and commitment of the staff teaching them. Whatever the reasons for entering academia, support is needed to build the confidence and skills of new nurse academics. This is a two-way process which not only relies upon a level of enthusiasm for education from the nurse academic, but also comprehensive support from the institution. If this is lacking there is little benefit to anyone, and before long, tired academics flounder, burn out, and begin to deliver poor quality education. Being informed and passionate about students' education, and embracing research and scholarly activity, even if this feels particularly anxiety-provoking, could be the formula to a long and happy career in academia.

Conclusion

By the time this chapter is published, I will once again have moved countries and therefore roles. I anticipate that wherever I will go, the move from professional practice into academia will continue to present both opportunities and challenges. My suggestions to those seeking an academic career from clinical practice is to seek out roles where there is a culture of support and respect for your professional background, but also one which will push you to develop as an academic. If you have a passion for education, you are in demand and new ways of working have the potential to open more opportunities for your academic career than ever before. However, you need to be clear about the reasons for your move into academia and you need to be aware that you are embarking on a new career. It is a disservice to both your future students and colleagues to come into academia for a break; you must want to teach. Be passionate, be collegial, and only try to control what you can. The life of an academic can be full of joy and opportunity. You just need to find the right place and the right people to work with.

Points for Reflection

- Hodgson emphasises the importance of mentoring and peer support during transitions. Is this something you relate to? Consider examples of when you have been supported by a mentor and how they helped you.
- The challenge of engaging with scholarly activity whilst teaching on a practice-focused course is elucidated in this chapter. Consider the ways in which continuing professional development and scholarly activity may be balanced.

References

Anderson, J. K. (2009). The work-role transition of expert clinician to novice academic educator. *Journal of Nursing Education, 48*(4), 203–208. https://doi.org/10.3928/01484834-20090401-02

Bandura, A. (2002) Social Cognitive Theory in Cultural Context. *Applied Psychology, 51*(2), 269–290. https://doi.org/10.1111/1464-0597.00092

Benner, P. (1982) From novice to expert. *American Journal of Nursing, 82*(3), 402–407.

Boyd, P., & Lawley, L. (2009). Becoming a lecturer in nurse education: The work-place learning of clinical experts as newcomers. *Learning in Health and Social Care, 8*(4), 292–300. https://doi.org/10.1111/j.1473-6861.2009.00214.x

Brown, T., & Sorrell, J. (2017). Challenges of novice nurse educator's transition from practice to classroom. *Teaching and Learning in Nursing, 12*(3), 207–211. https://doi.org/10.1016/j.teln.2017.03.002

Cartledge, S. (2019). A balancing act: From clinical practice to research. *British Journal of Cardiac Nursing, 14*(4), 1–3. https://doi.org/10.12968/bjca.2019.0015

Cleary, M., Horsfall, J., & Jackson, D. (2011). Mental health nursing: Transitions from practice roles to academia. *Perspectives in Psychiatric Care, 47*(2), 93–97. https://doi.org/10.1111/j.1744-6163.2010.00280.x

Dempsey, L. M. (2007). The experiences of Irish nurse lecturers role transition from clinician to educator. *International Journal of Nursing Education Scholarship, 4*(1). https://doi.org/10.2202/1548-923X.1381

Fisher, M. T. (2005). Exploring how nurse lecturers maintain clinical credibility. *Nurse Education in Practice, 5*(1), 21–29. https://doi.org/10.1016/j.nepr.2004.02.003

Geraghty, S., & Oliver, K. (2018). In the shadow of the ivory tower: Experiences of midwives and nurses undertaking PhDs. *Nurse Education Today, 65*, 36–40. https://doi.org/10.1016/j.nedt.2018.02.017

Glover, H. A., Hitt, A., Zills, G., Darby, W., Hall, C., & Kirkman, T. (2021). Nurturing novice faculty: Successful mentorship of nurse practitioners. *The Journal for Nurse Practitioners, 17*(10), 1271–1275. https://doi.org/10.1016/j.nurpra.2021.07.015

Grassley, J. S., Strohfus, P. K., & Lambe, A. C. (2020). No longer expert: A meta-synthesis describing the transition from clinician to academic. *Journal of Nursing Education, 59*(7), 366–374. https://doi.org/10.3928/01484834-20200617-03

Hunter, J., & Hayter, M. (2019). A neglected transition in nursing: The need to support the move from clinician to academic properly. *Journal of Advanced Nursing, 75*(9), 1820–1822. https://doi.org/10.1111/jan.14075

Jeffers, S., & Mariani, B. (2017). The effect of a formal mentoring program on career satisfaction and intent to stay in the faculty role for novice nurse faculty. *Nursing Education Perspectives, 38*(1), 18–22. https://doi.org/10.1097/01.NEP.0000000000000104

Kenny, G., Pontin, D., & Moore, L. (2004). Negotiating socialisation: The journey of novice nurse academics into higher education. *Nurse Education Today, 24*(8), 629–637. https://doi.org/10.1016/j.nedt.2004.08.002

Korkosz, J. A., Fuller, A. J., Sheehy, S. B., Taylor, L. A., Seibert, D. C., & Johnson, H. L. (2020). Taking the leap from clinical practice to academic faculty: A beginner's guide. *Journal of the American Association of Nurse Practitioners, 32*(9), 630–637. https://doi.org/10.1097/JXX.0000000000000320

Laari, T. T., Apiribu, F., Gazari, T., Akor, M. H., Mensah, A. B. B., Atanuriba, G. A., et al. (2021). Strategies adopted by novice nurse educators to facilitate their transition from practice to academia: A qualitative study in Ghana. *SAGE Open Nursing, 7*. https://doi.org/10.1177/23779608211035209

McDermid, F., Peters, K., John Daly, J., & Jackson, D. (2013). 'I thought I was just going to teach': Stories of new nurse academics on transitioning from sessional teaching to continuing academic positions. *Contemporary Nurse, 45*(1), 46–55. https://doi.org/10.5172/conu.2013.45.1.46

McDermid, F., Peters, K., Daly, J., & Jackson, D. (2016). Developing resilience: Stories from novice nurse academics. *Nurse Education Today, 38*, 29–35. https://doi.org/10.1016/j.nedt.2016.01.002

McDermid, F., Mannix, J., Jackson, D., Daly, J., & Peters, K. (2018). Factors influencing progress through the liminal phase: A model to assist transition into nurse academic life. *Nurse Education Today, 61*, 269–272. https://core.ac.uk/download/pdf/220157602.pdf

Miner, L. A. (2019). Transition to nursing academia: A positive experience. *The Journal of Continuing Education in Nursing, 50*(8), 349–354. https://doi.org/10.3928/00220124-20190717-05

Murray, C., Stanley, M., & Wright, S. (2014). The transition from clinician to academic in nursing and allied health: A qualitative meta-synthesis. *Nurse Education Today, 34*(3), 389–395. https://doi.org/10.1016/j.nedt.2013.06.010

Power, P. J., & Warren, G. M. (2021). The leap to faculty in the time of COVID19. *Journal of Professional Nursing, 37*(1), 34–37. https://doi.org/10.1016/j.profnurs.2020.11.008

REF. (2022). *What is the REF?* https://www.ref.ac.uk/about-the-ref/what-is-the-ref/

Ruiz, D., & Gonzales, M. (2021). Transition to practice and Back again: The journey into nursing academia. *Nursing Education Perspectives, 42*(6), E81–E82. https://doi.org/10.1097/01.NEP.0000000000000836

Singh, C., Jackson, D., Munro, I., & Cross, W. (2021). Work experiences of nurse academics: A qualitative study. *Nurse Education Today, 106*, 105038. https://doi.org/10.1016/j.nedt.2021.105038

Smith, S., Karosas, L., & Beauchesne, M. A. (2019). Preparing for the transition from clinical practice to academia. *Journal of the American Association of Nurse Practitioners, 31*(2), 82–84. https://doi.org/10.1097/JXX.0000000000000190

Specht, J. A. (2013). Mentoring relationships and the levels of role conflict and role ambiguity experienced by novice nursing faculty. *Journal of Professional Nursing, 29*(5), e25–e31. https://doi.org/10.1016/j.profnurs.2013.06.006

Stamps, A., Cockerell, K., & Opton, L. (2021). A modern take on facilitating transition into the academic nurse educator role. *Teaching and Learning in Nursing, 16*(1), 92–94. https://doi.org/10.1016/j.teln.2020.04.002

Stanley, M. J., & Martin, C. (2021). Guiding elements for success in the nurse educator role. *Nursing Education Perspectives, 42*(6), E86–E88. https://doi.org/10.1097/01.NEP.0000000000000741

Summers, J. A. (2017). Developing competencies in the novice nurse educator: An integrative review. *Teaching and Learning in Nursing, 12*(4), 263–276. https://doi.org/10.1016/j.teln.2017.05.001

Viveiros, J., Schuler, M., Chung, J., & D'Esmond, L. (2021). A cohort model of mentoring as facilitator to the transition to an academic nurse faculty position following completion of a PhD. *Nursing Education Perspectives, 42*(5), 315–317. https://doi.org/10.1097/01.NEP.0000000000000852

Wenner, T. A., Hakim, A. C., & Schoening, A. M. (2020). The work-role transition of part-time clinical faculty: Seeking to validate the nurse educator transition model. *Nurse Educator, 45*(2), 102–105. https://doi.org/10.1097/NNE.0000000000000704

Dr Suzanne Hodgson is a nursing academic at Unitec- Te Pukenga in Auckland, New Zealand. She has a background in both children's nursing and public health nursing in the UK and in New Zealand spanning the last 30 years. Her research interests centre on transitions to fatherhood and paternal perinatal mental health. Suzy has taught interprofessional education and public health to all levels of university students for the past ten years and has collaborated with colleagues to design and deliver innovative educational approaches. She has been part of the Hallam Pracademia community of practice for the past four years and is passionate about supporting new nursing academics as they commence their careers in higher education.

Chapter 4
The Pracademic: Where Practice Meets Theory. The Value of Practitioner Experience when Teaching and Researching in a Higher Education Environment

Michelle Stirk

Abstract This chapter is in three parts: considering the pracademic from three different dimensions, past, present and the future. It is set within an accounting and finance discipline, which is usually incorporated within a business school of a Higher Education Institution (HEI). The chapter provides a personal examination of the skills and knowledge a practitioner brings from their *past* as they enter academia. In this case, a qualified accountant that has already worked in industry for many years. It then looks at how these skills and knowledge can be leveraged in Higher Education (HE), in the *present*. It focuses on the key skills that the pracademic can draw upon to navigate their path through HE, including some practical tips and key areas for reflection. This section also examines some of the less widely discussed areas upon securing an academic position, such as, types of assessment and the importance of student self-evaluation. The chapter concludes by considering how practice and theory are embodied in a pracademic. It discusses how both practice and theory are equal for a pracademic, with neither having primacy over the other. This concise evaluation of a pracademic's background, their present and *future*, highlights associated skills that provide a strong foundation for further growth and success.

Keywords Assessment · Authentic assessment · Experience · Real world · Reflection · Mentor · Career transitions · Accounting

M. Stirk (✉)
Nottingham University Business School, University of Nottingham, University Park, Nottingham, UK
e-mail: Michelle.Stirk@nottingham.ac.uk

© The Author(s), under exclusive license to Springer Nature Switzerland AG 2023
J. Dickinson, T.-L. Griffiths (eds.), *Professional Development for Practitioners in Academia*, Knowledge Studies in Higher Education 13,
https://doi.org/10.1007/978-3-031-33746-8_4

At a Glance
- Primarily aimed at pracademics, some of the reflections, discussions, and recommendations may also be relevant for more experienced academics and other higher education professionals.
- Provides practical suggestions to enhance learning and teaching environments for students and pracademics, by implementing elements of practitioner experience and insight.
- Includes reflections from an accounting and finance subject perspective, but may have relevance to other disciplines.

Introduction

This chapter evaluates pracademic experience from three lenses: the past, the present, and the future. It provides supportive guidance and helpful tips for navigating the Higher Education (HE) sector and Higher Education Institutions (HEIs). It is primarily aimed at very new pracademics, or those still in practice who may be considering making the transition to HE but some of the reflections, discussions, and recommendations may also be relevant for more experienced academics and other HE professionals.

Newer pracademics may lack confidence in their academic voice, particularly if they are yet to publish in academic journals, or do not have a higher degree. They may feel that they will be playing 'catch up' for the rest of their academic career, to regain the position of knowledge and expertise that that had in practice. However, I will explore how pracademics can bring value to their new academic role and realise their unique perspective within their HEI.

Key Themes

The Past

Lecturers with first-hand practitioner experience, or pracademics (Panda, 2014), are widely considered to have authority about their subject, whether they realise it or not. They have invested a significant part of their working life into their career to date. This may have included completing a professional qualification out in practice after they finished an undergraduate degree. This professional qualification (for me, an accountancy qualification, and thereafter, membership of an internationally recognised professional accounting body) demonstrates that they have achieved a level of understanding and developed a set of skills to carry out the tasks associated with their profession. While they have been out in practice, they have had opportunities to put these skills to use and, in doing so, may have learned many more.

Here, I would like to draw your attention to a teaching methodology that is regularly adopted in medical surgery education and teaching which is the model of 'See One, Do One, Teach One' (SODOTO) (Kotsis & Chung, 2013). The essence of this approach is to learn 'by doing', in three dimensions. First, the learner *observes* the task/activity; second, the learner *executes* the task/activity for themselves; and third, the learner *teaches* another person to execute the task/activity. Like many things in academia (and life), there are debates for and against using the approach. However, the reason that the framework (and consequently its derivatives) is still being used in medical education, is because it elevates the learner from passive learning to an environment where they must participate and become engaged. In a similar way, the discipline of accounting and finance can be detailed, complex, and technical. To succeed in this field, a student needs to be able 'to do' as this is an essential skill that employers value.

Can you imagine being operated on by a surgeon who has never done any surgery before, or being given legal advice from a solicitor who has only ever read the law in books and statutes, or indeed, business advice from a consultant who has never worked in business? There is a learning gap between what can happen in theoretical terms and what can (and does) happen in practice: that learning gap is 'real world' experience. Similar to other disciplines, accounting is a 'doing' discipline. I have learned, via my own journey, that learning is about being engaged, taking responsibility, and not being a 'passenger'.

Furthermore, the students are preparing themselves through HE for an 'onward' journey, although they may, at times, forget this. It is for us, as educators, to remind students about why we are teaching them the subjects that they study. Dickinson et al. (2022) highlighted that pracademics report that they feel a responsibility to teach the 'next generation' of professionals, but they also are critical of existing practice and want to encourage change. I find that frequently using opportunities within the teaching environment to highlight this next generation purpose often refocuses students' attention and interest. Pracademics' experience is essential in giving the students an insight into what is awaiting them once they leave university, and how what is covered in the curricula will be relevant to their onward journey, whether in practice or academia (Race, 2005). Pracademics provide an important contribution towards completing the missing link that cannot be accessed in textbooks – the real-world context and application – which is what makes pracademics potentially very powerful and credible educators.

Academic colleagues, without experience of working in industry, may draw on two dimensions of the SODOTO methodology, namely 'See One and Teach One'. Pracademics, on the other hand, have the potential for embodying the SODOTO philosophy by employing all three elements – learning, executing/doing, and teaching. This may facilitate a deeper understanding of their discipline and their ability to teach becomes practice-informed rather than wholly academic. Indeed, pracademia is the point where experience (practice) meets theory (academia).

An approach that I have always found interesting and useful for reflecting on my own teaching and learning is that of experiential learning. Kolb (2015, p. 49) defines learning as 'the process whereby knowledge is created through the transformation of experience'. Kolb conceptualises the transformation of experience as a cyclical model that utilises four modes: active experimentation, concrete experience, reflective observation, and abstract conceptualisation. This model resonates with me because having experience is fundamental within the discipline of accounting. Furthermore, this approach reinforces the importance of experience, and it can give pracademics more confidence in the value that they bring to the HE sector, as well as providing a useful pedagogical tool. Within accounting, for example, there are many calculations to learn to do and understand, and employers seek graduates who have experience of undertaking those calculations. During teaching, there is an opportunity to mobilise this model. For example, students can experience a concept via a numerical illustration that is used by me as the lecturer. Then, I encourage students to make an attempt themselves, either in groups or individually. This facilitates a refocus on the learner and encourages reflection on the ideas that have been discussed, and active experimentation on a question/problem. This approach ensures that all four modes of the learning cycle have been met, and the benefit and learning to the student optimised. In addition, this provides a breathing space for individual learners who have diverse learning preferences because not all students process learning in the same way (Kolb, 2015). Whilst there are no perfect models for learning for me, I believe that it is essential that anyone wanting to learn anything needs to be able to experience it, reflect on it, amend, and then try it out for themselves.

Race (2005) takes the learning cycle and transforms it into a model likened to ripples on a pond, emanating from a central origin. The origin represents the basic need or want of learning that occurs and, just as ripples originate from this central point, so do the other related aspects of learning, such as the doing, digesting, and feedback. It is the origin that generates the other ripples. As the concentric circles move out from the centre, deeper learning is facilitated. As an academic, my goal is to inspire students to want to learn or, alternatively understand why they need to learn, a particular topic or calculation. This is where I find my pracademic experience valuable, because I know what is required for a career in practice and the importance of what needs to be learned and why. So, to help secure students' engagement, I explain why the topics to be covered in the curricula are important to their future careers. However, I understand that not all learners are sure of their career paths and can be impacted by career self-doubt (Wong & Kaur, 2018). Still, the advantage of employing this way of learning and teaching from a pracademic perspective, is that we do not have to create examples or scenarios in our minds, because we have 'experienced' the application of the learning in practice. As former/current practitioners, we can see how the benefit of what is learned in the HE arena is applicable to 'real world' scenarios that the students could be facing in a few short years. Pracademics bring a unique insight into what needs to be taught, and more significantly, why. If a student is unaware of 'why' something is to be learned, they are unlikely to be motivated to learn it.

In summary, experience of industry can help pracademics to understand more fully, and meet, significant, present-day challenges, such as writing student assessments, incorporating the different needs of learners and potential employers, and evaluating student learning. Designing appropriate assessments is a creative process and thought needs to be given as to what needs to be assessed. These considerations are discussed in more detail in the following section. Lastly, pracademics could optimise and operationalise their practical experience through making time to reflect on how their practical experience aligns with their teaching (see reflective activity at the end of the chapter).

The Present

The night before giving my first lecture every academic year, my stomach is in knots, and I am very nervous. I thought that, by now, having delivered hundreds of lectures and presentations, I would have developed nerves of steel. It has not happened. This experience is a part of teaching that, until recently, I had hoped, would have faded. However, this very feeling ensures that I am (as far as possible) delivering my best every academic year and that I continuously strive to become a better educator, scholar, and learner. Others may feel the same. Perhaps this is normal, and it shows that we care about our practice and the learning environment that we facilitate. In fact, according to Cox, "nervousness is essential for peak performance" (1994, p. 64) and Wilkinson (2020) suggests strategies for dealing with it, amongst other personal reflections and experiences that new pracademics may find interesting.

Although lectures, seminars, and tutorials are largely delivered in 'real time' (that is, production and consumption are simultaneous), the assessment and the learning outcomes of teaching need to be considered carefully, and ahead of time. Boud suggests that while "students can, with difficulty, escape from the effects of poor teaching, they cannot (by definition, if they want to graduate) escape the effects of poor assessment" (1995, p. 35). There are two main types of assessment: formative and summative assessments. Both are important in the context of HE and each of them serves a different purpose. Formative assessments provide feedback to the student whilst they are learning, and part of their purpose is to nurture improvement. Summative assessment occurs at the end of a period of learning, and it evaluates the extent of what the students have learned (Biggs & Tang, 2011). The point that Boud (1995) makes (see above) concerns the inconsistency of learning and assessment, and the messages that are sent to students via the selected forms of assessment. The type of assessment used on a course or a programme should optimise learning and be aligned with the intended learning outcomes. The concept of constructive alignment (Biggs, 1996) is a helpful idea to broach at this juncture. Constructive alignment puts the student at the centre of the learner journey and pushes at the boundaries of traditional assessments. Constructive alignment can be thought of as evaluating students' learning via a range of methods and a range of assessors. Broadly speaking, in HE, one evaluator that is seldom considered is the student.

The concept of the learner assessing their own work may be familiar to pracademics. It is a skill that they are likely to have developed (in some instances, rather quickly) during their time in practice. I remember starting a new role as a practitioner. Looking back, this was a role that defined me, as it was here that I learned and polished many of my accounting skills. I remember my manager, sitting with a neon colour highlighting pen, reading the financial reports that I had produced. The manager would circle the mistakes that were present in my work and hand the report back to me. Of course, I would be embarrassed as some of my mistakes were obvious and should have been corrected before I submitted the report. Thankfully, as I became more familiar with the role, and made time for self-evaluation before submitting my reports to my manager, fewer errors were highlighted to me. This taught me a valuable lesson: I needed to concentrate on finishing the report swiftly but also *carefully*, and to *evaluate* my own work before submitting it to my manager as complete and finished. This also developed my resilience; something that is important for students to develop, whatever pathway they choose. Anecdotes such as the one above, can be shared in on-to-ones with learners to demonstrate resilience-building journeys. Students can become preoccupied with deadlines and assessments without leaving much time for the very important element of evaluation – an aspect that is essential as a practitioner. Pracademics need to support students in developing evaluation skills in addition to practising self-evaluation in their own work (Schön, 1983).

Self-evaluation is raised by Tai et al. (2018), who suggest that students need to be able to evaluate their own work before leaving university, and that HEIs should consider the use of evaluative judgement. Tai et al. note that incorporating this aspect into assessment can help students to develop self-regulated learning (Sitzmann & Ely, 2011). Pracademics may realise the importance of being able to judge their own work, because in practice, they could not expect to rely on their manager to do so. The ability (and confidence) to judge one's own work is a key skill worth developing in students. Furthermore, this skill helps to lay the foundation for being able to evaluate the work of others. As learners begin to understand the reference points for good quality work, they will also develop an understanding of the good quality markers and indicators required as and when they may eventually become managers themselves.

Another aspect to consider, and incorporate within current teaching practice, is group working/peer learning. Brandes and Ginnis (1986) (amongst others, including Hall & Buzwell, 2013; Mutch, 1998; Myers, 2012; Poort et al., 2022) make a persuasive argument for the benefits, advantages, and value of group working. They suggest that group working can act as a mechanism by which the ownership of learning can pass from the teacher to the student. They suggest that ownership is central within the context of education and that students themselves should own their learning. Furthermore, they conceptualise ownership as a culmination of possession and responsibility, which extends to "the motivation for care, maintenance, and development of that which is owned" (Brandes & Ginnis, p. 25).

Students, particularly in the first year of a degree programme, may be accustomed to a learning environment where (school) teachers have owned the students' learning. Students may even perceive that their teachers have previously decided what they need to study and talk about, the tasks they need to complete, and the resources that will be needed. Therefore, students coming into HE from school may think, similarly, that the person standing at the front of the classroom also has ownership of their learning. The use of group work/peer learning directs the focus away from the teacher to the student/s (Boud et al., 2001). This responsibility for learning and group cooperation is a useful skill to develop for a career in practice. Pracademics' industrial experience may have taught them to take ownership of their own learning and to develop and maintain networks with our colleagues. As pracademics, we need to prepare students for the challenges of a working life where we do not necessarily work with our friends, where we need to discover things on our own, and where we have to develop a professional attitude and follow an accepted etiquette. By working in groups, the lecturer is no longer the centre of attention and ownership of learning is transferred to the student and the collective student body. Of course, academics/lecturers are there to guide, although the students remain autonomous. Pracademics understand the value of developing an independent learning approach, because in industry they may have had opportunities to learn from a range of colleagues, in addition to their direct manager/s. Students too need to be aware of the learning enrichment that other sources and people can provide.

Pracademics have a key role to play in supporting students with development of good working relationships, given that a part of their learning is nurtured and nourished through their relationships with professional networks. The conversations with former colleagues from practice, networking activities at professional conferences, and reading professional publications and academic literature all enrich scholarly activity and personal learning. Pracademics do not have to cut all ties with the professional/practitioner community. Maintaining these important links will give insights into the current conversations in the field, thereby informing teaching and enriching students' experience of the subject. A study of pracademics by Dickinson et al. (2022) highlighted the close relationship of 'real world' applicability and the development of innovative syllabus content and teaching designs. Furthermore, it may also indicate areas of interest that pracademics wish to study and research. Part of the way in which these elements coalesce for me, is through my personal reflections and reflection activity.

Rogers (2001) suggests that, although there has been an increased focus on reflective skills across HE, there needs to be a deeper understanding of how they can be applied to (and incorporated into) teaching and learning. One way of facilitating reflection within current teaching practice is to consider how much time is included within the module activities for reflection, for both the facilitator and the students. Pracademics can crystallise their learning from experience by reflecting on what they have done in their industry careers. This can be deliberate, or it can arise as thoughts meander through memories for different reasons. I still experience moments that connect my past practical experience to what I read and teach in academia in the present. Processes of learning about ourselves, about teaching, and about learning, form a continuous journey and at times can be non-sequential. Surely, that is part of why pracademics are pursuing academic careers because they like learning and developing. Biggs and Tang (2011) explain reflective teaching in a simple way, using excellent examples for those who are new (and not so new) to teaching. I am always surprised at how much can be discovered and distilled through the power of reflection.

In summary, if you are a pracademic, this is your first year of teaching, and you feel that your head is spinning and academic life is not what you imagined, you should not worry: many pracademics have felt this way (Dickinson et al., 2022). You may have had to write your notes from scratch, set assessments, complete marking, and you will have had to learn a whole new vocabulary, but it does get easier. By reflecting on your own learning journey, and how you want to facilitate students' understanding via assessments, examples from your time in practice, and group work amongst other things, you will be able to create a good learning environment for your students.

The last section considers topics that may become significant to the pracademic in the future. It discusses how they could harness these to optimise learning and development for themselves and, of course, their students.

Conclusion

The Future

Below are some thoughts about future directions on which pracademics may wish to reflect. They are the use of technology for student learning, teaching and reflection; keeping abreast of developments in practice; and the role that mentors can play.

We have experienced a seismic shift in how we operate as a society, and in our need for, and use of, information technology (IT) and social media (Burns, 2017). Social media has provided vehicles for individuals to voice their opinions and thoughts. Celebrities, politicians, and academics use such media to share their ideas and perspectives. Over the years, this form of communication and sharing has increased significantly. Burns (2017) provides a comprehensive overview of the social media space and gives a helpful reference point for understanding some of its characteristics. HE has also experienced a change in its relationship with IT and digital development (Farias-Gaytan et al., 2022) and one that is, perhaps, here to stay. Furthermore, the harnessing of technology in the HE sector has been expedited via the effects of the COVID-19 pandemic (Gamage & Perera, 2021).

Social media can also be very useful to students and, as educators, we should look to incorporate some of these areas within the teaching and learning opportunities that we provide to students. One form that this could take is the use of blogs and blogging. Oravec (2002, p. 618) suggests that "the weblog has many dimensions that make it well suited to students' unique voices… empower[ing] students to become more analytical and critical". The reason for this is that to develop and sustain a clear and confident voice, one must carefully formulate and stand by one's opinions. Pracademics may realise the importance of being confident in our opinions because after an opinion is voiced in practice, it most likely precipitates an action. The action arises because the opinion has value, and the value is a product of practical knowledge, experience, and evidence. In an accounting context, it could be the selling price of a product or the application of an accounting technique. For further discussions about social media for learning, see Dagli et al., 2020.

Pracademics understand the significance of supporting their opinions with evidence. This is a useful skill to develop in students too, because in the workplace, an idea that is supported using evidence may carry more weight than one without. Meyer (2003) suggests that when opinions and ideas are conveyed in an online setting, versus a face-to-face setting, the quality of the discussion can improve. Meyer's study found that "often more thoughtful [and] more reasoned perspectives would be voiced" (2003, p. 61).

Online discussions would have more structure, be more persuasively argued, and better supported by evidence (potentially an academic's dream). In effect, online fora allow more time for reflection and thinking, which is not always readily available in face-to-face sessions, where participants can be competing for limited time. When writing an opinion, it is likely to be based on some type of evidence, so that it can be defended. This demands a structured and planned strategy for conveying an opinion, as it will appear in black and white. Furthermore, having an online forum to share opinions means that students are not bound by lecture and seminar/tutorial times, thus providing them with flexibility. This is also something that has been brought to the fore by the transition to online learning, necessitated by the pandemic (Gamage & Perera, 2021). An online discussion thread allows students to access and write their points of view (possibly after reflection and based on evidence) at a time when it suits them. This also gives the academic an insight into the subjects/discussions that students find interesting and topical, which consequently can generate more engagement and discussion when they deliver their next face-to-face classes.

Another key priority is to develop and enhance digital literacy and competency for students. Shopova (2014) posits that digital capabilities can support students in honing information gathering and communication skills, leading to increased competitiveness when applying for jobs. Hence, part of the modern skills' set is digital competence and ensuring that students keep pace with digital developments. Sharpe et al. (2022) provide an informative collection of discussions that explore HE through a digital lens. Digital skills are also an essential component for enhancing student employability. For me, there is some technical knowledge that I draw upon years after I learned it, because as mentioned above, learning is not always sequential. Being human means that we can access memories (and learning) long after they have faded into the mists of our own individual timeline. An example of this for me is my proficiency on the spreadsheet application, Microsoft Excel. Excel for me is a joy, but I never thought I would ever say that. The first time that I encountered Excel was in my undergraduate degree course, and I remain grateful to the designers of that undergraduate programme. When I was being interviewed for my first job after graduation, I was able to talk about what I had learned to do in Excel. As a potential employee, I would therefore have been a more attractive prospect than a candidate with no prior experience. Since securing my first role, I have spent many hours in practice as an accountant, working on Excel. Pracademics should try to incorporate digital systems and applications that are used in practice within programme curricula, where appropriate, to ensure that students are equipped to meet employer and industry expectations (Morgan et al., 2022).

Over time, the focus of HE will inevitably change, depending on the topics that become fashionable, just as in any other sector. For example, the current emphasis on reflection and digitisation within the curriculum (see above) may decrease and something else will be highlighted. Although this can be destabilising for any lecturer, it could be particularly challenging for a pracademic given that it may add to the feelings that they may already be experiencing around the need to play catch up. However, one of a pracademic's skills can be their ability to navigate changing environments like a "chameleon" (Dickinson et al., 2022, p. 298) just as they may have done in practice, the key difference being that things may shift much more slowly in HE. This more gradual rate of change enables a more measured and thoughtful long-term plan, such as undertaking a teaching qualification or contemplating a higher degree or undertaking research to contribute to knowledge. HE may provide pracademics with opportunities to survey the landscape, reflect, and make decisions that deliver a rewarding and enriching academic experience not only for the students, but also for them.

I have completed a Postgraduate Certificate in HE (PGCHE), and this has been a valuable tool in developing my pedagogic practice and facilitating my registration with Advance HE, the UK-based professional development organisation for HE. As an active member, I can follow and embrace good practice found in the sector and disseminate it. The PGCHE was a worthwhile programme because it introduced me to educational vocabulary, and helpful learning and teaching frameworks. By combining understanding gained through the PGCHE with my practical experience, I felt 'more rounded' as a scholar and educator. I still access materials and information through Advance HE and I find it very useful. For examples of other reflections on the value of a teaching qualification, see Ginns et al. (2008).

I maintain strong networks within academia, the profession, and the wider business community. I try to attend online webinars and in-person events organised by professional accounting bodies and HE organisations that align with my areas of interest and research. Although this is tricky to manage alongside my academic role, it does ensure that I have a good overview of current issues. Having networks within these spheres enables knowledge exchange, creativity, and supports continued personal and professional development (Ansmann et al., 2014). Additionally, it provides an opportunity to make a difference by transcending professional and academic boundaries. For me, this has meant writing for a practitioner journal and providing strategic support for a learned society, amongst other things. Newer pracademics could get in touch with the editor/s of the publication they want to write for and ask if they would be interested in publishing some of their writing. Another useful tip in the journey forward is to select some mentors to provide a system of feedforward and feedback – a sounding board, if you like. Newer pracademics are likely to be doing a lot of thinking (after all, they are an academic), and on occasion, it is useful, if not essential, to incorporate insights from others, with whom they may have reciprocal respect and trust. This may help develop a grounded view of the immediate context and have some perspective when planning. Many HE institutions have formal mentoring programmes where mentors can be allocated, or, alternatively, prospective mentees could approach a colleague with whom they feel a natural affinity. Manuel and Poorsattar (2021) provide some excellent guidance for successful mentoring and mentor selection. Two key tips that they highlight (amongst others) are, first, to choose your own mentor, and second, to build a network of mentors to draw upon, thus providing a diverse range of skill and input.

By deciding to read this collection of insights, it indicates that you may be open to suggestions, and new ways of thinking. Not all of these recommendations may work for everyone, but the idea is to select the ones that might, and adapt them to what *does work* for you. There is a little bit of trial and error in everything. If everything was a success all the time, then every academic would be perfect, but alas, we are all a work in progress.

Finally, a note to newer pracademics – welcome. I wish you every success as you begin another phase in your career.

Points for Reflection
- Stirk champions the experience that pracademics bring with them into academia. To what extent might your previous experience, as a student, practitioner, and/or academic have shaped your current approach?
- The chapter emphasises the importance of evaluation and reflection. How do you assess your own practice, and foster an evaluative approach in others? How could regular reflection enhance your professional development and practice, and what opportunities are available for you to do this?
- Stirk emphasises the importance of continual development for academics and students. How could you use your role to support colleagues and students with their future endeavours?

References

Ansmann, L., Flickinger, T. E., Barello, S., Kunneman, M., Mantwill, S., Quilligan, S., Zanini, C., & Aelbrecht, K. (2014). Career development for early career academics: Benefits of networking and the role of professional societies. *Patient Education and Counseling, 97*(1), 132–134. https://doi.org/10.1016/j.pec.2014.06.013

Biggs, J. (1996). Enhancing teaching through constructive alignment. *Higher Education, 32*(3), 347–364. https://doi.org/10.1007/BF00138871

Biggs, J., & Tang, C. (2011). *Teaching for quality learning at university* (4th ed.). Open University Press.

Boud, D. (1995). Assessment and learning: Contradictory or complementary? In P. Knight (Ed.), *Assessment for learning in higher education* (pp. 35–48). Kogan Page.

Boud, D., Cohen, R., & Sampson, J. (2001). *Peer learning in higher education: Learning from & with each other*. Kogan Page.

Brandes, D., & Ginnis, P. (1986). *A guide to student-centred learning*. Blackwell.

Burns, K. S. (2017). *Social media: A reference handbook*. ABC-CLIO.

Cox, B. (1994). *Practical pointers for university teachers*. Kogan Page.

Dagli, G., Altinay, F., Altinay, Z., & Altinay, M. (2020). Evaluation of higher education services: Social media learning. *The International Journal of Information and Learning Technology, 38*(1), 147–159. https://doi.org/10.1108/IJILT-03-2020-0032

Dickinson, J., Fowler, A., & Griffiths, T.-L. (2022). Pracademics? Exploring transitions and professional identities in higher education. *Studies in Higher Education, 47*(2), 290–304. https://doi.org/10.1080/03075079.2020.1744123

Farias-Gaytan, S., Aguaded, I., & Ramirez-Montoya, M. S. (2022). Transformation and digital literacy: Systematic literature mapping. *Education and Information Technologies, 27*(2), 1417–1437. https://doi.org/10.1007/s10639-021-10624-x

Gamage, K., & Perera, E. (2021). Undergraduate students' device preferences in the transition to online learning. *Social Sciences (Basel), 10*(8), 288. https://doi.org/10.3390/socsci10080288

Ginns, P., Kitay, J., & Prosser, M. (2008). Developing conceptions of teaching and the scholarship of teaching through a graduate certificate in higher education. *The International Journal for Academic Development, 13*(3), 175–185. https://doi.org/10.1080/13601440802242382

Hall, D., & Buzwell, S. (2013). The problem of free-riding in group projects: Looking beyond social loafing as reason for non-contribution. *Active Learning in Higher Education, 14*(1), 37–49.

Kolb, D. A. (2015). *Experiential learning*. Pearson.

Kotsis, S. V., & Chung, K. C. (2013). Application of the see one, do one, teach one concept in surgical training. *Plastic and Reconstructive Surgery, 131*(5), 1194–1201. https://doi.org/10.1097/PRS.0b013e318287a0b3

Manuel, S., & Poorsattar, S. (2021). Mentoring up: Twelve tips for successfully employing a mentee-driven approach to mentoring relationships. *Medical Teacher, 43*(4), 384–387. https://doi.org/10.1080/0142159X.2020.1795098

Morgan, A., Sibson, R., & Jackson, D. (2022). Digital demand and digital deficit: Conceptualising digital literacy and gauging proficiency among higher education students. *Journal of Higher Education Policy and Management, 44*(3), 258–275. https://doi.org/10.1080/1360080X.2022.2030275

Meyer, K. A. (2003). Face-to-face versus threaded discussions: The role of time and higher-order thinking. *Asynchronous Learning Networks, 7*(3), 55–65. https://doi.org/10.24059/olj.v7i3.1845

Mutch, A. (1998). Employability or learning? Groupwork in higher education. *Education & Training, 40*(2), 50–56. https://doi.org/10.1108/00400919810206884

Myers, S. A. (2012). Students' perceptions of classroom group work as a function of group member selection. *Communication Teacher, 26*(1), 50–64. https://doi.org/10.1080/17404622.2011.625368

Oravec, J. (2002). Bookmarking the world: Weblog applications in education. *Journal of Adolescent and Adult Literacy, 45*(7), 616–621.

Panda, A. (2014). Bringing academic and corporate worlds closer. *Management and Labour Studies, 39*(2), 140–159. https://doi.org/10.1177/0258042X14558174

Poort, I., Jansen, E., & Hofman, A. (2022). Does the group matter? Effects of trust, cultural diversity, and group formation on engagement in group work in higher education. *Higher Education Research and Development, 41*(2), 511–526. https://doi.org/10.1080/07294360.2020.1839024

Race, P. (2005). *Making learning happen*. Sage.

Rogers, R. (2001). Reflection in higher education: A concept analysis. *Innovative Higher Education, 26*(1), 37–57. https://doi.org/10.1023/A:1010986404527

Schön, D. A. (1983). *The reflective practitioner*. Temple Smith.

Sitzmann, T., & Ely, K. (2011). A meta-analysis of self-regulated learning in work-related training and educational attainment: What we know and where we need to go. *Psychological Bulletin, 137*(3), 421–442. https://doi.org/10.1037/a0022777

Sharpe, R., Bennett, S., & Varga-Atkins, T. (2022). *Handbook of digital higher education*. Edward Elgar Publishing.

Shopova, T. (2014). Digital literacy of students and its improvement at the university. *Journal on Efficiency and Responsibility in Education and Science, 7*(2), 26–32. https://doi.org/10.7160/eriesj.2014.070201

Tai, J., Ajjawi, R., Boud, D., Dawson, P., & Panadero, E. (2018). Developing evaluative judgement. *Higher Education, 76*(3), 467–481. https://doi.org/10.1007/s10734-017-0220-3

Wilkinson, C. (2020). Imposter syndrome and the accidental academic: An autoethnographic account. *The International Journal for Academic Development, 25*(4), 363–374. https://doi.org/10.1080/1360144X.2020.1762087

Wong, Z. Y., & Kaur, D. (2018). The role of vocational identity development and motivational beliefs in undergraduates' student engagement. *Counselling Psychology Quarterly, 31*(3), 294–316. https://doi.org/10.1080/09515070.2017.1314249

Dr. Michelle Stirk is an Associate Professor in Accounting, at the University of Nottingham's Business School. Her research focuses on how sustainability and business organisations intersect, this has included research projects in the area of management control, modern slavery and renewable energy. She is a chartered management accountant and previously held a number of senior accountant posts in both the public and private sectors. Her research is interdisciplinary and draws upon her wealth of practical and academic experience gained over 25 years.

Chapter 5
Imposter Syndrome and the Non-pracademics: A Joint Autoethnographic Account

Catherine Wilkinson and Samantha Wilkinson

Abstract This chapter adopts a joint autoethnographic approach as the authors reflect on their own everyday experiences as non-pracademics teaching across Education Studies, Early Years, Early Childhood Studies and Childhood Studies programmes at two UK Higher Education Institutions (HEIs), Liverpool John Moores University and Manchester Metropolitan University. At these HEIs, the aforementioned programmes are taught predominantly by former professionals, for instance primary school teachers, nursery owners, managers and workers. The authors focus on feelings on imposter syndrome as 'non-pracademics', having never worked in professional settings outside of academia related to children and young people. Using excerpts from their fieldnote diaries, the authors reflect on expectations from students that academic staff possess knowledge of the structures and processes involved in practice and have networks with professional settings. This leads the authors to reflect that some students may value more highly academics with practitioner expertise, and the resultant feelings of imposter syndrome stemming from beliefs of being lesser or lacking they felt as non-pracademics.

Keywords Imposter syndrome · Non-pracademic · Pracademia · Higher education sector · Joint autoethnography · Field journal · Student experience · Academic collaboration

> **At a Glance**
> - Adopting a joint autoethnographic approach, this chapter provides personal reflection on the authors own everyday experiences as non-pracademics teaching across Education Studies, Early Years, Early Childhood Studies, and Childhood Studies programmes at two United Kingdom (UK) Higher Education Institutions (HEIs).

(continued)

C. Wilkinson (✉) · S. Wilkinson
School of Education, Liverpool John Moores University, Liverpool, UK
e-mail: C.Wilkinson@ljmu.ac.uk; samantha.wilkinson@mmu.ac.uk

© The Author(s), under exclusive license to Springer Nature
Switzerland AG 2023
J. Dickinson, T.-L. Griffiths (eds.), *Professional Development for Practitioners in Academia*, Knowledge Studies in Higher Education 13,
https://doi.org/10.1007/978-3-031-33746-8_5

- Focusses on feelings of imposter syndrome given that the authors, as 'non-pracademics', have never worked in professional settings outside of academia related to children and young people.
- Reflects on expectations from students that academic staff possess knowledge of the structures and processes involved in practice and have networks with professional settings.

Introduction

This chapter adopts a joint autoethnographic approach as the authors reflect on their own everyday experiences as non-pracademics teaching across Education Studies, Early Years, Early Childhood Studies, and Childhood Studies programmes at two United Kingdom (UK) Higher Education Institutions (HEIs); namely, Liverpool John Moores University (Catherine) and Manchester Metropolitan University (Samantha). Departing from typical use of the term 'career academic', we use the term 'non-pracademic' in this chapter, which to our knowledge has not been previously used in academic literature. We have chosen to use this phase as two 'accidental academics' (see Wilkinson, 2020), believing that 'career academic' sounds more strategic and premeditated in reaching our career stage. Career academic is a phrase used by Pilcher et al. (2017) and Tennant et al. (2015) to describe research-led staff employed at HEIs who enter academia with limited or no industrial or practical experience. So-called career academics have often been welcomed by hiring committees for their potential for grant capture and publishing of high impact journal articles, thereby being celebrated for enhancing institutional reputation. By contrast, the phrase 'pracademic' (see for instance Volpe & Chandler, 2001; Posner, 2009) has been used to describe someone who is both an academic and a practitioner in their subject area, and examples of different practitioner-academics or academic-practitioners permeate this edited collection. Arguably, the phrases career academic and pracademic are rather limiting and binary; for instance, an academic is also a practitioner though the weight of their practice is in Higher Education (HE).

Our use of the phrase 'non-pracademics' in this chapter refers to the fact that we have no professional experience in children's education or early childhood settings, and as such our knowledge of these subjects comes from education and through consulting scholarship only. This is discordant with the fact that at our respective institutions the aforementioned programmes are taught predominantly by former professionals, for instance primary school teachers, nursery owners, managers and workers. In this chapter, we focus on feelings of imposter syndrome as 'non-pracademics'. Using excerpts from our fieldnote diaries, we reflect on expectations from students that academic staff should possess knowledge of the structures and processes involved in practice and have networks with professional settings. This leads us to reflect that some students may value academics with practitioner expertise more highly, resulting in feelings of imposter syndrome stemming from beliefs of being lesser or lacking as non-pracademics.

This chapter is structured as follows. First, we provide a position statement. We then identify the scholarly void to which this chapter aims to contribute; namely, the discussion of imposter syndrome in relation to pracademia and specifically non-pracademics. Following this, we detail our methodological approach of a joint auto-ethnography. Then, we discuss two key themes identified through our analysis: lack of lived experience, and networks and ties. We conclude with two key recommendations for institutional change to enable synergy between pracademics and non-pracademics for the benefit of both groups, and their students.

Position Statement

Following graduation from our degree programmes, we both completed master's degrees and then began our PhDs in 2012, submitting and being conferred in 2015. Having completed our doctorates, we moved into temporary research positions. Within one year of working in these roles, we secured lecturing posts in 2016 (Catherine at Edge Hill University and Samantha at Manchester Metropolitan University, UK). Currently, Catherine is employed as Reader in Childhood and Youth Studies at Liverpool John Moores University and Samantha as a Senior Lecturer in Childhood and Youth Studies at Manchester Metropolitan University. Neither of us has worked outside of academia in professional settings related to children and young people. Having provided a brief position statement, we now move on to highlight the scholarly void to which this chapter aims to contribute.

Situating Imposter Syndrome in Debates on Pracademia

'Imposter syndrome', coined in 1978 by Clance and Imes (1978), refers to a psychological phenomenon characterised by intense feelings of intellectual fraudulence. Imposter syndrome suggests that you believe your success was down to luck and soon your lack of ability will be exposed as underserving of your position (Kauati, n.d.). Pressures of perfectionism, increasing social comparisons, and a fear of failure are suggested to contribute to imposter syndrome (Sakulku, 2011). Imposter syndrome has been well documented in the academy, ranging from research studying the incidence and impact of the phenomenon (Hutchins & Rainbolt, 2017), to a focus on imposter syndrome as related to doctoral students (Craddock et al., 2011) and teaching evaluations (Brems et al., 1994).

For the individual who experiences it, imposter syndrome can be debilitating; bias and exclusion can exasperate feelings of doubt (see Tulshvan & Burey, 2021). It can have wide-reaching career implications. Laux (2018) reports on flawed perceptions of the promotion process and implications of this for women academics experiencing imposter syndrome. Further, Robertson (2017) tells us how the anxiety and stress provoked by imposter syndrome can lead people to give up their academic careers. Imposter syndrome can have wider implications beyond the workplace, including sleep disruption (Wilkinson, 2020).

Whilst imposter syndrome has been discussed and debated extensively in the literature related to HE, there is a lack of academic literature that connects discussions of imposter syndrome to pracademia, and specifically to the notion of being 'non-pracademics', or even the conventional term of career academics. It is to this specific gap in the literature that this chapter contributes, with an emphasis on the experiences of two women in academia. Existing research explores transitions made by former or current practitioners who are now university academics (pracademics) (see, for instance, Dickinson et al., 2020), but there is a lack of research focussed on non-pracademics. Scholarship on 'career' academics' is predominantly in the fields of construction and engineering education (see Pilcher et al., 2017; Tennant et al., 2015), and not in the areas of early childhood studies or childhood and youth studies.

Having highlighted the scholarly void to which this chapter aims to contribute, we now outline the methodology.

Methodology

As self-reflexive inquiry, autoethnography can be used to recall, retell, and reveal bodily embodiment (Allbon, 2012). The process of autoethnography combines characteristics of ethnography and autobiography that allows individuals to explore cultural understanding through self-observation, which results in individual narratives (Chang, 2008). As a methodology, autoethnography enables us to "open up to the possibility of seeing more of what we might ignore in both ourselves and others, asking why it is ignored, and what we might need to do about it" (Dauphinee, 2010, p. 818).

This chapter reports on a joint autoethnography. Joint autoethnography, sometimes termed collaborative autoethnography, is a "multivocal approach" (Lapadat, 2017, p. 589), in which two or more researchers work together to share personal encounters and interpret the pooled autoethnographic data. This chapter builds on existing, published, autoethnographic work by the authors (Wilkinson, 2019, 2020) which reflected on earlier data from our research diaries. These papers include honest accounts of our lived experiences of imposter syndrome as academics, and specifically women working in UK HEIs. We argue that joint autoethnography is a valid methodology through which to achieve the kind of reflexivity required to reflect on and represent our experiences as 'non-pracademics'.

Diary-Keeping

From January 2019–December 2020 we recorded, in individual personal diaries, observations, thoughts, feelings, and interactions of our everyday experiences (Dewalt & Dewalt, 2002) in academia. In our diaries, we were concerned with the ordinary, banal everydayness of events and interactions; paying attention to taken-for-granted practices in our roles. Our diaries contained subjective accounts that we reflected upon, individually and together, periodically.

Data Analysis

We adopted an interactive, thematic approach to analysing our diary entries. We analysed by hand as we believed that this would facilitate greater closeness to the data, considering this "human as analyst" (Robson, 2011, p. 463) stance important, due to the autoethnographic nature of our study, where the researcher is both a tool of data collection and analysis, and the subject of that data collection and analysis. After reading through our data set multiple times, first we undertook open coding, using verbatim words from our diary entries. We dismissed any preconceived data categories and loosened the initial focus of the study to "generate as many codes as possible" (Emerson et al., 1995, p. 152). We used memos to comment on parts of our diaries that intrigued us, or that we considered particularly important. This was followed by a second coding of data (axial coding). MacLure (2008) speaks of the pleasure derived from manual analysis, particularly "poring over the data, annotating, describing, linking, bringing theory to bear, recalling what others have written, and seeing things from different angles" (p. 174). Crucially, this enabled us to ask questions about what had emerged through the data. As a result, we changed and made links between some codes, and dropped and added others. We returned to the data multiple times, adopting a process of constant comparison, grouping some of the open codes together under a single code, and comparing our individual analyses to ensure thorough interrogation of data and thematic concordance (Silverio et al., 2020). Below, we introduce you to the key themes yielded from selective coding.

Findings

The key themes identified in our analysis are lack of lived experience; and networks and ties. We discuss these respectively below.

Lack of Lived Experience: "No Time Behind the Wheel"

Lack of lived experience was a recurring theme within our field diaries. Lived experience refers to personal knowledge about the world gained through direct, first-hand involvement in everyday events, rather than through representations constructed by other people. This lived experience within a professional setting, for instance through paid employment or volunteer work, is considered to bring authenticity to the role of a pracademic (see Dickinson et al., 2020). "Time behind the wheel" is a metaphor used to describe the value placed on learning 'on the job' (see Posner's, 2009 discussion of re-engaging practitioners and academics). As academics with no experience in professional practice related to children and young people, our field diaries were replete with examples where we believed that our lack of lived experience was evident to students. For instance, we did not know some of the language or structures of practice settings which were much more familiar to our pracademic colleagues. As an example, in a discussion during a workshop with students, the following situation unfolded:

> Today during a session with my Early Childhood Studies student, a student asked me whether their Early Childhood Studies degree would enable them to progress to the role of Nursery Manager. I honestly did not know the answer to the question or what qualifications were needed. This was further complicated as the student was from Northern Ireland and I was also not sure if the qualifications needed there were the same or different as in England. This gave me the opportunity to tell the student I would need to look into this. I did some research into this and emailed the student later in the day to tell them what I had found out, but I reflected on how this would be much more common knowledge for my colleagues who had worked in or managed nurseries. (Catherine, 22nd April 2020, field diary)

Along the same theme, Samantha reports on an incident in her field diary where it became apparent that the technical terminology related to early years' settings was not familiar to her:

> Lecturing on Early Years and Childhood Studies, we often have students undertaking placement experience in nursery settings. Discussing their placement experiences with me, students use terms such as 'key person' and discuss platforms such as 'Tapestry' that I am not familiar with, having never worked in a nursery setting myself. I felt like students assumed I would have this knowledge, but I used it as an opportunity to make students feel like the experts and asked them to share their knowledge and to commend them on the knowledge they held. (Samantha, 2020, field diary)

Above, we both reflect on how we did not possess knowledge of professional structures or language related to practice settings. We considered our pracademic colleagues, on the other hand, as being able to 'walk the talk', having on-the-ground practice experience (see Talbot, 2020). Without this, we believed that it could be seen by students that we are lacking intellectual capital (see Bontis, 1998; Cuozzo et al., 2017), or at least this is what our imposter syndrome led us to believe, as Catherine articulates with reference to a different scenario below:

> Today a student asked me how the Early Years Foundation Stage (EYFS) is assessed in practice. I refer to the EYFS a lot in my lectures, in fact it is integral to the Early Childhood Studies degree programme, as we introduce students to the characteristics of effective learning, and the prime and specific areas etc. However, I did not know the specifics of 'how' the EYFS is assessed in practice. I was co-teaching the session, so I referred the student to my colleague, a former nursery worker. I watched as the student listened attentively to my colleague's answer, and I felt a huge sense of failure, like I didn't belong in this subject area. (Catherine, 2020, field diary excerpt)

This sense of failure and feelings of incompetence is also captured by Samantha:

> One of the key readings for one of my units with an assignment focusing on professionalism in practice is a book that many staff who have professional experience in early years and / or childhood studies have contributed to. I have written a host of texts, but these are predominantly theoretical or methodological. I think students really enjoy reading work published by their lecturers and it makes me feel a bit of an outsider that I wasn't able to signpost students to anything helpful I had written in this regard. (Samantha, 2020, field diary)

In our field diary excerpts, we can both be seen to reflect on how we believed students valued our academic colleagues with practitioner expertise more highly. This led to feelings of being lesser or lacking in comparison to our pracademic peers. These colleagues were former professionals: for instance, primary school teachers, nursery owners, managers, and workers. However, it should be considered that pracademics' knowledge may be perceived as outdated by students, owing to time spent away from professional settings (see Dickinson et al., 2020). Further, whilst we consider our knowledge field to be limited in the respects we note above, it is expansive in other areas. Here, we refer the reader to Barth's (1995) discussion of other knowledge and other ways of knowing, which is beyond the scope of this chapter.

Imposter syndrome permeates our field diary accounts as we reflect on feelings of being undeserving of our positions, and feelings of intellectual fraudulence (see Clance & Imes, 1978). This is particularly interesting when considering Volpe and Chandler's (2001) discussion that pracademics often encounter suspicion from students because of their perceived or actual stake as members of the academic community. Though it should be noted that Volpe and Chandler's (2001) study was within the specific context of conflict management, which will have directly impacted on the perception of pracademics by students, our joint autoethnography has shown that, as non-pracademics, we experience (or perceive to experience) similar suspicion from the student body. Having presented our analysis in relation to 'lack of lived experience', we now present the second and final identified theme.

Networks and Ties: "It's Not What You Know, It's Who You Know"

The second and final theme identified within our field diaries relates to networks and ties. According to Granovetter (1973, p. 1364) weak ties, or "bridges", are infrequent contacts that are often without emotional content. Granovetter (1973, 1983) positions weak ties as a powerful feature of human relationships, useful for the acquisition of information and for societal integration. Within our field diaries, we often reflected on how we did not possess as many ties as our pracademic colleagues. Take the following excerpt from Catherine's diary as an example:

> In a session today I reminded students that they must start thinking about where to undertake their Level 5 placements. A student approached me at the end of the workshop to express their worry at finding a placement and asked if I had any connections they could use. Whilst I could divert this student to another staff member and to placement services within our university, I did not have any personal connections I could use to support this student and I felt like the student expected me to hold these connections. (Catherine, 2019, field diary excerpt)

The above excerpt is significant when considering Jarrett et al.'s (2005, p. 52) finding that ties to "resource-rich adults" can assist young people towards further education and employment opportunities. Catherine reflects on how, unlike many of her pracademic colleagues, she was resource-poor in terms of the ties that she could foster for her students. This further relates to previous literature (see, for example, Posner, 2009; Powell et al. 2018) which discusses how pracademics can play bridging roles; serving as network brokers bridging the ivory tower and practice and creating new channels to enhance cooperation and communication across the academic-practitioner divide. Samantha documents a similar scenario to the one recounted by Catherine:

> I am the international exchange coordinator for the Early Years and Education Schools, which involves helping set incoming international students up with a placement experience; this is really useful for them to gain an awareness of cultural differences in education provision. However, I have no connections with any nurseries or primary schools in the area, and always have to ask my colleague who undertakes the equivalent role to me in the School of Primary Education to use her connections to help these students find placements. I feel inferior and as if I am not doing very well at my job because I lack these useful networks. (Samantha, 2019, field diary)

Above, Samantha acknowledges the strength of 'weak ties', acquaintances within one's network, (see Granovetter, 1973, 1983) for connecting students to new networks. Yet, she reflects on how she does not possess many relevant ties. As academic staff, we have the power to function as what McLaughlin (1993, p. 660) refers to as "brokers, catalysts, and coaches" for our students; making the contacts necessary and providing the introductions to make such opportunities possible. As non-pracademics, we experienced feelings of being lesser or lacking than our pracademic colleagues.

It was not solely links to placement opportunities which highlighted our lack of ties. Catherine recounts similar sentiments in her discussion of organising guest speakers:

> During a staff meeting today regarding a module I co-teach on with a former secondary school teacher and an early years professional, we were discussing options for guest speakers to come in to give inspiring talks to our students. I started suggesting the names of academics who I have seen present at conferences and considered them to be captivating and engaging. Part way through the conversation I realised that whilst my mind had immediately gone to academic guest speakers, my colleagues were actually looking for recommendations for professionals from within the local community, such as nursery managers, educators, and play therapists. When I couldn't suggest any such professionals, I felt I had nothing to contribute to the discussion and felt a sense of intellectual fraudulence. (Catherine, 2020, field diary excerpt)

The following excerpt from Samantha's field diary also emphasises this, with a focus on the impression that this may leave on colleagues:

> I am currently co-organising for international partners to visit my institution and we are planning talks by experts in the morning (e.g., a forest school leader) and visits to nurseries and primary schools in the afternoon. I feel like I am taking a backseat in the organising and may not appear all that helpful as I do not have any real connections with any local forest schools/nurseries/schools to invite guest speakers or arrange visits. (Samantha, 2020, field diary)

Notably, whilst we have referred to this theme as 'lack of ties', it is interesting that we both possess an abundance of ties with international academic colleagues, which may be incredibly useful to our students. Thus, whilst our specific lack of ties to individuals working in practice settings led to perceived fraudulence and feelings of self-doubt and personal incompetence, as we write this chapter, with the benefit of time and reflection, we realise that we have many ties of which our students can take advantage – not least those wanting to progress onto postgraduate study or academic careers.

Having presented both key thematic areas identified through our joint autoethnographic research, we now draw the chapter to a close.

Conclusion

In this chapter, we have presented findings from a joint autoethnography whereby we reflected on our own everyday experiences as non-pracademics teaching across Education Studies, Early Years, Early Childhood Studies, and Childhood Studies programmes at two UK HEIs. Using excerpts from our fieldnote diaries, we reflected on expectations from students that academic staff possess knowledge of the structures and processes involved in practice, and to hold networks with professional settings. This led us to reflect that some students may value academics with practitioner expertise more highly, resulting in feelings of imposter syndrome stemming from our beliefs of being lesser or lacking as non-pracademics.

Through our narrative presented in this chapter, we have developed a collective understanding of the experiences of two academic staff who do not possess experience in practice, or what we term 'non-pracademics'. We propose the following two key recommendations for institutional change:

Consider the benefits of implementing team teaching, where non-pracademics can team up with those teaching staff who possess practical expertise (pracademics) for student benefit.

Facilitate staff internships to different practice settings to enable non-pracademics to gain experience to inform course content and curriculum development, and to enable them to learn about language and structures in practice as part of their continuing professional development.

Through implementing these recommendations, the imposter syndrome experienced by non-pracademics can be alleviated and students may well benefit from this dual approach in terms of different kinds of knowledge. Future research could build on the experiences that we present herein, using in-depth interviews with other non-pracademic colleagues. Further, it would be interesting to interview students to gain their perspectives on their non-pracademic tutors, to see if these correspond with our presumptions, or if these presumptions are indeed clouded by imposter syndrome.

Points for Reflection
- The authors suggest that labelling different groups of academics may be unhelpful. Do you agree? Do you think that this practice may contribute to feelings of imposter syndrome?
- Is there anything which universities as organisations can do to manage some of the issues raised in this chapter? How might course/departmental leaders help promote collaboration between different groups of academics?
- With collaboration between academics the goal, what knowledge, skills, or networks do you possess that might be unique amongst your colleagues?

References

Allbon, C. (2012). "Down the rabbit hole" – "Curiouser and curiouser": Using autoethnography as a mode of writing to re-call, re-tell and re-veal bodily embodiment as self-reflexive inquiry. *Journal of Organizational Ethnography, 1*(1), 62–71.

Barth, F. (1995). Other knowledge and other ways of knowing. *Journal of Anthropological Research, 51*(1), 65–68.

Bontis, N. (1998). Intellectual capital: An exploratory study that develops measures and models. *Management Decision, 36*(2), 63–76.

Brems, C., Baldwin, M. R., Davis, L., & Namyniuk, L. (1994). The imposter syndrome as related to teaching evaluations and advising relationships of university faculty members. *The Journal of Higher Education, 65*(2), 183–193.

Chang, E. (2008). *Autoethnography as Method.* West Coast Press.

Clance, P. R., & Imes, S. A. (1978). The imposter phenomenon in high achieving women: Dynamics and therapeutic intervention. *Psychotherapy: Theory, Research & Practice, 15*(3), 241–247.

Craddock, S., Birnbaum, M., Rodriguez, K. L., Cobb, C., & Zeeh, S. (2011). Doctoral students and the imposter phenomenon: Am I smart enough to be here? *Journal of Student Affairs Research and Practice, 48*(4), 429–442.

Cuozzo, B., Dumay, J., Palmaccio, M., & Lombardi, R. (2017). Intellectual capital disclosure: A structured literature review. *Journal of Intellectual Capital, 18*(1), 9–28.

Dauphinee, E. (2010). The ethics of autoethnography. *Review of International Studies, 36*(3), 799–818.

Dewalt, K. M., & Dewalt, B. R. (2002). *Participant observation: A guide for fieldworkers.* AltaMira Press.

Dickinson, J., Fowler, A., & Griffiths, T. (2020). Pracademics? Exploring transitions and professional identities in higher education. *Studies in Higher Education, 47*(2), 1–15.

Emerson, R., Fretz, R., & Shaw, L. (1995). *Writing ethnographic fieldnotes.* The University of Chicago Press.

Granovetter, M. (1973). The strength of weak ties. *American Journal of Sociology, 78*(6), 1380–1380.

Granovetter, M. (1983). The strength of weak ties: A network theory revisited. *Sociological Theory, 1*(1), 201–233.

Hutchins, H. M., & Rainbolt, H. (2017). What triggers imposter phenomenon among academic faculty? A critical incident study exploring antecedents, coping, and development opportunities. *Human Resource Development International, 20*(3), 194–214.

Jarrett, R. L., Sullivan, P. J., & Watkins, N. D. (2005). Developing social capital through participation in organized youth programs: Qualitative insights from Three Programs. *Journal of Community Psychology, 33*(1), 41–55.

Kauati, A. (n.d.). *The imposter syndrome and academic life*. http://www.interparadigmas.org.br/wp-content/uploads/2015/06/N1.EN_.KAUATI.pdf

Lapadat, J. C. (2017). Ethics in autoethnography and collaborative autoethnography. *Qualitative Inquiry, 23*(8), 589–603.

Laux, S. E. (2018). *Experiencing the imposter syndrome in academia: Women faculty members' perception of the tenure and promotion process*. Doctoral dissertation, Saint Louis University.

MacLure, M. (2008). Classification or wonder? Coding as an analytic practice in qualitative research. In R. Coleman & J. Ringrose (Eds.), *Deleuze and research methodologies* (pp. 164–183). Edinburgh University Press.

Pilcher, N., Forster, A., Tennant, S., Murray, M., & Pilcher, N. C. (2017). Problematising the 'career academic' in UK construction and engineering education: Does the system want what the system gets? *European Journal of Engineering Education, 42*(6), 1467–1485.

Posner, P. L. (2009). The pracademic: An agenda for re-engaging practitioners and academics. *Public Budgeting & Finance, 29*(1), 12–26.

Powell, E., Winfield, G., Schatteman, A. M., & Trusty, K. (2018). Collaboration between practitioners and academics: Defining the pracademic experience. *The Journal of Nonprofit Education and Leadership, 8*(1), 62–79.

Robertson, J. (2017). Dealing with imposter syndrome. In J. Roberton, A. Williams, D. Jones, L. Isbel, & D. Loades (Eds.), *EqualBITE: Gender equality in higher education* (pp. 146–151). Sense Publishers.

Robson, C. (2011). *Real world research*. Wiley.

Sakulku, J. (2011). The impostor phenomenon. *International Journal of Behavioral Science, 6*(1), 75–97.

Silverio, S. A., Wilkinson, C., & Wilkinson, S. (2020). Further uses for grounded theory: A methodology for psychological studies of the performing arts, literature and visual media. *QMiP Bulletin, 29*, 8–19.

Talbot, D. (2020). *'Pracademics': A new generation of academics who walk the talk*. https://www.pioneerspost.com/news-views/20200929/pracademics-new-generation-of-academics-who-walk-the-talk

Tennant, S., Murray, M., Forster, A., & Pilcher, N. (2015). Hunt the shadow not the substance: The rise of the career academic in construction education. *Teaching in Higher Education, 20*(7), 723–737.

Tulshyan, R., & Burey, J. A. (2021). Stop telling women they have imposter syndrome. *Harvard Business Review, 31*, 1–7.

Volpe, M. R., & Chandler, D. (2001). Resolving and managing conflicts in academic communities: The emerging role of the "pracademic". *Negotiation Journal, 17*(3), 245–255.

Wilkinson, S. (2019). The story of Samantha: The teaching performances and inauthenticities of an early career human geography lecturer. *Higher Education Research & Development, 38*(2), 398–410.

Wilkinson, C. (2020). Imposter syndrome and the accidental academic: An autoethnographic account. *International Journal for Academic Development, 25*(4), 363–374.

Dr Catherine Wilkinson is Reader in Childhood and Youth Studies at Liverpool John Moores University. Prior to this, Catherine was a Senior Lecturer in Education at the same institution and continues to teach across the Education Studies and Early Childhood Studies degree programmes. Catherine completed her PhD in Environmental Sciences at University of Liverpool (2012–2015), funded by an ESRC CASE award. Catherine works at the intersection of a range of research approaches, including mixed methods, ethnographic and participatory research. Catherine's primary research interests are children, young people and identity; young people and community radio; and children and young people-friendly research methods. Catherine has an established reputation for making cutting-edge contributions, conceptually and methodologically, to research 'with' children and young people and uses this research to inspire teaching she delivers.

Dr Samantha Wilkinson is a Senior Lecturer in Childhood and Youth Studies at Manchester Metropolitan University. Samantha teaches and leads on a range of modules from Foundation to Masters level. Samantha is an interdisciplinary researcher and has undertaken research on a diverse range of themes including young people's alcohol consumption practice and experiences; Airbnb; home care for people with dementia; and university students and conceptualisations of place. Samantha completed a PhD in Human Geography at The University of Manchester (2012–2015). Her doctoral research explored young people's (aged 15–24) alcohol consumption practices and experiences. The research Samantha conducts draws on both traditional and innovative methods and she has published extensively on the use of novel, participatory and ethnographic methods with children and young people. Methods Samantha employs include autoethnography, joint autoethnography, participant observation and mobile phone methods.

Chapter 6
Grappling with Pracademia in Education: Forms, Functions, and Futures

Paul Campbell, Trista Hollweck, and Deborah M. Netolicky

Abstract This chapter begins by critically examining the origins and possibilities of the concepts of the pracademic and pracademia as both an identity marker and space of operation respectively. Drawing upon the previous scholarly work and reflections of the authors, broader themes and possibilities relating to the form, function, and future of pracademic identities and spaces are explored. Exploring the identities and spaces of pracademia through the lenses of power and agency (Friesen Journal of Professional Capital and Community 7(1):71–82, 2022) emphasises this process of exploration as sense-making and emancipatory in nature. It reveals new insights into forms, functions, and possible futures of the pracademic and pracademia.

This chapter concludes by highlighting how greater conceptualisation of pracademia and the pracademic in the field of education offers both a reflective and futures-oriented framework that can be applied to the interaction of policy, practice, and research, while also speaking to broader concerns of the role and purpose of higher education and the work of those predominantly based in higher education settings for broader society.

Keywords Identity · Community · Learned societies · Professional learning · Networks · Networking

P. Campbell (✉)
Education University of Hong Kong, Hong Kong, SAR, PRC

T. Hollweck
University of Ottawa, Ottawa, ON, Canada

D. M. Netolicky
Murdoch University, Murdoch, WA, Australia

© The Author(s), under exclusive license to Springer Nature Switzerland AG 2023
J. Dickinson, T.-L. Griffiths (eds.), *Professional Development for Practitioners in Academia*, Knowledge Studies in Higher Education 13,
https://doi.org/10.1007/978-3-031-33746-8_6

At a Glance

- Examines how professionals with membership and recognised expertise in a range of communities can exercise unique influence and forms of knowledge mobilisation.
- Explores the concepts of pracademia and the pracademic, and recognises the plurality of spaces, and the space itself, occupied by those interacting within, between, and beyond the domains of practice and academia.
- Highlights how pracademia involves three key components of exploration: identity, community, and engagement.
- Understands the possibilities of the pracademic and pracademia, and imagines the possibilities of working within, and across, commonly understood constructions of the boundaries between practice, policy, and research.

Introduction

Discussions about bridging research, policy, and practice, and the relationship between the academy and professions, are long-standing. In fact, relationships between the forms of knowledge, and how they are connected and applied, can be traced to Plato and Aristotle. Craft or domain-specific knowledge with a functional purpose was presented by Plato as *techne*. Aristotle, however, made a distinction between this functional knowledge and what he articulated as *phronesis*; the professional knowledge needed for those engaged in moral or value-implicated work in public spaces, which considered the complexity required to interact with a range of people (Dunne, 1997). Following on from the development of these ideas, society in Ancient Greece developed a shared appreciation for the importance of education, while also establishing distinctions between practice and theory (Wyse et al., 2020).

In modern times, how we comprehend and negotiate the distinct understandings and positioning of practice and theory, or practice and research, as well as what this means for professions and professionals, remains vibrant and worthy of critical consideration (Brookfield, 2017). There is also a need to challenge the discursive and organising tools that have come to characterise Western ideas of progress and modernity and the associated certainties of what constitutes knowledge and knowing (Harrison & Luckett, 2019). Indigenous knowledge and systems of beliefs often reflect a more holistic approach to understanding phenomena. Rather than making discipline-specific distinctions to observations and learning, there is "a world made up of constantly forming multidimensional cycles in which all elements are part of an entangled and complex web of interactions" (Mazzocchi, 2006, p. 464). This worldview challenges us, as authors, to consider how we understand knowledge and learning, and can help us to rethink the role of individuals, places, spaces, and their boundaries in the pursuit of learning. Concomitantly, it has implications for our conceptualisation of the pracademic and pracademia which we recognise is a

Western, hierarchical, and systematised one. We anticipate, and hope, that other approaches to knowing could open up this conceptual development in new and important ways.

As societies across the globe grapple with the challenges of our time, characterised by constitutional uncertainty, climate crisis, war and forced migration, and conflict of values, all within a post-truth era, the demands placed upon professions and education across phases continue to increase in volume and complexity (Campbell, 2020). With this comes both an opportunity and a need to understand how educators, and the professions that they represent or support, not only develop needed skills and capabilities, but also how they interact and collaborate across practice, research, and policy spaces to respond to the complex challenges they face.

Emerging through conferences, social media platforms, and more recently in academic writing, the concepts of pracademia and the pracademic in education are beginning to be conceptualised, theorised, and mobilised. In doing so, the literature is pursuing understanding of the new possibilities that these concepts offer for how we understand the interaction of practice, policy, and research, and how knowledge is created and deployed in more nuanced and imaginative ways (Hollweck et al., 2022a). To explore these prospects, this chapter begins by critically examining the origins of, and the opportunities presented by, the concepts of the pracademic and pracademia as an identity marker and space of operation respectively. Building on the published work and reflections of the authors, broader themes and possibilities relating to the form, function, and future of pracademic identities and spaces are explored. We draw upon our own doctoral work (on social ecology, communities and landscapes of practice, and professional identity) and our recent co-edited Special Issue for the *Journal of Professional Capital and Community* (JPCC) on "Pracademia: Exploring the possibilities, power and politics of boundary-spanners straddling the worlds of practice and scholarship", and contributed article (see Hollweck et al., 2022a, b). Exploring the identities and spaces of pracademia through the lenses of power and agency (Friesen, 2022) emphasises this process of investigation as sense making and emancipatory in nature.

This chapter explores the idea and concept of pracademia and the pracademic within education, with the authors drawing upon their own professional experience working within both schools and universities, as well as their individual and collective, empirical and conceptual development work. While we believe that the contribution has meaningful application across professional fields and disciplines, debates continue about knowledge organisation within education, and the extent to which it should be described as a field or a discipline (Wyse et al., 2020). For Krishnan (2009), research and study within education demonstrates disciplinarity through how it develops, draws upon, and encourages a particular focus, specialist knowledge, specific terminologies, and associated research methods. With this comes the possibility to explore and develop ideas that transcend sectors and fields within the discipline of education, instead considering ideas, possibilities and application that relate to shared concerns of learning and knowledge. Learning from, and through, research derived from the field, and then critically reflecting on its impact and contribution to not only theoretical and methodological development (Wyse et al., 2020) but also to professional practice, resonates across fields and disciplines.

We conclude this chapter by highlighting how greater conceptualisation of pracademia and the pracademic in the field of education offers both a reflective and futures-orientated framework. This can be applied to the interaction of policy, practice, and research, while also speaking to broader concerns of the role and purpose of higher education (HE) and the work of those predominantly based in such settings for broader society.

Key Themes

Forms: The Origins of the Pracademic and Pracademia

As authors of this chapter, we are currently, or have been, professionals in senior leadership positions in varied school, district, and systemic contexts within the field of education, while also gaining doctoral degrees, writing, and publishing through journals, books, and policy texts, engaging in academic and professional fora, and holding various official and unofficial roles in HE. With these experiences has come an appreciation, and broader understanding, of the mobilisation of ideas across spaces of research, policy, and practice. Commonly, this can be understood as being part of specialised roles within systems or universities, or the domain of an institution's engagement with the profession or field, and vice versa. This understanding relies on the commonly understood parameters and discourse around what constitutes practice and research (Hollweck et al., 2022b). Through the lived realities and reflections of the authors, it has become clear that common understandings of the relationship between research and practice rely heavily on forms of engagement and dissemination. There must also be a focus on the interaction and influence needed to mobilise and build ideas with others in a variety of positions and contexts (Hollweck & Doucet, 2020).

Tseng (2012) highlights that a broader consideration of the social ecology of research use must account for the relationships, contexts, and political and policy influences that frame the work of those engaging with, or in, research. The common focus on the "cognitive, affective, and motivational processes" of research engagement oversimplifies the complexity of how individuals acquire, understand, and apply knowledge or learning across the boundaries of their communities (Tseng, 2012, p. 7). Aspects of this complex process can include individual's identity, the nature and scope of their professional work, and significance of their contribution to the field (Hollweck et al., 2022b).

The terms 'pracademic' and 'pracademia' combine the terms practitioner or practice, and academia or academic. Drawing upon the work of Panda (2014) and Posner (2009), practice could refer to the spaces in which practice-based professionals primarily operate, such as schools, and across governance and policy making within an education system. Academics could refer to those situated primarily within the university. The pracademic is consequentially represented as an individual who may primarily be situated in either practice or academia, but who exercises influence across both practice and academic-based places and spaces.

Articulating pracademia and the pracademic as a space and an identifying community respectively, emphasises the complex relationships, networks, expertise, and recognition that individuals can enjoy across domains within a field like education. Often, this is done in the pursuit of learning, improvement, change, and goals that are particularly relevant when societies around the world are facing such complex, persistent, and sustained challenges. Within pracademia, multiple membership and collaboration are valued and the pracademic's ability to forge relationships and leverage networks across domains can lead to change. It is the complementary knowledge, experience, and established networks that those in the space and work of pracademia bring to their collaboration with, and between, practice-based professionals, policy makers, and academics, that is their biggest contribution (Willis, 2016).

We define pracademia as characterising the plurality of spaces, and the space itself, occupied by those interacting within, between, and beyond the domains of practice and academia (Hollweck et al., 2022b). For us, pracademia involves three key components that are described in more detail below: identity, community, and engagement.

Functions: Identity

Considering identity in pracademia means considering the complex, enduring process of situating and understanding self, and how this relates to the communities that we interact with (Hollweck et al., 2022b). Identities are flexible, multiple, fluid, shifting, and shaping over time depending on contexts, situations, experiences, and relationships (Netolicky, 2018). Holland et al. describe identities as "imaginings of self in worlds of action" (1998, p. 5) and Netolicky expresses them as the "situated, ongoing process through which we make sense of ourselves, to ourselves and to others" (2020, p. 19). The complexity and dynamism of identity is complicated further by the tendency for education professionals to inextricably tangle identity and work, personal, and professional senses of self (Netolicky, 2018).

If we consider our own author identities as imaginings of self in worlds of action, we reflect on the following.

Paul, as a professional in the field of education and Vice Principal of a school, sees his roles as being less about professional choice or duty, and more an opportunity to contribute to the advancement of communities and society overall. Key identity markers for him include school leadership, writing, researching, thinking, influencing, and collaborating. Paul traces these markers back to a central belief that education should be about developing a sense

(continued)

of self, our communities, and how we can take action within and across them. As such, his day-to-day work is driven by these goals rather than through established norms or expectations for particular roles. This spans practice, policy, and research, through paid and voluntary roles in practice, HE, research, and professional networks. The identity marker of the pracademic holds less importance for Paul individually, but understanding and exploring the complexity of the space that could be understood as pracademia is important for him in understanding the possibilities for the type of work that he does.

Trista has always struggled to explain her professional identity and provide a clear answer to the question about what she does as an educator. She has had experience in schools and systems as a teacher, Vice Principal, school board consultant, teacher induction programme developer, teacher trainer, and coach. In academia, her roles include an adjunct professor, researcher, network leader, and most recently, a research fellow. Often many of these roles overlap. The term 'pracademic' has been a useful identity marker for Trista as it captures her passion for professional engagement in – and unwillingness to choose between – roles across both practice and academic domains. Currently situated in HE, Trista works closely with teachers, leaders, and policy makers from across Canada and the globe; designing and leading networks to help them learn with, and from, one another to ultimately improve teaching and learning for students. Trista's academic role as a research fellow is new at the university and sits outside traditional tenure track positions. As the sole individual in this role, and remaining an 'outsider', Trista values the community that she has developed with other pracademics. This is because of the sense of belonging that she gains, but also for the validation of the existence of pracademia as a liminal space with real potential to contribute to the work of educators and the field of education.

Deb is anchored in her work by a sense of moral purpose to serve her school community and the wider education community, and to make a positive difference in the lives of young people. Her 'teacher' identity sits at the core of who she perceives she is, although she has taught less and less as she has moved, over the 23 years of her career, into more and more senior leadership positions in schools. The word 'teacher' does not encompass the multi-faceted-ness of Deb's professional experience, including as a teacher and leader in schools (now as a school Principal) as well as researcher, author, school Board Chair, blogger, podcaster, speaker, and member of a range of professional networks and education groups nationally and internationally. Collaborative academic writing, conferences (academic and professional), podcast conversations, and group membership, afford her opportunities to learn from, and with, educators from a variety of contexts and knowledge systems. Deb has been called a 'pracademic' by others, and has since been considering to what extent the label reflects her place in the education world, and the work in which she engages.

We offer our above autoethnographic author reflections to share our positionality as well as illuminate the shifting and interleaving nature of personal and professional identities in education, and particularly for those in education who work across or between traditional or official spaces. These brief reflections reveal the complexity of the identity work of those operating between, and across, spaces in their field. As we have spoken to colleagues about pracademia, people have expressed to us their desire to feel a sense of self, a way of associating, and a group and place within which they may belong. There is more to identity, however, than resonance with an appropriate label. As identities exist in motion, in action, in context, and in community, they interact with feelings of agency and efficacy. Agency can be understood as the means through which an individual can act through the environments they occupy, resulting from the complex interplay between individual effort, available resources, and contextual and structural influences that affect the spaces within which they operate (Biesta & Tedder, 2007). Behaviour can be influenced by the ways in which an individual understands their own capacity to influence or make decisions and actions, and the extent to which they are empowered or coerced (Cameron, 2005). Identities interacting with the concept, and space, of pracademia allow us to consider the ways in which power is enacted and embodied rather than possessed, and is in a constant state of negotiation and change (Gaventa, 2003). This continuous exchange is reflected by Mynott and Zimmatore (2022) when they write about the unease, contradiction, and duality of their pracademic identities, which they situate as crossing boundaries, and existing within, and between, communities. They add that negotiating and reflecting upon identities has the effect of forming agency and moments of productive professional friction.

Functions: Theorising Pracademia Through Communities and Landscapes of Practice

In defining pracademia and the pracademic through the lenses of identity, community, and engagement, we intentionally avoid the binary thinking that has come to characterise the discourse around the relationship between theory and practice. Dewey (1938, p. 17) noted that "mankind likes to think in terms of extreme opposites. It is given to formulating its beliefs in terms of Either-Ors, between which it recognizes no intermediate possibilities". Aligning with characteristics of philosophical pragmatism (Dewey, 1938), and post structural thinking (Hetherington, 2013), we favour a *both/and* logic, reflecting the varied engagement that constitutes professionals' work, the diverse communities and spaces within which this happens, and the consequences that this has for the (re)forming of identities within, and across, spaces and communities (Hollweck et al., 2022b).

Commonly, endeavours to develop research engagement or research informed practice with practice-based professionals do not reach their intended aims, with research and practice remaining disconnected (Butler & Schnellert, 2008). In understanding the complex interplay of identity, community, and engagement, and the varied experiences of each one of these, pracademia is positioned at the nexus of the domains of practice, policy, and research. As such, it offers an important opportunity to understand the potential for the wider ecological dimensions of professions, professional work, and associated HE.

Paul, as a professional primarily based in a site of practice, has always attributed value and importance to research. The focus of this has not only been about what research can offer practice, but how research engagement can enable a process of sense-making for the self, as well as illuminate communities and networks that support career-long learning, a sense of belonging, and professional fulfilment that differs from what is possible in day-to-day professional roles. This is where Paul has come to develop an interest in understanding the nature and possibilities of how pracademia can be understood as a space within which many may operate in unique ways, just as the three authors do, but with a common emphasis on transcending boundaries that typically demarcate the domains of practice, policy, and research.

For Trista, pracademia helps capture the importance she places on problems of practice driving her research agenda, using and implementing the learning and recommendations derived back into practice, and then using research methods to surface new problems and questions. Her current pracademic work is focused on the design and development of national and international learning networks, while simultaneously researching their influence, relationality, and sustainability, using social network analysis in order to improve.

Deb came to research from the desire to inform her practice. Since undertaking her PhD – which sought to bridge the gap between scholarship and the daily work of teachers and school leaders – she found that engaging in the liminal space of pracademia has benefits beyond providing a research-informed approach to practice. Engaging between, and across, the spaces of practice and academia builds networked connections and rich communities between unlikely collaborators who challenge one another's ways of being, thinking and operating. This agitation of the status quo, and disruption to accepted ways of working in either the practice space or the academe, open alternative lenses to apply to scholarship, and alternate ways of approaching problems of practice.

The role of, and possibilities for, the pracademic and the spaces within which they operate can be understood through conceptions of communities and landscapes of practice, as defined by Wenger (1998). To be a 'true' community of practice, Wenger emphasises three crucial elements that must be combined and developed: domain, community, and practice. Individuals coming together within a community of practice have a shared domain of interest through commitment and competence, and engage in joint discussions and activities as a group. Additionally, as a practice, members develop a repertoire of common resources comprising language, styles, and routines, through which they express their identities. Communities of practice can be formal or informal, and are an integral part of daily life. They can be understood within professions through their associated spaces of practice, policy, and research. Research shows that a strong community can wield the power to enact policies or subvert them, foster change or resist it, and spread innovation or impede it (Schlager & Fusco, 2003). As Wenger states, communities of practice "are a force to be reckoned with, for better or worse" (1998, p. 85).

Communities of practice theory is best described as a socially situated, practice-based approach to learning. Individuals develop knowledge as they interact with each other, as well as with materials and representational systems (Cobb & Bowers, 1999). Learning within, and between, communities of practice is best understood as a process of "attunement" (Fenwick, 2014). As newcomers enter and join communities of practice, they adjust themselves, and adapt their web of beliefs and practice, according to what goes on within that community. However, the "'body of knowledge' of a profession is not understood as a reified curriculum, but rather as a 'landscape of practice', consisting of a complex system of communities of practice and the boundaries between them" (Wenger-Trayner & Wenger-Trayner, 2015, p. 13). It is through the relationships, the practice, artefacts, and the wider social organisation that growth and transformation of identities emerges. At the same time, the newcomer changes the community and its practices through their participation. The attunement of both the community and its individual members can be seen as collective learning. Professional occupations are constituted by a complex landscape of different communities of practice, all of which have their own histories, domains, and regimes of competence (Wenger-Trayner & Wenger-Trayner, 2015).

Although there are many formal learning structures in professions and organisational contexts, learning also happens through the many informal social networks that arise within professions. For the Wenger-Trayners, competence in the landscapes of practice theory is described as "the dimension of knowing, negotiated and defined within a single community of practice" (2015, p. 13). To be competent in a community of practice, individuals learn how to participate in its discourse, norms, and practices in order to gain full membership status or "mastery" (Lave & Wenger, 1991, p. 22). Knowledgeability, on the other hand, refers to "the complex relationships people establish with respect to a landscape of practice which make them recognizable as reliable sources of information or legitimate providers of services" (Lave & Wenger, 1991, p. 22). Thus, individuals are deemed knowledgeable in organisations when they understand the different regimes of competence, and how to negotiate and attune themselves to these practices. Participation in a landscape of practice is "a dance of the self" (Wenger-Trayner & Wenger-Trayner, 2015, p. 24); individuals are shaped by their journeys through the landscape, and they shape the landscape by their experiences. Amongst the different communities of practice that exist in schools, school districts, and HE, there are clear power dynamics at play. They combine the fluid, mutually transformative interactions between individual and community of practice; just as the individual influences the community, the community influences the individual. Within the landscape, professionals can identify or dis-identify with a number of communities of practice. When a new-comer enters a community, there is a process of alignment and realignment that occurs between competence and personal experience. As the community's regime of competence pulls, challenges, and transforms the newcomer, they can also refuse, or be refused by, the community, which may leave them marginalised. Thus, "[l]earning to become a practitioner is not best understood as approximating better and better reified body of knowledge. Rather it is developing a meaningful identity of both competence and knowledgeability in a dynamic and varied landscape of relevant practices" (Wenger-Trayner & Wenger-Trayner, 2015, p. 23).

Naturally, in a landscape of practice, hierarchies exist. The relationships and boundaries between the different communities of practice are in constant negotia-tion and "boundary crossing and boundary encounters are crucial aspects of living in a landscape of practice" (Wenger-Trayner & Wenger-Trayner, 2015, p. 19). For educators who are new to respective communities of practice, the reflective sense-making, connection with others who are also navigating various boundaries, and shared 'cross boundary experiences' are essential. As stated by the Wenger-Trayners "[w]hether the competence of a community is recognised as knowledge depends on its position in the politics of the landscape" (2015, p. 16). Ultimately, schools and similar learning organisations are socially and culturally constructed sites that (re) produce and (trans)form learning and encompass complex relations (Netolicky, 2016). In understanding the possibilities of the pracademic and pracademia, the landscapes of practice theory can be a useful lens to explore the complexities inher-ent in working within, and across, commonly understood constructions of the boundaries between practice, policy, and research. It is also important to recognise here how such boundaries, their constructions, and their consequences reflect or manifest complicity in processes of the marginalisation of voices, insights, knowl-edge and ways of knowing. Harrison and Luckett suggest that:

> higher education needs to rethink its practices to reflect multiple (and contradictory) voices in knowledge construction and curricula. It needs to lead the self-reflexive deconstruction of received orthodoxies and canons and open up membership of expertise communities in ways that are transparent, inclusive and humble. (2019, p. 269)

How we conceptualise the pracademic and pracademia more broadly emphasises the plurality of group membership and the related socially embedded identities, which highlights the importance of community and communities (Kuhn, 2002; Posner, 2009). Well-documented in the fields of education and public policy is the importance of community membership and interaction in forms and evaluation of knowledge mobilisation efforts, and the partnership working aimed at brokering relationships and knowledge exchange across spaces of practice, policy, and research (Chapman et al., 2016; Lieberman et al., 2016). Considering the boundary-spanning work that pracademics engage in, and the possibilities that can result in terms of influence, recognised expertise, and contribution to multiple spaces, iden-tifying and exploring the work of the pracademic adds a new dimension to the debate on the research and practice divide. Theorising the possibilities of the praca-demic and pracademia takes the exploration of the relationships or tensions between practice, policy and research beyond the traditional either/or binaries that have characterised the debate to date. It reaches a more nuanced and sophisticated understanding of the complex ecological dimensions of the work of professionals that enjoy recognised expertise, membership of multiple, varied communities, and the knowledgeability to be able to act with influence within, and across, them.

Paul noticed that throughout his time engaging in postgraduate and doctoral study while still teaching and leading in schools full time, not only was it the knowledge, expertise, and capacity for critical and analytical thinking that developed over time, but so did his knowledge of, exposure to, and confidence in, accessing spaces and networks traditionally reserved for those operating in spaces of academia. In doing so, he was forced to reflect on the extent to which your primary site of professional responsibility or practice, such a school or a university, is important, and whether or not one of these sites makes boundary-spanning, influence, recognition of expertise, and consequential membership easier. This is something that Paul continues to problematise and reflect on, and he remains curious as to what a blurring or shifting of the boundaries between sites and spaces may offer, the different perspectives and questions that could be possible rather than simply an answer to the comparatively simple question of where influence, recognition, and membership may (or may not) be easier.

Like Paul, Trista found the academic networks that she developed during her postgraduate and doctoral studies not only contributed to her critical and analytical thinking and confidence but also informed future research projects. However, the professional networks that she built through her work as a teacher, Vice Principal, and consultant were also invaluable for pushing her thinking about the value, impact, and purpose of the research. Ultimately, it was the interplay, interweaving, and boundary crossing between these networks and spaces that she believes brings greater depth and insight to her practice and research work.

For Deb, the connections that she built through academic conferences, research collaborations, and membership of academic communities, are enriching and challenging. Conversations, and the deep collaborative work of academic writing, presenting, and connecting, have deepened and fundamentally altered Deb's ways of thinking and operating in her daily work in schools. Yet, there is also something isolating about being an outsider in academic spaces, while developing ways of knowing, thinking, and being that are unusual for, and not shared by, those within your daily place of work.

When moving into new communities or spaces, the alignment and realignment that happens between norms of reference, personal experience, and perceived or actual competence can result in a sense of personal discomfort. The feeling of 'fitting' within a community, or the attribution of value to aspects of an individual's professional identity or expertise that contrasts the dominant expertise expected within that space can create tensions and challenges, or, in some cases, result in a process of marginalisation (Hollweck et al., 2022b). This has implications for the nature of the engagement that is possible within the community or space, and the extent to which influence can be exercised, and the degree of impact that can be had.

Through understanding this complexity, and emphasising the possibilities that can result, it is possible to envisage a process of reforming how individuals understand themselves, and who they want to be, and their preferences around engaging in collaboration and knowledge exchange. With this, comes possibilities to reconsider the form, function, and future of pracademic identities and spaces, and the implications that this has for practice, policy and research across professional domains.

Futures: Grappling with Pracademia and the Pracademic

The emergence of the pracademic as an identity marker, and pracademia describing a space of operation and action, is becoming increasingly common. There is growing conceptual development, and empirical exploration, of pracademia happening across fields. This is evident in conflict resolution, negotiation and mediation (Avruch & Nan, 2013; Susskind, 2013; Volpe & Chandler, 2001; Vuković, 2017; Wilson, 2019), law (Schneider, 2013), nursing (Andrew & Wilkie, 2007), policing (Braga, 2016; Willis, 2016), political science (McDonald & Mooney, 2011; Posner, 2009), project management (Walker, 2010), public administration and non-profit management (Powell et al., 2018; Vrentas et al., 2018), organisational studies (Panda, 2014), environmental health and protection (LaPorte & Opp, 2016; Runkle, 2014), and public and foreign policy (Brans & Pattyn, 2017; Murphy & Fulda, 2011). However, in the field of education, it has traditionally remained explored in the blogosphere and on social media, with growing development through academic writing emerging in recent years (Hollweck, 2018; Hollweck et al., 2022a, b; Hollweck & Doucet, 2020; Netolicky, 2020).

The importance of the connection, collaboration, and co-creation that professionals experience, or engage in, is well-established in the field of education (Goodlad, 1975; Lieberman, 1992). In HE, over time, the pressure has increased for greater, and more varied forms of, research impact, and community engagement in scholarship as a means of knowledge mobilisation (Briscoe et al., 2015; Campbell et al., 2017; Cooper et al., 2018). This can be through forms of action research that emerge in sites of practice, or academics who emphasise forms of participatory research and knowledge mobilisation that foster close collaboration with practice-based professionals (Hollweck et al., 2022b). However, the pracademic, and the space of pracademia, are distinct from this common understanding of research of practice or a practitioner as researcher stance (Cochran-Smith and Lytle, 1999, 2009). The pracademic is active and influential in both spaces, and the space between these remains a contested and negotiated site (Jansson et al., 2010; Macduff & Netting, 2010; Reed, 2009). This emphasises the common, and important, concerns when discussing and understanding the interaction between, and across, these spaces of methodological rigour and immediate practical relevance, characterised by Panda as "a tussle between scientific rigour and practical relevance" (2014, p. 143).

Social media platforms such as Twitter are being explored as pracademic spaces that foster collaboration across the domains of practice and research (Kolber & Heggart, 2022). This links with how Friesen (2022) describes pracademia as a form of praxis; action informed through critical reflection, and an understanding of common needs and interests in the community within which this takes place (Greene, 1978). The role of the pracademic is one that emphasises collaboration and the negotiation of the 'liminal space' between theory and practice or the academy and the profession. Through these processes, individuals can "question, critique, and challenge educators, educational researchers, and theorists to think and act beyond the familiar and conventional boundaries of learning, teaching, and leadership practices" (Friesen, 2022, p. 75). Chaaban et al. (2022) found that in the context of HE and education policy and practice in Qatar, pracademics took on the role of the 'missing link' to bridge the divide between them.

Forms, Functions and Futures of Pracademia

For Campbell (2022, p. 101) the conceptual development of pracademia and the pracademic is "a quest for clarity in a messy reality". She calls for continued empirical effort on developing the conceptual and deep ethnographic and qualitative work, as well as larger scale studies of the "why, what, who, how and so what of pracademia and pracademics" (Campbell, 2022, p. 106). It is hoped that this chapter contributes to this endeavour, while also highlighting possible avenues for continued work and means of understanding the complex reality of the pracademic and pracademia with a focus on HE.

Bringing together our articulations around identity and community formation, broader theorisation through the lens of communities and landscapes of practice, and the emerging possibilities of the pracademic and pracademia throughout the chapter, we present Fig. 6.1. This represents how we can begin to make sense of the complex realities of those that identify as a pracademic or their work within a space of pracademia.

Figure 6.1 represents a rebuttal to the long-standing debate that positions theory and practice, or academic and practice domains in a dichotomous way. It highlights that the conceptual, theoretical, and empirical development of the concepts of pracademia and the pracademic are not about developing a hierarchical view of the contributions made by different individuals within a professional domain or field. Instead, it is about making sense of the realities of these contributions and attributing value to the coalescence, collaboration, and intentional multiplicity (Hollweck et al., 2022a).

Historical debates around the research and practice divide, or how we close the gap between the academy and practice, rely on language and arguments of logic and comparison across, and within, fields (Lyotard, 1984). This too often serves to set

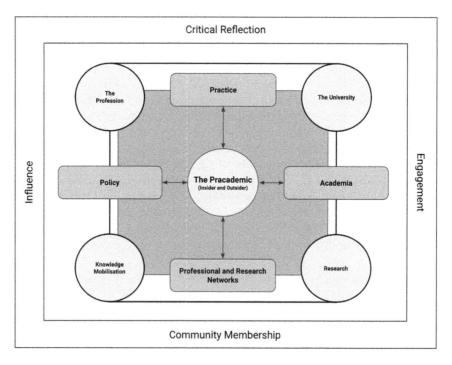

Fig. 6.1 Understanding the pracademic and pracademia

the parameters of what is possible, what is deemed the norm or expectation, and discussions around factors of identity, community, and engagement that make up an individual's professional role. With this comes the construction, and reconstruction, of norms as to what should drive particular forms of collaboration, and who should be engaging in them and when. It is important to acknowledge, and critically reflect on, the complex interplay between different aspects of professional spaces and fields, and the individuals that are engaging in, and influencing them, through their communities. It enables a (re)examination as to the forms, functions, and futures of the relationship between not just academia and practice, but how the professional, as both an insider and outsider within spaces of practice, policy, research, and broader networks, engages in these spaces, exercises influence, and makes sense of their roles, functions, and impact through critical reflection. In doing so, it offers new possibilities as to the relationship between the profession, the university, research, and knowledge mobilisation through the forms of collaboration that are possible, and the approaches to knowledge generation and exchange that emerge through multi-community membership. This aligns with the contention of Xu (2017) that researchers, depending on their purposes, and individual circumstances, can experience a fluidity of status as an insider and outsider, rather than relying on traditional notions of fixed boundaries. While this is not solely attributed to those who may self-identify as pracademics or operate in spaces of pracademia, the purpose of its conceptualisation is to emphasise the complementary knowledge, experience, and networks that pracademics can bring in collaboration with, and between, practice-based professionals, policy makers, and academics (Willis, 2016).

Tseng (2012) highlights that a broader consideration of the social ecology of research use must account for the relationships, contexts, and political and policy influences that frame the work of those engaging with or in research. The common focus on the "cognitive, affective, and motivational processes" of research engagement oversimplifies the complexity of how individuals acquire, understand, and apply knowledge or learning across the boundaries of the communities they are a part of (Tseng, 2012, p. 7). This was personally significant for the authors, evident in their narrative reflections, as they gradually became increasingly involved in research, policy, and practice networks, as their professional roles changed, and as they began to move between the domains of practice, policy, and research more confidently. This forms the basis of their engagement with the emerging concept of pracademia and the pracademic in education.

Conclusion

Throughout this chapter, in exploring the complexities, nuances, and implications inherent in grappling with the concepts of pracademia and the pracademic, it is clear there is a need to continue the pursuit of conceptualisation and broader theorisation of these concepts, and engage in further empirical exploration through the lenses of power, agency, and legitimacy. In this chapter, we have illuminated the complex interplay between identity, community, and engagement in the pursuit of understanding the pracademic and pracademia. We believe that the opportunity arises to rethink the forms, functions, and futures of HE, professional work, and policymaking, and the implications that this could have for the advancement and betterment of communities and society more broadly.

Points for Reflection
- The authors present an argument for the elimination of binary categorisations between academia and practice domains. Referring to Fig. 6.1, how does this approach manifest in your consideration of your professional identity?
- Within the chapter, a number of benefits related to the occupation of a 'liminal space' are elucidated by the authors. Can you identify with these and/or suggest any additional benefits?
- Power and community are two themes which arise repeatedly in this chapter. Consider how the various forms of community engagement highlighted by Campbell, Hollweck, and Netolicky can support the emancipation of knowledge.

References

Andrew, N., & Wilkie, G. (2007). Integrated scholarship in nursing: An individual responsibility or collective undertaking. *Nurse Education Today, 27*(1), 1–4.

Avruch, K., & Nan, S. A. (2013). Introduction: The constraints and opportunities of practicing conflict resolution from academic settings. *Negotiation Journal, 29*(2), 205–212.

Biesta, G. J. J., & Tedder, M. (2007). Agency and learning in the lifecourse: Towards an ecological perspective. *Studies in the Education of Adults, 39*, 132–149.

Braga, A. A. (2016). The value of 'pracademics' in enhancing crime analysis in police departments. *Policing, 10*(3), 308–314.

Brans, M., & Pattyn, V. (2017). Validating methods for comparing public policy: Perspectives from academics to 'pracademics'. *Journal of Comparative Policy Analysis, 19*(4), 303–312.

Briscoe, P., Pollock, K., Campbell, C., & Carr-Harris, S. (2015). Finding the sweet spot: Network structures and processes for increased knowledge mobilization. *Brock Education Journal, 25*(1), 19–34.

Brookfield, S. (2017). *Becoming a critically reflective teacher* (2nd ed.). Wiley.

Butler, D., & Schnellert, L. (2008). Bridging the research-to-practice divide: Improving outcomes for students. *Education Canada, 48*(5), 36–40.

Cameron, D. H. (2005). Teachers working in collaborative structures: A case study of a secondary school in the USA. *Educational Management, Administration, & Leadership, 33*(3), 311–330.

Campbell, P. (2020). Rethinking professional collaboration and agency in a post-pandemic era. *Journal of Professional Capital and Community, 5*(3/4), 337–341.

Campbell, C. (2022). Afterward? Moving onwards for developing pracademia and pracademics in education. *Journal of Professional Capital and Community, 7*(1), 98–108.

Campbell, C., Pollock, K., Briscoe, P., Carr-Harris, S., & Tuters, S. (2017). Developing a knowledge network for applied education research to mobilise evidence in and for educational practice. *Educational Research, 59*(2), 209–227.

Chaaban, Y., Sellami, A., Sawalhi, R., & Elkhouly, M. (2022). Exploring perceptions of pracademics in an Arab context. *Journal of Professional Capital and Community, 7*(1), 83–97.

Chapman, C., Chestnutt, H., Friel, N., Hall, S., & Lowden, K. (2016). Professional capital and collaborative inquiry networks for educational equity and improvement? *Journal of Professional Capital and Community, 1*(3), 178–197.

Cobb, P., & Bowers, J. (1999). Cognitive and situated learning perspectives in theory and practice. *Educational Researcher, 28*(2), 4–15.

Cochran-Smith, M., & Lytle, S. (1999). Relationships of knowledge and practice: Teacher learning in communities. *Review of Research in Education.* https://doi.org/10.2307/1167272

Cochran-Smith, M., & Lytle, S. (2009). *Inquiry as stance: Practitioner research for the next generation*. Teachers College Press.

Cooper, A., Rodway, J., & Read, R. (2018). Knowledge mobilization practices of educational researchers across Canada. *Canadian Journal of Higher Education/Revue canadienne d'enseignement superieur, 48*(1), 1–21.

Dewey, J. (1938). *Logic: The theory of inquiry*. Holt, Rinehart & Winston.

Dunne, J. (1997). *Back to the rough ground: Practical judgement and the lure of technique*. University of Notre Dame Press.

Fenwick, T. (2014). Sociomateriality in medical practice and learning: Attuning to what matters. *Medical Education, 48*(1), 44–52.

Friesen, S. L. (2022). Dwelling in liminal spaces: Twin moments of the same reality. *Journal of Professional Capital and Community, 7*(1), 71–82.

Gaventa, J. (2003). *Power after Lukes: An overview of theories of power since Lukes and their application to development*. Participation Group, Institute of Development Studies. https://www.powercube.net/wp-content/uploads/2009/11/power_after_lukes.pdf

Goodlad, J. I. (1975). *The dynamics of educational change*. McGraw-Hill.

Greene, M. (1978). *Landscapes of learning*. Teachers College Press.

Harrison, N., & Luckett, K. (2019). Experts, knowledge and criticality in the age of 'alternative facts': Re-examining the contribution of higher education. *Teaching in Higher Education, 24*(3), 259–271.

Hetherington, L. (2013). Complexity thinking and methodology: The potential of 'complex case study' for educational research. *Complicity: An International Journal of Complexity and Education, 10*(1/2), 71–85.

Holland, D., Lachicotte, W., Skinner, D., & Cain, C. (1998). *Identity and agency in cultural worlds*. Harvard University Press.

Hollweck, T. (2018). A pracademic's exploration of mentoring, coaching, and induction in the Western Quebec school board. *CollectivEd, 4*, 31–40.

Hollweck, T., & Doucet, A. (2020). Pracademics in the pandemic: Pedagogies and professionalism. *Journal of Professional Capital and Community, 5*(3/4), 295–305.

Hollweck, T., Netolicky, D. M., & Campbell, P. (2022a). Guest editorial: Pracademia: Exploring the possibilities, power and politics of boundary-spanners straddling the worlds of practice and scholarship. *Journal of Professional Capital and Community, 7*(1), 1–5.

Hollweck, T., Netolicky, D. M., & Campbell, P. (2022b). Defining and exploring pracademia: Identity, community, and engagement. *Journal of Professional Capital and Community, 7*(1), 6–25.

Jansson, S. M., Benoit, C., Casey, L., Phillips, R. I., & Burns, D. (2010). In for the long haul: Knowledge translation between academic and nonprofit organizations. *Qualitative Health Research, 20*(1), 131–143.

Kolber, S., & Heggart, K. (2022). Education focused pracademics on twitter: Building democratic fora. *Journal of Professional Capital and Community, 7*(1), 26–44.

Krishnan, A. (2009). *What are academic disciplines?* Some observations on the disciplinarity vs. Interdisciplinarity debate. https://eprints.ncrm.ac.uk/id/eprint/783/

Kuhn, T. (2002). Negotiating boundaries between scholars and practitioners. *Management Communication Quarterly, 16*(1), 106–112.

LaPorte, T., & Opp, S. M. (2016). APSA pracademic fellowship: The third epoch: A pracademic view of the EPA's office of policy. *Political Science and Policy, 49*(4), 923–926.

Lave, J., & Wenger, E. (1991). *Situated learning: Legitimate peripheral participation*. Cambridge University Press.

Lieberman, A. (1992). The meaning of scholarly activity and the building of community. *Educational Researcher, 21*(6), 5–12.

Lieberman, A., Campbell, C., & Yashkina, A. (2016). *Teacher learning and leadership: Of, by, and for teachers*. Routledge.

Lyotard, J. F. (1984). *The postmodern condition: A report on knowledge*. University of Minnesota Press.

Macduff, N., & Netting, F. E. (2010). The importance of being pracademic. *International Journal of Volunteer Administration, 27*(1), 43–47.

Mazzocchi, F. (2006). Western science and traditional knowledge: Despite their variations, different forms of knowledge can learn from each other. *EMBO Reports, 7*(5), 463–466.

McDonald, M. P., & Mooney, C. Z. (2011). 'Pracademics': Mixing an academic career with practical politics: Editors' introduction. *Political Science and Politics, 44*(2), 251–253.

Murphy, A. M., & Fulda, A. (2011). Bridging the gap: Pracademics in foreign policy. *PS. Political Science and Politics, 44*(2), 279–283.

Mynott, J. P., & Zimmatore, M. (2022). Pracademic productive friction: Boundary crossing and pressure points. *Journal of Professional Capital and Community, 7*(1), 45–56.

Netolicky, D. M. (2016). Coaching for professional growth in one Australian school: "Oil in water". *International Journal of Mentoring and Coaching in Education, 5*(2), 66–86.

Netolicky, D. M. (2018). Elevating the professional identities and voices of teachers and school leaders in educational research, practice and policymaking. In D. M. Netolicky, J. Andrews, & C. Paterson (Eds.), *Flip the system Australia* (1st ed., pp. 9–18). Routledge.

Netolicky, D. M. (2020). *Transformational professional learning: Making a difference in schools.* Routledge.

Panda, A. (2014). Bringing academic and corporate worlds closer: We need pracademics. *Management and Labour Studies, 39*(2), 140–159.

Posner, P. L. (2009). The pracademic: An agenda for re-engaging practitioners and academics. *Public Budgeting and Finance, 29*(1), 12–26.

Powell, E., Winfield, G., Schatteman, A., & Trusty, K. (2018). Collaboration between practitioners and academics: Defining the pracademic experience. *Journal of Nonprofit Education and Leadership, 8,* 62–79.

Reed, M. I. (2009). The theory/practice gap: A problem for research in business schools? *Journal of Management Development, 28,* 685–693.

Runkle, K. (2014). I am an environmental health pracademic (and so can you!). *Journal of Environmental Health, 76*(10), 42–43.

Schlager, M., & Fusco, J. (2003). Teacher professional development, technology, and communities of practice: Are we putting the cart before the horse? *The Information Society – TIS, 19*(3), 203–220.

Schneider, A. K. (2013). Pracademics: Making negotiation theory implemented, interdisciplinary, and international. *International Journal of Conflict Engagement and Resolution, 1*(2), 108–202.

Susskind, L. (2013). Confessions of a pracademic: Searching for a virtuous cycle of theory building, teaching, and action research. *Negotiation Journal, 29*(2), 225–237.

Tseng, V. (2012). The uses of research in policy and practice. *Social Policy Report, 26*(2), 1–24.

Volpe, M. R., & Chandler, D. (2001). Resolving and managing conflicts in academic communities: The emerging role of the 'pracademic'. *Negotiation Journal, 17,* 245–255.

Vrentas, C., Freiwirth, J., Benatti, S., Hill, C., & Yurasek, A. (2018). Bridging the divide between the research and practitioners sectors: A new collaborative initiative between the alliance for nonprofit management and the association for research on nonprofit organizations and voluntary action: Pracademics section. *Journal of Nonprofit Education and Leadership, 8*(1), 93–103.

Vukovic, S. (2017). A "pracademic" jewel: A review of book conflict management in international missions: A field guide, by Olav Ofstad. *Peace and Conflict: Journal of Peace Psychology, 23*(1), 101–102.

Walker, D. (2010, October 10–13). *Being a pracademic–combining reflective practice with scholarship* [Conference presentation]. AIPM Conference, Darwin, Australia. https://leishman.conferenceservices.net/resources/266/2110/pdf/AIPM2010_0092.pdf

Wenger, E. (1998). *Communities of practice.* Cambridge University Press.

Wenger-Trayner, E., & Wenger-Trayner, B. (2015). Learning in a landscape of practice: A framework. In E. Wenger-Trayner, M. Fenton-O'Creevy, S. Hutchinson, C. Kubiak, & B. Wenger-Trayner (Eds.), *Learning in landscapes of practice: Boundaries, identity, and knowledgeability in practice-based learning* (pp. 13–10). Routledge.

Willis, J. J. (2016). The romance of police pracademics. *Policing: A Journal of Policy and Practice, 10*(3), 315–321.

Wilson, B. (2019). *'Pracs' and 'demics': Identifying pracademic subtypes in family mediation and other disciplines.* SSRN: https://ssrn.com/abstract=3404962 or https://doi.org/10.2139/ssrn.3404962

Wyse, D., Brown, C., Oliver, S., & Poblete, X. (2020). Education research and educational practice: The qualities of a close relationship. *British Educational Research Journal, 47*(6), 1466–1489. https://doi.org/10.1002/berj.3626

Xu, X. (2017). Researchers' positioning: Insider or outsider? *The Morning Watch: Educational and Social Analysis, 44*(1–2 Fall), 1–6.

Dr Paul Campbell based in Hong Kong, is Vice Principal of a large international primary school and a research engagement leader across a foundation of 22 schools. He is also a Scholar Practitioner Fellow of the Asia Pacific Centre for Leadership and Change (APCLC). Paul is an elected board member of the International Congress for School Effectiveness and Improvement (ICSEI), is Co-Coordinator of their Educational Leadership Network, and sits on the editorial board of the journals School Leadership and Management (SLAM) and Management in Education (MiE). He is also a Partner Tutor on Master of Education programmes at the University of Dundee, Scotland. His research centres around educational leadership, governance, and policy development.

Dr Trista Hollweck is a Research Fellow at the University of Ottawa's Faculty of Education. She is Director of ARC Education Project, a global policy learning network and co-lead of the Canadian Playful Schools Network. As a pracademic, Trista's work explores professional learning, leadership, teacher induction, mentoring, coaching, educational networks and systemic change. She is a proud mom of three and is committed to supporting schools and systems to improve education for all students within and across educational systems globally.

Dr Deborah M. Netolicky is an Australian school principal with a doctorate in professional identities, professional learning, and effective school change. She has more than 20 years of experience teaching and leading in schools in Australia and England, has hosted podcast The Edu Salon, and sits on national and international education committees. Her research, writing, and leadership have been consistently recognised through awards, such as the 2021 AERA Educational Change SIG Emerging Scholar Award, 2021 Michael Fullan Emerging Scholar Award, 2021 ACEL WA Certificate of Excellence in Educational Leadership. She is often invited to contribute to education conferences, peer-reviewed academic journals, books, and media. She is author of Transformational Professional Learning: Making a Difference in Schools, Editor of Future Alternatives for School Leadership: Diversity, Inclusion, Equity and Democracy, and co-Editor of Flip the System Australia: What Matters in Education.

Chapter 7
'Finding Your People': The Role of Networks in Pracademic Identity Construction

Helen Taylor

Abstract This chapter will consider the role of networks in enabling the construction of identity in a pracademic context. Focussing on early career pracademics, it uses the social model of identity construction to argue that 'finding your people' is an important part of supporting individuals to create a future sense of self. Proposing that early career pracademics occupy two liminal spaces of identity – between practice and academia and between student and professional/expert – it outlines the role of learned societies in supporting individuals to embrace the positivity of having multiple elements of identity and use this to create a robust conception of the self.

Keywords Professional development · Pracademic transitions · Doctorate · Digital skills · Levelling up · Barriers · Remuneration · In-house pracademic · On-boarding · Network · Buddy system · Knowledge transfer partnership · Industry liaison committee

At a Glance
- Highlights how pracademics can be understood to have multiple elements of identity, which should be considered a strength, but in reality this can lead to insecurities around occupying 'liminal spaces' and experiencing imposter syndrome.
- Considers how the social elements of identity construction can help pracademics more easily create future sense of selves, particularly those at the beginning of their careers.
- Reflects on how finding 'your people' can be a core part of future self-construction, and how, in some disciplines, learned societies can play a vital role in providing chances for individuals to network beyond their institutions.

H. Taylor (✉)
School of Education and Social Policy, Cardiff Metropolitan University, Cardiff, Wales, UK
e-mail: htaylor@cardiffmet.ac.uk

© The Author(s), under exclusive license to Springer Nature Switzerland AG 2023
J. Dickinson, T.-L. Griffiths (eds.), *Professional Development for Practitioners in Academia*, Knowledge Studies in Higher Education 13, https://doi.org/10.1007/978-3-031-33746-8_7

Introduction

This chapter will explore the utility of external networks in assisting identity construction in a pracademic context. Recognising the role of multiple (often seen as conflicting) elements of identity within pracademic identity construction, I will reflect on how engagement with individuals, groups, and networks beyond individuals' own institutions can support the development of a strong and positive identity. Applying the Social Model of Identity Construction (SIMIC) to the area of pracademia, I will suggest that the existence of multiple elements of identity should be considered a strength, rather than a weakness.

Learned societies will be used as an example of networks that support this form of identity construction. Specifically, the discussion will focus on the role of learned societies in supporting Early Career Pracademics (ECPs) to consider, and create future sense of selves. Not only do networks help support conceptions of the current self, but they are also important in enabling the construction of who individuals want to be in the future. This is particularly relevant in the context of Early Career Researchers (ECRs), or academics who work across practice and academia, where strong identity concepts might not be in place. I will provide an overview and reflection of my engagement with the Housing Studies Association (the learned society for Housing Studies as an academic discipline), from the beginning of my PhD to becoming Chair of the organisation, and the impact that this has had on my development of a pracademic identity. I will propose that learned societies often do, and explicitly should, play a role in supporting ECRs to build their professional identity, whether this sits within academia, practice, or both. Engaging with networks, and 'finding your people' can therefore be a key element to forming a strong and positive pracademic identity.

Key Themes

My Journey

After studying a philosophy degree at undergraduate level, I was employed as a support worker in a homelessness drop-in centre. The impact of changes to social policy in the form of welfare reform was obvious here, and I saw this as aligned with theories of (in)justice that I had been studying for the past 3 years. The motivation for me progressing to postgraduate study came from working in practice in this context and a desire to apply ideas around justice and equality from academic study to individuals' real-life experiences. My thesis was therefore a piece of applied philosophy; I intended to engage with those experiencing injustice on a day-to-day basis and use concepts from political philosophy to analyse this. It involved creating a philosophical conceptual tool to apply to social policy, with a case study on a piece of homelessness legislation.

I was based in a Languages and Politics School, and then a Law and Politics School within the Politics Department, and had two political theorists as my supervisory team. The core conceptual underpinning of my thesis was situated within political philosophy, however, it also involved data collection, something unusual in this context. Additionally, I was analysing contemporary devolved Welsh legislation[1] and working part-time within a policy organisation to support my studies. This engagement with another type of practice informed my research, and I was able to use the knowledge from this role to inform the PhD. Although undertaking a philosophical piece of work, I considered myself as also working in two areas of practice: Welsh politics, and housing and homelessness. I believed this engagement with both theory and practice as key to my academic and professional identity at the time.

Reflecting on my PhD experience from a pracademic perspective, I felt out of place: occupying a "liminal space" (Wood et al., 2016, p. 230) between academia and practice. My work was too applied to be valued as pure political philosophy, and I was seen as disconnected from practice as I was engaged in academia. I was situated in a "plurality of spaces" (Hollweck et al., 2021, p. 13) but I did not consider this to be a strength. Instead, I felt that I fitted in neither academia nor practice.

Pracademia

The definition of pracademia and individuals as being pracademics has been well-rehearsed in recent journal editions (Hollweck et al., 2021) as well as previous chapters in this book. I will therefore only provide a short discussion of one definition of pracademia to set the context for further discussion.

As Hollweck et al. (2021) outline, the phrase 'pracademia' can be used as both a noun and an adjective, and there is no consistent definition or identification criteria. They outline three metaphors for understanding pracademia:

(i) The Bridge – this is the simplest understanding, where individuals are perceived to be active in both scholarly and practical activity. Here, there is an implicit assumption that there is a gap between academia and practice, and that pracademics identify with, and work in, multiple spaces.

(ii) The Mobius Strip – this metaphor focusses on the connectedness of practice and academic identities, rather than seeing them as separate and distinct. On this account, individuals have two connected and inseparable identities, which inform all decisions and choices about their work.

(iii) Dismantling the wheel – this final metaphor provides a challenge to the traditional conceptualisation of roles and spaces within education, and proposes a new way of understanding multiple identities within processes and structures.

---

[1] Devolved Welsh legislation is created by the National Assembly for Wales in accordance with the Government of Wales Act 1998, following the affirmative devolution referendum in 1997 (Gov. uk, 2018).

Here, the aim is to dismantle and rebuild a network/community that focusses on multiple identities and "offers recognition, legitimacy, and attribution of value to those who choose to remain working simultaneously within, between, and beyond the demarcated spaces of practice, policy, and academia" (2021, p. 12).

After exploring these metaphors, Hollweck et al. arrive at a definition of pracademia as "characterizing the plurality of spaces, and the space itself, occupied by those interacting within, between, and beyond the domains of practice and academia" (2021, p. 13).

Within this definition, are three key threads: identity, community, and engagement:

 (i) Identity – pracademics are involved in an ongoing and complex process of situating and understanding the self.
 (ii) Community – the community memberships and sense of connection that individuals do, or do not, hold relates to their conceptualisation of self.
(iii) Engagement – there is an active interplay between the conceptualisation of self, the positioning of this within communities, and the actions that result from this engagement.

What is clear from both the definition and the key threads that run throughout this, is the focus on the continual project of identity construction within pracademic experiences and the multi-layered nature of this. Authors discuss and define the position of pracademics as operating within a "liminal state" (Wood et al., 2016, p. 230) in either both, or neither, practice nor academia. This can lead to "fragile academic selves" (Knights & Clarke, 2014). Implicit in this discussion, then, is the idea that individuals have multiple identities, various community memberships, and competing elements of self-conceptualisation which can lead to issues around robust identity construction for pracademics. This focus on manifold elements of identity within the pracademic context can be seen (or more importantly felt) to be a weakness (Forster et al., 2017; Pilcher et al., 2017). For example, this can manifest as "imposter syndrome" (Clance & Imes, 1978) where individuals feel that they belong in neither practice nor academia. Pracademics report adapting the description of their identities depending on their context, acting like "chameleons" (Dickinson et al., 2020, p. 299).

This multi-dimensional context of self-conceptualisation, however, can also be a strength. As Dickinson et al.'s (2020) research demonstrates, pracademics can experience an academic validation when their practitioner expertise and identity is recognised. This understanding of multiple elements of identity as a strength is also recognised in the Social Identity Model of Identity Change (SIMIC). This outlines how individuals who are able to access multiple social identities are better able to cope with a range of life transitions. As Ballentyne et al. (2021, p. 203) note, "access to multiple social identity groups provides resources to navigate the challenges that a new environment presents". Furthermore, this ability to create continuity in identity leads to a more overall coherent sense of self. In the context of career development and pracademia, transitions and new environments could present themselves; for example, when moving between different jobs and roles, or between student and professional or 'expert'. The experience of both pracademics and ECRs is often full of transitions, and experiences of balancing different identities, and focussing on future self-identity construction. Two liminal spaces can be seen in this context: identities that fall between practice and academia, and identities that are being constructed at the beginning of an academic career. The SIMIC is therefore a useful model to look to here.

As the name suggests, the SIMIC emphasises the social element of identity construction – the consideration of ourselves and our self-concept in relation to others. Miscenko and Day (2016) outline how identity is constructed in relation to a larger collective, and that a person's sense of self can be shaped and strengthened through both engagement and identification with others. This reflects the discussion of communities of practice within the professional development literature (Wenger, 1998), and Iyer et al.'s (2009) classification of life transitions as including a change in group membership. It is important to note that the 'social' element of the SIMIC encompasses both engagement with others (this could be around a variety of issues and be positive or negative), and identification with others. This element of identification with others is important in the context of a discussion of early career pracademia; here, the SIMIC can relate to individuals being able to construct their future selves through interactions with others with whom they identify.

Conscious that I felt I neither belonged to academia nor practice, I actively engaged with a wide range of opportunities across both spheres to develop a network, as well as creating a Twitter account for myself (@practademia). I actively tried to 'find my people'.

Future Self-Construction and PhD Supervision

In terms of 'finding your people' as a PhD candidate, your supervisory team would seem to be a good starting point. Bentley et al. (2019) applied the SIMIC to ECRs' relationships with their PhD supervisors. The authors outline three models in which their research participants identified with their supervisors:

(a) The Doing Model – here, ECRs identify with their supervisors based on the skills that the supervisors have, and those that the ECRs wants to develop.
(b) The Guidance Model – here, the supervisor can provide personal advice and guidance that the ECR feels that they require.
(c) The Being Model – here, the supervisor is someone who embodies the ideal or elements of the desired future self of the ECR.

The findings of the research showed that ECRs who relied on a single academic identity experienced more confusion and frustration about who they were, and their career trajectory, than those who report multiple identities. Those with multiple elements to their identity had a stronger and more positive sense of how their PhD identity contributed to their broader chosen career pathway. The multiple identities, in the context of past and present self, enabled a stronger development of future identity. The role of the supervisor was important as:

> Research into people's connections with those who act as models for a profession suggests that these individuals, by providing a concrete representation of a future professional identity, can also contribute to a sense of continuity between present and future selves (Bentley et al., p. 6).

Those candidates with multiple identities were more likely to identify connections between their ideal future self and their supervisors, whereas those who experienced incompatibility between their current and future identity and their supervisors, were limited in their ability to construct a future identity. Bentley et al. conclude that "it is only by embedding students in diverse networks of professionals (both inside and outside universities) and peers… that universities are most likely to support candidates in their attempts to construct the future career identities that underpin thriving and later success" (2019, p. 9).

The key points to note here are that:

- Identity can be understood in a social context, through both engagement and identification with others.
- Those with multiple elements to their identity may be more able to cope with both transitions in life and more specifically, the development of a future sense of self.
- In the context of academia and ECRs, the identification of multiple elements to one's self-concept and the relationship with an ECR's supervisor play a role in the ability of the ECR to create a future sense of self.
- Universities therefore should enable ECRs to identify, and engage with, individuals and networks, both inside and outside of their institution, which will assist them in constructing a future identity.

Although I was successful in writing and defending my thesis, my experience of supervision did not fit into the 'doing', 'guidance', or 'being' models. The team did not undertake the same type of applied research as me and, as I did not see myself as a political philosopher, were not role models for my future career. Neither the supervisory team nor I thought of our relationship as one that should involve pastoral care and guidance. Considering the SIMIC model in this context, I had a multi-dimensional professional identity that did not match that of my supervisory team or broader role models within the research group. The elements of my identity involved working in homelessness and within the sphere of devolved Welsh politics, and being committed to using my academic knowledge to critically analyse policy, and try to create change. I had networks and role models across these different fields, but had not met an individual or group who worked across all three and could provide a model for future self-construction.

Finding My People: Finding My Discipline

Aligned to balancing multiple identities across academia and practice, I also struggled with identifying my place within academia – in particular, the discipline that I should be part of. Whilst completing my PhD and considering professional development, finding a 'home' within a discipline was both important to me and elusive. However, undertaking data collection for the case study element of the PhD also functioned as networking and, through this, I heard of an individual doing similar academic work as myself. I contacted them, we met to discuss our shared research interests, and she encouraged me to join the Housing Studies Association (has). Having had a similar experience around engaging with philosophical concepts in the policy sphere, she emphasised how the HSA provided a network for individuals who were theoretically engaged with issues around housing and homelessness.

The area of 'housing studies' as an academic discipline or sub-discipline is contested. Ahashe HSA website notes, membership of the organisation is relevant for individuals from different areas who are interested in housing-related research. This can be from within academia, practice, or policy organisations. The core element to the study of housing and housing studies education is its focus on functional knowledge (Manzi & Richardson, 2017). The creation and dissemination of knowledge in this context, then, is so that it can be applied and used. Within the broad range of housing research (whether this is in academia or practice), there is a clear commitment to use this knowledge to influence society. When research is undertaken in the practice context, this is largely to inform organisations who provide housing, such as housing associations or private landlord groups. Similar research is undertaken in academia, where the production of new knowledge is often focussed on influencing policy.

Within academia, debate concentrates on whether housing studies can be understood as an academic discipline in its own right, or whether housing studies researchers purely bring knowledge and methodologies of other academic disciplines to topics related to housing. Allen defines the concept of housing studies research as an "epistemological fallacy" (2009, p. 54). Allen highlights that within housing studies, we see academics returning to their disciplines (for example, economics, sociology, philosophy, or planning) "to 'bring back' theories… into the analyses of housing phenomena" (2009, p. 54) rather than creating new conceptual frameworks. As Clapham (2018) notes "the complexity of housing has meant that it has been examined through the lens of different disciplines, each of which has offered important insights" (2018, p. 172).

Housing Studies could therefore be considered a discipline which consists of a large number of pracademics. The nature of the (sub)discipline includes a focus on functional knowledge and the application of theory to practice. It also relates to phenomena that we all experience, regardless of a professional or vocational interest. Anecdotally, there are several academics who have moved from practice or third sector organisations to academia, and there is a significant focus on work that occurs within the housing studies sphere involving collaboration with different organisations, with an aim of informing or creating change. This focus on pracademia is evident in housing studies education. Although these qualifications at a higher education level have been in significant decline since the early 2000s, they bring together academic qualifications with professional accreditations (for example, a BSc Housing Studies includes an accreditation for the Chartered Institute of

Housing, the body for housing professionals in the UK). Built into housing studies education then, is a focus on pracademia – bringing together the rigour and knowledge of academic discipline and issues that are experienced by individuals in relation to their housing.

Discovering housing studies as an academic discipline therefore led to me strongly identify with a discipline. Rather than saying I did political philosophy 'but…', I was able to situate my research within housing studies. Core to this, was the ability to apply different theoretical frameworks to particular housing-related problems, but also draw on functional knowledge and an understanding of problems in order to propose solutions – the focus on pracademia.

The Housing Studies Association

As Bentley et al. (2019) highlight, this type of social support for ECRs can occur both within and outside institutions. One type of network that provides opportunities for ECRs to meet individuals whom they identify with are learned societies. Hopkins (2011) notes that there is no single definition of a learned society, and there is little literature exploring these types of organisations. He outlines that the phrase has historically been used as an umbrella term for a variety of different organisations or groups. These started in Renaissance Italy but have consistently been concerned with the pursuit of knowledge and its dissemination to a broader audience. In the eighteenth century, these organisations were local and did not fund research, but in the nineteenth century they refined their focus to particular areas of intellectual enquiry. Modern learned societies have focussed in again on a particular discipline, sub-discipline, or field. For example, the Political Studies Association, Socio-Legal Studies Association, and Regional Studies Society are all active in the UK, holding conferences, seminar series, and providing support for ECRs in terms of bursaries for event attendance and networking opportunities.

Hopkins (2011) outlines that modern learned societies can be conceptualised in the context of knowledge exchange. This can be between researchers working in different institutions and/or between those working in academia and those working in practice. Hopkins describes learned societies as "geographically far-reaching organisations that occupy an interstitial space that draws together disciplines, sub-discipline or field-focussed individuals from their broad-focussed geographically static institutions" (2011, p. 260). Members of these groups are therefore brought together by shared research interests and skills, providing an opportunity for the development and strengthening of identity through engagement with others. Hopkins highlights that learned societies provide "means for their members to network and communication both within specialised intellectual area and to society at large" (2011, p. 260–261). It is this element of communicating to society at large, beyond the membership, that Benande (2016) asserts differentiates a learned society from a professional body for practitioners. Professional bodies are more insular, Benande notes, focussing purely on their membership. Learned societies, however, have retained the historical focus on the promotion of knowledge beyond the academy.

Considering the SIMIC model in the context of learned societies, it is clear that these provide the opportunity for individuals to consider themselves in a professional context in relation to others and, importantly, engage with those who could provide models of the future self. It therefore enables individuals to create an identity beyond their institution amid peers with similar research or career interests. Members can both solidify their current conception of self, as well as use social interaction to develop their future sense of self. As previously noted, this is particularly important for ECPs who can be seen to be occupying two liminal spaces. I will now consider the role of the Housing Studies Association (HSA), the learned society for Housing Studies as a discipline in the UK, in my future self-construction.

The HSA was created in 1991 to support the creation and dissemination of knowledge related to the field of housing studies. The organisation defines itself as "the forum for housing-related research and debate" with the below aims:

- To promote the study of housing.
- To bring together researchers, practitioners and policy makers interested in housing research and education.
- To encourage the practical application of social research to the field of housing studies.
- To represent the interests of those researching or teaching housing studies in higher education to funding and development organisations and to government.

The organisation was created as a response to a significant growth in housing education and academic research in the 1980s. Membership spans across academia, practice, and policy organisations, and includes individuals in both the UK and internationally. Typically, the HSA runs an annual conference and an Autumn lecture each year and provides support for individuals involved in housing-related research to run their own events or attend HSA events. The organisation is governed by a voluntary committee, and strategic priorities are defined by the Chair who holds office for 2 years. The organisation, therefore, fits in with the definition of a learned society as it is involved in the support of production and dissemination of knowledge within a particular field/sub-field.

Finding Your People: Future Self-Construction

As noted, prior to joining the HSA I had not understood housing studies to be an academic discipline. Some time after becoming a member, I joined the executive committee – the group of volunteer members who govern and drive the activities of the organisation. I then became the Communications Officer (2017–2019), then Vice Chair (2019–2021) and I am currently Chair (2021-). During this time, I secured a permanent lecturer position at Cardiff Metropolitan University in Housing Studies (2015) and I credit the engagement with the HSA as giving me confidence to pursue an academic career. It was through joining the HSA, that I was able to envisage a future self within academia, which combined the current three elements of my professional identity: working in homelessness, policy, and academia.

Bentley et al. (2019) have applied the SIMIC to professional development in academia, focussing on the process of future self-construction in the experience of ECRs. They state that this process "may have less to do with pragmatic 'doing' concerns, and more to do with an experiential sense of who one *wants to be*, or more importantly, *who one thinks one is able to become*" (2019, p. 628–629). Here the focus on identification with others within the SIMIC is important. Larson et al. (2014) outlines that the process of identity construction for ECRs has become increasingly problematic due to the increase in numbers of individuals completing PhDs and the decline in the number of academic positions. This is aside from broader issues around career development within academia such as those relating to the 'leaky pipeline', inequalities, class, and social capital. Applying the SIMIC in the context of future identity construction is useful as "if multiple groups can facilitate a sense of continuity from past to present, they may also act as a bridge to the future" (Bentley et al., 2019, p. 3). Bentley et al. (2019) present two key questions in relation to identity:

 (i) Who do you want to be?
 (ii) Who can you really become?

This positive impact of social identification on identity construction is mirrored in Iyer et al.'s (2009) discussion on social identity theory and self-categorisation theory. They note that "group memberships help define the individual self and form the building blocks of people's social identities" (Iyer et al., 2009, p. 708). Again, this social element of identity has been observed to assist individuals in coping with change and challenges, and it is noted that "self-categorisation as a group member offers a new sense of belonging and provides individuals a tool for meaning-making" (Iyer et al., 2009, p. 708). As well as enabling future self-construction, identification with others makes individuals more willing to give and receive support and resources – further contributing to successful development.

I was able to match up my answer to the second of Bentley et al.'s (2019) questions to my answer to the first:

 (i) Who do you want to be?

    (a) Answer: an academic who is engaged in housing and homelessness practice and policy change

 (ii) Who are you able to become?

    (a) Answer: an academic who is engaged in housing and homelessness practice and policy change

By 'finding my people' within the membership of the HSA, I was able to reconceptualise the multiple strands of my professional identity from a weakness to a strength. It provided the opportunity to engage in future self-construction by meeting those who had professional identities that matched my hoped-for future self, as well as provide a network of support for being able to attain this. Instead of my multiple elements of identity across academia and practice leading to a "fragile academic self" (Knights & Clarke, 2014), I was able to create a strong sense of self through social interaction with others.

Conclusion

This chapter has outlined how 'finding your people' can play a key, positive, role in identity construction for pracademics. Engaging with individuals, groups, and networks beyond one's institution or organisation, enables pracademics to find individuals with similar identities to strengthen the current conception of self, or provide examples for future selves. As pracademics occupy a liminal space between practice and academia, looking beyond places of work can provide opportunities to meet, network, and work with others who have similar research interests and who also provide examples of how individuals can develop professionally. In this context, Early Career Researchers (ECRs) can be seen to occupy a second liminal space. Therefore, finding networks that provide opportunities for social identity construction can be seen to be particularly important for Early Career Pracademics (ECPs).

Looking to where these networks might exist, learned societies have been outlined as a key place for ECPs to be able to construct a future sense of self. I reflected on my involvement with the HSA as an example of how early career academics can be supported in professional identity construction through learned societies. As well as benefitting career development, the support that learned societies provide for ECRs can also be seen as a core part of identity construction when considering this from a social aspect. If pracademics are working in institutions that contribute to, rather than counteract, their "fragile academic selves" (Knights & Clarke, 2014, p. 335), finding networks beyond these can enable them to recognise the multiple elements of their identity as positive, and subsequently help strengthen both current and future senses of self.

Points for Reflection
- In this chapter, Taylor identifies the benefits of building networks to 'find your people'. This doesn't necessarily mean within the same discipline; it could be aligned to individual values or life experiences. How could you seek out opportunities where you might make such connections?
- Taylor particularly highlights how membership of learned societies can be beneficial for developing contacts. Thinking about your own field, what societies may be the most beneficial for you to join? If you are already a member of a society, could there be opportunities for becoming more involved, for example through joining their leadership committee?

(continued)

- Throughout this chapter, multiple elements of identity are presented as a strength. Reflect on the different components of your own professional identity. How could you draw on them to make a positive contribution to your work and profession?

References

Allen, C. (2009). The fallacy of "Housing Studies": philosophical problems of knowledge and understanding in housing research. *Housing, Theory and Society, 26*(1), 53–79. https://doi.org/10.1080/14036090802704429

Ballentyne, S., Drury, J., Barrett, E., & Marsden, S. (2021). Lost in transition: What refugee post-migration experiences tell us about processes of social identity change. *Journal of Community and Applied Social Psychology, 31*(5), 501–514. https://doi.org/10.1002/casp.2532

Benande, L. (2016). Learned societies, practitioners and their 'professional' societies: Grounds for developing closer links. *Educational Philosophy and Theory, 48*(14), 1395–1400. https://doi.org/10.1080/00131857.2015.1104953

Bentley, S., Peters, K., & Haslam, S. A. (2019). Construction at work: Multiple identities scaffold professional identity development in academia. *Frontiers in Psychology, 10*(628), 1–13. https://doi.org/10.3389/fpsyg.2019.00628

Clance, P. R., & Imes, S. A. (1978). The imposter phenomenon in high achieving women: Dynamics and therapeutic intervention. *Psychotherapy: Theory, Research & Practice, 15*(3), 241–247. https://doi.org/10.1037/h0086006

Clapham, D. (2018). Housing Theory, Housing Research and Housing Policy. *Housing, Theory and Society, 35*(2), 163–177. https://doi.org/10.1080/14036096.2017.1366937

Dickinson, J., Fowler, A., & Griffiths, T. (2020). Pracademics? Exploring transitions and professional identities in higher education. *Studies in Higher Education, 47*(2), 290–304. https://doi.org/10.1080/03075079.2020.1744123

Forster, A. M., Pilcher, N., Tennant, S., Murray, M., Craig, N., & Copping, A. (2017). The Fall and Rise of Experiential Construction and Engineering Education: Decoupling and Recoupling Practice and Theory. *Higher Education Pedagogies, 2*(1), 79–100. https://doi.org/10.1080/23752696.2017.1338530

Gov.uk. (2018, September 10). *Guidance devolution settlement: Wales.* UK Government. https://www.gov.uk/guidance/devolution-settlement-wales

Hollweck, T., Netolicky, D. M., & Campbell, P. (2021). Defining and exploring pracademia: Identity, community, and engagement. *Journal of Professional Practice and Community, 7*(1), 6–25. https://doi.org/10.1108/JPCC-05-2021-0026

Hopkins, J. (2011). The role of learned societies in knowledge exchange and dissemination: The case of the regional studies association, 1965–2005. *History of Education, 40*(2), 255–271. https://doi.org/10.1080/0046760X.2010.518161

Iyer, A., Jetten, J., Tsivrikos, D., Postmes, T., & Hasman, S. A. (2009). The more (and the more compatible) the merrier: Multiple group memberships and identity compatibility as predictors of adjustment after life transitions. *British Journal of Social Psychology, 48*(4), 707–733. https://doi.org/10.1348/014466608X397628

Knights, D., & Clarke, C. A. (2014). It's a bittersweet symphony, this life: Fragile academic selves and insecure identities at work. *Organization Studies, 35*(3), 335–357. https://doi.org/10.1177/0170840613508396

Larson, R. C., Ghaffarzadegan, N., & Xue, Y. (2014). Too many Ph.D. graduates or too few academic job openings: The basic reproductive number R0 in academia. *Systems Research and Behavioural Science, 31*(6), 745–775. https://doi.org/10.1002/sres.2210

Manzi, T., & Richardson, J. (2017). Rethinking Professional Practice: The Logic of Competition and the Crisis of Identity in Housing Practice. *Housing Studies, 32*(2), 209–224. https://doi.org/10.1080/02673037.2016.1194377

Miscenko, D., & Day, D. (2016). Identity and identification at work. *Organizational Psychology Review, 6*(3), 215–247. https://doi.org/10.1177/2041386615584009

Pilcher, N., Forster, A., Tennant, S., Murray, M., & Craig, N. (2017). Problematising the 'Career Academic' in UK construction and engineering education: Does the system want what the system gets? *European Journal of Engineering Education, 42*(6), 1477–1495. https://doi.org/10.1080/03043797.2017.1306487

Wenger, E. (1998). *Communities of practice: Learning, meaning and identity.* Cambridge University Press.

Wood, C., Farmer, M. D., & Goodall, D. (2016). Changing professional identity in the transition from practitioner to lecturer in higher education: An interpretive phenomenological analysis. *Research in Post-Compulsory Education, 21*(3), 229–245. https://doi.org/10.1080/1359674 8.2016.1195173

Dr Helen Taylor is a Senior Lecturer in Housing at Cardiff Metropolitan University. She is currently the Chair of the Housing Studies Association and has held board positions with housing organisations including Cymorth Cymru, Tai Pawb, and Newport City Homes. Helen's academic interests lie in social policy issues such as homelessness and exploring these through conceptual frameworks around justice. These research interests are informed by previous experience working in the homelessness sector.

Part II
Professional Development

Chapter 8
Pracademics: Facilitating Smooth Transition from Industry to Academia

Funmi Obembe

Abstract The decision to move from an established industry career to academia is, in most cases, one that is not taken lightly, and the factors that contribute to this decision vary from person to person. In a world with an increasing demand for universities to produce professionals that are industry-ready, and able to make positive contributions in the workplace and wider sector, having educators with industry experience who understand the needs of the sector can be invaluable. This is particularly so in practice-oriented disciplines, such as Technology. However, in most cases, for those trying to make the transition, it is not a straightforward process. There are often stumbling blocks and factors that stand as deterrents to making this transition. Drawing on practical experience, this chapter will discuss how transitions into academia can be eased by starting with part-time or visiting academic roles whilst still in industry, prior to taking up full-time academic positions. Additionally, the chapter will explore how the undertaking of a relevant doctorate whilst still working in industry can help to smooth the transition. Finally, the author makes recommendations for how HEIs can assist in mitigating some of the deterrents to the transition process.

Keywords Pracademic · Professional identity · Academic Practitioner · Career transitions · Barriers

At a Glance
- Draws on practical experience to discuss how transitions into academia can be eased by starting with part-time or visiting academic roles whilst still in industry, prior to taking up full-time academic positions.

(continued)

F. Obembe (✉)
Faculty of Arts, Science and Technology, University of Northampton, Northampton, UK
e-mail: funmi.obembe@northampton.ac.uk

© The Author(s), under exclusive license to Springer Nature
Switzerland AG 2023
J. Dickinson, T.-L. Griffiths (eds.), *Professional Development for Practitioners
in Academia*, Knowledge Studies in Higher Education 13,
https://doi.org/10.1007/978-3-031-33746-8_8

- Explores how undertaking a relevant doctorate whilst still working in industry can help to smooth the transition to an academic role.
- Suggests how Higher Education institutions (HEIs) can assist in mitigating some of the barriers to the transition process.

Introduction

The term 'pracademic' was first used over three decades ago (Hollweck et al., 2022; Owens, 2016). It has since been given various definitions, mainly all in the context of industry and academia (Chaaban et al., 2022; Dickfos, 2019). Posner used the term "broker" to describe the role of pracademics, and speaks of them as "breath[ing] life into networks" and "serv[ing] as the glue that holds networks together" across practice and academia (2009, p. 16).

The gap between academia and practice has been widely discussed (Bartunek & Rynes, 2014; Hollweck et al., 2022; Panda, 2014). Several proposals have been made over the years for bringing these two realms more closely together. These include promoting research for practice, and exploring the role that intermediaries can play to convene, facilitate, and support the bridging of the gap between research and practice (Bansal et al., 2012; Treby & Shah, 2005). The championing of both research-informed teaching and practice-informed research further illustrates that this could be a two-way process (Chynoweth, 2013; Joseph-Richard et al., 2021).

There continues to be an increasing demand on universities to produce graduates, from both traditional degree courses and non-conventional academic programmes, who are industry-ready, for example through the UK Government's Levelling Up initiative (Department for Levelling Up, Housing and Communities, 2022) and the Bridging the Digital Skills Gap programme (Department for Digital, Culture, Media, & Sport, 2021). First, the Levelling Up initiative is one of the UK Government's flagship priorities and aims to address inequality with a focus on a number of key areas for change. These include education, and universities are said to have a crucial role to play here. This is likely to involve implementing some non-traditional ways of educating and engaging with communities, and pracademics could play an important part in developing these initiatives (Department for Levelling Up, Housing and Communities, 2022). Secondly, the Bridging the Digital Skills Gap programme aims to increase digital and technical skills in areas where there is a gap in these skillsets. In response to this government agenda, various universities are involved in the development of short courses, apprenticeships, work-based learning, and so on, and pracademics who previously worked in relevant roles in industry are well-equipped to make meaningful contributions here. Pracademics can also support the employability requirements within HEIs due to their proximity to industry. Clearly, the pracademic can add value by bringing together both disciplinary theory and practical application within teaching and research. However, for those who want to transition from industry to academia, the journey is not always smooth. For the purposes of this chapter, I define the 'pracademic'as an academic who has industry experience prior to moving into academia. Within this chapter, I will explore some of the barriers to making the transition from industry to academia and suggest ways to mitigate against them. These include undertaking relevant doctoral studies and taking up part-time or visiting academic roles prior to making the transition. I will conclude this chapter with several additional recommendations to help ease the career move from industry to academia.

Methodology

This chapter is a conceptual exploration that builds on existing literature within the field. It also draws on the experiences of both the author and ten other pracademics who completed an in-depth survey about their experiences. Adopting a purposive sampling method to source a broad range of views (Campbell et al., 2020), I invited academics with practitioner experience from three HEIs in the UK to participate. These HEIs are all post-92 universities[1] with strong, practice-focussed cultures.

In terms of demographics, there were six male and four female participants. Two were Black/African/Caribbean/Black British and seven were White (one participant declined to provide this information). Six participants had more than 20 years of industry experience whilst the rest had between 11 to 20 years. The participants' disciplines included: Information Systems (4 participants), Marketing (1 participant), Computer Science (2 participants), Operational Management and Entrepreneurship (1 participant), Engineering (1 participant), and Accounting (1 participant). More detailed demographic information about the participants is provided in Table 8.1.

The survey instrument consisted of 25 multiple choice and short answer questions. The questions covered seven main areas, starting with the participants' demographic information. The next category focused on their industry experience. This was followed by questions on: motivations for making the transition from industry to academia; barriers to the transition; mechanisms that helped with the transition; experiences during the transition; and finally, occurrences after the transition had been made. I used thematic analysis to draw out reoccurring and relevant themes (Kiger & Varpio, 2020), which I have reported on in the subsequent discussion.

In terms of the data and research, it is useful to explain my positionality. I am a pracademic with 18 years of industry experience, primarily in the Technology/ Health sector prior to moving into full-time academia. In the last 3 years prior to this transition, I worked as a part-time lecturer in parallel with my industry role as a senior manager. In academia, I have been able to bring together both theoretical aspects of Technology and their practical applications in teaching and research.

---

[1] Former polytechnics, central institutions or colleges of HE that were given university status through the Further and Higher Education Act 1992.

Table 8.1 Participants' demographics

Pseudonym	Sex	Ethnic group	Industry years	Industry level of experience	Transition period	Discipline
P1	Female	Black/African/Caribbean/Black British	11–20	Senior or executive level	between 2016 and 2020	Information Systems
P2	Male	White	>20	Senior or executive level	between 2016 and 2020	Marketing
P3	Male	White	>20	Senior or executive level	between 2016 and 2020	Computer Science
P4	Male	Prefer not to say	>20	Mid-level	between 2000 and 2009	Computer Science
P5	Male	Black/African/Caribbean/Black British	11–20	Mid-level	between 2016 and 2020	Information Systems
P6	Male	White	>20	Senior or executive level	between 2000 and 2009	Operational Management and Entrepreneurship
P7	Male	White	>20	Intermediate	between 1990 and 1999	Engineering
P8	Female	White	11–20	Mid-level	between 2010 and 2015	Accounting
P9	Female	White	11–20	Mid-level	between 2000 and 2009	Information Systems
P10	Female	White	>20	Mid-level	between 1990 and 1999	Information Systems

De Montfort University Research Ethics Committee reviewed and approved this research. I also obtained informed consent from all individual participants involved in the study.

Findings

The analysis of the survey data revealed the following three key themes: the rationales for making the move from practice into academia; some of the barriers that may be faced; and the benefits of pracademia for various stakeholders. Each of these will be explored in turn.

Rationales for Making the Move from Practice into Academia

The decision to make the transition from a well-established industry career to academia is taken by people for various reasons. Some of these have been covered extensively in the existing literature and include, for example, the desire to: teach, undertake a lifestyle change, conduct research, be able to plan ahead, and also reduce stress (Garrison, 2005; Reitbauer et al., 2022). Table 8.2 (below) cites the reasons that the participants included in this study gave for making the transition from industry into academia.

These findings align with the existing literature that examines the motives for making this career change, including Mouratidou (2020) who discovered that some perceive teaching as a calling.

Barriers

For those who want to move careers from practice to academia, whatever their reason for doing so, there are some reported barriers. Examples that have been identified in the literature include: changes in professional identity, differences around organisational culture, feelings of alienation, and lack of support (Herman et al., 2021). A summary of participants' responses on the issue of barriers is included in Table 8.3.

As outlined in Table 8.1, all participants (except one) had been at either mid-level or senior/executive level in industry prior to making their transition into academia. However, they revealed (and this again aligned with findings from the literature) that this did not necessarily correspond to the level that they were placed at after moving into academia. Mabry et al. (2004) discuss how the most difficult part of the move for one of their authors was the switch to starting over on the career ladder,

Table 8.2 Participants' reported reasons for making the transition from industry to academia

Reasons for making the transition from industry to academia	Participants who selected this statement
"To give back to society/younger generation"	(P1, P2, P3, P5, P6 and P7)
"For a sense of purpose/fulfilment"	(P1, P2, P3, P5, P7 and P8)
"To teach"	(P1, P2, P4, P7 and P9)
"For a better work – life balance"	(P1, P3, P6, and P7)
"For the flexibility"	(P1, P3, P5 and P7)
"For the autonomy"	(P1, P3, P7 and P10)
"For the stability"	(P4 and P7)
One free-text response to 'Other': "to have a wider influence in the industry beyond one employer"	

Table 8.3 Participants' reported barriers to making transitions from industry to academia

"Remuneration. Industry experience not fully taken into account with starting point in academia" (P1)
"Better work life balance" (P6)
"Lack of knowledge of and trust in the academic institution. Lack of IT and software skills and knowledge" (P7)
"commuting distance, pay, academic qualifications" (P8)
"There were no deterrents. However, my industrial experience was ignored when setting my initial grade, but my skills gained in industry was used. I went for a job where I could fit in with my children's holidays" (P9)
"to be able to have a wider influence in the industry through research and consultancy" (P10)

one which included a lower salary and loss of some autonomy. Overall, the participants did seem to have a more positive experience in terms of the extent to which their industry experience was taken into account than is generally demonstrated by much of the existing literature that touches on this issue (Garrison, 2005; Wilson, 2014). Most participants reported that their industry experience was either 'considered' or 'partially considered' by the recruiting HEI. Future research could explore what is meant by a HEIs' 'consideration' of prior practitioner experience, and some recommendations are also made in the concluding section of this chapter around this aspect.

As seen in Table 8.1, all of the participants in this study had spent between 11 and 20 years in industry before moving into academia. These are substantial lengths of time and if the value of such prior experience is not recognised, this could present a significant barrier to making the career transition, particularly for those in senior roles. As one participant noted:

> a mindset change is needed amongst non-industry academics; there is a feeling that many view practitioners as inferior if they do not have research credentials. When I applied for a senior role, I was openly informed by a colleague that he had applied to stop me, a non-researcher, getting the role. He also said there had been a discussion 'amongst the researchers' as to who should stand against me to have a better chance of success. Aside: I got the role, so senior management did not have the same mindset. (P8)

In this case, although colleagues who were career academics did not seem to appreciate the value that this pracademic brought to the role, fortunately the management did. Another participant reflects on other potential challenges with making this career transition:

> Academia needs to value and set initial grades that reflect industrial experience and skills. A mentoring scheme should be in place to support transitioning to academia. When transitioning from industry you do not know things like how to develop new modules, or student learning styles or even your own teaching style. I was dumped into teaching with no experience and limited support, just 2 weeks after I had started - it was a case of sink or swim. (P9)

Figure 8.1 summarises the participants' answers to the question '*Was your industry experience considered doing the recruitment process?*'. The answers are grouped by the year range in which the participants made the transition from practice into academia.

Participant	Was your industry experience taken into account?	What year did you transition to an academic role?
P1	Partially	between 2016 and 2020
P2	No	between 2016 and 2020
P3	Yes	between 2016 and 2020
P4	Yes	between 2000 and 2009
P5	Partially	between 2016 and 2020
P6	Partially	between 2000 and 2009
P7	Yes	between 1990 and 1999
P8	Yes	between 2010 and 2015
P9	No	between 2000 and 2009
P10	Yes	between 1990 and 1999

Fig. 8.1 Participants' responses around whether their industry experience was taken into account doing the recruitment process? (Grouped by year range of transition from practice into academia)

Figure 8.1 demonstrates how the year of transition had no influence on participants' perceptions as to whether their industry experience was considered by their HEI during the recruitment process into academia. Two participants who had moved into academia between 1990 and 1999 believed that it had been considered. More recently, a participant, who had made the transition between 2016 and 2020, perceived that their industry experience was taken into consideration. Based on this sample, it does not appear that much has changed in this area in the past decade. However, there are other factors to be considered and this could be an area for further exploration.

There is more consistent evidence that students value the experience that pracademics can bring to their teaching. This has been witnessed first-hand by the author for many years and is also widely reported in extant literature (see, for example, Massie, 2004). From their survey completed by 15,221 students in UK universities, Neves and Hillman (2016) found that 47% of the students said that it was very important that teaching staff have relevant industry or professional expertise.

In terms of renumeration, all of the participants recorded a reduction in salary after moving from practice into academia that was either 'greatly reduced' or 'reduced'. Again, this is in line with what is seen in the literature. Garrison (2005) found that 75% of pracademic participants experienced a reduction in salary.

Another barrier for some who want to make the transition is the need to have a higher degree, typically a doctorate. This is not the case in all disciplines but is becoming increasingly common across many fields and universities (Baker, 2018). An illustrative search on an academic jobs site like jobs.ac.uk shows that for many roles, even in highly practice-based ones like Computer Science, a doctorate is necessary. There is continued discussion over whether such a higher degree should be required for certain disciplines, particularly for practice-based subjects (Dann et al., 2019; Baker, 2021). However, where it is essential, this can be a barrier to a professional who may have many years of practical, hands-on industry experience in the sector but who does not have a doctorate. A final barrier, raised by one participant in the survey, is the lack of HEI teaching experience. On the other hand, for a number of those who chose to make the transition, as seen in the responses to the question 'what motivated you to make the move', a desire to teach is seen as an impetus and not a barrier. This was also the case for me.

In the next section, I consider some of the benefits of pracademia for stakeholders before exploring potential ways to mitigate against the various barriers raised above to help smooth the transition.

Benefits

Pracademics add significant value to academia and its programmes (Dickfos, 2019). As mentioned earlier, this is recognised by students. Pracademics bring unique skillsets and knowledge that, if leveraged in academia, would benefit all stakeholders. In the study, participants were asked if the industry/practitioner experience they had was relevant to their academic role, and all participants answered 'yes'. Furthermore, when asked if they believed that their industry experience had contributed positively to their impact as academics, again all of the participants agreed. Table 8.4 highlights a selection of particular responses:

There is increasing demand for universities to produce graduates that are industry-ready and able to make meaningful contributions in the workplace and wider sector. Pracademics bring with them skillsets, experience, and knowledge bases that they can draw on to support students' development, as they have first-hand insight into industry and understand the needs of the sector. When it comes to universities' standing in league tables, student employability can be a key factor. Graduate career prospects are an important metric. For instance, in the Complete University Guide league table, one of the factors is 'Graduate Prospects' which is based on the HESA graduate outcomes survey (Oliver, 2022). In addition to student

Table 8.4 Participants' responses around how their industry experience has contributed positively to their academic career

'Helps me teach relevant and up to date material. Helps me in developing my students to be well rounded industry relevant professionals' (P1)
"The ability to understand exactly what is needed in teaching marketing subject area, and the relevance of marketing assessments. Also, employability" (P2)
"Taught how to manage and organise in a non-academic environment. This is translatable to an academic environment, not convinced the reverse would be true" (P4)
"Being able to connect with business and business leaders taking post graduate qualifications at the university. Being able to tell real life stories to under graduates how the real world works and how they can best make a success for their future career in industry" (P6)
"Able to encourage students and point them along ways of working and thinking that will assist their careers" (P7)
"my management experience has led to rapid promotion within academia; my practical experience assisted greatly in making my teaching come to life" (P8)
'I gained a lot of transferrable skills in industry such as project management, leading a team and blue-sky research where you could see the positive impact of your work. I could write reports, plan projects and handle project finances. I would always recommend that students gain industrial experience before moving into academia' (P9)
'can talk from personal experience, have lots of examples to use. Know what really happens in practice beyond the simplicity of textbook' (P10)

employability, pracademics are generally also able to leverage industry connections to bring in guest lecturers, and organise sessions that bring professionals and academics together to further students' knowledge and understanding of industry. An example of this is an annual event that I organise for students called 'A Day in the Life of a Data Professional' where alumni who work as data professionals and industry experts are invited to speak at a session with students. During the event, they share key industry insights with the students, followed by a question-and-answer session. It is always extremely popular and student feedback demonstrates perceptions that they gain immensely from it. Pracademics, particularly those who stay in contact with industry after transitioning to academia, are also invaluable when it comes to keeping curricula relevant both currently and for the future (namely maintaining alignment of curricula with industry requirements). Pracademics also bring in diverse perspectives. At times, these perspectives are sought in other ways, for example through periodical industry liaison committees, which have a remit to help ensure that curricula are relevant to current and future industry needs. However, the in-house pracademic is even more valuable. If empowered, the in-house pracademic may help by developing well-rounded graduates who meet industry expectations and workforce needs. This is buttressed by a quote from one of the survey's participants:

> there is a lot that academia can learn from industry to help student employability. (P10)

In the UK HEI system, as mentioned in the introduction, there are also some areas which are increasingly being prioritised as a result of Government initiatives. These include Levelling Up, Bridging the Digital Skills Gap programme, and accreditation of programmes by professional bodies. These are areas where pracademics are well suited for supporting HEIs.

Smoothing the Transition

Having discussed some of the barriers to transitioning from industry to academia, this section makes recommendations for facilitating smoothing the transition. These are considered under three main headings: Before, During and After the transition.

Before

For disciplines that require a doctorate, this may be something for the potential pracademic to consider undertaking alongside their industry role before they make the transition into academia. This is the route that I took, and I found that it helped immensely years later when I made the decision to transition into a full-time academic role. 50% of the survey participants revealed that they had similarly completed doctorates prior to transitioning into academia, and all of them described it as helpful for the transition process. A summary of all of the participants' responses is provided in Table 8.5.

Table 8.5 Participants' responses to the question: *would you recommend acquiring a PhD prior to moving into full time academia?*

"Yes, it's a great foundation to build an academic career on" (P1)
"Not necessarily. A strong level of industry experience can provide wider academic team with the reality of what skills are needed in business. 1% of students will progress to be an academic researcher, and 99% go to university to get a job." (P2)
"Yes. An important part of the role is supervising PhD students, so it helps to have been in that position." (P3)
"Not relevant within my particular area, which provides almost vocational training with little research focus." (P4)
"Facilitate some common grounds with colleagues in academia." (P5)
"Business Schools need practitioners with experience as much as people with PHDs. Other qualifications might be more relevant." (P6)
"Possibly although the PhD is rarely central to what is going on in industry." (P7)
"no; entering academia can provide access to obtaining a PhD without having to self-fund" (P8)
"Yes - it is essential because you will not be given enough time to complete your PhD as the time taken for teaching is underestimated." (P9)
"yes. There is not time to do a PhD when in a full-time academic role." (P10)

The responses highlighted a few interesting and important points about completing a doctorate prior to making the career move and how it can help smooth the transition:

- It is not applicable to all disciplines but, for disciplines where a doctorate is a requirement, it can help the transition process; P1 and P5 alluded to this.
- P3 mentioned how it would help in the role in terms of supervising doctorate students, this also applies to research-heavy roles.
- Part of the smoothing process could be that it immediately gives common ground with colleagues in academia (P5)
- Combining studying for a doctorate with an academic role (after transitioning) can be challenging timewise. This was mentioned by two of the ten participants (P9 and P10)
- Finally, there was the comment by participant P7 who observed that the doctorate is rarely central to what is going on in industry. In some sectors, such as the one that I worked in, this is very true and the decision to complete doctoral studies must be an intentional and strategic one, particularly when a person decides that at some point in the future they are likely to make the transition to academia.

Another way to smooth the transition from practice to academia, and perhaps to even sense-check the decision to do so, is to take up part time or visiting academic roles whilst still in industry but recognising that this may not necessarily result in a higher starting position (Garrison, 2005). Such partial involvement in academia may provide the professional with first-hand insights into the role to help support their decision-making around a career transition. It can also help to gradually build up their experience of teaching and learning at a more comfortable pace, and to build and further develop networks. This would likely translate to a less steep

Table 8.6 Participants'
response to question: *If
taking on a part-time or
visiting academic role helped
your transition, how did
it help?*

Responses	Number of Participants
Helped provide impetus to make the transition	3
Building networks	2
Gaining experience	5
Not applicable	3

learning curve when the practitioner eventually makes the transition to a full-time role. In my case, I held a part-time role for 3 years prior to transitioning to a full-time role. The result was that the career change went smoothly and, in terms of the actual tasks and work entailed in the role, the move was a very pleasant process.

In terms of responses from the survey, seven (70%) of the participants took on part time or visiting academic roles prior to transitioning. When asked how this helped smooth the transition, the majority (n = 5) of those who had part time/visiting academic roles prior to transitioning cited gaining experience as something that had helped smooth the transition for them (see Table 8.6).

When asked whether they would advise others who may be looking to make the transition from industry into academia to consider undertaking a part time or visiting academic role, all but one of the participants who had done so selected 'yes' that they would. One participant selected 'maybe'.

Finally, when participants were asked how they would rate their overall experience of transitioning from industry to academia, choosing from 1 (very easy) to 5 (very difficult), the average value over the ten participants was 2.6. Facilitating smooth transition through adopting the recommendations outlined at the end of this chapter, and through similar processes, is likely to result in a positive shift in the experiences of those transitioning.

During

This sub-section focuses on the application and interview process. If a part time or visiting academic role has been undertaken, the professional would already have networks in place that can potentially help in terms of putting together applications, references, and ultimately lead to successful recruitment. It may also be that those professionals are best- placed to apply for any full-time role that becomes available in their university where they are already known. To smooth the transition, the candidate needs to map their skillsets to the requirements of the person specification. Even though their skills, experience, and knowledge might not align directly with the requirements (which may be written with a career academic in mind), the professional needs to remember that they still have a very rich and valuable experience that they bring from industry. There is a need for this to be similarly recognised during the recruitment process by the HEI, and in the section on recommendations, this is discussed further.

After

To smooth the process after the transition, the university needs to have in place on-boarding processes that are tailored to the needs of staff who do not have a traditional academic background but do have significant industry experience. One of the participants from the survey mentioned this:

> When transitioning from industry you do not know things like how to develop new modules, or student learning styles or even your own teaching style. I was dumped into teaching with no experience and limited support, just 2 weeks after I had started – it was a case of sink or swim. (P9)

This is particularly important for those who have previously never worked in academia and who did not take on a part time or visiting role prior to transitioning. It may be very easy for institutions to assume that everyone who comes into academia has knowledge about the relevant systems and processes (as mentioned by P9 in the quote above); for example, the development of new modules, student learning styles, and teaching. There should be processes in place for those who need this additional support, and it should be visible and easily accessible to the new staff member. Additional recommendations are made in the final section below.

Conclusion

To help mitigate against the various barriers discussed in this chapter, maximise the benefits for HEIs in embracing pracademics, and generally smooth the transition process for those seeking to move from industry to academia, several recommendations are offered.

In terms of recognising the benefits of engagement and collaboration with industry, some progress has been made over the years. For instance, a search on jobs.ac.uk for academic roles, which include industry experience as a criterion, brought up several opportunities.

The impact of this can also be seen in the additional career pathway that increasing numbers of universities have already introduced or are introducing. Traditionally, universities have always had alternative career progression pathways; teaching and learning, research pathway, or a hybrid of these two. Now, universities are beginning to introduce the enterprise pathway, which focusses on collaboration, impact, and engagement with industry. Whilst this is a major headway, it is interesting to note that for all of the participants in the survey, the enterprise career pathway was not available in any of the universities when they were recruited. Those universities that do have this essential new route are to be celebrated, but arguably more still needs to be done. This leads us to the first recommendation.

For disciplines where the recruitment and retention of pracademics present a clear advantage, formal models should be developed to help map industry skillsets and experiences to pay grades. This would help to ensure that practitioner backgrounds are considered during the recruitment process in a non-subjective manner. For example, in recruiting into practice-oriented disciplines such as computer science and information systems, the model would map years of industry experience to pay grades that also consider technical certifications and other relevant skillsets. When it comes to the mapping of skillsets from academia to industry, there are numerous examples available (Gehr et al., 2020; Shankararaman & Gottipati, 2016; Talboy, 2020). However, the same does not appear to hold true for the reverse. This implies a clear area of development for HEIs that are interested in recruiting from industry.

The next recommendation focuses on the provision of HEI support for those who transition to academia from industry. This career move can represent a significant change in terms of culture, identity, and expectations (Herman et al., 2021; Wilson et al., 2014). Having a strong support network in place, which ideally includes academics with previous/current practitioner experience who can relate to their new colleague, could be invaluable. If applicants were made aware of the support system in place, this could serve as a potential impetus for deciding to make the transition. Making this support available to prospective applicants, where feasible, would go a long way in smoothing the transition. In this study, participants were asked what would have helped in smoothing the transition. A few (P1, P8, and P9) mentioned that a buddy system, for example where "academic staff in similar situations previously, provide informal help network" (P8), would have been useful, but none of their HEIs had one.

Based on existing literature, and the experiences of the survey participants, this does not appear to be happening on a large scale. In HEIs where buddy systems are in place, or where mentors are assigned to new members of staff, thought may not have been given as to who pracademics are allocated as buddies. Having a mentor who has taken the same career path can be truly invaluable and could reduce assumptions, the potential for miscommunication, and provide tailored support.

Another recommendation is that HEIs should actively promote a culture that values pracademics, and their contributions, as part of a diverse academic community. Any change in culture and mindset of an organisation needs to be driven from the top down (Muls et al., 2015). For change to occur, it must become a priority for the leadership team who should proactively embed the message across the entire organisation. This could include championing examples of pracademics who make valuable contributions to the university in, for example, the holistic development of graduates.

The final recommendation is that HEIs should put in place systems and processes that encourage and empower pracademics to draw on their unique skillsets and industry knowhow; for instance, in their teaching, mentoring of both students and colleagues, continued industry engagement through schemes (such as knowledge transfer partnerships and industry liaison committees), enterprise lead roles, short courses, and continuing professional development. A quote by the late Steve Jobs helps to illustrate further why this important: "It doesn't make sense to hire smart people and tell them what to do; we hire smart people so they can tell us what to do". (Lipman, 2018). With regards to industry skillsets and knowledge, universities should ensure that they give those with the knowhow the freedom and required support to leverage them.

The results of this research demonstrate that there are ways to smooth the transition for those who make the choice to move from industry to academia. In terms of renumeration, those who decide to make the transition may find that they need to accept a reduction in salary. However, as reported, there are mitigating factors such as opportunities to give back to society/younger generation, developing a sense of purpose/fulfilment, and to teach. In time, as universities continue to build on industry engagement in areas like the enterprise career pathway, this might cease to be a barrier. Other challenges, such as the mapping across of industry experience, are ones that HEIs should address urgently. There is a strong need for pracademics in the sector, and if the pathway from industry to academia is not smoothed, it could be detrimental to universities, students, and ultimately society as a whole.

Points for Reflection
- In this chapter, Obembe identifies how the recruitment of pracademics can offer potential benefits for stakeholders. Reflecting on your own context, what do you consider could be a primary advantage of engaging pracademics in higher education, and why?
- Some of the barriers that pracademics may face in making their career transition from practice into academia are highlighted in this chapter. Which of these challenges might be the most significant, and why? Can you think of any others?
- In drawing the chapter to a close, Obembe proposes recommendations that could help those who may be looking to make a career transition from industry to academia. Reflecting on your particular context, which of these do you believe could make the most impact, and why? Can you identify any other steps that could be taken?

References

Baker, S. (2018, March 8). Mandatory PhD policies lead to boom in academics with doctorates. *The Times Higher Education.* https://www.timeshighereducation.com/news/mandatory-phd-policies-lead-boom-academics-doctorates

Baker, S. (2021, June 2). Complete PhD coverage for lecturers 'undesirable', says professor. *The Times Higher Education.* https://www.timeshighereducation.com/news/complete-phd-coverage-lecturers-undesirable-says-professor

Bansal, P., Bertels, S., Ewart, T., MacConnachie, P., & O'Brien, J. (2012). Bridging the research-practice gap. *Academy of Management Perspectives, 26*(1), 73–92. https://doi.org/10.5465/amp.2011.0140

Bartunek, J. M., & Rynes, S. L. (2014). Academics and practitioners are alike and unlike: The paradoxes of academic-practitioner relationships. *Journal of Management, 40*(5), 1181–1201. https://doi.org/10.1177/0149206314529160

Campbell, S., Greenwood, M., Prior, S., Shearer, T., Walkem, K., Young, S., Bywaters, D., & Walker, K. (2020). Purposive sampling: Complex or simple? Research case examples. *Journal of Research in Nursing, 25*(8), 652–661. https://doi.org/10.1177/1744987120927206

Chaaban, Y., Sellami, A., Sawalhi, R., & Elkhouly, M. (2022). Exploring perceptions of pracademics in an Arab context. *Journal of Professional Capital and Community, 7*(1), 83–97. https://doi.org/10.1108/JPCC-11-2020-0091

Chynoweth, P. (2013). Practice-informed research: An alternative paradigm for scholastic enquiry in the built environment. *Property Management, 31*(5), 435–452. https://doi.org/10.1108/PM-04-2013-0028

Dann, R., Basford, J., Booth, C., O'Sullivan, R., Scanlon, J., Woodfine, C., & Wright, P. (2019). The impact of doctoral study on university lecturers' construction of self within a changing higher education policy context. *Studies in Higher Education, 44*(7), 1166–1182. https://doi.org/10.1080/03075079.2017.1421155

Department for Digital, Culture, Media & Sport. (2021). *Quantifying the UK data skills gap – full report*. UK Government. https://www.gov.uk/government/publications/quantifying-the-uk-data-skills-gap/quantifying-the-uk-data-skills-gap-full-report

Department for Levelling Up, Housing and Communities. (2022). *Levelling up the United Kingdom*. UK Government. https://www.gov.uk/government/publications/levelling-up-the-united-kingdom. Published 2 February 2022

Dickfos, J. (2019). Academic professional development: Benefits of a pracademic experience. *International Journal of Work-Integrated Learning, 20*(3), 243–255.

Garrison, C. P. (2005). Who moves from industry to academia and why: An exploratory survey and analysis. *Education, 125*(3), 414+.

Gehr, S., Garner, C. C., & Kleinhans, K. N. (2020). Translating academic careers into industry healthcare professions. *Nature Biotechnology, 38*, 758–763. https://doi.org/10.1038/s41587-020-0552-x

Herman, N., Jose, M., Katiya, M., Kemp, M., le Roux, N., Swart-Jansen van Vuuren, C., & van der Merwe, C. (2021). Entering the world of academia is like starting a new life': A trio of reflections from health professionals joining academia as second career academics. *International Journal for Academic Development, 26*(1), 69–81. https://doi.org/10.1080/1360144X.2020.1784742

Hollweck, T., Netolicky, D. M., & Campbell, P. (2022). Defining and exploring pracademia: Identity, community, and engagement. *Journal of Professional Capital and Community, 7*(1), 6–25. https://doi.org/10.1108/JPCC-05-2021-0026

Joseph-Richard, P., Almpanis, T., Wu, Q., & Jamil, M. G. (2021). Does research-informed teaching transform academic practice? Revealing a RIT mindset through impact analysis. *British Educational Research Association, 47*(1), 226–245. https://doi.org/10.1002/berj.3681

Kiger, M., & Varpio, L. (2020). Thematic analysis of qualitative data: AMEE Guide No. 131. *Medical Teacher, 42*, 1–9.

Lipman, V. (2018, September 25). *The best sentence I ever read about managing talent*. Forbes. https://www.forbes.com/sites/victorlipman/2018/09/25/the-best-sentence-i-ever-read-about-managing-talent/?sh=444207accdfb

Mabry, C. K., May, G. L., & Berger, N. (2004). Moving from practice to academia: Three perspectives. *Human Resource Development International, 7*(3), 395–402.

Massie, W. W. (2004, June 20–23). *Bringing Practitioners and Practice into the Curriculum. Proceedings of The American Society for Engineering Education (ASEE) Annual Conference. USA*.

Mouratidou, M. (2020). Moving from industry to academia. In M. Antoniadou & M. Crowder (Eds.), *Modern day challenges in academia: Time for a change* (pp. 16–30). Edward Elgar.

Muls, A., Dougherty, L., Doyle, N., Shaw, C., Soanes, L., & Stevens, A. (2015). Influencing organisational culture: A leadership challenge. *British Journal of Nursing, 24*(12), 633–638.

Neves, J., & Hillman, N. (2016). *The 2016 student academic experience survey*. Higher Education Academy. https://www.advance-he.ac.uk/knowledge-hub/hepi-hea-student-academic-experience-survey-2016

Oliver, C. (2022, September 29). *University and subject league tables methodology.* The Complete University Guide. https://thecompleteuniversityguide.co.uk/sector/insights/university-and-subject-league-tables-methodology?amp=true

Owens, L. W. (2016). Reflections of a pracademic: A journey from social work practitioner to academic. *Reflections, 22*(1), 37–43.

Panda, A. (2014). Bringing academic and corporate worlds closer: We need pracademics. *Management and Labour Studies, 39*(2), 140–159. https://doi.org/10.1177/0258042X14558174

Posner, P. L. (2009). The pracademic: An agenda for re-engaging practitioners and academics. *Public Budgeting & Finance, 29*(1), 12–26. https://doi.org/10.1111/j.1540-5850.2009.00921.x

Reitbauer, M., Fürstenberg, U., Kletzenbauer, P., & Marko, K. (2022). Teaching is therapy for me. The subjective wellbeing of Austrian ICLHE teachers: Learning to balance challenges and resources through teacher development. *Innovation in Language Learning and Teaching, 16*(4–5), 366–380. https://doi.org/10.1080/17501229.2022.2064468

Shankararaman, V., & Gottipati, S. (2016). Mapping information systems student skills to industry skills framework. Proceedings of The *IEEE Global Engineering Education Conference (EDUCON).* United Arab Emirates. https://doi.org/10.1109/EDUCON.2016.7474561.

Talboy, A. (2020, February 19). Five ways your academic research skills transfer to industry. *Microsoft.* https://www.microsoft.com/en-us/research/blog/five-ways-your-academic-research-skills-transfer-to-industry/

Treby, E., & Shah, A. (2005). Bridging the gap between academia and practitioners: Training coastal zone managers. *Planet, 14*(1), 16–17. https://doi.org/10.11120/plan.2005.00140016

Wilson, M. (2014). Down the Rabbit hole: Navigating the transition from industry to academia. *Macquarie University, University of Tasmania, and University of Queensland.* https://ltr.edu.au/resources/SD12_2534_Wood_Information%20Booklet_2014.pdf

Wilson, M. J., Wood, L., Solomonides, I., Dixon, P., & Goos, M. (2014). Navigating the Career Transition from Industry to Academia. *Industry and Higher Education, 28*(1), 5–13. https://doi.org/10.5367/ihe.2014.0189

Dr Funmi Obembe is Head of Technology at the University of Northampton, UK where she leads on the strategic development and operational management of the subject area which covers Computing, Engineering and Games programmes. Prior to going into full time academia, she worked in the technology industry/health informatics sector for over 18 years and is also a data development and analytics specialist. Funmi is passionate about bringing together in teaching and research both theoretical aspects of technology and their practical applications. Her main research areas are in technology enhanced learning, open data/big data analytics, knowledge management, and machine learning algorithms for knowledge representations.

Chapter 9
The Value of Objects: How Artefacts Can Enrich Professional Reflection and Reflexivity

Jill Dickinson ⓘ and Teri-Lisa Griffiths ⓘ

Abstract This chapter will explore how artefacts can be utilised to support reflection on professional identities and promote reflexivity. With origins in material culture and sociomateriality (Orlikowski & Scott The Academy of Management Annals 2:433–474, 2008), the exploration of how objects can demonstrate aspects of professional identity has previously been explored in the social work context (Scholar Qualitative Social Work 16:631–648, 2017; Doel The British Journal of Social Work 49:824–841, 2019). The authors utilised this concept more widely in their own research, exploring the identities and transitions of pracademics from diverse subject areas and at various stages of their academic careers (Dickinson et al. Studies in Higher Education 47:290–304, 2020). Beginning with an exploration of objects and their link to identity, this chapter will develop to consider the utility of artefacts in professional reflection and reflexivity. Readers will be encouraged to consider how selecting and reflecting on their own artefacts can contribute to their understanding of their motivations to transition to Higher Education and how they can take a values-led approach as their professional identity evolves post-transition.

Keywords Reflexivity · Reflection · Professional identity · Sociomateriality · Artefacts · Objects · Professional values · Career transitions · Totems

J. Dickinson (✉)
School of Law, University of Leeds, Leeds, UK
e-mail: j.dickinson1@leeds.ac.uk

T.-L. Griffiths
Department of Law & Criminology, Sheffield Hallam University, Sheffield, UK

J. Dickinson, T.-L. Griffiths (eds.), *Professional Development for Practitioners in Academia*, Knowledge Studies in Higher Education 13,
https://doi.org/10.1007/978-3-031-33746-8_9

At a Glance
- Explores how artefacts may be used to encourage reflection and reflexivity on professional development and career transitions between practice and Higher Education.
- Defines artefacts very broadly to include objects and tools that are made by humans, whether tangible or not, for example, a phone, a website, or a corporate strategy.
- Draws on a combined theoretical framework of professional identity and sociomateriality (the dynamic relationship between humans and artefacts).
- Makes recommendations as to how universities could support pracademics' professional development and career transitions for the benefit of the academic community, students, and the institution.

Introduction

This chapter draws on the concepts of both professional identity and sociomateriality to explore how artefacts can facilitate reflection and reflexivity to support pracademics' navigations of their career transitions, and future professional development.

First, professional identity includes knowledge, philosophy, professional roles and expertise, attitudes, behaviours, and interactions with other professionals (Woo et al., 2014), and collectively, professional identities play a key role in organisational behaviour (Hay et al., 2021). Broadly, organisational behaviour comprises an entanglement of relationships around, for example, space and place, instruments, policies and procedures, reference points, groupings, systems, and specialisms (Orlikowski & Scott, 2008). In short, professional identity is about more than internal concepts of the professional self. We have previously explored the "fluid and context-dependent" nature of professional identity (Dickinson et al., 2020, p. 290), and further studies suggest how it comprises both self-perception and others' views of the individual "as a particular sort of person in a particular context at a particular time" (Beltman et al., 2015, p. 226). Within education, researchers have observed how the professional identity of academics within a teaching-specific context comprises feelings around being valued, a sense of belonging, self-efficacy, dedication, and visualising career development (van Lankveld et al., 2016). Further to this, it is important to recognise the potentially multi-faceted role of academics who are frequently required to publish research in addition to their teaching responsibilities. Within the broader context, across Higher Education (HE) within the UK, academic staff face increased scrutiny through performance evaluation programmes and associated metrics, focussed on research outputs and teaching quality. Mula et al. (2021) warn that this working environment could particularly influence the professional identity development of early career academics to the extent that they may develop unethical approaches to research whilst trying to navigate the multiple challenges presented around staff-student relations, work-life balance, and job security (Schaap et al., 2021).

Beltman explores how internal and external opinions about the future self are particularly important at any stage of an individual's professional development given that action plans for "becoming" are founded upon them (2015, p. 225). Related to this, Khapova et al. (2007) demonstrate how professional identity in terms of both connection to, and networks within, a particular field can be a significant predictor for career change. There are also suggestions that those with the ability to 'access multiple identity resources [a]re more likely to perceive a navigable pathway to a future professional self' (Bentley et al., 2019), for example from practice into academia to become a pracademic (Posner, 2009). Pracademics can play an important role in challenging norms, driving forward change (Friesen, 2022), and facilitating symbiotic theory and practice-development (Panda, 2014). Yet, research from Dickinson et al. (2020) illustrates how pracademics may face underlying personal challenges around their sense of professional identity. Their research reports findings of pracademics feeling the need to develop "liquid identities" and "shape-shift", for example as they introduce themselves to different audiences, perhaps as an academic, a lecturer, and/or a practitioner (2020, p. 300). Within the next section of this chapter, we consider the second concept of sociomateriality before we then draw on both concepts to explore how artefacts can be used to support processes of reflection and reflexivity for professional development.

Sociomateriality presents a distinct perspective in the context of organisational development. Broadly, sociomateriality perceives the relationship between humans and materials as an "entanglement... of continuously performed intra-relations" (Hultin, 2019, p. 92). It is important to distinguish notions of sociomateriality from discussions around material culture theory. Whereas material cultural theory explores the relationship between humans and materials at a *particular* moment in time (Prown, 1982), sociomateriality focuses on the *dynamic* interface between humans and materials (de Moura & de Souza Bispo, 2019). Sociomateriality is therefore particularly relevant for this chapter as we encourage reflection on the development of professional identity over time. Orlikowski and Scott (2008) note how the sociomateriality approach examines three interrelated elements: technology (which is broadly defined to include any material tools used for work); work (including the actors within an organisation); and the organisation itself. This chapter draws on sociomateriality to consider the central role played by the material world in developing understandings around professional identity.

Humans have historically assigned meaning to material objects. In the eighteenth century, the British philanthropist, Thomas Coram, opened the Foundling Hospital in London. In recognition of the living conditions of the poor at that time, it was a place where mothers, without the resources to care for their children, could leave them in the charge of the hospital. For the first twenty years of the hospital's operation, mothers were each invited to leave a token to enable them to identify their children should they ever have the means to reclaim them into their care. These objects included buttons, coins, padlocks, and scraps of fabric. Also referred to by Doel (2017), this example demonstrates how the meaning which humans ascribe to material (non-human) objects can have the effect of changing or transforming the object itself. What might, to the unknowing eye, appear to be unwanted, worthless items, instead become poignant symbols of familial love and identity.

The importance of artefacts is similarly apparent within the context of professional identity. Doel (2019) designed a project that used objects to tell the story of social work. Inviting anyone with a relationship to social work to submit objects with an accompanying story, the project revealed aspects of social work practice and culture beyond the professional context (Doel, 2019). In parallel with the meaning making of the Foundling Hospital mothers, Doel acknowledged how the narrative accompanying each object is critical to the construction of its meaning in the social work context. Within the same field, Scholar (2012) identifies how qualified social workers who supervise, educate, and assess students perceive dress and self-presentation as key elements of their professional identities. The importance of objects within the workplace has also been recognised within other disciplines. In their examination of the ways tables are used in various work settings, including roundtables and countertops, Conrad and Richter (2013) posit that "material artefacts like the table intervene in human interaction by structuring activities, promoting certain activities and restraining others." (2013, p. 134) For instance, they suggest that table shapes can impose degrees of integration between participants. Round tables may invite discussion on an equal footing, whereas rectangular tables can be utilised to reinforce hierarchies. Lundin and Nulden (2007) explored the importance of workplace tools within the Swedish police service, such as communications technology and pepper spray, for generating conversations that facilitate organisational learning. In their study of chefs' tools, Robinson and Baum (2019) acknowledge the mutable nature of the chef's role and explored how the significance of artefacts (i.e. tools of the trade) can change according to temporal and spatial contexts. Their findings that chefs would keep artefacts as mementos after they finished using them for work is pertinent to the pracademic context.

Adopting these dual concepts of professional identity and sociomateriality, previous studies have employed artefacts to generate additional dimensions. The literature defines the term 'artefact' very broadly to include "any product of human activity" (Scholar, 2017, p. 634). Svensson and Gluch similarly argue that tangibility is not a pre-requisite; noting how "a mission statement, a strategic plan, an organizational chart, or an algorithm" could all be reified as objects as they may affect human agency within the institutional setting (2022, p. 42). Lundin and Nulden (2007) explain how 'intellectual' artefacts, such as language and behaviours, can provide novice practitioners with a route into understanding their contribution within the professional community.

Whilst the adoption of artefacts within the research setting has become increasingly common, it is important to understand the rationale. Artefacts are often used because of their human-made, representative, instrumental, and deliberate nature (Czerwinski, 2017), and their importance may also lie within their sense of permanence (Friedman, 2007). Yet, artefacts need to be brought to life, or vitalised, through human narrative (Makela, 2007) to trigger memories, reflection, and storytelling (Lundin and Nulden, 2007). However, researchers also need to be mindful that using artefacts may unduly narrow the discussion and risk missing consideration of the broader context (Birkhead, 2021).

Artefacts can be used to encourage processes of reflection in broader contexts such as teaching and learning, and personal and professional development. There is a range of evidence demonstrating the importance of reflecting on experience for developing professional identity. Feucht et al. suggest how "mindful introspection, dialogues with peers about relevant and critical issues, and more systematic and rigorous participation in action research" can together "embod[y] the essence of being a professional" (2017, p. 234). They also advocate for such reflective practice to be combined with processes of reflexivity (namely considering the wider context of experiential learning) to change "practices, expectations, and beliefs" (p. 234). Alongside self-identity and resilience, reflexivity has also been classed as a "fundamental resource" for career development, particularly for driving more values-aligned decision-making (Tomassini, 2015, p. 275) which, as we will demonstrate, could prove particularly pertinent within the context of pracademia.

Against this backdrop, the chapter combines the concepts of professional identity and sociomateriality to explore how artefacts can be used to foster reflective and reflexive practice and help develop pracademics' self-identification with their "knowledge, sets of skills, ways of being and values" (Trede et al., 2012, p. 380). It considers how and why pracademics may retain, discard, and/or further develop elements of their professional identity as they navigate their career journeys into HE.

Methodology

The data reported in this chapter is from a case study conducted at a large, post-1992,[1] HE institution in the UK. We put out an open call for pracademics within the institution to take part in one of six focus groups. Forty-two participants came forward from a range of disciplines and at different stages of their academic careers. Our research design was inspired by the work of Doel (2019) and aligns with the socio-material approach described above. Recognising how artefacts can support communication, and illustrate and illuminate phenomena (Thornquist, 2015), we invited each participant to bring an artefact which they felt represented their career transition from practice to academia. Out of the forty-two pracademics who participated in the focus groups, seventeen participants brought an artefact with them (which is something we will discuss further on in this section). Within each focus group, we encouraged participants to draw on their artefacts in generating insights into their experiences and the related cultural framework (Elliott, 2005). Findings from the focus group discussions centre around two key themes of practice-informed teaching and professional identities. This chapter specifically focuses on the participants'

---

[1] Former polytechnics or Higher Education colleges that were granted university status in the United Kingdom through the Further and Higher Education Act 1992.

choices of artefacts and the meanings behind them in terms of their professional identity development. We deliberately asked each participant to select an artefact ahead of their focus group to encourage pre-reflection and generate further insights during the discussions.

Following calls for social researchers to clarify their positionality (see, for example, Unluer, 2012), we feel that it is important to note our status as insider researchers at this point. We have both made the career transition from practice into academia; one as a lawyer and the other as a careers adviser, and we both now hold academic roles within UK universities.

Before specifically considering some of the artefacts that the participants brought with them, it is useful to consider why some participants failed to bring an object to their focus group. Participants revealed how one of the reasons why they struggled with the task was a perception of clear divisions between their practice and their current teaching role.

> Artefacts: yeah, the reality is that I think most artefacts that represent the work that I did sort of stayed at the office when I left it, I didn't take anything with me. So, all the artefacts I have are all to do with what I'm doing now really. I mean I've got certificates and stuff, but I have struggled to come up with something that was really relevant or that would have been something I could have brought with me here. (Participant A, focus group 1)

This account can provide some insight into the fluctuation of professional identity; this participant 'didn't take anything' with them from practice and any object that they could have produced is 'to do with what I'm doing now'. It is worthy of note that this participant had been a lecturer for a longer period than they were in practice, and their comments may suggest that they have made a secure transition from their previous professional identity (van Lankveld et al., 2016). Yet, the professional identities of pracademics may not necessarily be so dichotomous; perhaps they may be better conceived as comprising layers that an individual builds up over time. It is possible that such seams of professional identity may remain separate; for example, the quote above suggests very clear distinctions between professional identities that this participant has developed in practice and academia. Perhaps such layers of identity may also be woven together sometimes when individuals adapt elements of their professional identity from practice for the academic setting, whether knowingly or not.

In the next section of this chapter, we will explore the artefacts chosen by seven of our participants and situate them within the context of the literature around both professional identity and sociomateriality.

Findings

The participants' selection of artefacts included both organisational artefacts that enabled efficient working practice (Eriksson-Zetterquist et al., 2009) (for example, a mobile phone, a reference text, and a scale rule), and "totems" or "trophies" that held symbolic meaning (Robinson & Baum, 2019, p. 165) (for example, a doll, a thank-you letter, and a charm).

Congruent with the literature, some participants preferred to reflect on more symbolic 'tools', often involving either senses and/or skills that they had developed in their previous profession and which they could relate to their current context.

> The artefact that I've brought is my ears [. . .] I mean because obviously as a journalist for many years, it's about listening to people [. . .] and following things up all the time and just listening for the clues, picturing what people are saying to you in order to make your programmes or do your interviews. I would like to think that I use that here as well, because part of my role as the joint course leader is pastoral, is the pastoral side and you know, following the students up who are not attending, finding out why they're not, and finding out that range of problems that are keeping them from coming in, and listening to them and devoting time to actually listen to them. (Participant G, focus group 5)

This participant has outlined how their existing professional skills assisted them with providing pastoral support in the transition to their role as a lecturer. This is arguably in contrast to Mula et al.'s study (2021) which focussed on postdoctoral identities and concluded that early-career academics experienced insecurity and uncertainty. Other participants similarly noted how they used specific senses that they had established in their previous practice to explore and reflect on their approach to teaching.

> I'm also very aware that we learn incredibly well with our eyes, and I think that I'm incredibly mindful about the type of images I display in my class and how I use images as a means of generating an emotional response, a deeper layer of connectivity with the subject. So, I do spend a lot of time thinking about what I'm showing students because psychologically we're affected quite significantly by what we see, the subliminal messages. We're controlled [. . .] some architects design to make us feel how they want us to feel, to move us on quickly, to make us confused so we stay and maybe buy things, to make us want to buy things. There is a kind of- a level of how our surroundings influence us and how our images. So actually, if we can teach visually as well as verbally, I think that that's a skill that I've learnt." (Participant B, focus group 5)

Participant B has considered the importance of 'seeing', both as a mode of learning and how visual contexts influence the practice of architecture. This participant has employed their professional values as an architect to help them to make sense of their conceptualisation of the academic role. In a similar way to the proceeding example, this account diverges from previous research that deems experience acquired before the academy as insufficient to support professional development as academics within a teaching-specific context (van Lankveld et al., 2016). As previously illustrated, the symbolic nature of these artefacts is not unusual. Doel (2019, p. 12) similarly had "metaphysical" submissions which fell outside of the scope of conventional objects, but which illuminated an aspect of practice or professional culture.

Those participants who brought material objects to their focus group selected a mixture of tools or items which had either practical use in their previous professional practice roles and/or symbolic significance for them. One participant highlighted how a certain tool was so integral to their professional practice that they had incorporated it into their teaching and assessment approaches.

My artefact is my phone because it's an essential tool of the journalist, because you film on it, you can record on it, talk to people on it, you talk to the office and every student has got one. So, I don't tell them to put phones away in lectures. [. . .] I tell them it's an important thing and you should always have it switched on. So that's a really good way of identifying with them and we use phones a lot. They use their own phones in their assessments. (Participant F, focus group 5)

Here, the participant is exploiting their professional knowledge, and potentially their students' awareness of their previous practice as an asset. It also supports the notion that tools are important to the development of practice. Lundin and Nulden (2007) conclude that talking about tools is an important method for teaching new recruits about practice. Participant F has retained the knowledge of their previous practice to support the development of those preparing to enter that profession, through identifying and encouraging the use of a specific 'tool of the trade'. Another participant had collected items that they had used in their work as a community safety officer.

The reason why I brought these as my artefacts is because it brings back some memories actually, some quite good memories of that time, because I did enjoy being a practitioner, but I think that from a teaching perspective, I think that they really highlight how you need to know the theory to be able to put things in to practice [. . .] So, all of these different materials are aimed at preventing crime and relate to something called the crime triangle, so routine activities theory. So, the premise is very basic level criminology, that for a crime to occur there need to be three things that happen at a single point in time: a motivated offender, a suitable target, and the lack of a capable guardian. So, all of these things some-where try and break that crime triangle, by demotivating a motivator [. . .] and so I try and use those types of examples with students when I talk crime prevention about bringing a theory from the classroom and how it can translate, and you need to still be thinking about that theoretical side when they get a real-life job. (Participant D, focus group 2)

This example is ostensibly demonstrating how the participant wishes to emphasise to their students how theory can be applied in practice through real-world experi-ence and the tools used in work. However, the participant is also revealing some-thing of their professional values, namely that practice should be informed by theory. This values-first approach was something that the researchers saw repeat-edly through the artefacts that participants produced.

I brought a little thank you that I got from a young person that I was working with who, we used to do quite a lot of longer-term work, so it's someone that I spent a lot of time with [. . .] I always keep that with me on my desk as a bit of a reminder of my time there [. . .] The reason why it influences me now is that when I'm working with the students in our child-hood studies course a lot of them are going to go and work in some capacity with children [. . .] So, I just really try and hold that–how important it is really for them to do the best they can for every child and young person and family that they work with. That sometimes, well not sometimes, usually, systems get in the way of doing the best work you can and how important it is for them to just really try and, I guess, advocate for all those children that they're working with [. . .] and how that they can make a difference, even when it might feel like they can't. (Participant A, focus group 4)

Both preceding participants highlight the important role that values play in the way that pracademics reconceptualise their professional experiences and apply them to their teaching and research practice. Again, this challenges earlier research that focusses on the transition from practice into academia as disruptive in the context of professional values (Shreeve, 2011; Wood et al., 2016). These findings highlight how pracademics may find constancy and security from the value-base developed in their previous practice (Dickinson et al., 2020). The artefact selected by Participant A also highlights another facet of the objects selected; namely, their totemic, rather than utilitarian, appeal as symbolising the participants' experience and values. One participant explained how their totemic artefact instilled them with confidence when making the transition from practice into academia.

> My [previous] colleagues bought me a star charm to make me remember as I left, what skills and attributes I'd got and that I was still a star. For me, this will sound quite weird, I've worn it [. . .] walking into a lecture theatre for the first time with a hundred students, to remember that I am actually still an expert in my field and in that department, when a lot of colleagues are talking about PhDs and research, which overwhelms me still I have to say, but keeps me remembering that I have got those skills and I have got something to give to learners, peers, colleagues. So, I do wear it on a daily basis. (Participant D, focus group 5)

Here, the participant reveals experiences which align with the disruptive nature of the pracademic transition reported in prior research (Gourlay, 2011). Finding themselves in a new, unfamiliar working environment and culture where 'colleagues are talking about PhDs and research', the participant discloses their need for reassurance about their worth. They suggest that their totemic artefact helps by reminding them how they were held in esteem by their former colleagues and that they 'have got something to give' within their new academic setting. This aligns with the authors' previous calls for universities to recruit pracademics and support their professional development to extol the benefits of a diverse academy (Dickinson et al., 2020). The theme of transition was similarly prominent for other participants. One reflected how their artefact (a Dictaphone they would use for transcription whilst they were in practice) prompted them to recall a moment of realisation.

> I was sat in a multidisciplinary sort of department with people next to me who weren't lawyers and they certainly weren't from the sort of corporate background that I was from and suddenly I started not only to realise that there are other ways of being a professional, but that also I started to understand what I had been and what I had become and how I'd been trained into a particular type of beast. (Participant H, focus group 5)

These three examples of the gift from the young person, the star charm, and the Dictaphone together illustrate how artefacts can be selected for their symbolism in terms of the participant's feelings towards the transitional process and what it means for them. The spatial dimension of this final reflection, with the participant experiencing an instant of comprehension once they had transitioned to their new 'multidisciplinary' working environment, aligns with previous findings around how the meaning of artefacts changes along with the working circumstances of the individual (Robinson and Baum, 2019). Pracademics, with their experience of "being in two camps" (Shreeve, 2011, p. 79), are uniquely placed to draw on any artefacts that they bring with them from practice into academia to support processes of reflection and reflexivity in developing their professional identities. This aspect will be explored within the discussion and conclusion that follows.

Conclusion

We will reiterate and draw together the key points made within this chapter around using the dual lenses of professional identity and sociomateriality.

First, recent attention has highlighted issues around the purpose of pracademics, and some of the challenges and opportunities arising from their potential roles (Campbell, 2022). Eacott (2021) similarly notes how the pracademia narrative is gathering momentum but cautions against perceptions of the pracademic's role as a panacea. Against this backdrop, the chapter has presented a timely discussion around how the dual notions of professional identity and sociomateriality are inextricably interweaved within this context, and how combining these concepts, as we have done here, can be used to further develop understanding. The chapter has drawn on this theoretical framework to illuminate the distinctive, multifaceted, and iterative nature of pracademics' professional identities as they seek to navigate their career transitions from practice into academia whilst also retaining aspects of the professional identities that they developed as practitioners.

Second, the chapter has highlighted the importance of artefacts, and particularly within the broader workplace environment including, but not limited to, academia. We have identified how people may retain artefacts for a variety of reasons including: to remind them of their tacit knowledge and skills, to recall memories of previous practice, and to evoke important professional values. The findings have also demonstrated how the purpose for which artefacts are retained may change over time; for example, a once useful item in the professional practice setting may be kept as a totemic reminder of the pracademic's career development and professional values. The findings from the case study have evidenced the potential for drawing on artefacts to support taking a reflective and reflexive approach to decision-making around professional development and career transitions. Whilst the case study designed-in artefacts to encourage focus group discussions within the research setting, there is potential for similarly using artefacts to support professional development discussions, for example within a mentoring or coaching setting. The research has evidenced how artefacts can be used to add another dimension to such sessions by encouraging recall, and reflective and reflexive practice around previous experience to help colleagues locate and understand their professional identity and sense of worth, and develop their thoughts and ideas around further professional and careers development.

Third, the findings have illustrated the extent to which perhaps previously self-assured practitioners may rely on totems acquired from their time spent in practice to remind them of all that they have to offer, and what is important to them, as the make the transition into the academic environment. Our previous research called for university leaders to explicitly recognise the skills, knowledge, and experiences that pracademics bring with them and to nurture and support the further development of these attributes within the academic setting (Dickinson et al., 2020). Whilst there is evidence that some initiatives have been developed which may help to address these concerns (for example, the online Pracademia Network as part of Advance HE Connect, and the Academic Careers Framework, which equates practice experience and engagement with research development (Sheffield Hallam University, 2020), this chapter highlights the potential for developing other opportunities. These could include, for example, adopting similarly creative approaches to developing induction and training programmes. Such opportunities could also serve to crystallise what newer pracademics wish to convey about their professional values and identity in their new academic role.

Finally, it is important to identify a potential limitation of the case study. As highlighted within the methodology, only forty percent of participants brought an artefact with them to the focus groups. Whilst we earlier suggested some rationale for such a decision, for example because the pracademic has made a full transition from practice to academia and no longer sees the relevance of their past professional identity, there may also be other reasons for non-engagement with this element. As Dickinson et al. (2022) suggest, creative methodologies can create uncertainties for participants about what is required. Cultural differences may also play a factor, with participants questioning the implication and value of objects for understanding their experience. There is scope for future research to explore this further.

> **Points for Reflection**
> - In this chapter, participants selected a variety of artefacts to represent their professional journey, including tools, totems, and trophies. If you were asked to select an object which represents your professional life, what would you choose?
> - Think about why you selected your chosen object. Does it provide some insight into your professional identity? Is it a tangible or a symbolic item?
> - Dickinson and Griffiths invite readers to draw on artefacts to develop understandings around motivations for career journeys, adopting a values-led approach as professional identity evolves post-transition. If you are preparing to transition into a new profession, or you have done so previously, what knowledge, skills and values could you bring with you from your practice?

References

Beltman, S., Glass, C., Dinham, J., Chalk, B., & Nguyen, B. (2015). Drawing identity: Beginning pre-service teachers' professional identities. *Issues in Educational Research, 25*(3), 225–245.

Bentley, S. V., Peters, K., Haslam, S. A., & Greenaway, K. H. (2019). Construction at work: Multiple identities scaffold professional identity development in academia. *Frontiers in Psychology, 10*, 628. https://doi.org/10.3389/fpsyg.2019.00628

Birkhead, A. (2021). Exploring the identity negotiation of early career mathematics teachers: A pilot study. *Proceedings of the British Society for Research into Learning Mathematics, 41*(2), 1–5.

Campbell, C. (2022). Afterward? Moving onwards for developing pracademia and pracademics in education. *Journal of Professional Capital and Community, 7*(1), 98–108. https://doi.org/10.1108/JPCC-01-2022-104c

Conrad, L., & Richter, N. (2013). Materiality at work: A note on desks. *Ephemera: Theory & Politics in Organization, 13*(1), 117–136.

Czerwinski, A. M. (2017). Artifact selection. In M. Allen (Ed.), *The SAGE encyclopedia of communication research methods* (pp. 57–59). Sage.

de Moura, E. O., & de Souza Bispo, M. (2019). Sociomateriality: Theories, methodology, and practice. *Canadian Journal of Administrative Sciences, 37*(3), 350–365. https://doi.org/10.1002/cjas.1548

Dickinson, J., Fowler, A., & Griffiths, T. (2020). Pracademics? Exploring transitions and professional identities in higher education. *Studies in Higher Education, 47*(2), 290–304. https://doi.org/10.1080/03075079.2020.1744123

Dickinson, J., Griffiths, T., & Austen, L. (2022). Collaborative methodological reflection: Disrupting the ethical practices of a creative method in higher education research. *Social Research Practice, 12*(Spring), 22–31.

Doel, M. (2017). *Social work in 42 objects (and more)*. Kirwin Maclean Associates.

Doel, M. (2019). Displaying social work through objects. *The British Journal of Social Work, 49*(3), 824–841. https://doi.org/10.1093/bjsw/bcy086

Eacott, S. (2021). Pracademia: an answer but not the answer to an enduring question. *Journal of Professional Capital and Community, 7*(1), 57–70. https://doi.org/10.1108/JPCC-12-2020-0100

Elliott, J. (2005). *Using narrative in social research: Qualitative and quantitative approaches*. Sage.

Eriksson-Zetterquist, U., Lindberg, K., & Styhre, A. (2009). When the good times are over: Professionals encountering new technology. *Human Relations, 62*(8), 1145–1170. https://doi.org/10.1177/0018726709334879

Feucht, F. C., Brownlee, J. L., & Schraw, G. (2017). Moving beyond reflection, reflexivity and epistemic cognition in teaching and teacher education. *Educational Psychologist, 52*(4), 234–241. https://doi.org/10.1080/00461520.2017.1350180

Friedman, K. (2007). Behavioural artifacts: What is an artifact? Or who does it? *Art, 1*(1), 7–11. https://doi.org/10.1080/17493460600610764

Friesen, S. L. (2022). Dwelling in liminal spaces: Twin moments of the same reality. *Journal of Professional Capital and Community, 7*(1), 71–82. https://doi.org/10.1108/JPCC-11-2020-0095

Gourlay, L. (2011). New lecturers and the myth of 'communities of practice'. *Studies in Continuing Education, 33*(1), 67–77. https://doi.org/10.1080/0158037X.2010.515570

Hay, G. J., Parker, S. K., & Luksyte, A. (2021). Making sense of organisational change failure: An identity lens. *Human Relations, 74*(2), 180–207. https://doi.org/10.1177/0018726720906211

Hultin, L. (2019). On becoming a sociomaterial researcher: Exploring epistemological practices grounded in a relational, performative ontology. *Information and Organisation, 29*(2), 91–104. https://doi.org/10.1016/j.infoandorg.2019.04.004

Khapova, S. N., Arthur, M. B., Wilderom, C. P. M., & Svensson, J. S. (2007). Professional identity as the key to career change intention. *Career Change International, 12*(7), 584–595. https://doi.org/10.1108/13620430710834378

Lundin, J., & Nuldén, U. (2007). Talking about tools–investigating learning at work in police practice. *Journal of Workplace Learning, 19*(4), 222–239. https://doi.org/10.1108/13665620710747915

Makela, M. A. (2007). Knowing through making: The role of the artefact in practice-led research. *Knowledge, Technology, and Policy, 20*(3), 157–163. https://doi.org/10.1007/s12130-007-9028-2

Mula, J., Rodriguez, C. L., Segovia, J. D., & Cruz-Gonzalez, C. (2021). Early career researchers' identity: A qualitative review. *Higher Education Quarterly, 76*(4), 786–799. https://doi.org/10.1111/hequ.12348

Orlikowski, W. J., & Scott, S. V. (2008). Sociomateriality: Challenging the separation of technology, work and organization. *The Academy of Management Annals, 2*(1), 433–474. https://doi.org/10.1080/19416520802211644

Panda, A. (2014). Bringing academic and corporate worlds closer: We need Pracademics. *Management and Labour Studies, 39*(2), 140–159. https://doi.org/10.1177/0258042X14558174

Posner, P. L. (2009). The pracademic: An agenda for re-engaging practitioners and academics. *Public Budgeting & Finance, 29*(1), 12–26. https://doi.org/10.1111/j.1540-5850.2009.00921.x

Prown, J. D. (1982). Mind in matter: An introduction to material culture theory and method. *Winterthur Portfolio, 17*(1), 1–19.

Robinson, R. N. S., & Baum, T. (2019). Work(ing) artefacts: Tools of the trade, totems or trophies? *Human Relations, 73*(2), 165–189. https://doi.org/10.1177/0018726719828447

Schaap, H., van der Want, A. C., Oolbekkink-Marchand, H. W., & Meijer, P. C. (2021). Changes over time in the professional identity tensions of Dutch early-career teachers. *Teaching and Teacher Education, 100*(103283), 1–13. https://doi.org/10.1016/j.tate.2021.103283

Scholar, H. (2012). Dressing the part? The significance of dress in social work. *Social Work Education, 32*(3), 365–379. https://doi.org/10.1080/02615479.2012.667798

Scholar, H. (2017). The neglected paraphernalia of practice? Objects and artefacts in social work identity, practice and research. *Qualitative Social Work, 16*(5), 631–648. https://doi.org/10.1177/1473325016637911

Sheffield Hallam University. (2020, September 1). *Welcome to the Academic Careers Framework (ACF) website*. Sheffield Hallam University. https://blogs.shu.ac.uk/acf/#

Shreeve, A. (2011). Being in two camps: Conflicting experiences for practice-based academics. *Studies in Continuing Education, 33*(1), 79–91. https://doi.org/10.1080/0158037X.2011.521681

Svensson, I., & Gluch, P. (2022). Materiality in action: The role of objects in institutional work. *Construction Management and Economic, 40*(1), 41–55. https://doi.org/10.1080/0144619 3.2021.2014063

Thornquist, C. (2015). Material evidence: Definition by a series of artefacts in arts research. *Journal of Visual Art Practice, 14*(2), 110–119. https://doi.org/10.1080/14702029.2015.1041713

Tomassini, M. (2015). Reflexivity, self-identity and resilience in career development: Hints from a qualitative research study in Italy. *British Journal of Guidance & Counselling, 43*(3), 263–277. https://doi.org/10.1080/03069885.2015.1028890

Trede, F., Maklin, R., & Bridges, D. (2012). Professional identity development: A review of the higher education literature. *Studies in Higher Education, 37*(3), 365–384. https://doi.org/1 0.1080/03075079.2010.521237

Unluer, S. (2012). Being an insider researchers while conducting case study research. *The Qualitative Report, 17*(58), 1–14.

van Lankveld, T., Schoonenboom, J., Volman, M., Croisit, G., & Beishuizen, J. (2016). Developing a teacher identity in the university context: A systematic review of the literature. *Higher Education Research & Development, 36*(2), 325–342. https://doi.org/10.1080/0729436 0.2016.1208154

Woo, H., Henfield, M. S., & Namok, C. (2014). Developing a unified professional identity in counseling: A review of the literature. *Journal of Counselor Leadership and Advocacy, 1*(1), 1–15. https://doi.org/10.1080/2326716X.2014.895452

Wood, C., Farmer, M., & Goodall, D. (2016). Changing professional identity in the transition from practitioner to lecturer in higher education: An interpretive phenomenological analysis. *Research in Post-Compulsory Education, 21*(3), 229–245. https://doi.org/10.1080/1359674 8.2016.1195173

Dr Jill Dickinson is an Associate Professor in Law at the University of Leeds. A former Solicitor specialising in Real Estate, Jill's research interests encompass place-making, learning landscapes, and professional development. As an SFHEA, Jill was selected to review the Advance HE Global Teaching Excellence Awards and her approach to research has been recognized through the Emerald Literati Awards.

Teri-Lisa Griffiths is a Senior Lecturer in Criminology at Sheffield Hallam University. Her teaching is focused on the development of student employability and academic skills, working with external partners to provide relevant and high-quality experiences for students. Her research interests are student engagement and professional development. As a former careers adviser, Teri-Lisa is interested in how education and professional identity can influence career and development choices. She is a co-founder of the pracademia community of practice.

Chapter 10
From Practice to Theory: The Pracademic and the PhD

Caroline Hunter and Helen Carr

Abstract Law schools in the UK have had a shifting relationship with practice with consequences for the status, expectations, and career progression of pracademics. The make-up of staff in law schools has changed as the expectation that academics will have a PhD and be research-active has become established, with fewer now having a legal practice background. But it is not clear how many staff in Law Schools have a PhD, or whether they are required for all or some posts. Nor is it clear how pracademics feel about requirements for a PhD.

This chapter seeks to fill this knowledge gap and explore the challenges for practitioners employed by law schools who choose, or are required to embark upon, a PhD. Empirical research for the chapter explores two questions:

1. To what extent do law schools require applicants to have, or undertake, a PhD?
2. What is the experience of those practitioners who have undertaken a PhD?

Keywords Legal education · PhD · Research · Growth of law schools · Faculty profiles · Career development

C. Hunter (✉)
School of Law, University of York, York, UK
e-mail: caroline.hunter@york.ac.uk

H. Carr
Southampton Law School, University of Southampton, Southampton, UK
e-mail: h.p.carr@soton.ac.uk

© The Author(s), under exclusive license to Springer Nature
Switzerland AG 2023
J. Dickinson, T.-L. Griffiths (eds.), *Professional Development for Practitioners in Academia*, Knowledge Studies in Higher Education 13,
https://doi.org/10.1007/978-3-031-33746-8_10

At a Glance

- Focuses on the role of PhDs in the transition from practice to academia.
- Draws on empirical data collected from pracademics working within law schools across the UK.
- Explores the changing context of law schools, the extent to which law schools require practitioner applicants to have or undertake a PhD, and the experiences of those practitioners who have undertaken a PhD.
- Reflects upon the complex, contradictory, and competitive environment of the contemporary law school in the UK and suggests that the status of pracademics remains problematically unresolved.

Introduction

Lecturer wins unfair dismissal case after being told to get PhD.

The headline above is from a 2021 Times Higher Education report of the victory of a senior lecturer, who was a professionally qualified accountant, against the University of Huddersfield in the UK (Baker, 2021). In 2013, the university introduced a policy that all full-time, permanent lecturers should have a PhD, or study to obtain one. The policy is "controversial" (Lavigueur, 2021), but provides an extreme example of how universities have prioritised research. As Dickinson et al. (2022) acknowledge, the Research Excellence Framework (REF)[1] has resulted in some Higher Education Institutions (HEIs) preferring to recruit those primarily involved in producing high quality research outputs, namely 'career academics', putting in doubt the role of practitioners in higher education (HE), despite the vocational content of some courses.

In this chapter, we focus on lawyers who have moved from legal practice to law schools ('pracademics') and who have, or are undertaking, a doctorate. Law schools in the UK have had a shifting relationship with practice (Bradney, 2003) with consequences for the status, expectations, and career progression of pracademics. Cownie and Jones (2021) suggest that the make-up of staff in law schools has changed as the expectation that academics will have a PhD and be research-active has become established, with fewer now having a legal practice background. In 2011, Twining suggested that "the PhD has gradually replaced membership of a practising profession as an almost necessary qualification" (2011, p. 167). But it is not clear how many staff in Law Schools have a PhD, or whether they are required for all or some posts. Nor is it clear how pracademics feel about requirements for a PhD.

---

[1] In the UK, the REF is undertaken by the UK higher education funding bodies to provide accountability for public investment in research and to allocation funding.

This chapter seeks to fill this knowledge gap and explore the challenges for practitioners employed by law schools who choose, or are required to embark upon, a PhD. Empirical research for the chapter explores two questions:

1. To what extent do law schools require applicants to have, or undertake, a PhD?
2. What is the experience of those practitioners who have undertaken a PhD?

We start by outlining the changing context of law schools in the UK before setting out our research methods. In the final section, we present our findings to the questions set out above, and then draw some conclusions about pracademics and PhDs.

The Changing Context of Law Schools

Contemporary writing on legal education has reflected on longstanding tensions in law schools, particularly between the "vocational and academic" (Sandberg, 2021, p. 4). For Leighton (2021, p. 411):

> The last 50 years have seen largely unbroken growth and diversification of legal education, especially in terms of its contribution to universities. However, many of the underlying tensions have remained, not least over the relationship between professional and academic legal education.

In this section, we chart some of the history of these tensions and what is known about the staffing of law schools over time. Given the different legal jurisdictions in Scotland and Northern Ireland, we focus on England and Wales, although some of the historic data does not differentiate between these jurisdictions. The history in England and Wales is complicated by the nature of legal education and bifurcation of the profession between solicitors and barristers.

A Short History of Law Schools

Using Leighton's lens of long-term growth and increasing diversity (2021), we trace law schools over the last 60 years or so. We start with the very useful survey of law schools that was undertaken in the mid-1960s for the Society of Public Teachers of Law (Wilson, 1966), which identified 23 universities across the UK offering undergraduate degrees and a range of academic post-graduate degrees. The biggest group, in terms of staffing, was the 'older provincial universities' (for example, Birmingham, Bristol, and Manchester). The survey found that "only 17% of law teachers held the PhD. degree, though 9% held the LL.D. or its equivalent. … 78% of law teachers held a professional qualification and that the ratio between the two branches of the profession was roughly four to one in favour of barristers" (Wilson, 1966, pp. 29–30). In addition, 68% of staff took the view that "law teachers should normally have had experience in professional practice" (Wilson, 1966, p. 31). At that time, the professional education (PE) on offer in England was through the Inns of Court School of Law (barristers) and the College of Law (solicitors), who oversaw professional examinations. Preparation for the examinations was also available in 'colleges of commerce in the provinces.'

A second survey was undertaken in 1973 (Wilson & Marsh, 1975). By that time, the Ormrod Committee (1971) had published its highly influential report on Legal Education. Although not all of its recommendations had been implemented (and indeed never were), Ormrod recommended that the profession in England and Wales should be a graduate profession, which did happen.

> It is salutary to remember that in 1971 only 40% of solicitors, though 80% of barristers, were graduates, but it is suspected that few had degrees in law. (Leighton, 2021)

This led to the growth of law degrees, which had become necessary for practice. Wilson and Marsh (1975, p. 241) note the consequences:

> perhaps the most significant development in this sector has been the appearance of nineteen polytechnic and technical college law schools offering law degree schemes....

The 23 law schools offering undergraduate degrees in law (LLBs) in 1966 had grown to 49, including 19 polytechnics and other local authority-maintained institutions. The number of students undertaking an LLB in England and Wales had risen from 4204 in 1965/6 to 7072 in 1974/5 (Wilson & Marsh, 1975). The Ormrod report set the now familiar pattern of three stages of legal education: first, the academic stage with compulsory qualifying subjects, then a period of PE, followed by a period of experiential training (Leighton, 2021).

The 1975 survey does not detail how many staff held PhDs. However, there is a sense that research had become more important. Conversely, continued involvement in legal practice was permitted, particularly in the polytechnics:

> All polytechnics, with one exception, allow full-time staff to engage in professional practice and other outside work and in some cases encourage this. Permission to engage in such work is, of course, subject to the limitation that it does not conflict with teaching or other duties. Two polytechnics have introduced a scheme whereby a full-time post can be divided between two persons so that half the time of each can be devoted to practice. (Wilson & Marsh, 1975, p. 274)

PE in England and Wales remained largely in the hands of the College of Law (solicitors) and the Inns of Court School of Law (barristers), although a number of polytechnics that had been colleges of commerce, offered the Law Society Part I course (for non-law graduates) and Part II finals (for all would-be solicitors).

The next major change for the HEI sector came in the 1990s when polytechnics became universities with degree awarding powers.[2] This can be understood as the beginning of the neoliberalisation of HE (Gibbons et al., 2015). Law schools continued to grow, with 86 offering an LLB in 2004 (Harris & Beinart, 2005). Another major change was the opening of the market of PE. At this time in England

---

[2] Throughout this chapter, we have differentiated between the ex-polytechnics the 'post-92 universities' (1992 was the year they received the right to award degrees) and older more established universities 'the pre-92 universities'. Historically the pre-92 universities have been more research active and received more government funding for research.

and Wales, there were 26 providers of full PE for solicitors, two of whom were not universities. Eight providers were offering the Bar vocational course.

Other changes in the legal landscape for HEIs in the 2000s encouraged private providers to offer undergraduate law courses. These included the major players in the PE – the University of Law (2006) and BPP University (2007) – who were granted degree awarding powers. The marketisation and competitiveness of legal education was further cemented by the removal of the cap on undergraduate numbers in 2015. As Maisuria and Cole (2017, p. 606) explain, this had two consequences:

> the expansion of the market to have a greater number of consumers [and] … individual providers of HE are pitted more directly in competition in a dog-eat-dog environment where, in the conditions of reduced government funding, the losers that fail to attract ever increasing numbers of students will be susceptible to closure.

The contradiction at the heart of university legal education became even more apparent in these conditions. Students were attracted by the ranking of law schools, which is heavily influenced by research (Gibbons et al., 2015) but also by the vocational element of the law degree (Nicholson & Johnston, 2021), so connections with practice became an important marketing feature. This explains Leighton's, 2021 position of growth – over 100 law schools with more than 99,780 students on undergraduate law degrees – and diversity. At the same time, recent developments have further embedded the tensions between research and practice, and have made effective resolution much more complex.

Research Excellence Framework

From the late 1980s, the research culture in universities has also changed with the Research Assessment Exercise (RAE), which became the REF. There is a suggestion from the 1990s that "the emphasis on research in determining career progression has gone too far, and this applies particularly to the way staff are being recruited or promoted to benefit an institution's RAE performance" (Court, 1999, p. 86).

More recently, Dickinson et al. reflected on evidence that the post-92 universities have responded to the REF. While some have emphasised their vocational excellence and links with practice, other evidence suggests that the REF has resulted in HEIs "preferring to recruit those primarily involved in producing high quality research outputs, namely 'career academics', at the expense of employing staff with relevant industrial experience" (2022, p. 291).

One response to the REF has been the creation of 'teaching only' posts (often referred to as 'teaching and scholarship'). These posts enabled institutions to manage high numbers of students without sacrificing research quality. Many of the posts are 'casual' – part-time and on short-contracts. However, from 2005/06 to 2018/19 the proportion of full-time workers among teaching-only staff has gradually increased (Wolf & Jenkins, 2021). Although starting from a lower base, the growth of teaching-only posts of all types has been most marked in research-intensive universities, namely pre-92 Universities (Wolf & Jenkins, 2021).

Clinical Legal Education

While research has been promoted generally in the HEI sector, there has been a concurrent push by law schools to offer clinical legal education (CLE). CLE is a broad church or indeed a "bazaar" (Bleasdale et al., 2020, p. 8). Giddings usefully defines it as learning activity:

> in which each student takes responsibility for legal or law-related work for a client (whether real or simulated) in collaboration with a supervisor. Structures enable each student to receive feedback on their contributions and to take the opportunity to learn from their experiences through reflecting on matters including their interactions with the client, their colleagues and their supervisor as well as the ethical dimensions of the issues raised and the impact of the law and legal processes. (2013, p. 14)

In 1987, Blake (1987, p. 3) commented that CLE in law schools had made little progress since the Ormrod Report. That is not the position today. In a survey of 78 law schools in 2019–20, 75% of respondents said that their pro bono offer included generalist advice and/or generalist advice with casework (Sandbach & Grimes, 2020). As live client cases are generally supervised by practising lawyers (with appropriate practice certificates), many law school clinics have had to employ dedicated staff to undertake this role (Bleasdale et al., 2020).

Summary

This very truncated history provides the background for our empirical data. It demonstrates growth and diversity of law schools – all offering undergraduate law courses, but a number also offering professional legal education. It demonstrates the growing importance of research which helps to explain why the composition of staff in law schools has shifted to an expectation that academics will have a PhD and be research-active, with fewer having a legal practice background (Cownie & Jones, 2021). At the same time, the growth of CLE as well as the market advantage of vocational degrees pulls in the other direction with a need to appoint practitioners and embed employability. One response to this has been the creation of teaching-only posts but the status of these posts is open to debate, whilst the question of what is at the core of legal education remains unresolved.

Methodology

We were interested in the extent to which law schools require applicants to have, or undertake, a PhD and the experience of those practitioners who have undertaken a PhD.[3]

---

[3] Ethics approval for the survey and the interviews was granted by ELMPS Ethics Committee at the University of York.

To explore our first question, a questionnaire was circulated to all the members of the Committee of Heads of UK Law Schools (CHULS). Membership of CHULS comprises Heads of Law Schools in HEIs across the UK that offer their own law degrees. Approximately 100 Heads were sent the questionnaire. 25 responses were received between 9 February and 16 March 2022. The responses were from a range of law schools. A number were research-intensive. Eight offered PE programmes. 71% (17) had submitted for the 2014 REF, while 7 had not. 80% (20) had submitted to the 2021 REF. This data was triangulated with data from job adverts posted on jobs.ac.uk on 24 April 2022. All details of adverts for permanent posts in law schools (that were not research-only) were collected and analysed for information on qualification requirements, particularly PhDs. 27 adverts were identified, some of which included more than one post.

For the second question, semi-structured interviews were undertaken with 13 permanent staff of law schools in the UK.[4] Nearly all had been in practice in the last 10 years (and had been in practice for at least 5 years)[5] and all had undertaken a PhD during the last 5 years or were currently undertaking such doctoral studies. Table 10.1 provides a more detailed picture of the interviewees in terms of: types of university; types of doctorate, whether undertaken before or during their permanent post; the types of contract they were on; and their teaching roles.

Findings

To What Extent Do Law Schools Require Applicants to Have, or Undertake, a PhD?

Given evidence of the growing use of teaching-only posts, we were interested to know if law schools were using different types of contracts for permanent staff. The majority (15–60%) were. It was more difficult to differentiate between the adverts. The majority, although generally advertising for lecturers or senior lecturers, did not specify the types of post. For a small number of pre-92 universities, the adverts clearly distinguished 'Research and Teaching' and 'Education' posts. Posts in Clinics (5 in total) either had distinct titles, for example 'Law Clinic Lead or Law Clinic Director', or were clearly advertised as teaching-only posts.

For posts that were labelled as including research, it was clear that practice qualifications were not sufficient. All the survey responses for that sort of post required a doctorate or registration for a doctorate, or the equivalent. Equivalent meant

---

[4] Interviewees were recruited via a call sent to a number of organisations: The Association of Law Teachers; The Socio-legal Studies Association; The Society of Legal Scholars. Some were then recruited via snowball methods. The interviews were undertaken on zoom and the interviews transcribed.

[5] A couple of interviewees has left practice more than 10 years ago. They had, however, continued to practice in a limited way while in a permanent academic post.

Table 10.1 Research interviewees

Interview number Interviewee	Type of HEI		Type of Doctorate		Doctorate full or part time (while on permanent academic post)		Type contract		Teaching roles: academic (A), clinic education (CLE), professional education (PE)
	Pre-92	Post-92	Law PhD	Professional doctorate	Full part	Part Time	Research and Teaching	Teaching and Scholarship	
1		✓	✓		✓		✓		A, CLE, PE
2		✓		✓		✓	✓		A, CLE, PE
3		✓		✓		✓	✓		CLE, PE
4	✓		✓		✓		✓		A
5	✓		✓		✓	✓		✓	A
6	✓		✓		✓		✓		A
7	✓		✓			✓		✓	A
8	✓		✓		✓		✓		A
9	✓		✓		✓		✓		A
10	✓		✓			✓		✓	A, CLE
11		✓	✓		✓	✓	✓		A, CLE, PE
12		✓	✓		✓	✓	✓		A, PE
13		✓	✓		✓	✓	✓		A, CLE, PE

experience in an HEI or evidence of publications. Amongst law schools that did not differentiate between types of contracts for permanent staff (10 responses), four would consider candidates with practice qualifications; however, the preference was for doctorates or equivalent. Apart from two responses citing professional qualifications, this meant publications.

The adverts demonstrated a similar position in terms of specifying a doctorate or equivalent experience. For some adverts, this included 'equivalent professional experience'. Essex was typical:

> Applicants will have a relevant doctoral level research degree or equivalent professional experience/practice or be close to completion of a PhD, as well as having an undergraduate/ postgraduate degree in law.

However, for many it was essential to have a doctorate. This were underlined by phrases such as:

> It is expected that in addition the post-holder will maintain a strong academic profile through research and publication. (Cambridge)

> [A] doctorate and a demonstrable intention to research is essential. (Leeds Beckett)

> A proven track-record and demonstratable potential for, internationally-excellent research in the Law of Evidence and Criminal Process/Criminal Justice, with a PhD or equivalent professional or other expertise. (Edinburgh)

A small number did not require a doctorate, for example Westminster – "Post-Graduate Degree or Professional Qualification".

London Metropolitan University had two adverts. The first was for a Lecturer or Senior Lecturer in Law (Commercial). For this post, a PhD, Professional Doctorate, or equivalent higher degree in a relevant subject was required. For the other post, a Lecturer in Law (LPC and SQE) focused on PE, the requirement was "to have relevant undergraduate qualifications". Apart from clinic posts, only one post was for teaching-only, at King's College, London. This was for Construction Law within a specialised Centre. The requirement was "relevant legal professional qualification or Masters in Law or equivalent experience".

For teaching-posts there are a larger spread of responses from the survey. Six required either a doctorate or to be registered for one, however four also considered practitioners and any practice qualification was counted as the equivalent of a doctorate by three HEIs.

As noted, several adverts were for roles in clinics. The survey indicates that for CLE posts it was much less likely that a completed doctorate was required (only one response indicated this). For the majority (73%), the requirement was for a practice qualification. This was reflected in the 5 adverts for clinical posts. All required a practice qualification, with a current practising certificate or the entitlement to obtain one. Only one advert (for a Law Clinic Director at Sunderland) included a reference to a PhD – a desirable requirement "to have or to be working toward a PhD".

The Experience of Those Practitioners Who Have Undertaken a PhD

One 2016 study around experiences of staff who had not entered academia via the traditional direct PhD route but joined early or mid-career from a 'practice'-based professional background showed that their identities were "largely self-constructed and consequently …often insecure and may not be highly valued by others within higher education." (Wood et al., 2016, p. 243). Another found that the "transition to lecturer was challenging and characterised at times by a degree of confusion, inauthenticity and isolation" (Gourlay, 2011, p. 76).

In our interviews of pracademics for this chapter, we were interested to explore the role of the PhD in this transition. We asked participants questions about why they undertook the PhD, their experiences of the PhD, what skills the PhD gave them, and whether, in their opinion, the PhD was worthwhile. How far does the PhD change their professional identity? (Dickinson et al., 2022).

Reasons for Undertaking the PhD

Half of those interviewed (6/13) had undertaken the PhD before starting a permanent academic post. For these interviewees, the PhD was a gateway into an academic career. Their academic orientation was obvious whilst they were in practice, with a number undertaking a masters degree during that time. Thus, for Participant 5, her law firm was:

> quite supportive of academic leanings, so solicitors were invited to contribute to papers and to speak at conferences. They were encouraged to join the Society of Legal Scholars, and actually, I completed my Masters whilst working at [law firm]. (Participant 5)

Some had also undertaken teaching or other pro bono work with universities whilst in practice.

> ...but I was really inspired by the teaching and by my students and I wasn"t sure how to make that transition into academia without kind of going back and getting a PhD, getting some formal research training and kind of going a traditional route into there. (Participant 4)

The decision to take a PhD was closely bound up with, and understood as necessary to, the decision to change career. Indeed, Participant 8 was not aware that it was possible to move into academia without a PhD.

> But I think that... it's kind of hard to say would I have definitely done the same if I'd have known that, but I think I might have done the same anyway because, as in still done a PhD, because I think that gives you the opportunity to be on the kind of research and education and research route which I think is probably the more interesting route for me, whereas I guess it would be quite difficult to get into the research path without having the PhD background. (Participant 8)

Of these six participants, five were in research and teaching posts. The sixth was completing her PhD part-time with an on-going permanent teaching-only post.

The participants who were already academics when undertaking the doctorate were all either in pre-92 universities on teaching-only contracts or in post-92 universities. Here, the reasons to undertake the PhD were very different. Three of the participants were, or had been, at universities that required them to undertake a PhD. That was their only reason for doing one:

> ...it would not be my choice to do a PhD at all and I'm doing it because I have to do it. It's a requirement for my job. (Participant 12)

> It was required, otherwise we have to leave. People were dismissed. (Participant 11)

> I only started because we had to do it. (Participant 13)

For the other four participants, although the PhD was not required, it was linked to careers and mobility. For some, this was implicit. For participant 7, who was on a teaching-only contract, there was nonetheless an expectation to publish. The PhD was a response to that:

> So, I wasn't sure whether to do a PhD because people said you don't need one, you can just publish. You can just (clicks fingers) publish, and I was like okay...how do you do that? I think when you come from a background where you trained to be a lawyer, you sort of think

that you ought to really understand the science of the thing or the art of the thing and I just kept thinking, well do I not need training in how to be a good academic? You know, I don't understand what it is that you need. (Participant 7)

Participant 3 expressed mixed reasons for undertaking a doctorate part-time.

Yes, so I mean I would have probably happily done it, even if it wasn't something the university wanted me to do. …I suppose my own intrinsic motivation … linked to what the university wanted me to do. …I didn't need it to get promoted because I hadn't completed [the doctorate] at the point I was promoted but my aim is to be further promoted again and I do think that in terms of career development it's important but I actually thought it was something good to have because our students… come out with a master's actually. (Participant 3)

All but one of the participants who were undertaking the doctorate part-time received some support towards fees. Some had time in their work allocation, although this was never sufficient.

I get 300 hours for doing the PhD and I work at home on a Friday… I learned very quickly, that does not even scratch the surface of what needs to be done so it is evenings, weekends, holidays. (Participant 12)

Participant 11 had to end her connection with practice:

…the time requirement meant that I could no longer do my returns to practice. I couldn't do both. (Participant 11)

The Experience of Teaching-Only Interviewees

Three of the participants had teaching-only contracts, all in different pre-92 universities. Two had major employability roles in their law school, and the third had a CLE role. All had been appointed because of their knowledge of, and links to, practice. For two of them, their teaching only contracts made them feel like second-class citizens.

…they don't value whatever I do is because I'm not REF returnable…in the REF created this two tier class of in academia, unfortunately. (Participant 10)

I want them to think that I'm good at my job. …I don't like being second class …and I think they do treat you as being second [class] …career-wise, where am I going? (Participant 7)

Participant 5 had not experienced that negativity, but she was just completing her PhD and contemplating her next career move.

[I am taking] a career researcher's employability course at the moment, which is [thinking] about …five to ten years' time…. I think the biggest question seems to be, here certainly – I don't know how it translates elsewhere – whether you follow a more teaching track or a more research track. I think, initially, I thought I had to do a research track because I'd done the PhD and that was what I ought to do. But actually, I do enjoy the teaching. (Participant 5)

Moving from a teaching-only contract did not seem possible for the two other participants at their current institutions.

What Has the Doctorate Given You?

We were interested to find out what the doctorate had given the participants in their academic lives. There were two types of responses.

First, for some, the doctorate provided generic skills. These included: specific research skills (data management and interviewing) and knowledge, critical thinking, time-management, and writing.

> It has taught me research skills; I think more it's taught me how to sort of condense work and refine writing. (Participant 13)

For participant 5, completing the doctorate had given her more confidence:

> I think the PhD helps in terms of, when you take part in discussion groups and things like that, I think it gives that little bit of confidence. You feel like you're talking as an equal. (Participant 5)

Second, it supported the participants' teaching. Mostly this played out in terms of communication with students:

> So I am a lot more empathetic, I think, as a teacher because I'm also a student… But I think I'm a lot more empathetic, and, also, I hope I'm a lot clearer now when I talk to students. (Participant 2)

> [As a student myself] I need to just take a step back from teaching and actually review how do I come across how do students perceive me as well, how do I convey the information, how do I have this dialogue with students about their, for example, final year a research project. (Participant 10)

That was particularly true for participants who supervised dissertations, whether at undergraduate or master's level. It also resulted in the subject of the PhD being included in modules. This ranged from specific amendments to the content of teaching materials, to a clinic project based on the PhD. However, for one participant, it had no effect on her teaching:

> Q: Have you used any of the skills from the PhD in your teaching, No, no, no. (Participant 12)

This participant did not teach in the area of her PhD. For her:

> My students are not interested in me having a PhD.

Some of her teaching was on professional courses. Another participant who also taught on professional courses made the same comment:

> We know that the students value practice experience over doctorates. (Participant 3)

Was the PhD Worth It?

The responses varied depending upon the very different circumstances that led to the participants to their doctoral studies. The three participants who had been required to undertake a PhD had very little positive to say about it.

Q: Do you still feel you're using the skills from the PhD?
A: to some extent, but I would have been better focusing on maintaining the practice side.
    (Participant 11)

[Once it is] done [I will not] be telling anybody, it will mean more to [my Dad] than it will
mean to me. It's taken something… this process. (Participant 12)

…it's just it's just been a real struggle and I don't really know if it was worth it, but I'm just
hoping to get over the final hurdle, and then it might seem like it was worth it. (Participant 13)

However, for most participants it led to the development of positive views about
themselves and their place in academia.

In terms of positioning myself as a proper academic, I think it's been very important across
the school to be able to have that doctorate there. (Participant 6)

…it would make sense in the bigger picture to have it because it's a sort of status mark.
(Participant 7)

I don't think I would be having the opportunity to do the research that I want to do now
without it. So, I think it's now …adding value and it's opening up things for me.
(Participant 1)

In turn, this was, or was seen as, important for careers or promotion.

…you don't have a gateway into those kind of jobs that involve research really without the
PhD. …however many years' experience you have in practice, I don't think people will
really take that as a substitute for having a PhD at this point. (Participant 8)

I think it's upskilled me, and in that respect …for promotion to Professor… (Participant 3)

Conclusion

Our research shows that the contemporary law school is competitive, complex, and
contradictory and that pracademics occupy an uneasy, liminal place within it.
Students want vocationally-oriented education with high employability outcomes
(Nicholson & Johnston, 2021). Pracademics can play an important part, not least
because of their work in CLE and their links with practice. The requirement for a
PhD for practice-oriented jobs seems unnecessary, and not just for CLE posts. At
the same time, high-quality research is also important to the law school – it is necessary for reputation, ranking, and funding, and the role of the pracademic here is less
clear. There are suggestions that the research agenda makes them feel second-class.
The PhD has the potential for better integration of pracademics – it may help support their professional identities and make them feel more highly-valued (Dickinson
et al., 2022; Wood et al., 2016; Gourlay, 2011). To an extent, our findings substanti-
ate this, but, as we also show, this is not inevitable. The challenge for law schools
(and we suspect other disciplines) remains the need to clarify the relationship
between practice and research in a highly competitive environment without rein-
forcing the hierarchy between teaching and research. It seems unlikely that any
clarity will be immediately forthcoming, but, without it, the role of pracademics and
their relationship with research remains unsatisfactory and potentially
destabilising.

Points for Reflection

- Hunter and Carr reveal how some HEIs provide support for those under-taking doctoral studies, whether in terms of fees and/or work allocation. To what extent should, or could, there be consistency in approach around the provision of support, both within the same HEI and across the sector?
- Reflect on the various routes to achieving a doctorate highlighted in this chapter; for example, a traditional thesis, by publication, and a Professional Doctorate. If you were to undertake a Doctorate, would you have a preferred route, and why?
- Hunter and Carr note how studying for a PhD can support the provision of teaching; for example, in terms of communicating with students, and also the development of modules. If you already have a doctorate, to what extent do, or could, you make links between your doctoral research and your academic practice?
- A selection of job adverts and their qualification requirements are explored in this chapter. With the balance shifting towards PhDs and away from practice, to what extent do you agree with this shift, and why? Reflect on your career goals, and your qualifications, experience, skills, and knowledge. Consider if a PhD would benefit your career journey.

References

Baker, S. (2021, April 30). Lecturer wins unfair dismissal case after being told to get PhD. *Times Higher Education*. https://www.timeshighereducation.com/news/lecturer-wins-unfair-dismissal-case-after-being-told-get-phd.

Blake, A. (1987). Legal education in crisis: A strategy for legal education into the 1990s. *The Law Teacher, 21*(1), 3–22. https://doi.org/10.1080/03069400.1987.9992677

Bleasdale, L., Rizzotto, B., Stalker, R., Yeatman, L., McFaul, H., Ryan, F., Johnson, N., & Thomas, L. (2020). Law clinics: What, why and how? In L. Thomas & N. Johnson (Eds.), *The clinical legal education handbook* (pp. 8–56). University of London Press, Institute of Advanced Legal Studies.

Bradney, A. (2003). *Conversations, choices and chances: The Liberal Law School in the twenty-first century*. Hart Publishing.

Court, S. (1999). Negotiating the research imperative: The views of UK academics on their career opportunities. *Higher Education Quarterly, 53*(1), 65–87.

Cownie, F., & Jones, E. (2021). Blackstone's tower in context. *Amicus Curiae, Series 2, 2*(3), 314–333.

Dickinson, J., Fowler, A., & Griffiths, T. (2022). Pracademics? Exploring transitions and professional identities in higher education. *Studies in Higher Education, 47*(2), 290–304. https://doi.org/10.1080/03075079.2020.1744123

Gibbons, S., Neumayer, E., & Perkins, R. (2015). Student satisfaction, league tables and university applications: Evidence from Britain. *Economics of Education Review, 48*, 148–164. https://doi.org/10.1016/j.econedurev.2015.07.002

Giddings, J. (2013). *Promoting justice through clinical legal education*. Justice Press.

Gourlay, L. (2011). New lecturers and the myth of 'communities of practice'. *Studies in Continuing Education, 33*(1), 67–77. https://doi.org/10.1080/0158037X.2010.515570

Harris, P., & Beinart, S. (2005). A survey of law schools in the United Kingdom, 2004. *The Law Teacher, 39*(3), 299–366. https://doi.org/10.1080/03069400.2005.9993189

Lavigueur, N. (2021, August 13). Huddersfield University 'flouting the law' as it defies judge who ordered sacked lecturer should get his job back. *YorkshireLive.* https://www.examinerlive.co.uk/news/west-yorkshire-news/huddersfield-university-flouting-law-defies-21293067

Leighton, P. (2021). Legal education in England and Wales: What next? *The Law Teacher, 55*(3), 405–413. https://doi.org/10.1080/03069400.2021.1939975

Maisuria, A., & Cole, M. (2017). The neoliberalization of higher education in England: An alternative is possible. *Policy Futures in Education, 15*(5), 602–619. https://doi.org/10.1177/1478210317719792

Nicholson, A., & Johnston, P. (2021). The value of a law degree – Part 3: A student perspective. *The Law Teacher, 55*(4), 431–447. https://doi.org/10.1080/03069400.2020.1843900

Ormrod Committee. (1971). *The report of the committee on legal education* (Cmnd. 4595). HMSO.

Sandbach, J., & Grimes, R. (2020). *Law School Pro Bono and Clinic Report 2020.* LawWorks and CLEO.

Sandberg, R. (2021). *Subversive legal history: A manifesto for the future of legal education.* Routledge.

Twining, W. (2011). Professionalism in legal education. *International Journal of the Legal Profession, 18*(1–2), 165–172. https://doi.org/10.1080/09695958.2011.634997

Wilson, J. F. (1966). Survey of legal education in the United Kingdom. *Journal of the Society of Public Teachers of Law (New Series), 9*(1), 1–144.

Wilson, J. F., & Marsh, S. B. (1975). Second survey of legal education in the United Kingdom. *Journal of the Society of Public Teachers of Law (New Series), 13*(4), 239–331.

Wolf, A., & Jenkins, A. (2021). *Managers and academics in a centralising sector: The new staffing patterns of UK higher education.* Nuffield Foundation.

Wood, C., Farmer, M. D., & Goodall, D. (2016). Changing professional identity in the transition from practitioner to lecturer in higher education: An interpretive phenomenological analysis. *Research in Post-Compulsory Education, 21*(3), 229–245. https://doi.org/10.1080/1359674 8.2016.1195173

Professor Caroline Hunter qualified as a barrister in 1985 and practised full-time for 5 years, before moving in academia (without a PhD) while keeping a door tenancy until 2012. Her practice and her research and teaching have been centred on housing law, policy, and practice. She was appointed a Professor at the (then) newly established York Law School in 2008. She was Head of School from 2013-2021. She has an on-going interested in legal education and was the editor of Integrating socio-legal studies into the law curriculum (Palgrave Macmillan, 2012).

Professor Helen Carr completed her PhD at the University of Kent after working as a solicitor in a law centre, a period teaching at a post-1992 institution, and secondment to the Law Commission. Her research interests are housing, homelessness and more broadly social justice. Her recent publications include with Ed Kirton-Darling and Dave Cowan, 'Marginalisation, Grenfell Tower and the voice of the social housing resident: a critical juncture in housing law and policy?' International Journal of Law in Context, 18(1), 10-24 and 'Exploring the Law/Bodies/Space Regulatory Conundrum' in (editors Didi Herman and Connal Parsley) Interdisciplinarities: Research Process Method and the Body of Law (Springer 2022). She is currently Professor of Property Law and Social Justice at Southampton Law School and Director of its Centre for People, Property, Community.

Chapter 11
Resilient Networking and Collaboration – Solving the Puzzle: How to Balance Being a Practitioner and a Researcher

Jan Gurung

Abstract This chapter explores the lived experience of a clinical practitioner who navigates the steps to become a practitioner who develops a research project and applies the research back into their professional field: a pracademic. It is written through the lens of a practicing psychotherapist, but many aspects will generalise to other types of practitioners. Practitioner researcher is used in this chapter to describe this activity. As a clinical psychotherapist working with students, in a university setting, with an abundance of research expertise and inspirational research projects with global reach, it would be easy to think the path to being a practitioner researcher would be straightforward. However, the reality of the lived experience is more complex.

I identify some likely challenges and strategies, providing a starting point for clinical practitioners who aspire to becoming researchers, including the barriers encountered, ways of building relational and personal resilience, the importance of collaboration, networking, and informal conversations, along with the role of mentors and critical friends. In addition, the practical psychological techniques offered, to help manage the brain's "negativity bias" (Rozin and Royzman, Pers Soc Psychol Rev 5(4):296–320, 2001) and imposter phenomenon (Clance PR, Imes SA. Psychotherapy 15(3):241–247, 1978. https://doi.org/10.1037/h0086006) and the key points are useful tools for any pracademic. The chapter also looks at how to balance and harness the different energies and focus required to engage with research and manage a practitioner caseload, and how the two can complement each other.

Keywords Pracademic · Personal resilience · Relational resilience · Clinical practitioner · Professional identity · Imposter phenomenon · Professional network · Mentoring · Professional development

J. Gurung (✉)
Sheffield Hallam University, Sheffield, UK
e-mail: j.gurung@shu.ac.uk

© The Author(s), under exclusive license to Springer Nature Switzerland AG 2023
J. Dickinson, T.-L. Griffiths (eds.), *Professional Development for Practitioners in Academia*, Knowledge Studies in Higher Education 13, https://doi.org/10.1007/978-3-031-33746-8_11

At a Glance

- Reports on the lived experience of a clinical practitioner who develops a research project and applies the research back into their professional field: a pracademic.
- Written through the lens of a practicing psychotherapist in a university setting, including excerpts from the author's research journal. "Practitioner researcher" (Robson, 2002) is used throughout this chapter to describe this activity.
- Provides a starting point, and practical psychological tools, for practitioners who aspire to become researchers.
- Considers how to balance and harness the different energies needed to manage a practitioner caseload and a research project, and how the two can complement each other.

Each lifetime is the pieces of a jigsaw puzzle.
For some there are more pieces,
For others the puzzle is more difficult to assemble.
Some seem to be born with a nearly completed puzzle.
And so it goes.
Souls going this way and that
Trying to assemble the myriad parts.
But know this. No one has within themselves
All the pieces to their puzzle…
Everyone carries with them at least one and probably
Many pieces to someone else's puzzle.
Sometimes they know it
Sometimes they don't. (Kushner, 2015, p. 69–70)

Introduction

The Clinical Practitioner's Puzzle

As a clinical psychotherapist working with students in a university setting, surrounded by colleagues with an abundance of research expertise and undertaking inspirational research projects with global reach, it would be easy to think that becoming a researcher would be straightforward. This chapter explores, and reflects on, the experience of the author and considers what is required for a clinical practitioner to become a "practitioner researcher" (Robson, 2002). As with researchers, psychotherapists are searching for insight to solve problems. Being curious and open, asking questions to seek understanding and clarification, and noticing patterns, are fundamental skills for therapists (Stafford & Bond, 2020). Coupling this approach with a desire to find better ways of practising makes rich and fertile ground for research creativity and inspiration. Clinical practitioners who become practitioner researchers are ideally placed to make valuable real-world contributions, by transferring research into practice and practice into research (Zundel & Kokkalis, 2010). In doing so, they can expand from helping individuals, to helping many. Yet, despite similarities, a leap of faith (Kierkegaard, 1992) is required to successfully vault the chasm from clinical practitioner to practitioner researcher.

In this chapter, I identify some likely challenges and strategies, and provide a starting point for clinical practitioners who aspire to become researchers. The chapter includes sections on taking the creative leap, finding belonging in the research community through relational resilience, adjusting to new ways of working, and building personal resilience. Personal accounts of my lived experience from my journal illustrate these sections. In addition, practical psychological tools are offered in the form of key points and coaching questions to help the practitioner researcher overcome barriers and access psychological resources. The chapter also considers how to balance and harness the different energies required to manage both research and a practitioner caseload, and how the two can complement each other.

The 'Creative Leap'

It is a risk for a practitioner who is experienced in their field to take the creative leap to start a research project. Creativity starts with curiosity, when a person thinks in an original way, sees a new pattern, or puts together existing components in a new combination (Milne, 2020). They also have the courage to question norms in their field. I have often found my clinical work a stimulating environment for generating potential research ideas (Florida, 2002). Where do these creative ideas come from and how do they form? Csikszentmihalyi's work on creativity suggests that there needs to be mastery of a field or domain where a gap or problem is identified, followed by an incubation period where connections are made and intuitively "pop out into awareness as an insight" (1996, p. 104).

Journal 2017: The Idea

On my day off, I was out running and processing some of my work from the week. I'd witnessed young people in distress and who were self-harming and suicidal. In contrast, I felt alive in that moment and present with nature; the mist rolling off the reservoir and blue sky breaking though. I started to wonder, what if those students were running with me right now? What if they could feel alive and vital with positive body chemistry and a sense of achievement at the end of the run? How would things change if they were encouraged to keep going when it gets tough? Would that make a difference in their therapy? I'd seen the transformation in one student whom I'd helped to start running; their suicide ideation subsided, they were achieving lots of running goals, and their self-esteem improved which transferred positively to their studies. If I put

(continued)

therapy and running together, what could that give my clients? The creative seed was there for a research project, a therapeutic running group for students.

This became MINDFIT, a running group with a difference. It was a wrap-around package with a psychologically trained and emotionally sensitive run leader, it used the NHS couch to 5 K initiative,[1] and it wasn't competitive. Runs were in nature, followed by hot drinks, healthy snacks, conversation, and psychoeducation, culminating with a celebration at parkrun after nine weeks; a coalescence of hundreds of hours counselling with young people, and a lifetime doing physical activity for my own wellbeing. This was combined with an increasing interest in research after a stimulating master's degree and a desire to find improved ways of working therapeutically.

Creative Idea to Implementation

To implement a creative research idea from clinical practice requires the practitioner to have self-efficacy (Bandura, 1997). This means that they require a deep interest in their subject and commitment to it. They also need to believe that they are competent enough to reach their desired goal and that they can be successful. The practitioner needs to have the capacity to take on new challenges, believing that they can learn, adapt, and perform well, creating a virtuous circle of increased self-belief. They cannot be put off easily because implementation takes time and effort and the demands of daily life often get in the way (Milne, 2020). Regulating emotions plays a part, with the ability to manage emotions when there are stressful situations, events, and obstacles to overcome (Gross, 2015). This is combined with the socio-cultural context within which they are operating and the support that they receive. As I developed my own competence, I needed to build psychological flexibility and inner reassurance (Harris, 2011) to manage the uncertainty and self-doubt of working in an unfamiliar context, with different values, language, rules, and processes. This was doubly so in the absence of an induction, a process map for new researchers, or a tangible research community.

Journal, 2018: Finding a Framework
I was looking for a framework to follow; an overview of the processes needed to set up a research project. I quickly realised that it was quite the opposite, I would have to piece this together. I had the shiny picture in my mind's eye of a research project to enable me to properly evaluate, but it was like I had emptied out the pieces of a large jigsaw puzzle. To master this goal would prove to be a test of my self-efficacy and endurance.

---

[1] The National Health Service (NHS) Couch to 5 is a running plan for absolute beginners (NHS, 2023).

Key Themes

Finding Belonging Through Relational Resilience

Recent research studies show that there are issues with academic culture, contributing to high levels of mental ill health and a negative effect on research outcomes. Building on the work of The Nuffield Council on Bioethics (2014) regarding the culture of scientific research in the UK, The Wellcome Trust launched #ReimagineResearch (Farrar, 2019). Diversity and inclusion are a priority and there is zero tolerance of bullying, with the aim of creating an overall fairer and kinder culture (Pickersgill et al., 2019). The Wellcome Trust has encouraged researchers to be heard by contributing their views in a survey, and invited engagement in an online research culture festival in 2021 to share new approaches and discussion cafés, to name but a few of their initiatives. Added to the negative issues of research culture, it is not obvious where the practitioner researcher fits, being neither a lecturer, a PhD student, nor a pure researcher. Without a defined career structure, and with few accessible role models, the practitioner researcher can find themselves isolated and left to fit the pieces together alone. To counter this, they need to find ways within which they can work across the boundaries of the traditional organisational structures where academic and professional services are separate entities (Whitchurch & Gordan, 2010).

> **Journal, 2018: Clicking Together**
> How as a pracademic do I tap into this elusive culture of innovation? Be proactive and bold, is my mantra. I start conversations, email people directly asking for their help and attend talks in the university. I activate previously learnt networking skills and I research the organisation, how it works and how things fit together, or don't. I am looking for collaboration, where the sum is greater than the parts. I don't seem to fit anywhere in the organisational structures, but I hold the belief that I have a potential research contribution to make in my field.

Developing relational resilience is one of the ways in which to become a member of the research community and access expert input and guidance, develop ideas, and contribute to the research conversation. As a clinical practitioner, building credibility and persuading colleagues, who are busy with their own deliverables, to listen to ideas informed by clinical practice, rather than scholarly activity, is challenging and important. Afifi (2018) acknowledges the attributes of personal resilience but suggests that the ability to adapt positively to adversity is most strongly influenced by social relationships. Jordan's Relational Cultural Theory (RCT) shows that psychological growth occurs in "growth fostering relationships" (2017, p. 231) which include empathy, courage, and empowerment; very different from relying on mental toughness. These qualities are at the heart of being a psychotherapist (Cooper, 2003), along with reciprocity, collaboration, and understanding the dynamics between people (Buber, 1970), providing excellent transferrable skills for research. With perseverance and authenticity, it is possible to attract people who want to collaborate, be critical friends or mentors, and form a research team.

Journal, 2018: Finding Critical Friends and Mentors

I forge ahead. As momentum builds with implementation, I put my marketing skills from my previous career to the test with publicity about the project. I receive valuable initial guidance from a Professor of Physical Activity and Health from Sheffield Hallam University (SHU) and reach a pivotal point at a SHU showcase event for projects. I leave the event buzzing, having met two key people. Another researcher with an interest in physical activity as a form of therapy and the project lead for Hallam Pracademia. The latter gives me a name to identify with and a way of describing what I'm doing. I now have both a critical friend and a research mentor. The pieces are fitting together, and I set up a longitudinal mixed methods study. For the qualitative research, I plan focus groups using semi-structured questionnaires and thematic analysis. For the quantitative, I plan to measure levels of depression and anxiety pre and post MINDFIT.

Key Points

- Find out who is in your organisation with similar research interests.
- Be bold and send speculative emails.
- If nothing comes back, don't take it personally, keep knocking on the doors, remember people are busy.
- Listen and observe to understand the landscape/context/politics.
- Attend talks and read about projects, internally and externally.
- Get your message out there at events.
- Prevent becoming overwhelmed by sifting information for what is important.
- Build credibility with authenticity.
- Understand resistance is a normal phenomenon with new initiatives.
- Thank, and appreciate, those who contribute, large or small.

New Ways of Working and Expectations

As I settled into new ways of working, two main socio-cultural themes stood out which were emotionally challenging and tested my personal resilience. They were the timescale and the pace required for a research project and the culture of peer review feedback.

Even though in clinical practice there may be long term therapeutic goals, I must make decisive clinical judgements in the moment, with a rationale which I can stand by. Reflection and debrief follow (Ferreira et al., 2017). There are frequent points of feedback directly from the client and markers of success which give a sense of closure after each session and the satisfaction of a job well done. The feeling that you have helped someone and made some progress can drive motivation and enhance feelings of competence and confidence (McBeath, 2019). This is quite different from the iterative process of research, requiring thinking time and planned progress towards a goal.

Journal, 2020: Different Ways of Working
I have the 'feel-good factor' from helping clients today in clinical practice and a feeling of satisfaction. My notes are written, all follow ups done and I have sense of completeness from the day and closure. There will be the ad hoc looking up of a specific area of theory or practice in readiness for clinical application, the usual unconscious processing overnight and the mental filing away until next time we meet. Of course, my clients pop into my mind and I wonder how they are getting on, but there is nothing I can do or need to do. Sometimes with distressing narratives it takes longer to work it through my system, but I have well practised strategies in these situations, good supervision and running in nature.

The practitioner researcher needs to be prepared to be patient, pause, take stock, and readjust, to incorporate new ideas. They need the ability to zoom in and out from the big picture to detail, take critique from peers, and deal with setbacks. There will be periods of productivity and flow (Csikszentmihalyi, 2002) with the accompanying satisfaction and times of frustration when things come to a grinding halt, and rest and recalibration is needed. It is rarely a straightforward trajectory, adding richness and validity to the process and results. As with PhD study, time and competing demands of general living are the biggest challenge (Beasy et al., 2021), along with any life events or episodes of illness. There are also the demands of managing workloads in clinical practice with self-care. Jackman et al. (2021) concur, in their systematic review on PhD study, that there are negative factors on mental health, including work-life imbalance.

Journal, 2020: Sorting the Pieces by Moving Back and Forth
With the research process being so different, I find myself carrying it daily, still present even when I am not focusing on it. There are many tensions. On the one hand, research gives me a feeling of progression, growth and exploring material otherwise out of range and yet there are always the distractions of clinical practice and family demands. It takes effort to pick up the threads after enforced putting down, followed by the ability to put the project down again once reabsorbed. Then there is the tension of the big picture vision,

(continued)

versus the detailed writing task. It's a balancing act of accepting these conflicts, being disciplined, channelling the contrasts, and going with the break throughs when things flow.

Receiving Feedback

Receiving feedback is a key part of the research process. Unlike the academic peer review process, once qualified, a psychotherapist clinical practitioner is not critically peer-reviewed. Therapists have high levels of autonomy in their work. There are formalised, well-developed, and reliable processes of clinical supervision and continuous professional development to ensure ethical practice, which is required for professional body membership (British Association for Counsellors and Psychotherapists, 2020). These processes are based on the principle of collaboration rather than critique, providing valuable opportunities for personal awareness, skill development, reflective practice, and self-care (Churchill, 2013). A good supervisor can have a very positive and transformative affect, leading to better outcomes for the supervisee and their clients (Watkins, 2020). The same principle could apply to research supervision and peer review and contribute to better research. Just as clinical practitioners "…do not come ready-made…but develop over time, and sometimes agonizingly so…", (Watkins & Callan, 2019, p. 27) pracademics may also go through a "painful transition" of finding their identity (Dickinson et al., 2022, p. 298). The long-term nature of research, the critical feedback, and any rejections can gradually reduce motivation and erode confidence in the possibility of success. At this point, the practitioner researcher may no longer value the original goal or may identify other activities with which they want to engage, and this may lead to a weighing up of values and options. This can result in them giving up; not necessarily because of a lack of will power but instead a redirecting of energy and motivation (Morton & Paul, 2019).

Journal, 2021: Dealing with Setbacks
The dark December night is settling over the city, it's been a busy clinical day. A quick check of emails before shutting down for the evening and dropped in the inbox is a harsh second peer review on our paper and cooling off from the publisher, who had originally seemed positive. The rational part of my brain is not working well, and I have lost perspective. Fatigued, dehydrated and with a raft of family responsibilities ahead of me in the evening, the feeling of rejection stings. My internal dialogue is loud and negative, "It's not worth the sacrifices. Is it even important anymore?" The big picture seemed feasible and a natural progression from my experience, but I question myself on why I ever thought I could do this; it feels now that I was naïve about what was involved, maybe under some sort of illusion about what was possible. At this point it would be easier to relinquish the difficult long-term goal and enjoy the easily gained pleasures in life, I could enjoy a night or two relaxing on the sofa watching Netflix, read a fiction book for pleasure, enjoy doing something for the sake of doing it.

Peer review is focused on the intellectual, with little regard for pastoral care for new researchers. It provides academic rigour and critique but often doesn't give feedback in emotionally sensitive ways to facilitate application into practice. Brewis (2021) describes this as emotional labour undertaken by the researcher with the need for emotional management. Peer review can also give rise to imposter phenomenon (Clance & Imes, 1978; Slank, 2019). This is experienced when the practitioner is building their professional identity but feels like they do not possess the talents and skills that are needed and believes that they will be exposed as fraudulent and unsuitable for the role (Gallagher, 2019). It often exists in both health care professions and academia where practitioners have the desire to serve and contribute to the greater good. Although some self-doubt is human and necessary to identify mistakes and grow (Salmons, 2021), holding this negative self-concept can affect confidence and wellbeing.

Methods of handling feedback vary across professional fields, with some taking more account of the psychology behind receiving feedback. Recent studies in medicine highlight the need for better practice and the recognition of the impact of imposter phenomenon and call for a "growth mindset" (Naik, 2021, p. 664). The Chartered Institute of Management (CIM) also emphasise the importance of good practice in giving feedback, how to provide it constructively, and how damaging it can be to confidence if presented badly (Hill, 2019). Motro et al. (2021) show the effects of negative performance feedback on emotions. They highlight how disappointment, and accompanying sadness from negative feedback, can affect future performance unless mediated by grit. In addition, relationships which grow and enrich intellectual development can strengthen resilience (Hartling, 2008). The humanitarian doctor, David Knott, is an inspiration and exemplary. In his book *War Doctor* (2019), he describes the joy and sense of achievement that he experiences when guiding junior surgeons to carry out new and difficult surgical procedures. He witnesses their euphoria and mastery, knowing that he has passed on skills, enabling them to go on to make a bigger contribution to medicine, and all of this accomplished in demanding conditions where rigour and safe practice are crucial to their success.

Journal, 2021: Staying Positive

The traditions of peer review contributed to my feelings of imposter phenomenon, but I had just enough perspective to give myself some space. Most importantly to remember why I embarked on this, which was to create an intervention to help students with their mental health and to find out if it worked. I always knew setting up a mental health intervention as a research project was ambitious. For some parts I was drawing on my therapeutic skills, but many parts took me outside my comfort zone and all alongside the demands of clinical practice. Remembering this helped. I valued the support of my more experienced pracademic friends who pointed out that this kind of peer review experience was not uncommon and reframed the feedback, maybe I hadn't found the right home for my work. There was much invested, and the

(continued)

research results were good. I still believed there was something worth sharing in my field. I was not done yet and I strengthened my resolve to rework the paper. Research is a steep learning curve. The rules are very different to my previous professional experience and as with a puzzle, some parts which originally seemed to fit now needed reworking. On reflection, I am still observing the rules of business and clinical practice where the guiding principle of feedback is to enhance performance. I understand the need for academic rigour, but the anonymous and critical nature of peer review and lack of discussion sits in stark contrast to my person-centred values and beliefs of encouraging growth.

These painful experiences of transition to being a practitioner researcher are a contrast to well-honed clinical expertise which contributes to the professional identity of the clinical practitioner. Becoming a practitioner researcher means dovetailing this expertise with newly developing researcher skills. The hierarchy of values can shift and change, redefining what is important and what gives meaning (Dilts, 1999). This can lead to a struggle with the duality of identities and the necessary reshaping to find a pracademic identity (Dickinson et al., 2022; Hollweck et al., 2022). Initially this was uncomfortable but, over time, I am integrating the conflicting parts to be a "blended professional" accepting my mixed and unique portfolio (Whitchurch, 2008, p. 378).

Key Points

- Think about how you relate to the timescale as compared with clinical practitioner milestones. Overestimate how long your project will take
- Recognise and plan for periods of productivity and periods of rest or pause
- Be proactive in creating a writing space as a boundary from daily reactive tasks
- Step away and let creative ideas emerge
- Pause, give space, and reflect after receiving feedback
- Set goals, including short-, mid- and longer-term goals
- Notice how far you have progressed and celebrate along the way

Growing Personal Resilience Through Challenge

Cultures change slowly and, although there are moves to shift academia to be kinder and more inclusive (Farrar, 2019; Shaw & Ward, 2014), it is important to develop personal resilience. This is needed not only to survive in the face of challenges, but to thrive, adapt, pursue goals, and grow despite adversity (Hanson & Hanson, 2018). 'Grit', which is synonymous with resilience, also includes passion and perseverance and it is important for the achievement of long-term goals (Hill et al., 2016; Morton & Paul, 2019). All of these characteristics are essential for the practitioner researcher.

Throughout this project, I have drawn on my clinical skills to understand what I was experiencing to boost my own personal resilience and to stay connected to my goals and values. Seligman and Csikszentmihalyi's (2000) model of positive psychology provides ways of countering self-doubt by focusing on how people can flourish and achieve their goals even in the face of challenges. It cites the importance of optimism, along with encouraging and developing a person's strengths. Frankl (2004) and Baumeister (1991) concur that personal growth in the face of challenges and activities, which are meaningful and goal-oriented, enable a person to flourish. Although these are important models, it is also helpful in times of challenge to have practical techniques to boost resilience.

Practical Techniques

An understanding of how the brain and body works when under stress is helpful and for this, we can draw on basic neuroscience. The brain's natural tendency towards negative thinking is an instinctive protective mechanism to help us notice a perceived threat. This protects us from danger and is technically known as the negativity bias (Rozin & Royzman, 2001). When there is a threat, we experience an emotional charge which is processed by the amygdala. When the amygdala is activated in this way, the rational part of the brain, called the prefrontal cortex, which is involved in planning, organising actions, and making decisions doesn't function as well and perspective can be lost (Hanson, 2008). Our nervous system, commonly known as our "flight and fight" (Cannon, 1929) and "freeze" response (Rothschild, 2017) is also activated. The way that our body works means that when barriers or rejections are experienced, it is easy to react to them as threats and fall into negative distorted and generalised thinking, which can lead a person to catastrophise.

Acceptance and Commitment Therapy (ACT) (Harris, 2019), Emotional Freedom Technique (EFT) (Church & Marohn, 2013) and Taking in the Good Course (TGC) (Hanson et al., 2021) are psychological techniques which help to diffuse negative thoughts and stimulate the emotional centre of the brain in positive ways. This supports us to look for the positive possibilities and can prevent us from ruminating, getting stuck, and repeating patterns of behaviour which aren't helpful. This is possible because the brain has neuroplasticity, which means that it can change and modify, updating old emotional memories with new positive experiences (Ecker, 2015). Refer to the 'Coaching Techniques' box below for simple tools to help manage emotions, boost resilience, and enable the rational part of the brain to function more effectively when faced with threats.

Coaching Techniques: Regulate Your Nervous System and Build Your Resilience

- Notice difficult thoughts and imagine putting them on clouds or in balloons and letting them drift away.
- Notice your feelings – are there uncomfortable sensations in your body, a knot in your stomach, and/or a tightness in your chest? Take three deep breaths and on the out breath send kindness to the sensations.
- Create space by diffusing difficult thoughts/feelings using the techniques below:
  - **Validate and diffuse**
    You can write down or say to yourself, "even though I have difficult thoughts/feelings which are holding me back and I think I am not good enough; essentially, I am going to fail. (You can input your own difficult thoughts/feelings). This is understandable and I may be able to accept these thoughts and know they are only thoughts/feelings."
  - **Move to positive possibilities**
    "There is a possibility that I may be able to develop my confidence and trust myself in this process." (Input your own positive thoughts).
  - **Develop gratitude**
    To help you filter for positive things. These can be very small things; for example, notice a blue sky, have a chat with a friend, a walk in the woods, or observe a beautiful flower.
  - **Finish with an overall positive search statement** using the set-up of 'what if I can', for example, be productive today and/or develop as a researcher.

Informed by Church and Marohn (2013), Hanson et al. (2021), Harris (2011).

Which of These Inner Strengths and Qualities Do You Exhibit? Which Can You Develop?

- Perseverance, determination, and grit
- Maintain a sense of humour
- Activate Gratitude
- Emotional awareness and sensitivity
- Compassion for self and others
- Inspiration
- Manage the brain's tendency towards negative thinking
- Maintain perspective and ability self soothe and calm your brain
- Discipline of daily practice to build and embed positive thoughts and resilience
- Awareness of personal value Informed by Hanson (2023)

Conclusion

It has been five years since I started my endeavour to be a practitioner researcher. I find myself ruminating at times, weighing up the opportunities that I have turned down because of investing my energy on this project and thinking about some of the struggles. Sometimes I ask myself, knowing what I know now, would I do it again? I would, for these reasons.

From an intervention and research outcomes perspective, I recruited 4 groups. By the fourth, there were 25 regular runners. At this stage, MINDFIT was paused because of the COVID-19 lockdown. The research findings were positive, with qualitative findings showing that MINDFIT created a community which reduced isolation and social anxiety for students. The presence of a run leader who was a counsellor created safety, which helped students to engage and achieve mastery of a goal. Attainment and retention were also positively affected. Quantitative measures of depression and anxiety levels showed promising reductions at the end of the programme.

Through the project, I have advanced my research skills and met many people, not least the students. I've witnessed their magical moments, moving from struggling with anxiety, low mood, and isolation, to flourishing and belonging to a community through MINDFIT. I noticed too how I shared a parallel process with them, of finding my research community. At first, I felt like an imposter who did not belong, before establishing supportive relationships, where I have shared enjoyment, growth, and developmental conversations. As with a jigsaw puzzle, I had to make sense of messy disorganised pieces, create the outline, develop and re-work parts, persevere, walk away, come back refreshed and view the situation from a new perspective, ask for help, and share the joy when large chunks of the puzzle clicked together.

With self-awareness and an understanding of the academic system and its implicit and explicit rules, a reciprocal relationship can be established between clinical practice and research, bringing fresh energy and stimulation, which can help to prevent burnout or boredom. It does require the ability to tolerate some disorientation and discomfort when moving between the two. It provides many opportunities for growth, both scholarly and personal with similar effect to adversarial or posttraumatic growth. The challenge of the latter can lead to readjustment and functioning at a higher level (Tedeschi & Calhoun, 2004). I think about Victor Frankl's (2004) seminal text *Man's Search For Meaning* and how MINDFIT aligns at the level of purpose and values for me. It brings therapeutic healing and growth through physical activity, dovetailing four passions of running, therapy, nature, and research. Being proactive, keen to shape things, and complete what I've started when in project mode, I can be in a rush. I have realised how rush isn't possible when balancing being a clinical practitioner and a practitioner researcher. As with most worthwhile and valuable endeavours, it takes time to unfold. I now see my research as continually evolving rather than having an end point, and the enforced break caused by COVID-19 has reinforced this. Reinvigorating MINDFIT post-pandemic is a work in progress, with the paper now published and the possibility of a bigger research project in the future (Gurung et al., 2023). Just as becoming a mature and seasoned clinical practitioner takes years, it is the same with research. I hope that my lived experience offers some insights and ways forward, at the very least to know that the practitioner researcher is not alone in their endeavour and can find belonging with other pracademics.

Points for Reflection
- Gurung shares her process of becoming a practitioner researcher and her identification with the label of pracademic. Do you have a professional journey you would like to embark on? What is it's purpose, and what will it give you?
- If you identify with the role of a pracademic, what is important to you about being a pracademic? How does becoming a pracademic represent who you are?
- Gurung elucidates the importance of working in accordance with her values. As your professional journey evolves, to what extent are you still aligned to your purpose and values, and why?

References

Afifi, T. D. (2018). Individual/relational resilience. *Journal of Applied Communication Research, 46*(1), 5–9. https://doi.org/10.1080/00909882.2018.1426707

Bandura, A. (1997). *Self-Efficacy: the exercise of control*. Freeman and Company.

Baumeister, R. F. (1991). *Meanings of life*. Guilford Press.

Beasy, K., Sherridan, E., & Crawford, J. (2021). Drowning in the shallows: An Australian study of the PhD experience of wellbeing. *Teaching in Higher Education, 26*(4), 602–618. https://doi.org/10.1080/13562517.2019.1669014

Brewis, J. (2021). Rolling with the punches: Receiving peer reviews as prescriptive emotion management. *Culture and Organization, 27*(3), 267–284. https://doi.org/10.1080/1475955 1.2020.1837829

British Association for Counselling and Psychotherapy (BACP). (2020). *Introduction to supervision (public version)*. https://www.bacp.co.uk/media/10210/bacp-intro-to-supervision-caq-gpia064-nov20.pdf

Buber, M. (1970). *I and Thou* (W. Kaufman, Trans.). Charles Scribner's Sons.

Cannon, W. B. (1929). *Bodily changes in pain, hunger, fear and rage: An account of recent researches into the function of emotional excitement* (Vol. 22, p. 870). D. Appleton & Company.

Church, D., & Marohn, S. (2013). *Clinical EFT handbook: A definitive resource for practitioners, scholars, clinicians and researchers*. Psychology Press.

Churchill, S. (2013). Transformational Supervision. *Therapy Today, 24*(6). https://www.bacp.co.uk/bacp-journals/therapy-today/2013/july-2013/articles/transformational-supervision/

Clance, P. R., & Imes, S. A. (1978). The imposter phenomenon in high achieving women: Dynamics and therapeutic intervention. *Psychotherapy, 15*(3), 241–247. https://doi.org/10.1037/h0086006

Cooper, M. (2003). *Existential therapies*. Sage.

Csikszentmihalyi, M. (1996). *Creativity flow and the psychology of discovery and invention*. Harper Perennial.

Csikszentmihalyi, M. (2002). *Flow. The classic work on how to achieve happiness*. Rider Publishing.

Dickinson, J., Fowler, A., & Griffiths, T. (2022). Pracademics? Exploring transitions and professional identities in higher education. *Studies in Higher Education, 47*(2), 290–304. https://doi.org/10.1080/03075079.2020.1744123

Dilts, R. B. (1999). *Sleight of mouth: The magic of conversational belief change*. Meta Publications.

Ecker, B. (2015). Memory reconsolidation understood and misunderstood. *International Journal of Neuropsychotherapy, 3*(1), 2–46. https://doi.org/10.12744/ijnpt.2015.0002-0046

Farrar, J. (2019, December 20). *Why we need to reimagine how we do research*. Wellcome Trust. https://wellcome.ac.uk/news/why-we-need-reimagine-how-we-do-research

Ferreira, J. F., Basseches, M., & Vasco, A. B. (2017). Guidelines for reflective practice in psychotherapy: A reflection on the benefits of combining moment-by-moment and phase-by-phase mapping in clinical decision making. *Journal of Psychotherapy Integration, 27*(1), 35–46. https://doi.org/10.1037/int0000047

Florida, R. (2002). *The rise of the creative class*. Basic Books.

Frankl, V. E. (2004). *Man's search for meaning*. Rider Publishing.

Gallagher, S. R. (2019). Professional identity and imposter syndrome. *The Clinical Teacher, 16*(4), 426–427. https://doi-org.hallam.idm.oclc.org/10.1111/tct.13042

Gross, J. J. (2015). *Handbook of emotion regulation* (2nd ed.). The Guilford Press.

Gurung, J., Turner, J., Freeman, E., Coleman, C., Iacovou, S., & Hemingway, S. (2023). An evaluation of MINDFIT—A student therapeutic running group as a multi-layered intervention in the United Kingdom. *Nursing Reports, 13*(1), 456–469.

Hanson, R. (2008). *Peace of mind: Emotions, the limbic system, and equanimity*. Rick Hanson, Ph.D. https://www.rickhanson.net/peace-of-mind-emotions-the-limbic-system-and-equanimity/?highlight=limbic

Hanson, R. (2023). *Grow inner strengths*. Rick Hanson, Ph.D., https://www.rickhanson.net/grow-inner-strengths/

Hanson, R., & Hanson, F. (2018). *Resilient: How to grow an unshakeable core of calm, strength, and happiness*. Harmony books.

Hanson, R., Shapiro, S., Hutton-Thamm, E., Hagerty, M. R., & Sullivan, K. P. (2021). Learning to learn from positive experiences. *The Journal of Positive Psychology, 18*(1), 142–153. https://doi.org/10.1080/17439760.2021.2006759

Harris, R. (2011). *The confidence gap, from fear to freedom*. Robinson Publishing.

Harris, R. (2019). *ACT made simple* (2nd ed.). New Harbinger Publications.

Hartling, L. M. (2008). Strengthening resilience in a risky world: It's all about relationships. *Women & Therapy, 31*(2–4), 51–70. https://doi.org/10.1080/02703140802145870

Hill, E. (2019, December 4). *How to give feedback constructively*. Chartered Institute of Management. https://www.managers.org.uk/knowledge-and-insights/article/how-to-give-feedback-constructively/#author

Hill, P. L., Burrow, A. L., & Bronk, K. C. (2016). Persevering with positivity and purpose: An examination of purpose commitment and positive affect as predictors of Grit. *Journal of Happiness Studies, 17*, 257–269. https://doi-org.hallam.idm.oclc.org/10.1007/s10902-014-9593-5

Hollweck, T., Netolicky, D. M., & Campbell, P. (2022). Defining and exploring pracademia: Identity, community, and engagement. *Journal of Professional Capital and Community, 7*(1), 6–25. https://doi.org/10.1108/JPCC-05-2021-0026

Jackman, P. C., Jacobs, L., Hawkins, R. M., & Sisson, K. (2021). Mental health and psychological wellbeing in the early stages of doctoral study: A systematic review. *European Journal of Higher Education, 12*(3), 293–313. https://doi-org.hallam.idm.oclc.org/10.1080/21568235.2021.1939752

Jordan, J. V. (2017). Relational-cultural theory: The power of connection to transform our lives. *Journal of Humanistic Counselling, 56*(3), 228–243. https://doi-org.hallam.idm.oclc.org/10.1002/johc.12055

Kierkegaard, S. (1992). *The concept of anxiety: A simple psychologically orientating deliberation on the dogmatic issue of hereditary sin* (R. Thomte & A. B. Anderson, Trans.). Princeton University Press. (Original work published 1844).

Knott, D. (2019). *War Doctor Surgery: On the Front Line*. Picador.

Kushner, L. (2015). *Honey from the Rock* (2nd ed.). Jewish Lights Publishing.

McBeath, A. (2019). The motivations of psychotherapists: An in-depth study. *Counselling and Psychotherapy Research, 19*(4), 377–387. https://doi.org/10.1002/capr.12225

Milne, J. (2020). What is creativity? *British Journal of Nursing Tissue Viability Supplement, 29*(12), 54. https://doi.org/10.12968/bjon.2020.29.12.S4

Morton, J. M., & Paul, S. K. (2019). Grit. *Ethics, 129*(2), 175–203. https://doi.org/10.1086/700029

Motro, D., Comer, D. R., & Lenaghan, J. A. (2021). Examining the effects of negative performance feedback: The roles of sadness, feedback self-efficacy, and grit. *Journal of Business and Psychology, 36*, 367–382. https://doi.org/10.1007/s10869-020-09689-1

Naik, H. (2021). On imposter syndrome and feedback: A resident's reply (letter). *Medical Education, 55*(5), 664. https://doi-org.hallam.idm.oclc.org/10.1111/medu.14472

National Health Service (NHS). (2023, October 2). *Get running with couch to 5k.* https://www.nhs.uk/live-well/exercise/running-and-aerobic-exercises/get-running-with-couch-to-5k/

Nuffield Council on Bioethics. (2014, December). *The culture of scientific research in the UK.* https://www.nuffieldbioethics.org/publications/the-culture-of-scientific-research

Pickersgill, M., Cunningham-Burley, S., Engelmann, L., Ganguli-Mitra, A., Hewer, R., & Young, I. (2019). Challenging Social Structures and changing research cultures. *The Lancet, 394*(10210), 1693–1695. https://doi-org.hallam.idm.oclc.org/10.1016/S0140-6736(19)32635-2

Robson, C. (2002). *Real world research a resource for social scientists and practitioner-researchers* (2nd ed.). Blackwell Publishers.

Rothschild, B. (2017). *The body remembers volume 2: Revolutionizing trauma treatment.* W.W. Norton & Company.

Rozin, P., & Royzman, E. B. (2001). Negativity bias, negativity dominance, and contagion. *Personality and Social Psychological Review, 5*(4), 296–320. https://doi.org/10.1207/S15327957PSPR0504_2

Salmons, P. (2021). Imposter syndrome: A degree of doubt is essential. *British Medical Journal, 374*(1706). https://doi.org/10.1136/bmj.n1706

Seligman, M. E. P., & Csikszentmihalyi, M. (2000). Positive psychology: An introduction. *American Psychologist, 55*(1), 5–14. https://doi.org/10.1037/0003-066X.55.1.5

Shaw, C., & Ward, L. (2014, March 6). Dark thoughts: Why mental illness is on the rise in academia. *The Guardian.* https://www.theguardian.com/higher-education-network/2014/mar/06/mental-health-academics-growing-problem-pressure-university

Slank, S. (2019). Rethinking the imposter phenomenon. *Ethical Theory and Moral Practice, 22*, 205–218. https://doi.org/10.1007/s10677-019-09984-8

Stafford, M. R., & Bond, T. (2020). *Counselling skills in action* (4th ed.). Sage.

Tedeschi, R. G., & Calhoun, L. G. (2004). Post traumatic growth: Conceptual foundations and empirical evidence. *Psychological Inquiry, 15*(1), 1–18. https://doi.org/10.1207/s15327965pli1501_01

Watkins, E. C. (2020). Psychotherapy supervision: An ever-evolving signature pedagogy. *World Psychiatry, 19*(2), 244–245. https://doi.org/10.1002/wps.20747

Watkins, E. C., & Callan, J. (2019). Psychotherapy supervision research: A status report and proposed model. In S. G. DeGolia & K. M. Corcoran (Eds.), *Supervision in psychiatric practice: Practical approaches across venues and providers* (pp. 25–36). APA Publishing.

Whitchurch, C. (2008). Shifting and blurring the boundaries: The Emergence of the *Third Space.* Professionals in UK Higher Education. *Higher Education Quarterly, 62*(4), 377–396. https://doi.org/10.1111/j.1468-2273.2008.00387.x

Whitchurch, C., & Gordan, G. (2010). Diversifying academic and professional identities in higher education: Some management challenges. *Tertiary Education and Management, 16*(2), 129–144. https://doi.org/10.1080/13583881003757029

Zundel, M., & Kokkalis, P. (2010). Theorizing as engaged practice. *Organization Studies, 31*(9–10), 1209–1227. https://doi.org/10.1177/0170840610374405

Jan Gurung is an accredited Psychotherapist with the British Association for Counselling and Psychotherapy (BACP), working in a university setting and private practice. Jan works with people who are experiencing difficulties with their mental health, typically anxiety, social anxiety, and depression, and specializes in rapid trauma techniques, using Eye Movement Desensitization Reprocessing (EMDR) and Emotional Freedom Technique (EFT). Loneliness is at the heart of both her therapeutic and research work, along with finding innovative solutions to build supportive communities and increase belonging to improve mental health. She also has a special interest in the way physical activity can be used therapeutically. Jan is the founder of MINDFIT, a running group for students. MINDFIT is a transformational, experiential programme, which brings together two powerful therapeutic agents, running and a counselling approach. Jan also works with the Sheffield Hallam Centre for Loneliness Studies, contributing to research projects and is an active member of the Sheffield Hallam University's Pracademic Community.

Chapter 12
How Pracademics Can Help to Address the Rigour-Relevance Gap in Business and Management Schools

Steve Johnson and Mark Ellis

Abstract Growth in the number of pracademics in business schools can make a significant contribution to addressing the 'rigour-relevance gap', which has long been a concern of business and management schools. Influential commentators have argued that business and management research is overly concerned with achieving scholarly impact, primarily through journal publications, to the detriment of relevance to practice. Likewise, teaching and learning in many business schools is regarded as too theoretical and does not prepare students adequately for the 'real world' of business. Not all observers accept this view, but there can be little doubt that the career paths of most business and management academics tend to emphasise doctoral qualifications and scholarly outputs rather than practical experience of management and leadership. The authors reflect on their experiences as practitioners and academics, working with colleagues with backgrounds within and outside academia. The increasing influence of pracademia can facilitate business research, teaching, and learning that has impact beyond the academy. However, there are several barriers to the achievement of this potential, requiring radical and creative solutions. Proposals include enhancing the status of professional doctorates, reforming academic career structures to reward the distinctive contributions of pracademics and creating genuinely 'porous' business schools.

Keywords Pracademic · Pracademic career development · Business school · Management · Rigour · Relevance · Doctorate · Commercial relevance · Imposter syndrome · University recruitment

S. Johnson (✉)
School of Business, Leeds Trinity University, Leeds, UK
e-mail: st.johnson@leedstrinity.ac.uk

M. Ellis
Department of Management, Sheffield Hallam University, Sheffield, UK
e-mail: m.ellis@shu.ac.uk

J. Dickinson, T.-L. Griffiths (eds.), *Professional Development for Practitioners in Academia*, Knowledge Studies in Higher Education 13,
https://doi.org/10.1007/978-3-031-33746-8_12

At a Glance
- Highlights how pracademics make a significant contribution to addressing the widely discussed 'rigour-relevance gap' in business schools.
- Provides illustrations through the experiences of two business school pracademics, who highlight some positive achievements, but point out major cultural and systemic barriers.
- Recommends that recognition in recruitment and promotion processes of the value of practical experience, as well as academic qualifications and outputs, would be a major step forward.
- Notes how these proposed changes are essential if we are to create genuinely 'porous' business schools that combine the benefits of rigorous and relevant teaching, learning, and research.

Introduction

The 'rigour-relevance' debate has been a long-running one in relation to the role and impact of business schools,[1] notably in the context of research, but also in relation to teaching and learning. The most critical commentators argue that business schools have 'lost their way' by shifting from a model that is based primarily on professional or trade schools towards attempting to emulate established academic disciplines by emphasising scientific rigour over relevance to managerial practice (Bennis & O'Toole, 2005; Irwin, 2019). A corollary of this trend has been a rebalancing of the staff base of many business schools away from lecturers with experience of industry and commerce towards career academics with doctoral qualifications, records of publication in academic journals, and, typically, no experience of working in managerial roles outside the academic sector. This is recognized, for example, by AACSB, a leading accreditation body for business schools, which categorises academic staff into Scholarly Academics, Scholarly Practitioners, and Instructional Practitioners (AACSB, 2022).

Recent research has identified the existence and apparent growth of a group of people working in academic posts across the Higher Education sector who might be described as 'pracademics' (Dickinson et al., 2022; Hollweck et al., 2021; Susskind, 2013). Definitions vary and hard data is difficult to come by, but there are indications that this trend is being replicated in parts of the business school sector, typically in schools that emphasise the applied focus of their teaching and research activities (Panda, 2014). This is certainly the case within the institution in which the two authors worked together and reflects the experience of one of the authors who

---

[1]We use the term 'business school' as a shorthand to describe academic schools that teach and research topics related to business and management. Some such organisations are known as schools or departments of management, or similar.

has held academic and research leadership positions in five United Kingdom (UK) business schools over the past 20-plus years.

The apparently increasing significance of business school pracademics raises the prospect of a (perhaps partial) solution to the rigour-relevance conundrum. Put simply, academic staff with practical experience, but without advanced qualifications such as doctorates, are regarded as unlikely to possess the academic credibility and approach that is necessary to deliver a university-standard educational experience or to publish research findings in high-ranking journals. Conversely, as noted earlier, 'pure' academics without business experience have the qualifications and experience required to produce research outputs, but have a limited basis on which to explore practical implications with students, or to work with managers to understand the practical implications of their research.

The 'rigour-relevance' debate tends to characterise academics who are focused on scholarly research, and those concerned primarily with impact on practice, as "two tribes" (Gulati, 2007, p. 775) with their own distinctive languages and cultures that make it difficult or impossible for them to work together (Kieser & Leiner, 2009). It can be argued that 'pracademics' with varying combinations of academic and practitioner backgrounds, represent a potential 'middle way' that can challenge the pessimistic prognosis suggested by the 'two tribes' model. Panda (2014) identifies several key differences between academic scholars and research executives, which pose a challenge to those who propose that the two approaches be reconciled:

> The academic scholars are mandated to create knowledge, whereas corporate executives are expected to create wealth ... The academic scholars are rational in their thinking process, whereas corporate executives rely on both rational and intuitive thought processes ... Sense of urgency is valued more in the corporate community compared to in the academic community ... Academic scholars tend to prefer complex language laden with academic jargons, whereas corporate executives prefer simple language. (Panda, 2014, p. 144)

Of course, these depictions of academics and practitioners are – as the authors recognise – generalisations that do not do justice to the wide range of backgrounds, experience, and cultures both within and between these idealised groups. Of course, there are academics who are excellent at engaging with business and there are practitioners with high quality research outputs in leading journals. However, the academic-practitioner-pracademic model broadly reflects the observations and experiences of the two authors of this chapter, both of whom have worked inside and outside of academia over the course of their careers, interacting with colleagues and stakeholders from a variety of backgrounds.

Pracademics who offer a combination of academic and practitioner backgrounds, experience, and competences, have the potential, in theory, to make a significant contribution to bridging the gap between rigour and relevance. The literature to date on the pracademia phenomenon is limited and focuses primarily on disciplines with strong professional links, such as law, architecture, public policy, and education. In addition to Panda's (2014) auto-ethnographic paper mentioned above, McNatt et al. (2010, p. 15) argue for the development of a "pracademic paradigm" as one possible approach to addressing the gap between the 'academic world' and the 'practitioner world' in relation to management research.

As is often the case with relatively new (or recently discovered) phenomena, definitions of pracademics or pracademia vary and the nature of the concept is influenced, arguably, by the disciplinary and professional context which is being considered. Some pracademics simultaneously run private practices and teach in universities (Susskind, 2013) whereas others are engaged in educational or public policy-related activities. For example, Hollweck et al. (2021) focus on the education sector and their definition of pracademics includes practising teachers who are undertaking part-time university programmes. After reviewing a range of definitions, they "conceptualize pracademia as the dynamic connecting or liminal space between educational research and the classroom, school, and policymaking" (Hollweck et al., 2021, p. 7).

This conceptualisation can, in principle, be translated to a business and management context. Pracademics in this field could be described as occupying a 'liminal space' between academia and business, although the extent to which business school pracademics are actively involved in management outside academia is typically limited. A more common model, in the authors' experience, is for business school pracademics to retain links with professional and business networks and to be actively involved with business engagement activities, such as student placements, guest lectures, consultancy, and knowledge exchange projects. Business schools are increasingly building links with practising managers through Entrepreneurs in Residence or Executives in Residence, and by the engagement of business representatives on advisory boards and curriculum development processes. Guest lectures by business professionals are relatively common and many part-time adjunct or associate teaching staff are practising business owners or managers.

These trends suggest that pracademia is becoming an important influence on teaching, learning, and research across many business schools, in the UK and internationally. It might be expected that the combination of pracademics in academic roles, and increasing external engagement with business school activities, would result in an observable narrowing of the gap between rigour and relevance. This would be evident, for example, in more practically-based teaching and learning programmes, and research that has a demonstrable impact on policy and practice. While there are examples of movement in these directions (Chartered Association of Business Schools (CABS), 2021), commentary by leading professional organisations and influential commentators suggest that there is still a long way to go (RRBM, 2022). The experiences and observations of the authors suggest that significant barriers remain to the effective reconciliation of rigour and relevance through pracademia in business schools.

Key Themes

A Pracademic's Tale

The Fairy Tale

I had done it, after many weeks of preparation and much hard work, I had managed to secure a job as an academic. I was over the moon. I had even managed to negotiate a position as a Senior Lecturer, based on my twenty plus years of management experience. The future was bright. OK, so I might not change the world, but at least I would be in a position to contribute positively toward society and maybe have an impact. Whereas I had become jaded and cynical in the commercial world, I now had purpose.

I recalled these elated emotions as I ascended the stairs to meet my new Subject Group Leader on my first day at work. Now, some ten years further down the road, and a PhD behind me (and still an academic), I know the reality of academia is more complex. I also know that the potential is just as real as I first imagined.

When I reflect on the two worlds of academia and business, each seems to have a view of the other as challenging to engage with and significantly opaque. A sweeping generalisation maybe, but I would also counter this with the view that at the confluence of these two worlds pracademics really can make a difference. Here's how.

The Value of Analogies

In my early days as an academic, I had significant imposter syndrome. My rhetoric and an MBA had got me through the door, but now I had to actually know what I was doing. I did lots of reading in an attempt to be as learned as my established scholarly colleagues, which helped. But, what soon became apparent within my teaching was the value of analogies built from my experiences. Where I would be introducing a concept and associated theory, this would often be met with stony silence or quizzical expressions from the students. I realised they weren't really getting it, so I flipped my approach to telling them about a situation in the business world and then built the theory around this; taking them from a social construct they understood to a new way of looking at this from a theoretical perspective. They got it, and moreover, were keen to chat about it and explore further. With over twenty years of business experience in a wide range of areas, I had an almost limitless supply of stories that I could relate from my experiences which have added as much value as my reading. It also occurred to me that the vast majority of our students aspire to be practitioners, not academics, so when we talk about cold theory, this does not have the same engagement factor as tales from the coalface.

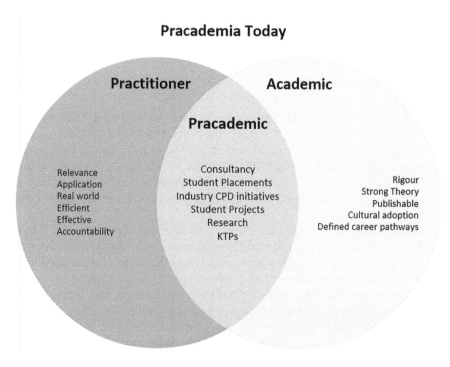

Pracademia Today

Practitioner   **Academic**

Pracademic

Relevance	Consultancy	
Application	Student Placements	Rigour
Real world	Industry CPD initiatives	Strong Theory
Efficient	Student Projects	Publishable
Effective	Research	Cultural adoption
Accountability	KTPs	Defined career pathways

Fig. 12.1 Pracademia today

Pracademics as Interpreters

The commercial world is not too concerned about the academic merit of research (for example, contribution to the Research Excellence Framework[2]). It wants research to be validated in some way, but more than this, businesses need to be able to see the relevance and benefits. Simultaneously, academic research is driven by publication, ranking, impact, and esteem, all of which might well coalesce into a neat Venn diagram (Fig. 12.1).

However, both sides will likely retain their self-interested focus, not to a point of win-lose, more win-whatever. But the potential here is staggering. During my time as a leader in a medium sized management consultancy, we had a significant influence on the UK business community, more so than the local business schools. We did this with perhaps 5–10% of the staffing of a business school, with the vast majority having significantly less academic knowledge than my academic colleagues. Of course, supporting business is not the main priority for universities, but engaging with it is a must. As pracademics, we have a window into both worlds and their specific needs around rigour and relevance, and it is from this standpoint that

---

[2] 'The Research Excellence Framework is the UK's system for assessing the quality of research in UK higher education institutions.' (REF, 2022).

we need to engage and seek out the win-win opportunities and capitalise on the vast potential at the nexus of academia and business.

Challenging the Paradigm and Bringing Common Sense

Higher Education Institutions (HEIs) are oil tankers, small and medium-sized enterprises are speed boats, and public limited companies are cruise ships; each operating in the same seas but with vastly different capabilities and aspirations. Universities have long histories and traditions that are reinforced by hierarchies and structures, perpetuating that which has gone before. The commercial world operates on the concept of the survival of the fittest and most adaptive. These two cultures drive very different approaches. Meetings in academia can, at times, seem to be without focus or outcome, where I have witnessed colleagues take no notes on allocated actions and then simply not follow through on them, with no accountability. Were this to occur in the commercial world, 'words' would be had, and disciplinary actions might follow. Of course, this type of behaviour is not ubiquitous across HE, but neither is it uncommon. I have to admit, that after 10 years as an academic, I have in part 'gone native' and am more relaxed in driving meetings and projects forward compared to my consultancy days. However, the challenge for effective and efficient systems in large and complex organisations like universities is significant where, once again as pracademics, we must attempt to retain our broader experiences and bring common sense and professionalism to bear in a culture where tradition and hierarchies are often more prevalent. This may not be easy. I have witnessed pracademics come into HE and soon become exasperated by the culture, only to head back into industry or 'go native' themselves. HEIs may well be missing a trick here by not capitalising on good practice of those coming in from industry and simply expecting the individuals to adapt to HE with no value placed on reciprocity.

Pracademia Tomorrow?

Strong sectoral cultures lead to tunnel vision for both academics and business practitioners, resulting in missed opportunities for both parties. Synergies across these two worlds can be facilitated by pracademics who have an intimate cultural understanding of both. As indicated in the 'Pracademic Today' diagram (Fig. 12.1), HEIs currently do this with a range of initiatives such as Knowledge Transfer Partnerships (KTPs) and student projects. However, this is only scratching the surface. Even the suggested evolution of this model to 'Pracademia Tomorrow' (Fig. 12.2), itself aspirational, will still fall short of the true potential of a cultural revolution within HEIs. This could be a culture where it is expected, and seen as the norm, to have a balance of research and practice-based staff, recognising the value of industry experience and what it can bring to academia. Indeed, where HEIs are well-placed to develop practitioners' academic knowledge and skills, they should also consider the reverse and investigate and incentivise routes for academic-focused colleagues to gain and

Pracademia Tomorrow?

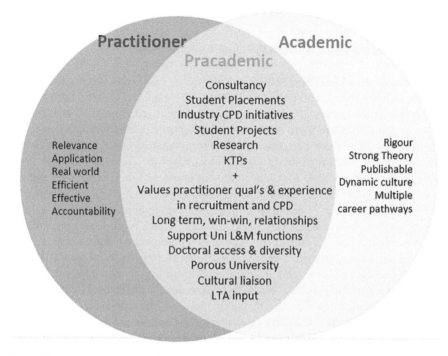

Fig. 12.2 Pracademia tomorrow?

maintain industry experience. This notion of both populations learning from each other, and this being recognised as positively contributing to career progression, would be a significant culture change signal internally and externally. I could see a future where *all* academics undertake a significant industry sabbatical every few years; creating vast opportunities and kick starting the culture change that is needed. Industry professionals could reciprocate and be hosted by HEIs for a period where they are supported to research the solutions to the business challenges of the day. We could build a culture where a KTP is just as valued as a high-ranking journal publication, where a professional doctorate has parity of esteem as a PhD, and a seasoned chief executive officer is as valued as a professor.

A Research Leader's Tale

My academic career has been far from typical, although I have spent most of the past 40 years of my working life in academic institutions. Much of my early career was spent on short-term research contracts in three university-based research centres, funded almost entirely by external grants and contracts. I did not complete my doctorate, started in 1980, until 27 years later when I was already in a senior position in one of these research centres. In between research contracts, I had three periods of working in economic consultancies, finally becoming research director of a small consultancy business. My first 'proper' academic post came in 2011, when I was appointed as senior lecturer in a research-intensive business school. I have since taken up research leadership roles, including five years as Associate Dean in a business school, with a mission to 'transform lives' through applied research, teaching, and learning.

Reflecting on my own journey, I would not describe myself as a typical pracademic, despite having spent around 10 years working in commercial organisations, nor have I followed a traditional academic career path. Until 10 years ago, my working environment was more akin to private sector consultancies, and the skills that I acquired were helpful when I entered the 'real' consultancy sector. Performance was measured in relation to income targets, financial contribution, and client satisfaction, rather than publications or scholarly impact. Fortunately for my academic career, I produced sufficient academic outputs to enable me to obtain a doctorate by published works and eventually be awarded the title of Professor.

I often reflect that, had I entered the academic world for the first time during the past 10 years or so, it would have been highly unlikely that I would have been appointed as a lecturer, let alone reach the level of professor and academic leader. Newly-appointed colleagues face enormous pressure to publish in well-regarded journals while simultaneously providing high quality teaching and learning, and achieving 'impact' through engagement with external stakeholders. For those entering business schools following a sometimes-prolonged period of working in business, public sector or not-for-profit organisations, the pressures can be even more intense, to the point of negating the potentially positive contribution that these colleagues can make to research, teaching, learning, and external impact.

My co-author's experience of imposter syndrome is reflected in my own feelings, despite having spent a considerable proportion of my career in academic institutions. My lack of a doctoral qualification, and a publication record that contains a large number of 'non-standard' outputs, put me at a disadvantage – or so I felt – in relation to many of my peers. It did not occur to me that my experience of winning research grants and consultancy projects, managing these projects, liaising with partners and clients, managing teams of highly qualified colleagues, and meeting challenging deadlines within tight resource constraints, were potentially valuable in the academic world. Unfortunately, neither did this occur to many institutional leaders, who viewed research success primarily in terms of publications, research grants, and successful supervision of doctoral students (incidentally something that can be difficult for pracademics to achieve).

In my long experience in academia and consultancy, I have worked with many colleagues who might have been labelled as 'pracademics', even before the term became popular in the academic literature. Some of the most effective teachers in fields such as marketing and business strategy, entered academia from business or professional practice, in most cases without doctorates or records of academic publications. Several of these colleagues quickly returned to practice, whereas others became immersed in the academic world, becoming published authors, and in some cases attaining senior academic or professorial status. But these colleagues are in the minority. Many remain in academia as highly effective, popular, and hard-working colleagues, who go largely unnoticed by the academic hierarchy. Their achievements in relation to business engagement, networking, and knowledge exchange tend not to be recognised in recruitment or promotion criteria. As a result, the cultural shifts that are necessary to reduce the rigour-relevance gap are extremely slow in emerging, and the existing academic culture dominates in most business schools.

Many of my colleagues in applied research and consultancy had the potential to develop into effective academics or pracademics if they so wished. In most cases they did not do so, preferring to remain in consultancy or to move into leadership roles in the not-for-profit, social enterprise, or public sectors. Whether this is by choice, or whether structural factors inhibited moves into the academic world, I would argue that many of these former colleagues could make significant contributions to business school research and teaching, had the pracademic route been more open to them at the time. The concept of the "porous" university (Stewart, 2015) is highly relevant to the business school mission, and many of my former colleagues could – in principle – play a significant role in bringing together the worlds of academia and business leadership.

My experience of working with, and latterly leading, colleagues with non-standard academic career histories reflects both my own and my co-author's observations that business schools are not, in general, making the most of the potential of pracademics to help to address one of the most pressing strategic issues facing business schools. There is a need to maintain high academic standards, while addressing wider societal challenges and preparing students for the complex and challenging world of the future (Cornuel et al., 2022; Moratis & Melissen, 2022). While there are many examples of business schools achieving societal impact with the contribution of pracademics (CABS, 2021), there are equally many examples of unfulfilled potential, leading in some cases to pracademics returning to practice or going native by transforming into career academics focused on producing academic outputs in journals, with limited impact on practice.

Conclusion

Enhancing Pracademics' Contribution to Business School Success

Several institutions have put in place procedures and programmes to assist pracademics to transition into academic roles. For example, Sheffield Hallam University introduced an "Academic Careers Framework" that sets out three potential routes to promotion; Research and Innovation, Teaching and Learning, and External and

Professional Engagement (Sheffield Hallam University, 2020), with guidance and mentoring to support colleagues through the process. These initiatives have had varying degrees of success, but it is notable that their overwhelming focus is upon assimilating recruits with practice backgrounds into the culture, routines, processes, and expectations of academia. For example, newly-recruited pracademics are typically required, or encouraged, to attend refresher or conversion teaching courses and (like other new recruits) to participate in various courses designed to ensure that they are familiar with institutional rules, regulations, and processes regarding finance, equality and diversity, health and safety, and so on. The direction of travel, in terms of integration, is almost exclusively one way. There is little recognition of the experience and insights brought into the institution by recruits from outside of academia.

We argue, therefore, that academic institutions such as business schools have a lot to do to ensure that they are adapting to, and maximising the benefit from, the experiences, skills, and cultures that pracademics can bring to the academic world. Rebalancing the integration process to encourage two-way learning as well as one-way assimilation is essential, and this needs to be built into business school cultures and activities as pracademics become more embedded in, and influential on, teaching, learning, and research. We suggest the following as starting points for discussion.

More flexibility is needed around qualification requirements for lecturing posts, and simultaneously greater recognition of the value to business schools of business and related experience and qualifications. Most business schools now require a doctorate (completed or at least in progress) as a minimum qualification for entry-level lecturing posts. This immediately rules out many people with the potential to make a huge contribution to both rigour and relevance, and advantages those who have chosen the 'pure' academic route, potentially exacerbating the rigour-relevance gap.

Having said this, we recognise the importance of business school faculty obtaining higher-level qualifications, notably doctorates. This is reinforced, for example, by accrediting bodies such as The Association to Advance Collegiate Schools of Business, which expect most business school academics to be qualified to doctoral level. Almost by definition, pracademics have had fewer opportunities to undertake doctoral study which – in the UK at least – tends to be of limited perceived value in the business environment. Therefore, support, financial and in terms of time, for newly-appointed pracademics should be provided to complete doctoral qualifications. This has been the case in the authors' current business school, with several colleagues (including one of the authors) achieving doctorates while working as lecturers.

The conventional route to a doctorate, through 3- or 4-years' full-time study to achieve a PhD qualification, is not appropriate for most pracademics who have considerable professional and life experience, but limited time to undergo conventional PhD research. 'Non-standard' routes such as professional doctorates (for example, the Doctor of Business Administration), or doctorates by publication, represent more viable and appropriate routes, and indeed many pracademics have followed this path. However, there remains an often-unstated privileging of 'standard' PhDs over other routes among a sizeable group of academics, which can lead pracademic colleagues to believe that they are achieving an inferior qualification that has a lower status than a conventional PhD. This needs to change, and business schools have an important role to play in promoting the benefits of diverse routes to doctoral qualifications.

Academic institutions should be more open to recognising professional and business experience and qualifications in career development processes. Typically, such qualifications are of limited value to pracademics seeking promotion, especially through career pathways linked to research achievement. Even in the growing number of institutions – including the authors' – for which external engagement is seen as a legitimate route to promotion, qualifications, and experience gained outside of the academic environment tend to be treated less favourably than academic qualifications, outputs, and 'citizenship'.

Most business school pracademics have travelled in one direction – from practice to academia – with the flow from 'pure' academia to practice being relatively light. One reason for this is the limited practical value of doctoral qualifications, but it also reflects the difficulty of returning to academia after a period in practice. Research outputs, teaching experience, and citizenship all suffer, and experience outside academia is, as we have argued, not highly valued in promotion processes. One of the authors is unusual in that his career journey involved three 'return trips' from practice to academia, but this is not common. The creation of 'porous business schools' would be a significant step in the direction of making it easier for academics to move into non-academic roles outside HE, and to return to HE without detriment to their career ambitions in either context.

It is important to ensure that the skills and experience of pracademics are utilised effectively to improve business schools' processes and, where appropriate, to develop staff and student skills in areas such as project management, team leadership, and relationship management. Assigning pracademics, together with academics and professional service colleagues, to lead improvement projects, and recognising the value of this type of contribution in performance evaluation and promotion processes, would be a good way of capitalising on the experience of pracademics.

Business schools should approach industry-based research with a win-win focus, not just simply collecting data and vanishing. Pracademics can play a significant role in sharing analysis and results with external partners and exploring other opportunities for synergies. In so doing, business schools can enhance the value and recognition of building and maintaining links with industry for mutual benefit.

Routes for business and other stakeholders to access HE are still rather opaque, even for the most partnership-focused of business schools (Rybnicek & Königsgruber, 2019). There is much expertise in universities that can add value to practice, but businesses see HEIs as complex and bureaucratic; just finding the right person to talk to can be onerous and often a bridge too far. Pracademics, with their experience, background, context, and practice-driven approach to communication, can play an important role in helping businesses to navigate the complexities of collaborating with business schools, and vice versa.

Finally, as illustrated by one of the authors' experiences, pracademics should work closely with experienced academics in developing learning content, in particular building case studies from their experiences. This, of course, requires pracademics to develop their teaching and learning skills, but crucially it requires parity of esteem and mutual respect between academic and practice-based knowledge, adding value to the experiences of colleagues, students, and the wider business community. Building such a culture is central to addressing the rigour-relevance gap and to ensuring that business schools continue to be relevant to addressing the challenging issues that will face us all in future.

Points for Reflection
- Johnson and Ellis focus on pracademia within the context of business schools. To what extent might there be differences in the experiences of pracademics from more 'professional' disciplines such as education, law, or health?
- Within this chapter, a number of suggestions are made as to how HEIs could adjust to ensure that they are best-placed to maximise the benefits from pracademia. Could you suggest any other approaches for recognising and rewarding practical experience and qualifications in recruitment and promotion, while ensuring high academic standards?
- Johnson and Ellis highlight a number of routes to achieving a doctorate, including the professional doctorate and the doctorate by publication. How could the perceived value of such 'non-standard' routes to doctoral qualifications be enhanced?
- This chapter advocates for 'porous' business schools that bring together practice and academia. What could such schools look like and how can parity of esteem between academics and pracademics be achieved?

References

AACSB. (2022, July 1). *2020 AACSB Business Accreditation Standards*. https://www.aacsb.edu/-/media/documents/accreditation/2020-aacsb-business-accreditation-standards-jul-1-2022.pdf

Bennis, W. G., & O'Toole, J. (2005). How business schools lost their way. *Harvard Business Review, 83*, 96–104.

CABS. (2021). *Business schools and the public good*. Chartered Association of Business Schools. https://charteredabs.org/publications/chartered-abs-taskforce-report-business-schools-and-the-public-good/

Cornuel, E., Thomas, H., & Wood, M. (Eds.). (2022). *The value & purpose of management education: Looking back and thinking forward in global focus*. Routledge.

Dickinson, J., Fowler, A., & Griffiths, T. (2022). Pracademics? Exploring transitions and professional identities in higher education. *Studies in Higher Education, 47*(2), 290–304. https://doi.org/10.1080/03075079.2020.1744123

Gulati, R. (2007). Tent poles, tribalism, and boundary spanning: The rigor-relevance debate in management research. *Academy of Management Journal, 50*(4), 775–782.

Hollweck, T., Netolicky, D. M., & Campbell, P. (2021). Defining and exploring pracademia: Identity, community, and engagement. *Journal of Professional Capital and Community, 7*(1), 6–25. https://doi.org/10.1108/JPCC-05-2021-0026

Irwin, A. (2019). Re-making 'quality' within the social sciences: The debate over rigour and relevance in the modern business school. *The Sociological Review, 67*(1), 194–209. https://doi.org/10.1177/0038026118782403

Kieser, A., & Leiner, L. (2009). Why the rigour–relevance gap in management research is unbridgeable. *Journal of Management Studies, 46*(3), 516–533.

McNatt, D., Glassman, M., & Glassman, A. (2010). The great academic-practitioner divide: A tale of two paradigms. *Global Education Journal, 3*, 6–22.

Moratis, L., & Melissen, F. (2022, May 31). The future of business schools: Existential innovation or obsolescence? *GlobalFocus.* https://www.globalfocusmagazine.com/the-future-of-business-schools-existential-innovation-or-obsolescence/

Panda, A. (2014). Bringing academic and corporate worlds closer: We need pracademics. *Management and Labour Studies, 39*(2), 140–159. https://doi.org/10.1177/0258042X14558174

REF 2021: Research Excellence Framework. (2022). *About the REF.* https://www.ref.ac.uk/about-the-ref/

RRBM. (2022). A vision of responsible management in Business and management: Position paper. *RRBM network.* https://www.rrbm.network/position-paper/

Rybnicek, R., & Königsgruber, R. (2019). What makes industry–university collaboration succeed? A systematic review of the literature. *Journal of Business Economics, 89*, 221–250. https://doi.org/10.1007/s11573-018-0916-6

Sheffield Hallam University. (2020, September 1). *Academic Careers Framework v4.* https://blogs.shu.ac.uk/acf/files/2020/11/Academic-Careers-Framework-v4.pdf

Stewart, M. (2015, May 12). *The Porous University: Impact is not some added extra of academic life, but lies at the core of what we do.* Impact of Social Sciences. https://blogs.lse.ac.uk/impactofsocialsciences/2015/05/12/the-porous-university-michael-stewart/

Susskind, L. (2013). Confessions of a pracademic: Searching for a virtuous cycle of theory building, teaching, and action research. *Negotiation Journal, 29*(2), 225–237. https://doi.org/10.1111/nejo.12020

Professor Steve Johnson is Professor of Business and Innovation at Leeds Trinity University and Emeritus Professor at Sheffield Hallam University. He has held research leadership positions in three UK business schools, and he was director of a small economic and policy consultancy. Throughout his career Steve has operated at the intersection of research, practice and policy, and he is passionate about reforming research assessment and career pathways to recognise the diverse contribution and impact of the academic community. Steve sits on the Research Committee of the Chartered Association of Business Schools and is a Board member of the Institute for Small Business and Entrepreneurship.

Dr Mark Ellis joined academia in 2012 after more than twenty years as a leader and manager across several sectors (Adventure Education, Management Consultancy and International NGO work). His teaching focus is around Strategy, Innovation and Sustainability at both undergraduate and postgraduate level, where he also supervises PG and doctoral candidates. He works directly with SMEs in the Sheffield City region as an Innovation Expert on the Chartered Association of Business Schools Help to Grow programme. He is currently lead academic on a two-year knowledge transfer project with a Sheffield based manufacturer. His post-doctoral research is in the field of Responsible Leadership.

Part III
Teaching Practice

Chapter 13
The Value of Pracademics – Uniquely Placed to Enhance Student Employability

Sally Skea

Abstract This chapter aims to discuss the increasing value of pracademics in today's HE environment at a time when student employability is experiencing one of its most challenging periods. It will draw on relevant employability literature to examine the key areas of student employability that pracademics can enhance, and are increasingly needed by institutions for, to provide the industry insight and experience which the traditional academic teaching path may be less well-placed to offer. Throughout the chapter, the author will share experiences as an events management practitioner for 20 years, who, after combining part-time teaching with industry practice, made the career transition to academia just as the COVID-19 pandemic began and the global live events industry was reduced to almost nothing overnight. The author, by choice, works to a fractional teaching contract in order to keep industry experience and contacts active through a retained level of practice, and the chapter will explore the benefits and challenges of being a dual practitioner, offering practical tips and guidance to those considering how best to balance teaching with keeping practical knowledge and experience current. It also aims to consider the advice that pracademics can offer to aspiring pracademics contemplating entering the university environment.

Keywords Employability skills · Graduate employment · Pracademic · Industry · Professional practice · Practitioner · Dual identity · Experiential learning · Employability theory · Employability policy

S. Skea (✉)
School of Humanities and Performing Arts, De Montfort University, Leicester, UK
e-mail: sally.skea@dmu.ac.uk

J. Dickinson, T.-L. Griffiths (eds.), *Professional Development for Practitioners in Academia*, Knowledge Studies in Higher Education 13,
https://doi.org/10.1007/978-3-031-33746-8_13

At a Glance
- Outlines today's higher education (HE) environment in relation to student employability policy.
- Examines the pracademic's role in enhancing key aspects of student employability, via industry insight and experience.
- Explores the benefits and challenges of becoming a pracademic and dual practitioner, one who remains in practice and academia concurrently.
- Offers practical tips and guidance for balancing teaching with maintaining industry knowledge and experience, and to aspiring pracademics who may be contemplating entering the academic environment.

Introduction

Graduate Employability: What it Means and Where We Are Now

Graduate employability is a frequently discussed and contested topic. Some of the key issues central to this debate include whether graduates are 'work-ready', and if they possess the transferable skills and attributes needed for successful transition and career progression within the workplace (Chartered Management Institute [CMI], 2021a, b; Snowdon, 2011; Succi & Canovi, 2019; Swain, 2019; Yorke, 2006). From an employer perspective, this is key to business efficiency and is the oft-cited reason for the apparent disparity between the two environments; what employers need, and the attributes of university graduates (Institute of Student Employers [ISE], 2021; Webber, 2019). My experiences as an industry practitioner, where I have been in a position to witness new graduates embark on their first roles, has left me with similar questions.

The CBI/Pearson report of 2019, *Education and learning for the modern world,* found that businesses considered 17% of graduates were not 'workplace-ready' (CBI/Pearson, 2019). The 2021 CMI report two years later, *Work Ready Graduates: Building employability skills for a hybrid world,* ascertained that almost 80% of employers did not consider graduates to be 'work-ready'. This initial impression suggests a worrying downward trend in employer perceptions, one which may pose a significant challenge for universities today, with the skills gap projected to increase in a future digital and hybrid world (CMI, 2021a, b). However, this should also be balanced against the increasing visibility and understanding of employability arising from evolving economic conditions (Lowden et al., 2011), and the potential influence this may have on employer perceptions. Meanwhile, Yorke (2006), a leading authority in employability studies, suggests the significant adaptation required by students from education to work environments may often create a demand and supply disparity between the desires of employers for role-ready graduates, and the "preparedness" of graduates that higher education (HE) is able to provide.

To further understand the implications of these initial statistics, let us explore what it means to be 'workplace-ready', by considering Yorke's widely-regarded definition of employability as:

> a set of achievements – skills, understandings and personal attributes – that make graduates more likely to gain employment and be successful in their chosen occupations, which benefits themselves, the workforce, the community and the economy. (Yorke, 2004, p. 7)

Whilst acknowledging that his definition is founded on probability, rather than certainty, and context (Yorke, 2006), it still provides a useful benchmark for understanding the essence of employability in relation to graduates. Advancing the definition of employability specifically to the 'graduate employment' context, Firth (2020) defines this as:

> obtaining work or travel opportunities, where you are paid or trained within a specific sector or role. It does not relate to a specific salary or level of employment, but signals your ability to gain a contract of employment after completing your studies. (p. 51)

Yorke (2006) stresses the need to differentiate between the concepts of employability and employment, yet the consistent focus on ultimately gaining employment is clear. Firth's (2020, p. 51) subsequent attention to the "ability" of graduates to secure sector specific roles emphasises the industry agenda, reflecting the important voice of employers as decision-makers, and their perspectives of competency.

How Can 'Pracademics' Contribute to Student Employability?

Now we have established what is perceived by employers to be the current situation in graduate employability, let us turn our attention to the concept of pracademia, and more precisely, to the professionals at the centre of this field, 'pracademics', and what they may have to offer. In defining pracademics, Dickinson et al. (2020) seek to further the work of Posner (2009) by proposing pracademics to be "former and/or current practitioners who are now academics within HE" (Dickinson et al., 2020, p. 5). Specifically, the term neatly fuses industry practice with academia, describing a "scholar-practitioner who draws from both sides" (Wilson, 2015, p. 28). Therefore, with their dual insight of industry and academic environments, what is the role of the pracademic in enhancing student employability?

Of 11 key employability skills that are identified by the CBI (2021a, b), the three considered most important by employers are: team-working, critical thinking and problem-solving, and communication. Two of these skills (communication and team-working) were previously identified by Yorke (2006) as areas for development from the perspective of employers, demonstrating the importance placed over almost two decades on these key attributes. The discussion to follow will explore the contribution that pracademics can bring to these skills:

I. **Teamworking:** a fundamental component of workplace environments and an employability skill about which pracademics can convey first-hand experiences with theoretical underpinning. Pracademics can create learning environments which provide realistic, workplace teamwork opportunities that enable students to build their teamworking skills and philosophies on a cumulative basis through experiential learning, as reflective of a constructivist, pedagogical approach (Fry et al., 2009). Live experiences and opportunities for reflection using frameworks, such as The Kolb Learning Cycle (Fry et al., 2009), can be facilitated through team/group projects in the classroom with assigned roles and responsibilities, representative of industry, and linked to theory. Outside the classroom, this can also be achieved through team/group projects and realistic, workplace-relevant assessments (Dickfos, 2019), supporting Wilson's view that "theory needs to be arrived at through practical experience. Theory as knowledge is useful when engaged through experience—the real value beyond thinking" (2015, p. 29).

Pracademics can also facilitate the acquisition of teamwork skills through arranging volunteering experiences for students via industry contacts, thus providing students with hands-on opportunities to work with teams in a range of workplace environments and valuable experience to add to their CVs. The organisations also benefit from this arrangement through increased resource, whilst simultaneously gaining an important understanding of the emerging workforce generation and their attitudes towards work:

> By understanding them, the organizations can determine what can impact their recruitment and retention success through paying attention to what makes this generation tick in the workplace. (Gaidhani et al., 2019, p. 2804)

Organising volunteering experiences for students through my industry contacts and collaborations is something that I personally have chosen to adopt within my own pedagogical approach. For example, arranging volunteering at events at which I am also working as a contractor is an illustration of how education can meet industry for mutual benefit.

II. **Critical thinking and problem-solving**: an employability skill which is optimally developed through a constructivist approach to help students construct and accumulate their learning through direct experience of realistic workplace tasks which require the application of critical thinking and problem-solving skills. A pracademic's industry experience and contacts can be significant in guiding this learning need through workplace-relevant tasks, a view supported by Dickfos who discusses the positive contribution made by pracademics to developing student employability via "modelling, scaffolding and coaching employability skills gained through their pracademic experiences" (2019, p. 243).

III. **Communication**: a wide-ranging skillset for delivering and receiving information through a variety of written, listening, verbal, and non-verbal means. Professional experience of diverse working environments and stakeholders equips pracademics with extensive verbal and non-verbal communication skills to impart. This may also increase their ability to engage students from broad cultural backgrounds (Posner, 2009). Meanwhile, standard industry practices such as negotiation, cooperation, and mediation further contribute to a pracademic's capacity to impart experience, knowledge, and wisdom to students.

The ability to write professionally as well as academically is also a key skill that pracademics can support, by creating teaching and assessment activities involving realistic workplace reports and working with industry contacts to provide students with consultancy projects and 'live' briefs. Once again, this reflects the constructivist, experiential learning approach that is core to this topic of pracademic contribution (Fry et al., 2009). Nonetheless, it should be acknowledged that professional communication skills are not the exclusive domain of pracademics. Many career academics possess these skills through research activity and may also provide valuable support to students in these areas.

The Higher Education Sector Approach to Addressing Employability

As a sector, HE in the United Kingdom (UK) has made strides in embracing employability. The bedrock of the narrative, and subsequent university strategies, is reflective of Advance HE's *Embedding Employability model*, developed in 2019, and aimed at integrating employability throughout HE practice. The purpose of the model is to provide universities with a framework through which to consider their current employability practices and policies, and identify areas for introduction and change. Based on three underpinning principles of inclusivity, collaboration, and engagement, the application of the framework involves a four-stage process: (1) defining employability, (2) auditing and mapping, (3) prioritising actions, and (4) measuring impact. Meanwhile, the 'inner' sections provide a blend of ten core areas of focus and delivery that, collectively, are considered at the heart of graduate employability. The suitability of the model in responding to today's employability challenges is validated through the noticeable synergy of its ten core areas of focus with the 11 key skills identified by employers as the essential competencies of employability (CMI, 2021a, b).

These ten core areas of the framework are significant when considering the contribution that pracademics can make to HE. Several areas are discussed in this chapter as they illuminate the pracademic's practical 'tools of the trade', which can be usefully deployed in developing student graduate and employability skills, thus responding to employers' skills needs. Nevertheless, despite the growth of the pracademic movement in education in recent years (Eacott, 2022), the broader educational context would suggest a continuing decline in employer confidence of 'work-ready' graduates, indicating wider factors at play beyond the contribution of pracademics.

To advance the HE sector's insight and knowledge of employability, Advance HE published a comprehensive review of the literature surrounding employability from 2016 and 2021, concentrating on peer-reviewed journal articles (Dalrymple et al., 2021). The review seeks to ascertain the verifiable effects and 'impacts' of integrating employability within HE (Advance HE, 2021). Amongst its discoveries was that employability is now measured on an expanded range of qualitative criteria and outcomes beyond that of the original, and somewhat simplistic, means of graduate salary and associated factors. These new measurements consider wider-reaching metrics and scope, with a noticeable shift towards qualitative metrics relating to what are summarised as "personal constructs and self-defined measures" (Dalrymple et al., 2021, p. 15). These new factors include areas such as graduate role satisfaction in relation to aspirations, social contribution and personal values, and wellbeing, placing students and the differing situational influences that they face at the centre of the narrative, offering a more comprehensive interpretation of the data. Furthermore, the European Commission's acknowledgement of Covid-19's unparalleled effects on global HE and its range of emotional and psychological challenges to students (Farnell et al., 2021), indicates that these broader situational and environmental factors impacting students cannot be ignored.

A practical focus of Advance HE's review was to explore the links between opportunities for experiential learning activities (for example, placements, internships, volunteering), and employability outcomes. This evaluation of 'in-course provision' found notable evidence to suggest a correlation between those courses, which integrate experiential learning opportunities with improved employability outcomes. Specifically, beneficial links were demonstrated between 'embedded curricula internships' and reduced unemployment levels, as well as between placement opportunities and increased probability of securing suitable graduate roles and higher entry salaries. Student volunteering opportunities were also found to have beneficial consequences through the interpersonal skills acquired during social exchanges (Goodman & Tredway, 2016, as cited in Dalrymple et al., 2021).

As previously mentioned, pracademics are highly-suited to contributing towards 'in-course' provision of placements, internships, and volunteering through their close industry links and professional experience. The subsequently proven ability of in-course provision to enhance employability prospects (Dalrymple et al., 2021) further demonstrates the link between pracademics and enhancing student employability.

Key Themes

The Value of Pracademics; Personal Reflections of a 'New Recruit'

The focus of this chapter is an exploration of the contribution of pracademics to enhancing the employability skills of students. The following discussion will relate personal insights from my experience as a pracademic including, how and why

I chose this dual-industry identity, the value it holds in my discipline, and why I continue to choose this combination of roles today.

Prior to joining academia, I worked in the major events industry for 20-plus years, predominantly in the sports events sector. I worked in a range of full-time and part-time, employed, and self-employed or freelance roles, with a significant range of organisations and individuals whilst developing a valuable network of contacts. The period through which I operated as an event practitioner has spanned three decades, and for me personally, the journey to enter academia at a later stage in my career was made for several reasons. Firstly, I had reached a stage of life that 'giving something back' had become more important to me. Added to which, the reality of the events sector with its long hours and intense work periods (Event Academy, 2022) interspersed with 'career gaps' in work (intentional and circumstantial) did not attract and motivate me in the way that it once had, which led me to seek something more stable and consistent. At this point, alongside continuing industry freelance work, I decided to gain teaching experience as an hourly-paid associate lecturer and, at the same time, study for a Postgraduate Certificate in Teaching in Higher Education (PCTHE) in my own time. This was an ideal scenario for me as it enabled me to teach and study from September to May, and undertake freelance events work for the summer months.

As an associate lecturer teaching on events and marketing degree programmes, I discovered both my enjoyment of teaching and the opportunity to impart my experience with theoretical underpinning to aspiring professionals. At the same time, my personal experience of studying alongside teaching was very valuable and, having previously been away from HE for 20 years, it enabled me to truly understand what it means, and feels like, to be a student today. This, in turn, equipped me with experience and appreciation of the key aspects of the learning process, such as theory comprehension and reasoning skills (Fry et al., 2009), and the influence of context on learning styles (Firth, 2020). The experience helped me to acquire the technical skills needed both to learn and teach in the digital environment, and importantly to have a 'user' appreciation of virtual learning environment (VLE) functionality, including its strengths and weaknesses. This knowledge now helps to inform how I shape my teaching materials and VLE offering for my own students.

With a positive experience behind me, on graduating from the PCTHE, I made the decision to apply for a permanent, part-time role teaching Events Management in March 2020, whilst continuing to work for industry clients on a reduced, part-time basis. The timing of this career shift was significant, as what no one could predict at that time was the arrival of the Covid-19 pandemic, subsequent lockdown measures, and the huge impact on every facet of life; in particular, its destructive influence on the global events industries as one of the most significantly affected sectors (Madray, 2020). Restrictions imposed through lockdowns and social distancing measures resulted in the postponement or cancellation of live events and conferences (McGrath, 2022) and by as early as March 2020, $16.5 billion had been wiped off the global events industry's value (Fingar, 2021). Within the UK events sector alone, economic assessments in 2021 indicated business shortfalls could represent up to 81% of the industry's pre-pandemic value, and a value reduction from £70 billion to £57 billion overall (Business Visits and Events Partnership [BVEP], 2021).

For me personally in 2020, this meant an immediate loss of freelance work and simultaneously a renewed gratitude for the new teaching career that I had worked towards. As the pandemic progressed, I worked at a limited number of events in 2021, which returned with Covid-compliant measures to ensure the safe delivery of events in a controlled, modified environment to reduced audiences. As an events management pracademic, this practical, live experience of delivering events during a pandemic served as a unique experience to draw on and share with students, one which teaching colleagues who are not actively engaged in the industry may find difficult to match.

My industry experience was a key factor in being tasked to create and lead a new final year undergraduate module focused on employability in the events industry, which aimed to aid students with their events sector professional development. This type of employability module is commonly offered at universities in a generic way and is designed to prepare students for the 'education to workplace' transition. It also provides a useful example of Advance HE's Embedding Employability model (2019) in action. As this new module was bespoke to events management students, it provided me with an opportunity to use industry experience to design teaching and assessment materials related to the needs and skills of industry. From providing information on current industry trends and skills agendas; organising guest speaker sessions; sharing industry contacts, case studies, and practice-based anecdotes; highlighting volunteering opportunities; making LinkedIn connections; and a knowledge of graduate job vacancies, I was able to bring first-hand, professional insight for the students. This pedagogical approach was made possible through my continuation as a dual industry pracademic. It also addresses aspects of the industry engagement deficiencies identified in a pre-pandemic study of event management graduates (Barron & Ali-Knight, 2017) which found that respondents did not feel equipped with the necessary practical attributes for the working world, seeking "an increase in the opportunities for developing practical experience, perhaps through university organised industrial placements and enhanced industry engagement" (p. 37). Interestingly, Barron and Ali-Knight's (2017) study shows that, when reflecting on their academic provision, respondents also considered that their university programme had educated them well for future work. The study has acknowledged limitations in scope, being conducted at one Scottish university, yet it nevertheless provides useful insight into the perceptions of events management students, with regards to the educational development opportunities afforded to them.

As I write two years later, the effects of the pandemic have lessened, and the events industry is in recovery. During this period, I changed academic roles and moved to De Montfort University (DMU) which values industry experience and places employability as an integral element of its student offering. Recognised at the *National Undergraduate Employability (NUE) Awards* in 2021 with the award of Best University Careers/Employability Service, DMU offers a range of student support services including placement and volunteering opportunities, extra-curricular and co-curricular employability activities, and mentoring (Complete University Guide, 2021). These services reflect several of the 'inner' areas of Advance HEs *Embedding Employability model* (2019), most notably Career guidance and management and Experience and Networks.

When recruiting to my role, the university sought an individual with industry experience and contacts in addition to teaching proficiency, and on a part-time basis. Consequently, I now teach on sport management and events programmes, which specifically align to my ongoing industry role and contacts, whilst continuing to remain actively involved in industry. Key to the teaching role is working with industry contacts on experiential learning opportunities, including placements and volunteering, student consultancy projects, developing mentoring and employability skills, guest speaker sessions, and networking, all of which I can contribute to from first-hand experience, contacts, and knowledge as a pracademic.

The choice to remain a part-time teacher *and* part-time industry practitioner, and therefore 'active' in both areas, is a conscious one, and is what qualifies me a pracademic, a "scholar-practitioner who draws from both sides" (Wilson, 2015, p. 28). The primary reason for this is the mutual benefit I consider each role gains from the co-existence of the other. My pedagogical approach to teaching is informed, exemplified, and ultimately enhanced by my past and ongoing experience and professional identity as an industry practitioner (Dickinson et al., 2020), alongside contacts with potential employers. I consider myself equipped to be a better teacher of my discipline because of my industry role. Simultaneously, my industry work benefits from the insight that I have into the skills and aspirations of the young people in HE today whose aim it is to become the workforce of tomorrow.

Insight and Guidance for Those Considering the 'Dual Identity'

I will conclude this chapter by offering some thoughts on the benefits and challenges of becoming a dual practitioner and provide insight to those considering how best to balance teaching with ensuring that industry knowledge, contacts, and experience remain current.

Benefits and Rewards

Firstly, I feel fortunate to have the opportunity to work in two industries creating mutual and tangible benefits between them. It is a distinct and individual way of working, and not for everyone. Personally, I enjoy the distinction and variety of work, which allows me to do what I enjoy on three levels:

(a) Teach in the classroom and develop working relationships with students over time, using my experience to enhance their employability prospects and outcomes overall.
(b) Deliver live events within professional events teams in commercial environments and in varying locations.
(c) Combine the above – and work with industry contacts for mutual education and industry benefits, such as student volunteering, placements and projects, guest speakers, and networking opportunities.

Secondly, the two 'worlds' are very different and understanding this is key (Panda, 2014; Powell et al., 2018). Working in such diverse environments offers a unique opportunity to work with a cross-section of individuals, organisations, skillsets, cultures, mindsets, language, attitudes, management structures, leadership styles, and strategic directions. It requires adaptability, communication, and interpersonal skills. It is not always easy but is ultimately rewarding, whilst simultaneously providing continuing professional and personal development, as acknowledged by Dickfos who considers the pracademic experience as "an essential component of a comprehensive framework of continuing professional development" (Dickfos, 2019, p. 253).

There are also advantages that pracademics can bring to curriculum development. Possessing current industry insight and experience equips pracademics with the ability to provide a swifter level of responsiveness to meeting curriculum, macro environmental challenges, and 'gaps'. The relationship between curricula and industry is further explored by Dickfos (2019) who suggests that "teaching practices may improve as critical curriculum gaps are identified and the curriculum aligned with current professional practice" (p. 243). Designing teaching materials which address authentic environmental and sector challenges, in addition to writing assessment briefs which assess current workplace skills, are examples of the responsiveness that pracademics can offer to curricula development.

Finally, the dual identity of being a pracademic offers what I personally consider to be a potential vision of how HE and industry can successfully develop together. Those universities which have this vision, giving high regard and opportunity to teaching staff with professional skills and industry experience, may be in a position to capitalise on this expertise for the employability of their students and the benefit of industry. A contrary view is offered by Yorke (2006), who suggests that, rather than being responsible for students' preparedness for the world of work, the actual role of HE is as facilitator, and the end of the HE journey signifies a natural point of adaptation and challenge for students as they enter the workplace. Meanwhile, Collini (2012) proposes that the true raison d'être of universities is to be culturally and educationally diverse institutions with distinctive offerings and roles, rather than being economically-driven and measured. It is clear therefore that a range of views exist around the purpose and value of universities, and it is perhaps an individual perspective according to personal circumstance.

The Challenges for Pracademics Today

For balance, it is also important to discuss the challenges in relation to this career path with its characteristic dual professional identities. Being partially involved in two industries means that full immersion in either is hard to achieve, and the transition between them may prove problematic and disordered (Dickinson et al., 2020). Indeed, a level of self-acceptance is needed of the limitations that partial involvement in an industry brings, and that one cannot offer the same time commitment as a full-time individual can. Personal discipline is also required to ensure that the time spent on each role is balanced according to the contractual obligation. Peaks and troughs exist in every industry, so at times of work pressure in either industry (fortunately for mine, the peaks tend to be at different times of the year), achieving some level of control over one's time is very important.

Nevertheless, professional identities continue to evolve and develop over time, and in the case of the pracademic, through the ongoing fluidity between their dual industry and education sector roles. According to Dickinson et al. (2020), the inter-relationships between the roles mean that the pracademic may notice their attitude towards academia becoming shaped by their industry identity. This is a point with which I agree, although from personal experience I suggest that this is in fact a two-way process, with a pracademic's approach to industry also being influenced by their role in academia. For those entering HE from industry, there is a cultural and organisational adaptation to be experienced, and many of the processes, practices, and information sources can be distinctly different (Posner, 2009). What is standard procedure in HE may not be the case in industry, and vice versa. Whilst this takes adjustment, some may see these variants as an opportunity for self-development and knowledge-exchange, which can be considered a 'strength' when mutual appreciation exists in both the educational and industry environments (Posner, 2009).

Finally, Kitchener (2021) identifies an inconsistency between the reduced appreciation that HE traditionally has for professional, industry skills and knowledge, compared to the extent to which these attributes are valued by industries outside the HE sector. This may be impactful to the pracademic on initial entry to academia from industry roles. However, Kitchener (2021) also points to a fundamental and positive turning of the tide in HE which may be attractive to pracademics. This sees universities and academics being more closely-measured on broader key performance indicators (KPIs), in addition to employment outcomes. Examples of measures are the quality of student experience, teaching excellence, and diversity (Office for Students [OfS], 2022) as well as the student-centric "personal constructs and self-defined measures" identified by Dalrymple et al. (2021, p. 15). These are areas which, as demonstrated throughout this chapter, pracademics are well-placed to contribute value to.

Conclusion

During the course of this chapter, I have attempted to offer an understanding of the frequently discussed subject of graduate employability, coupled with an insight according to recent industry reports into employers' views of the preparedness of graduates for work. The definition and attributes of 'pracademics' have been explored, and the case made for acknowledging and embracing the contribution that pracademics offer to student employability in aspects of today's HE environment.

Clearly, pracademics cannot be held accountable for, or solve, the issue of ensuring the steady flow of 'work-ready' graduates from universities; indeed, through the discussion of other works, a range of factors and perspectives should be taken into consideration. Nevertheless, it is hoped that this chapter has helped to illuminate the value that pracademics can bring to HE, and do already provide, through their teaching and guidance.

The discussion of personal experiences as a 'new pracademic recruit' in the field of events management is intended to provide insight, and to support the decision-making of those who may be considering the rewarding route of 'dual identity'. I wish good fortune and professional satisfaction to those who embark on the journey!

Points for Reflection
- Skea's focus is on student employability. For the aspiring pracademic, what contribution could you make to HE and to enhancing student employability through your industry experience, knowledge, and contacts?
- For those currently in HE, what value do pracademics hold in your institution? Is this appropriately utilised and recognised? Could you make use of Skea's work to map the pracademic contribution against models of employability to support this work?
- The author holds a dual role, as an academic and practitioner. Consider some of the advantages and disadvantages of such a role within your own discipline.

References

Advance HE. (2019). *Essential frameworks for enhancing student success*. Advance HE. https://www.advance-he.ac.uk/sites/default/files/2020-05/Embedding%20Employability%20in%20Higher%20Education%20Framework.pdf

Advance HE. (2021). *Employability: A review of the literature 2016–2021*. Advance HE. Retrieved March 8, 2022, from https://www.advance-he.ac.uk/knowledge-hub/employability-review-literature-2016-2021

Barron, P., & Ali-Knight, J. (2017). Aspirations and progression of event management graduates: A study of career development. *Journal of Hospitality and Tourism Management, 30*, 29–38.

BVEP. (2021, September 6). *The shape of events*. Business Visits and Events Partnership. https://ukevents.org.uk/component/phocadownload/category/10-other?download=446:the-shape-of-events-bvep-report

CBI/Pearson. (2019, November). *Education and learning for the modern world: CBI/Pearson Education and Skills Survey report 2019*. https://www.cbi.org.uk/media/3841/12546_tess_2019.pdf

CMI. (2021a). *Work ready graduates: Setting the professional standard*. https://www.managers.org.uk/wp-content/uploads/2021/09/WorkReadyGrads_SettingTheStandard_Infographic_2021.pdf

CMI. (2021b, September). *Work ready graduates: Building employability skills for a hybrid world.* https://www.managers.org.uk/wp-content/uploads/2021/09/employability-skills-research_work-ready-graduates.pdf

Collini, S. (2012). *What are universities for?* Penguin Books.

Complete University Guide. (2021). *De Montfort University.* https://www.thecompleteuniversityguide.co.uk/universities/de-montfort-university/student-employability

Dalrymple, R., Macrae, A., Pal, M., & Shipman, S. (2021). *Employability: A review of the literature 2016–2021.* Advance HE. https://www.advance-he.ac.uk/knowledge-hub/employability-review-literature-2016-2021

Dickfos, J. (2019). Academic professional development: Benefits of a pracademic experience. *International Journal of Work-Integrated Learning, 20*(3), 243–255.

Dickinson, J., Fowler, A., & Griffiths, T. (2020). Pracademics? Exploring transitions and professional identities in higher education. *Studies in Higher Education, 47*(2), 290–304. https://doi.org/10.1080/03075079.2020.1744123

Eacott, S. (2022). Pracademia: An answer but not the answer to an enduring question. *Journal of Professional Capital and Community, 7*(1), 57–70. https://doi.org/10.1108/JPCC-12-2020-0100

Event Academy. (2022, February 28). *What working in the events industry is really like.* https://eventacademy.com/events/what-working-in-the-events-industry-is-really-like/

Farnell, T., Matijević, A., & Schmidt, N. (2021). *The impact of COVID-19 on higher education: A review of emerging evidence.* Publications Office of the European Union. https://op.europa.eu/en/publication-detail/-/publication/876ce591-87a0-11eb-ac4c-01aa75ed71a1/language-en

Fingar, C. (2021, May 4). *Covid continues to wreak havoc on the events industry.* Investment Monitor. https://www.investmentmonitor.ai/investment-monitor-events/covid-wreak-havoc-events-industry

Firth, M. (2020). *Employability and skills handbook for tourism, Hospitality and Events Students.* Routledge.

Fry, H., Ketteridge, S., & Marshall, S. (Eds.). (2009). *Teaching and learning in higher education* (3rd ed.). Routledge.

Gaidhani, S., Arora, L., & Sharma, B. V. (2019). Understanding the attitude of Generation Z towards workplace. *International Journal of Management, Technology and Engineering, 9*(1), 2804–2812.

Institute of Student Employers. (2021, March 17). *Graduates lack work-ready skills that businesses need during Covid era, reports ISE Student Development Survey.* https://ise.org.uk/page/graduates-lack-work-ready-skills-that-businesses-need-during-covid-era

Kitchener, M. (2021). *Supporting academics' full-time transition from professional practice to university. A qualitative study.* Unpublished EdD thesis, Oxford Brookes University.

Lowden, K., Hall, S., Elliot, D., & Lewin, J. (2011). *Employers' perceptions of the employability skills of new graduates.* Edge Foundation and University of Glasgow SCRE Centre Research. https://www.educationandemployers.org/wp-content/uploads/2014/06/employability_skills_as_pdf_-_final_online_version.pdf

Madray, J. (2020). The impact of COVID-19 on event management industry. *International Journal of Engineering Applied Sciences and Technology, 5*(3), 533–535.

McGrath, D. (2022, January 25). Live events after Covid: The hangover 'will last for years'. *AV Magazine.* https://www.avinteractive.com/markets/live-events/live-events-covid-hangover-will-last-years-25-01-2022/

Office for Students (OfS). (2022, July 26). *Student outcomes and teaching excellence.* https://www.officeforstudents.org.uk/publications/student-outcomes-and-teaching-excellence-consultations/

Panda, A. (2014). Bringing academic and corporate worlds closer: We need pracademics. *Management and Labour Studies, 39*(2), 140–159. https://doi.org/10.1177/0258042X14558174

Posner, P. L. (2009). The Pracademic: An agenda for re-engaging practitioners and academics. *Public Budgeting & Finance, 29*(1), 12–26. https://doi.org/10.1111/j.1540-5850.2009.00921.x

Powell, E., Winfield, G., Schatteman, A. M., & Trusty, K. (2018). Collaboration between practitioners and academics: Defining the pracademic experience. *Journal of Nonprofit Education and
Leadership, 8*(1), 62–79. https://doi.org/10.18666/JNEL-2018-V8-I1-8295

Snowdon, G. (2011, January 28). Almost half of graduates 'ill-equipped for world of
work'. *The Guardian.* https://www.theguardian.com/money/2011/jan/28/half-graduates-
ill-equipped-for-work

Succi, C., & Canovi, M. (2019). Soft skills to enhance graduate employability: Comparing students and employers' perceptions. *Studies in Higher Education, 45*(9), 1834–1847. https://
doi-org.proxy.library.dmu.ac.uk/10.1080/03075079.2019.1585420

Swain, H (2019, February 14). 'Universities stamp out creativity': Are graduates ready for work?
The Guardian. https://www.theguardian.com/education/2019/feb/14/universities-stamp-out-
creativity-are-graduates-ready-for-work

Webber, A. (2019, December 18). Graduates 'lacking key skills', HR managers say. *Personnel
Today.* https://www.personneltoday.com/hr/graduates-lacking-key-skills-hr-managers-say/

Wilson, D. M. (2015). Pracademia: The future of the lifelong learner. *About Campus, 20*(2), 28–31.
https://doi.org/10.1002/abc.21189

Yorke, M. (2004). Employability in the undergraduate curriculum: Some student perspectives.
European Journal of Education, 39(4), 408–427.

Yorke, M. (2006, May 1). *Employability in higher education: What it is – What it is not.*
Advance HE. https://www.advance-he.ac.uk/knowledge-hub/employability-higher-education-
what-it-what-it-not

Sally Skea is a Senior Lecturer in Sport and Cultural Events Management at De Montfort
University and a Fellow of Advance HE. She has 20 years' experience as an event operations practitioner in the sports sector, working in a range of roles for NGBs and organising committees,
including the 2022 Birmingham Commonwealth Games, ICC Cricket World Cup 2019, Glasgow
2018 European Championships, London 2017 World Athletics Championships, and London 2012
Olympics. She now continues this industry practice on a part-time basis alongside her roles in
higher education, having started working in the sector in 2018. Sally leads courses on Sport
Management and Cultural Events Management MSc programmes, where she specialises in embedding employability and professional skills into course delivery, teaching, and assessment.

Chapter 14
Those Who Can, Do (and Teach): Developing Simulations to Bring Practitioners and Students Together

Nichola Cadet

Abstract Despite students having some ideas about the occupations they may enter upon graduation, unless the course is vocational in nature, they may not have the opportunity to understand the realities of their chosen profession, the qualities required, and the opportunity to discover whether the occupation is the right fit for them. Academic departments may have staff with practitioner experience in their teams, but there can be anxieties about the currency of their applied knowledge and experience. By bringing existing practitioners into the classroom to take students through a simulated learning experience, both students and practitioners are able to benefit. However, the focus tends to be on the benefits for students. This chapter will explore from practitioners' perspectives, the benefits and challenges for teaching on a simulation module. Benefits include: reciprocity; pride in their expertise; opportunities to develop their own skills; and supporting the pipeline of future recruits. The chapter also outlines some challenges for delivering simulated learning, with pragmatic recommendations and considerations for academic staff who may wish to adopt such an approach.

Keywords Pracademic identity · Practice-theory gap · Experiential learning · Criminology · Faculty profiles · Pedagogy · Imposter syndrome · Career academics · Higher education policy

> **At a Glance**
> - Offers an account of developing a simulation module with active practitioners in the criminal justice system (CJS).
> - Reports research findings to understand practitioners' experiences of engaging in Higher Education delivery.

(continued)

N. Cadet (✉)
Department of Law and Criminology, Sheffield Hallam University, Sheffield, UK
e-mail: n.cadet@shu.ac.uk

© The Author(s), under exclusive license to Springer Nature   195
Switzerland AG 2023
J. Dickinson, T.-L. Griffiths (eds.), *Professional Development for Practitioners in Academia*, Knowledge Studies in Higher Education 13,
https://doi.org/10.1007/978-3-031-33746-8_14

- Benefits include reciprocity, pride, sharing expertise, opportunities to develop skills, and supporting the pipeline of future recruits.
- Challenges include understanding institutional processes, and aligning practitioner, staff, and student expectations.

Introduction

This chapter outlines the lived experiences of a group of nine criminal justice practitioners (CJPs) who were engaged in co-designing and delivering a simulation module for a criminology undergraduate course. Although descriptive in nature, the aim is to draw on a case study approach (McKernan, 2013) to identify potential challenges and benefits of engaging specialist practitioners whose expertise is their workplace knowledge. The findings are based on CJPs' experiences of engagement, rather than the subject matter, aiding generalisability to other disciplines. Their knowledge is distinguished from those who have moved full-time into the academy, those with substantive roles in both practice and academia, and equally, those participating on a one-off basis. The practitioners engaged in this module firmly viewed their identity in practice, with no aspiration to move into academia.

The rationale for developing the module is outlined, alongside the processes by which the module was developed, and an evaluation of the challenges and benefits of engaging practitioners. The chapter ends with a series of pragmatic recommendations for others who may be seeking to implement similar ways of deploying practitioners in applied settings.

The increased marketisation of universities has led to institutions enacting a plethora of initiatives and responses to supporting graduate outcomes (Crandall et al., 2021). Such activities are branded under 'university-industry collaborations'; adopting myriad approaches to developing applied interventions. These include mentoring, sandwich degrees, internships/placements, and bespoke collaborations within teaching delivery in the curriculum (Donovan and Jeung-Lee, 2018). Payne et al. (2003) also identified ad-hoc ways within which experiential learning was delivered in a criminal justice setting through 'ride-alongs' (where students are taken out in police cars to observe a shift in action), field trips, and guest speakers. These approaches critically integrate university study and professional practice to craft the application of disciplinary knowledge to real-world contexts (Smith & Worsfold, 2015).

Shreeve (2010) outlines five categories of professionals engaged in teaching. The first is identified as 'dropping in' – where the knowledge from practice is prioritised over teaching competences, and that expertise is sufficient to ensure knowledge transmission. The second category is 'moving across' where the emphasis is towards teaching and enabling students to understand how it feels to be a practitioner. In this group, curriculum design and learning activities are carefully crafted. Within the third classification of 'two camps', practitioners balance teaching and practice, but tensions are inherent, particularly where workload issues may inhibit the ability to perform practice or teaching satisfactorily. The fourth category, 'balancing', is similar. However, teaching and practice are more symbiotic with practitioners having the ability to enjoy both teaching and practice. The final group, 'integrating', is where practice and knowledge are inextricably bound together, and such practitioners are able to dovetail the two. There were aspects of the 'moving across', 'balancing', and 'integration' classifications evident in the delivery of our module.

A further development is the increased role within academia for individuals coming from practice into the classroom, or pracademics. Posner (2009) identified a continuum for pracademics, based on permanency and the length of time between each discipline. The experiences of pracademics have focused on the transition of experienced practitioners into the academy, and the attendant tensions and challenges that this presents (Dickinson et al., 2020). Similarly, evaluations of simulation activities have focused on the experiences of students, whereas this chapter focuses on the experiences of practitioners to understand the benefits and challenges of engaging in designing and delivering a simulation module from their perspective.

Methodology

This chapter draws on research findings from a questionnaire and telephone interviews completed by CJPs engaged on the module. In keeping with the university's ethos of providing applied experiences for students, the fieldwork was undertaken by a student researcher who had not taken the module. As a former practitioner, with "tacit lived experience" (Hollweck et al., 2021, p. 8), and actively engaged in policy, practice, and teaching, the module leader also felt it important to capture the views and experiences of those involved in developing and delivering the module, following informal conversations with practitioners. The module leader supervised the process, ensuring that ethics committee application procedures were completed in Summer 2017. The questionnaire was designed to briefly capture CJPs' demographic and professional backgrounds in addition to free-text responses related to their motivations and expectations for involvement; resourcing and administration of the modules; engagement and feedback; and suggestions for improvements. The questionnaire was thematically analysed to identify themes for semi-structured telephone interviews. The rationale for the two stages of questionnaire and interview adopted a pragmatic perspective (Denscombe, 2014); recognising how time-poor the practitioners are when managing their day-to-day professional demands. Of the participants, 62.5 percent were male, and the same proportion were working in the public/statutory and voluntary sectors. Their involvement with the module ranged from one to 4 years. Each practitioner delivered between six and twelve hours of face-to-face contact, in addition to preparation for the sessions.

Findings

Simulation as a Pedagogic Tool

According to the Higher Education Academy (now Advance HE) (Usherwood, 2015), simulations are "a recreation of a real-world situation, designed to explore key elements of that situation" (p. 4). Simulation has been used as a teaching technique for many years across a range of disciplines, including medicine, nursing, teacher education, management, and psychological counselling (Chernikova et al., 2020; Reese et al., 2010). Offering simulations can mimic and recreate important themes within different contexts, therefore enabling students to better understand real life scenarios and issues (Hagan, 1997).

In some disciplines, including criminology where students tend to be interested in careers in the CJS, constraints are inherent in providing students with first-hand experiences in workplace settings. This includes concerns about sensitive materials, confidentiality, ethics, and the vulnerabilities of service users (Davis, 2015). Therefore, to support experiential learning, alternative methods may be preferred. For example, mock law trials enable students to gain first-hand experience in learning about case development, as well as providing realistic settings to discuss topical, controversial, and morally difficult issues around the CJS (Farmer et al., 2013). In such settings, students gain a better understanding of the concerns surrounding morality and justice, as well as overcoming a lack of exposure to real life issues in the CJS such as 'cop culture', which informally shape the day-to-day experiences of policing and their organisational context.

> It gets them away from the purely academic side of things, and. . .listening to practitioners who day-by-day work at the coalface. . .and maybe a little bit of a taste of life and street-life and some of the clientele that you are dealing with. (CJP4)

Therefore, simulations can provide a safe environment to test out new ideas and concepts, moving the focus towards student-led learning (O'Neill & McMahon, 2005). Students have also expressed support for experiential learning opportunities in the classroom to provide them with real-world experiences (Kadee et al., 2021). Practical skills can be developed, such as public speaking, working in groups, persuasion, presentation skills, drafting documents, adaptability, and critical thinking (Kravetz, 2001). Therefore, research has found simulations to be a high impact practice which positively enhances student learning gain (Smith & Baik, 2021).

The rationale for developing our module was similar to that outlined in the research. The module takes place on a large, final year undergraduate programme, with around four hundred students per year across five law and criminology courses. The large cohort meant that a significant proportion of students were unable to obtain direct placement experiences, within the context of a university offer which required 'work related learning' to be available at every level. The module took students cumulatively through the criminal justice process, from a crime scene through to sentencing, all co-designed and delivered by CJPs.

When the module was first established following programme revalidation, an outreach event was held where practitioners worked collaboratively with academic staff to shape module content based on required learning outcomes. Additional sessions were facilitated for CJPs to refine the sequential nature of the simulation and the challenges that students would face. For example, the crime scene investigators and the police officers worked together to ensure that all aspects of the case study were set up to enable investigative processes to take place. This included integrating various artefacts; for example, fingerprint kits, crime scene reports, witness statements, blank indictments, and practice instructions. However, for practitioners who were engaged later in the process, they would have welcomed more opportunity to collaborate in developing the case study in advance of delivery:

> More interaction with other practitioners, maybe a more collaborative approach to building the module. (CJP4)

> Practitioners should meet up to discuss ideas and/or discuss the simulation case, to ensure that everyone's sessions are relevant to the case that the students are following. (CJP7)

The module commenced with a 'virtual crime scene' accessed by students via a bespoke app on a university tablet, co-designed with the crime scene investigators who taught on the module. Students were expected to engage in preparatory activities, including internet research, watching screencast lectures, and completing questions in their workbooks. Authenticity, that is the extent to which the learning environment has similarities to the real-world environment (Smith & Worsfold, 2015), was enhanced through asynchronous announcements sent to students about case progression, such as the return of forensic evidence and sightings of suspects, which were released on an ad-hoc basis, including evenings and weekends, to replicate the realities of undertaking investigations in the CJS (Chernikova et al., 2020).

The module deliberately engineered "ill-structured problems" (Shin et al., 2003, p. 6), designed to replicate the "swampy lowlands of practice" (Schon, 1983, p. 42) that are experienced daily by CJPs in responding to critical incidents and events. Therefore, the practitioners were actively engaged in designing all components of the module, and the sequencing of activities and dilemmas presented to students. Adopting a case method facilitated learning, critical thinking, and understanding among students (Kunselman & Johnson, 2010).

Although practitioners supported the development of learning outcomes for the module, they were unable to actively participate in assessment processes, and felt frustrated by a lack of flexibility in terms of university processes and procedures.

> We had some ideas around this, but the university were under strict guidelines with what they could do. (CJP5)

> We did have some ideas about assessments which were put forward but there were restrictions on what could be done. (CJP6)

Barriers included the timing of assessment tasks in the academic calendar, and an inability to use sub-tasks to assess learning incrementally. Enabling practitioners to have input into assessment design could form an important part of aligning future skills' needs with academic rigour.

Engaging Practitioners

Practitioners were identified through a range of mechanisms including academic contacts and networks, particularly from staff who had previously been in practice. In some instances, this included a combination of direct approaches to known individuals and in others, contact was made via an organisation. The practitioners who signed up to deliver the module included: crime scene investigators and police officers who delivered investigation sessions; Crown Prosecution Service solicitors, who outlined issues relating to criminal charges and trials; judges, who discussed issues relating to sentencing; and probation officers, who delivered sessions about pre-sentence reports.

The module was capped at 120 students, comprising three cohorts of 40 students. All teaching sessions were delivered in two-hour blocks on the same day to maximise efficiency for practitioners in terms of booking time off work, travel, and preparation.

Motivations for Practitioner Engagement

From a criminal justice perspective, Bordt (1999) identified three main motivations for CJPs to become involved in teaching: sharing experience and expertise, dispelling myths and misrepresentations, and financial gain. Research into other professions shows similar motivations. For example, Donovan and Lee (2018) cite benefits from engineering, including: ensuring relevance, the stimulating and rewarding nature of being involved in teaching, and future recruitment opportunities.

On our module, all of the practitioners stated that sharing information or experiences was a key motivator for becoming involved, particularly that dispelling myths or misrepresentations was an important factor.

> Having been taught by practitioners, in simulation and practical scenarios, in my degree, I know the positive impact this had on me; therefore it is a great experience to now be the practitioner imparting those experiences and impacting on students views of work in the real world. (CJP 1)

Practitioners also sought to dispel the myths and misrepresentations of the CJS, offenders, and victims that appeared in the media and society (Bordt, 1999) which led to inconsistencies between the fictions and the realities of the roles and responsibilities of the various agencies.

Research has also shown that practitioners felt that having a desire to inspire the next generation through sharing one's own experiences, knowledge, and expertise was important given the limited contact that practitioners tend to have with members of the general public (other than victims or offenders) (Smith, 2010). Additionally, they believed that a supplementary, real-life element would go beyond textbook learning, and explained how their passion for the job drove them to want to share and talk about their own experiences. In our module, all of the practitioners identified that being able to convey important information to future generations was a benefit, but they were less certain regarding the importance of having their own ideas and theories tested.

> To give future generations the experience to work in this environment (CJP5)
> To share real life practical experience. (CJP4)

Although a minority of practitioners offered their time voluntarily, generally when they had been put forward by their employer, most received some sort of financial payment or incentive for their time and/or travel costs (Bordt, 1999). This was expressed as an additional benefit but was not their primary motivation for participation. A quarter of practitioners stated that earning money influenced their involvement and three-quarters stated that self-satisfaction was a benefit.

> It was great to be paid but I would have done it for free anyway. (CJP 1)

> It was an added bonus. (CJP 3)

It was also acknowledged that remuneration is important in recognition of the time that people gave to the module.

> You give your time and it's good to be recognised for that time. (CJP 4)

Perceived Benefits to Students

All of the practitioners stated that opportunities to gain real life, first-hand experience, skills, and knowledge were beneficial to students. Almost all identified that being able to learn more efficiently and effectively through a more direct and practical method of teaching was a particular advantage, as was overcoming a lack of exposure to issues within the CJS. In particular, three-quarters of practitioners noted how exploring different career options, that students might have either not known about nor considered previously, was important.

> I hope that we've got more people who are interested in probation...I think that from the other agencies that were involved...they will also have got some interest in terms of people thinking that's a career and from probation I definitely wanted people to think "oh maybe I could be interested in that." (CJP 1)

> We had a lot of people contact us after the module who were interested in CSI and forensics but before the sessions never knew it was available to them...it opens them up to a lot of different experiences and opportunities rather than the few obvious ones that everyone thinks of such as police or probation. Also we had some people who thought they wanted to do CSI but then after exploring different areas they decided it might not really be for them as they were more interested in other aspects of the CJS. (CJP 5)

Related to piquing students' interest is the point that such modules help to enhance students' knowledge and skills which may place them at an advantage in their chosen career:

I did interviews for candidates who wanted to become probation officers and …it struck me that about half of them have a complete lack of awareness really about what the job entailed. (CJP1)

Getting the realities behind jobs and learning from practitioners will give you a better idea than a textbook or someone who hasn't even done that job. (CJP5)

They learn skills that would be expected in employment, skills and problem solving etc. (CJP6)

Perceived Benefits to Organisations

Additionally, practitioners identified several benefits for their organisations in terms of developing partnership awareness, inspiring future generations, and supporting students who are interested in the profession to derive relevant skills and knowledge.

It was talking about the organisation I was working for and letting them know about opportunities and how important volunteering is in that line of work because certainly when I've interviewed people who work in criminal justice a lot of them have degrees…but if they've got no first-hand experience of working with offenders, I'd be unsure about them. (CJP7)

However, the extent to which practitioners emphasised these benefits tended to differ based on their substantive role as employee: those with managerial roles tended to make more strategic links to organisational benefits, rather than personal motivations.

Challenges of Delivering Simulations

Despite the range of benefits, there are potential drawbacks to developing simulation activities. These include a limited ability to recreate and replicate reality, particularly within a classroom environment, due to lack of materials, space, or time (Bordt, 1999); ethical issues; students having little or no prior knowledge; and inflexibility or inaccessibility of materials and sessions (Bordt, 1999; Kravetz, 2001; Palys, 1978). The participants particularly cited the limitations of recreating and replicating reality.

It is difficult to replicate a case study in the classroom. (CJP3)

The crime scene aspect is difficult because you're not in 100% realistic setting: you're in a classroom. (CJP5)

Ethical issues surround CJPs being able to discuss with students' real-life cases or people (Palys, 1978), particularly in terms of confidentiality and anonymity of using cases relating to offenders, victims, and other CJPs (Pollock, 2014). This may mean extra effort, time and/or financial resources to gain ethical approval or create fictional situations to avoid the risk of harm to individuals. However, this poses questions for the authenticity and validity of the students' experiences. Other issues include the possible impact for students in terms of realising their own fears or personal experiences through participating in role play. For example, CJPs using specific crime types and events should take extra care and sensitivity when discussing emotive or distressing topics, such as being a victim of crime. Overall, this does not seem to be an issue on our module, although there have been instances reported elsewhere of students becoming upset or distressed when discussing topics in which they have personal experience (Cares et al., 2021; Pollock, 2014). To ameliorate the potential for students to experience harm, the module provided support resources, the general nature of the incident being investigated was made known to students ahead of selecting the module, and academic module staff were on-hand prior to, and following, sessions for debrief support. However, this relied on goodwill from academic staff who were resourced to deliver the module in the same way as other, more didactic approaches.

Where students have little or no previous knowledge or experience of the topic covered in the simulation, this may make it difficult for CJPs to cover issues and debates in detail within a reduced timeframe, either due to time, money, or space constraints (Bordt, 1999). This may mean that the students are only able to cover very basic content, rather than engage in detailed knowledge and discussion (George et al., 2015), and risks a danger of oversimplification (Usherwood, 2015). In our module, it was also acknowledged that if CJPs had a better understanding of students' current knowledge, this would enhance the benefits to students. Some practitioners felt that students had little or no prior knowledge despite the fact that all students had taken a 'criminal justice' module previously, which was designed to scaffold onto this module.

> Better knowledge of the students' knowledge of some basics prior to the sessions. (CJP1)

> We assumed people didn't have any prior knowledge at all so taught from the basics. (CJP6)

Although all practitioners felt that student attendance was good, they were more ambivalent about student engagement; in particular, students' preparation for the sessions, their level of knowledge about the case so far, and their willingness to actively participate in the sessions.

> As with always a case some had prepared and some hadn't, but I don't think it stopped them from benefitting from it if they hadn't done it. (CJP7)

> The thing is though they want to sit with their friends all the time and sit with the same groups but that doesn't happen in real life. You can't just sit with your friends all the time. (CJP5)

The final disadvantage includes inflexibility surrounding the teaching itself, such as timetable or space constraints (Bordt, 1999). This may make teaching students in detail difficult where the sessions are one-off, infrequent, or short. This may decrease the perceived advantages to stakeholders, such as students gaining in-depth knowledge, developing practical skills, and being able to critically assess theories, concepts, and ideas through gaining personal experience. All of these issues could potentially mean that the simulation is not as effective as first hoped; in fact, it could lead to students becoming disengaged due to a lack of detail and content being covered (George et al., 2015). Limited space or materials could also be an issue for some institutions as it could impact the potential for simulation, for example through reducing the number of students able to participate due to classroom sizes.

Resourcing

Research has shown that CJPs taking part in simulation prefer longer hours and more regular sessions, typically around two hours per week for at least a month depending on the subject content and level. This ensures that complex issues can be explored in greater depth (Bordt, 1999; George et al., 2015; Reese et al., 2010). For our module, practitioners advocated more frequent involvement in teaching than the current opportunity afforded them, with the most preferred length of sessions being a two-hour session.

> For the type of presentation I can deliver about case studies more time would give the students to question and probe issues of interest to them. (CJP3)

All practitioners felt that the class sizes of 40 were too large with 25 being the upper limit, and cited 15–20 as the ideal class size. This is borne out by other research which advocates for similarly smaller classes to maintain control and to set group work, if appropriate. Practitioners felt that such reduced numbers provided best engagement and attendance from students as they enabled interactivity yet were small enough to complete the work effectively (George et al., 2015; Starks et al., 2011). For our module, the sessions also had an academic member of staff in attendance. Their role was to provide context for the learning, introduce the speakers, support classroom management, and resolve any IT or related issues. Additionally, outside the classroom, these academics supported students with their assessments. One challenge for academic staff was helping students to catch up if sessions were missed, given that the case study sequentially followed the criminal justice process. Other research demonstrated how CJPs felt more able to tailor classes to previous learning or issues that students had found difficult to understand, whilst also allowing flexibility to deviate from the main topic to provide information on context or relevant and related issues. However, this is a source of potential conflict for academic staff who are required to ensure that learning outcomes are delivered.

Flexibility of classes was also an issue highlighted by the CJPs in terms of adhering to set, and often inflexible, timetables. This meant balancing their professional roles alongside the planned simulation sessions, and juggling multiple demands (Starks et al., 2011). They believed that more CJPs would take part in simulation if they had to work less around teaching. This was a key learning point from the first iteration of the module. Although sessions were scheduled on the same day, timetabling required CJPs to deliver sessions in different classrooms around campus. In later iterations, a single classroom was available for the whole day to eliminate the need for practitioners to navigate around campus. This was particularly important where students were using the crime scene app,[1] and where the practitioners were bringing in external materials, such as fingerprinting kits.

Our module made good use of additional IT for practitioners. They had access to the university's virtual learning environment; the Crime Scene Investigators worked with faculty to develop the crime scene app and support its introduction in a teaching session; and the policing sessions encouraged additional student engagement via online polling. However, another challenge for the practitioners included implementing university policies; for example, regarding the availability of learning materials ahead of the session to support student learning. Because of the simulated nature of the module, some information was inappropriate for students to be able to access in advance, for example, where new evidence was being presented. This has the potential to place students with additional learning needs at a disadvantage. However, practitioners were careful to share as much as possible ahead of the sessions to balance the need to maintain authenticity and support students. A complete suite of materials was available after each session. The content was also important to conduct simulation in a real-life scenario; for example, relevant legal documents or scenarios in order to provide role play, discussion, or debate (George et al., 2015; Starks et al., 2011).

Student Debrief and Feedback

Debriefing has become an integral part of simulation experience (Seropian, 2003). This method is most effective immediately after the simulation, in terms of focusing on positive aspects, as well as areas for change/improvement. The use of explicit student clinical reasoning during simulations enables debriefing to enhance student learning, as well as giving staff a better idea of which aspects of the sessions the students found most helpful (Rudolph et al., 2006). However, formal evaluations tend to be overlooked within simulations and therefore they could potentially lose their pedagogical value (Usherwood, 2015). Although evaluation took place utilising faculty processes at the end of the module, this was based on a standard questionnaire, which did not readily fit the pedagogical approach adopted in the module. The findings from the module evaluation were shared with practitioners, but they advocated more real-time provision of feedback. This is likely to be as a consequence of their practice environment where immediate feedback is provided or debriefing processes take place following incidents or case completion.

> One of the things I would absolutely change in terms of having formal feedback from the sessions that are done. (CJP1)

---

[1] A dedicated tablet application, which details the virtual crime scenes.

I think it's important that students should be given the chance to sort of fill in a form or something to say what they liked about a session, what they didn't like and any suggestions. (CJP3)

All of the practitioners identified that they received informal feedback from staff involved in the module, and highlighted the importance of having a regular, named contact to facilitate administrative processes around engagement alongside continuity within the module.

Implications for Developing Simulations with Practitioners

This chapter has highlighted some challenges associated with establishing a simulation module, that is co-designed and co-delivered with practitioners. Pragmatic considerations for others contemplating a similar approach include perceiving that the benefits of participating for organisations and individuals may not be the same, so understanding relevant drivers encourages buy-in. Developing a clear timeline from inception to delivery supports practitioners in meeting their professional commitments, and to know what they are signing up for. The timeline should also include considering resource implications, including: academic staff, IT access, timetabling, room allocations, sequencing, and contingencies. Additionally, CJPs were keen to share their experiences, but their remit may need clarifying, particularly if they have not had previous direct teaching or classroom experience. Practitioners are also perfectly placed to ensure the currency of course content, due to the changing statutory or policy landscape.

Considering the student experience is also vital. This includes induction activities to: manage student expectations, prepare them to understand their responsibilities as active learners, and engage appropriately. Mapping learning outcomes to future skills requirements enables students to make connections between theory and practice, and serves as an important scaffold for skills development and the demands of future employment. Finally, feedback and feedforward from both practitioners and students' alike shapes future iterations.

Conclusion

This chapter outlined the experiences of CJPs delivering a simulation module to law and criminology undergraduate students. Their first-hand accounts included their individual motivations, benefits for the organisations they worked for, and desire to provide the students with an opportunity to learn through experience.

Practitioners are keen to expand their involvement in delivering such modules, including, wherever possible: contributions to module design, innovative modes of delivery, collaboration with other practitioners, and engagement in assessment processes. However, pragmatic constraints, such as: resourcing issues for large programmes, the 'tyranny of the timetable', class size, and frequency of sessions were all potential barriers to simulations effectively enhancing student learning. Without fully appreciating the conditions by which immersion via simulation takes place, the positive outcomes can be more difficult to realise (Usherwood, 2015). If Higher Education institutions wish to realise the benefits of simulations, this needs to be appropriately resourced.

Simulation modules offer potential benefits for students to re-frame their attitudes and beliefs and consider the breadth of professions available to them upon graduation, through ensuring that learning takes place via an "interaction of expectation and experience" (Davis, 2015, p. 257). This interaction includes the academics, the students, and the practitioners, both within modules and potentially across a whole range of academic disciplines.

Points for Reflection
- Cadet notes how both organisations and individual practitioners are often keen to work with university institutions because it offers them a chance to give back; to nurture future talent pipelines, and to develop their skills along the way. Similarly, students appreciate the opportunity to engage with 'real life' practitioners, shaping their future career goals. What opportunities could there be for your institution to build further collaborations with external partners and practitioners?
- The chapter highlights how practitioners may struggle to balance their professional role with the expectations of delivering teaching at a university institution. What steps could be taken to help mitigate this at your institution?
- Cadet observes how simulation modules require additional support from academic institutions, alongside committed staff who are keen to foster and develop relationships in the field, and who can offer flexible opportunities for engagement. Consider what opportunities there may be for providing such resourcing within your institution.

References

Bordt, R. L. (1999). Simulation as a tool for teaching research methods in a criminology course. *Journal of Criminal Justice Education, 10*(2), 373–382.

Cares, A. C., Hernandez, A. M., Growette-Bostaph, L., & Fisher, B. S. (2021). For or against?: Criminal justice and criminology faculty attitudes toward trigger warnings. *Journal of Criminal Justice Education, 32*(3), 302–322. https://doi.org/10.1080/10511253.2021.1958884

Chernikova, O., Heitzmann, N., Stadler, M., Holzberger, D., Seidel, T., & Fischer, F. (2020). Simulation-based learning in higher education: A meta-analysis. *Review of Educational Research, 90*(4), 499–541. https://doi.org/10.3102/0034654320933544

Crandall, K. L., Buckwalter, M. A., & Witkoski, M. (2021). Show and tell: An examination of experiential learning opportunities in criminal justice courses. *Journal of Criminal Justice Education, 32*(2), 155–170. https://doi.org/10.1080/10511253.2021.1883695

Davis, J. (2015). Engaging criminal justice students through service learning. *Journal of Criminal Justice Education, 26*(3), 253–272. https://doi.org/10.1080/10511253.2015.1009478

Denscombe, M. (2014). *The good research guide: For small scale projects* (5th ed.). Open University Press.

Dickinson, J., Fowler, A., & Griffiths, T. (2020). Pracademics? Exploring transitions and professional identities in higher education. *Studies in Higher Education, 47*(2), 290–304. https://doi.org/10.1080/03075079.2020.1744123

Donovan, S. C., & Lee, J. (2018). University–industry teaching collaborations: A case study of the MSc in structural integrity co-produced by Brunel University London and the welding institute. *Studies in Higher Education, 43*(4), 769–785. https://doi.org/10.1080/03075079.2016.119954 2

Farmer, K., Meisel, S. I., Seltzer, J., & Kane, K. (2013). The mock trial: A dynamic exercise for thinking critically about management theories, topics, and practices. *Journal of Management Education, 37*(3), 400–430.

George, M., Lim, H., Lucas, S., & Meadows, R. (2015). Learning by doing: Experiential learning in criminal justice. *Journal of Criminal Justice Education, 26*(4), 471–492.

Hagan, F. E. (1997). *Research methods in criminal justice and criminology.* Allyn and Bacon.

Hollweck, T., Netolicky, D. M., & Campbell, P. (2021). Defining and exploring pracademia: Identity, community and engagement. *Journal of Professional Capital and Community, 7*(1), 6–25.

Kravetz, K. (2001). The mock trial course in justice education. *Journal of Criminal Justice Education, 12*(1), 147–168.

Kunselman, J. C., & Johnson, K. A. (2010). Using the case method to facilitate learning. *College Teaching, 53*(3), 87–92.

McKernan, J. (2013). *Curriculum action research: A handbook of methods and resources for the reflective practitioner* (2nd ed.). Taylor and Francis.

O'Neill, G., & McMahon, T. (2005). Student-Centred learning: What does it mean for students and lecturers? In G. O'Neill, S. Moore, & B. McMullin (Eds.), *Emerging issues in the practice of university learning and teaching.* AISHE.

Palys, T. S. (1978). Simulation methods and social psychology. *Journal for the Theory of Social Behaviour, 8*(3), 341–368.

Payne, B. K., Sumter, M., & Sun, I. (2003). Bringing the field into the criminal justice classroom: Field trips, ride-alongs, and guest speakers. *Journal of Criminal Justice Education, 14*(2), 327–344. https://doi.org/10.1080/10511250300085821

Pollock, J. M. (2014). *Ethical dilemmas and decisions in criminal justice.* Cengage Learning.

Posner, P. L. (2009). The pracademic: An agenda for re-engaging practitioners and academics. *Public Budgeting & Finance, 29*(1), 12–26.

Reese, C. E., Jeffries, P. R., & Engum, C. A. (2010). Learning together: Using simulations to develop nursing and medical student collaboration. *Nursing Education Perspectives, 31*(1), 33–37.

Rudolph, J. W., Simon, R., Dufrense, R. L., & Raemer, D. B. (2006). There's no such thing as a "non-judgmental" debriefing: A theory and method for debriefing with good judgment. *Simulation in Healthcare, 1*(1), 49–55.

Schön, D. (1983). *The reflective practitioner: How professionals think in action.* Basic Books.

Seropian, M. A. (2003). General concepts in full-scale simulation: Getting started. *Anesthesia and Analgesia, 97*(6), 1695–1705.

Shin, N., Jonassen, D. H., & McGee, S. (2003). Predictors of well-structured and ill-structured problem solving in an astronomy simulation. *Journal of Research in Science Teaching, 40*(1), 6–33.

Shreeve, A. (2010). A phenomenographic study of the relationship between professional practice and teaching your practice to others. *Studies in Higher Education, 35*(6), 691–703. https://doi.org/10.1080/03075070903254602

Smith, D. (2010). *Public confidence in the criminal justice system: Findings from the British crime survey 2002/03 to 2007/08*. Ministry of Justice. https://www.justice.gov.uk/downloads/publications/research-and-analysis/moj-research/confidence-cjs-british-crime-survey.pdf

Smith, C. D., & Baik, C. (2021). High-impact teaching practices in higher education: A best evidence review. *Studies in Higher Education, 46*(8), 1696–1713. https://doi.org/10.1080/03075079.2019.1698539

Smith, C., & Worsfold, K. (2015). Unpacking the learning–work nexus: 'Priming' as lever for high-quality learning outcomes in work-integrated learning curricula. *Studies in Higher Education, 40*(1), 22–42. https://doi.org/10.1080/03075079.2013.806456

Starks, B. C., Harrison, L., & Denhardt, K. (2011). Outside the comfort zone of the classroom. *Journal of Criminal Justice Education, 22*(2), 203–225.

Usherwood, S. (2015). *Simulations in politics: A guide to best practice*. Higher Education Academy. https://www.heacademy.ac.uk/system/files/resources/Simulations%20in%20Politics%20-%20a%20guide%20to%20best%20practice.pdf

Nichola Cadet is a Senior Lecturer in Criminology at Sheffield Hallam University. Her practice background was in the voluntary criminal justice sector where she managed a number of local, national, and international projects. As an academic, her teaching has focused on embedding employability in the curriculum and developing placement opportunities for students.

Chapter 15
Construction and Engineering Higher Education: The Role of Pracademics in Recoupling Classical Experiential Educational Norms

Alan M. Forster, Nick Pilcher, Mike Murray, Stuart Tennant, Nigel Craig, and Laurent Galbrun

Abstract This chapter considers the development of construction and engineering education that historically chartered an increasingly decoupled trajectory from being practical in nature, to include progressively more theoretical instruction. Indeed, over the last half century, construction and engineering education has become increasingly theoretical, and is now arguably delivered by academic staff with little practical experience of the discipline. This could be detrimental to those learning an inherently vocational subject, and perhaps understandably, calls to recouple theory and practice have recently gained traction, through vehicles such as Higher Education Apprenticeships. Whilst largely seen as positive, such recoupling may potentially create problems for the current staff base that are often characterised

A. M. Forster (✉)
School of Energy, Geoscience, Infrastructure & Society, Heriot-Watt University Edinburgh, Edinburgh, Scotland, UK
e-mail: A.M.Forster@hw.ac.uk

N. Pilcher
The Business School, Edinburgh Napier University, Edinburgh, UK

M. Murray
Department of Civil & Environmental Engineering, University of Strathclyde, Glasgow, UK

S. Tennant
School of Computing, Engineering and Physical Sciences, University of the West of Scotland, South Lanarkshire, UK

N. Craig
School of Engineering and Built Environment, Glasgow Caledonian University, Glasgow, UK

L. Galbrun
School of Energy, Geoscience, Infrastructure and Society, Heriot-Watt University, Edinburgh, UK

© The Author(s), under exclusive license to Springer Nature   211
Switzerland AG 2023
J. Dickinson, T.-L. Griffiths (eds.), *Professional Development for Practitioners in Academia*, Knowledge Studies in Higher Education 13,
https://doi.org/10.1007/978-3-031-33746-8_15

as 'career academics' with often limited 'real world' experience. Conversely, academics with industrial experience (or pracademics) are arguably better equipped to bridge theory and practice. Yet, 'pracademics' frequently feel an insecurity of identity associated with 'imposter syndrome' in a research-dominated Higher Education (HE) context. However, rather than being imposters, we argue 'pracademics' have a lineage going back centuries. We highlight the important role that pracademics play in bridging theory and practice and allude to their importance in achieving high quality, contextualised student focused experiential learning that is set to be an increasingly important aspect of HE provision.

Keywords Pracademic identity · Practice-theory gap · Experiential learning · Construction and engineering · Imposter syndrome · Career academics · Higher Education Apprenticeships · Higher education policy

At a Glance
- Examines the decoupling of academic theory and practice in construction and engineering higher education, and the adverse consequences for students receiving vocational instruction.
- Argues that this decoupling resulted in much education being delivered by academics with theoretical knowledge ('career academics') rather than practical workplace experience ('pracademics').
- Discusses the increasing anecdotal evidence of changing employment of pracademics and the drivers in recruitment patterns.
- Discusses the positive benefits of recoupling theory and practical knowledge, and how this can be facilitated.

Introduction

Over the last half-century, the decoupling of theory and industry practice in construction and engineering education has arguably resulted in increasingly decontextualized teaching and learning. This is manifest in many contemporary academic departments, their staff compositional mix, and institutional recruitment practices, both in the UK (Forster et al., 2017; Pilcher et al., 2020; Tennant et al., 2015) and worldwide (Norton, 2013; Schuster & Finkelstein, 2006). Indeed, historically, construction and engineering education was largely experiential in nature and intimately coupled with workplace practice. Here, we characterise construction and engineering education in three significant evolutionary stages: (1) fully experiential, (2) the voluntary dual system, and (3) experientially decoupled (Forster et al., 2017). Furthermore, at present, anecdotal evidence is beginning to suggest a fourth contemporary stage in the evolution of construction and engineering education delivery. This nascent phase strives to recouple theory with its experiential roots. This would align the education and training of engineering and construction with other disciplines that have a more experiential approach to departmental staff compositions such as nursing (Andrew et al., 2014) and policing (Braga, 2016).

Nevertheless, whilst such recoupling would be pedagogically beneficial for construction and engineering education (Evans et al., 2015; Forster et al., 2017), and for employability (Dalrymple et al., 2021), there are challenges for both academics and policy makers, seeking to recouple theory and practice within an institutional context that is biased towards theory (Olive, 2017). Such preference is manifest both through promoting and valuing individuals with theoretical experience and expertise (namely, those with a PhD and research-focused portfolio), and through institutionalised policy and procedures of recruitment and promotion that value theory (research publications and grant income) over practice (industrial experience) (Ferguson, 1992; Nuttall et al., 2013). Notably, in construction and engineering education, individuals with significant professional and practical experience (Andrew et al., 2014), or 'pracademics', have clear advantages over those with mostly PhD and research experience or 'career academics' (Tennant et al., 2015; Zaitseva & Finn, 2022). Pracademics can bring the outside world in (Evans et al., 2015); creating educational bridges between industry and theoretical instruction, and providing broader, professionally accredited syllabus design (Murray et al., 2017). They can function as the conduit between academia and industry; enhancing employability through creating authentic assessment and closer and more effective industry ties (Dalrymple et al., 2021). Conversely, career academics may feel unable to meaningfully incorporate practical examples of engineering and construction practice in their teaching (Craig et al., 2016; Pilcher et al., 2017).

Such fault lines are not new. These academic tensions reflect distinctions of ideas espoused by Ryle (1945) in what he termed the practical 'knowing how', and the theoretical 'knowing that', which may be forgotten in higher education (HE) pedagogical and epistemological constructs. The 'knowing how' constitutes the educational scaffolding for the subsequent 'knowing that'. Importantly, as Ryle noted, "doing things is never itself an exercise of intelligence, but is, at best, a process introduced and somehow steered by some ulterior act of theorising" (Ryle, 1945, p. 1). Thus, both the practical and the theoretical are integral to, and inform the development of each other; it is an individual's experience of both theory (knowing that) and practice (knowing how) that creates knowledge (cf. Kant et al., 2018). This is particularly relevant to construction and engineering; however, the current pedagogical approach conspires to decouple theory from practice. Such practice might induce feelings of imposter syndrome (Parkman, 2016) for many academics, especially if they are teaching students with significant construction experience when they themselves have none (Craig et al., 2016). Additionally, in terms of how best to support this, it may have policy implications for any higher education institutions (HEIs) needing to recalibrate their focus if confronted with a rapidly changing income funding landscape that prioritizes teaching and learning (Forster et al., 2017; Olive, 2017).

We do not endorse a return to past apprenticeship and historic learning practices. On the contrary, the intent is to harness the best of contemporary pedagogical practice for built environment students, ensuring that teaching and learning successfully manages to recouple both theory and practice. Indeed, in construction and engineering education, Higher Education Apprenticeships (known as Degree Apprenticeships in England and Wales, and Graduate Apprenticeships (GAs) in Scotland), and other experiential modes of study, such as part time learning, augmented by real-life contributions from Industry Advisory Panels, offer opportunities to capitalise upon the best of both educational realms (Forster et al., 2017). Nevertheless, the dual delivery strategy that we argue for here can only be meaningfully achieved by pracademics who are invested in design, delivery, and assessment, and, critically, who work in a system that promotes and values such individuals equally alongside those with theoretical expertise (Tennant et al., 2015). Employers (and professional bodies) could also perhaps be criticized for devolving formative professional educational responsibility to HEIs, yet simultaneously bemoaning the calibre of graduates that these institutions produce (Borg & Scott-Young, 2020). Importantly, experiential learning needs effective, carefully considered, and longitudinal work-based structures, with embedded educationally-rich activities, to contextualise theory, and meaningful industrial work-based mentorship (Zaheer et al., 2020). All of these aspects increase greatly any opportunity to meaningfully recouple.

The authors of this chapter have worked together for many years on this topic. The stimulus for what became a collective long-term research and writing collaboration was borne out of frustration with university recruitment policies, which seemed not to understand the critical importance of employing staff with significant industrial experience. Motivation was arguably from an understanding of what student learners were missing by not being taught (in part) by experienced pracademics. This was important given the inherently vocational nature of engineering and construction and how much is learned on-site through practical application. As authors, four of us have common industrial workplace experiences and pedagogical underpinning as construction apprentices. Upon completion of our apprenticeships, we then studied degrees in built environment programmes and entered the construction project management and building surveying professions. These formative years engrained an appreciation of the importance of experiential learning with a high regard for tutelage derived from those who had themselves undertaken onsite activities. Indeed, in academia, this was compounded by seeing older, former trade, and professionally very experienced, colleagues retiring, and new colleagues being recruited with limited or no practical experience but who possessed PhD qualifications and enhanced research attributes. We found ourselves both frustrated with government research strategy and HEI enactment of policy that appeared to bias research, and support theory over practice, in a discipline that logically requires both.

We describe the key themes of our work below, and conclude by suggesting that the emerging landscape is now starting to recognise the value of industrial workplace experience and HEIs are recruiting pracademics once again. Within the following discussion of key themes, the first Section, "Classical Patterns of Coupled

Built Environment Education", describes how education was historically coupled and focused on both theory and practice. The second Section, "Education in an Increasing Transitionary State of Decoupling", then outlines how decoupling began to tip the scales whereby theory took prominence over practice. The third Section, "The Gaining Employment Traction of the Career Academic and the Dominance of Research", considers the strong dominance of theory, evidenced by the rise of the career academic, and a system that championed theory over practice and research over teaching. The final Sections, "Recoupling Theory and Practice – The Rebalance Driven via the Teaching Excellence Framework" and "Returning to Classical Experiential Models – The Growth of a New Voluntary Dual System and the Key Role of Pracademics in Its Success", discuss how the system is attempting to recouple, and the challenges involved for those attempting to work in such a system, including policy makers.

Key Themes

Classical Patterns of Coupled Built Environment Education

Educational provision for those designing and constructing buildings has a long history. Classical education was born out of the 'master craft tradition' and was fully experiential in nature. Centre stage were the master masons and carpenters who designed and built cathedrals (Gimpel, 1961), palaces, and castles. Their education was characterised by a long apprenticeship with experiential learning at its core, but with supplementary theoretical input (Snell, 1996). Notably, this educational realm had both theoretical instruction and scholarly input, thereby combining the practical and the theoretical through instruction predicated on reading literature and through applying mathematical principles (geometry for complex structural masonry (Warland, 2015) and carpentry (Hewett, 1980)). Assessing the competency of the learner to effectively undertake the role was manifest through the production of the building within important parameters, such as time, cost, quality, and ultimately performance (compare Borg & Scott-Young, 2020; Zaheer et al., 2020).

Within this context, and underlining the importance of experiential and theoretical instruction was the work of Vitruvius, a 1st C. Roman architect and engineer writing in the reign of Augustus who wrote the seminal 'ten books on architecture'. These are considered the "Roman code of building practice" (Bowyer, 1993, p. 223) and were highly influential in architectural design for centuries from the renaissance and classicism, to neo-classicism (Summerson, 1983). Vitruvius stated:

> the architect ('Builder in Chief') should be equipped with knowledge and understanding of many different branches of learning, because they are required to judge the quality of artistic work. Architects ('Builder in Chief') who have manual skills and dexterity without scholarship are not able to reach the professional heights which their profession would warrant while those with scholarship and no practical skill hunt the shadow not the substance. Those who have a thorough knowledge of both practice and theory are in a position to obtain and wield authority (cited in Bowyer, 1993, p. 223).

The notion of such individuals has much cultural capital and is traditionally recognised within the term 'artisan', in so much as being academically learned in the craft itself. However, increasing complexity of design of building and civil engineering projects (for example, with growing need to understand tension forces in design) in the early modern period saw the birth of professional bodies and the emergence of professionalization in the construction,[1] engineering,[2] and architecture[3] sectors (Forster et al., 2017; Thompson, 1968). The training and education of those who undertook such increasingly complex projects was still characterised by the apprenticeship model, with instruction often being design and drafting-office based, but involving frequent site visits to oversee construction activities. Indeed, and reflecting this, "virtually all 'professional' engineers had acquired their skill-set by a process of pupillage in the office of an existing engineer" (Buchanan, 1985, pp. 218–219).

As training and education evolved, theoretical instruction began to be supplemented by evening classes in newly formed academic establishments. For example, mechanics institutes such as the School of Arts of Edinburgh (1821) (now Heriot-Watt University), and the Royal College of Science and Technology, Glasgow (1887) (now the University of Strathclyde) (Forster et al., 2017) pioneered the professional development of engineering and construction disciplines. This approach was known as the 'voluntary dual system', and represented the first formalised break from fully experiential modes of education (Snell, 1996). Here, industry looked after the practical training, and the colleges supported the theory to supplement workplace training (Snell, 1996, compare Ryle, 1945).

The voluntary dual system was however not free from issues (such as variable employer training input or decontextualized night class instruction from workplace activities), but the quality of experiential learning on offer was of fundamental importance for learning opportunities. That said, the length of apprenticeship remained such that it was logical that there was a high probability of learners who were experiencing a wide variety of practical exposure. Consequently, at this point in time, both theory and practice remained in healthy balance. However, retrospectively, an educational decoupling began taking place whereby colleges and industry took over specific roles previously undertaken in industry alone (Forster et al., 2017).

Education in an Increasing Transitionary State of Decoupling

Indeed, greater decoupling resulted from an increasing need for better scientific understanding of materials and structures (Buchanan, 1985). This became alarmingly evident through tragic incidents, such as the collapse of the Tay Bridge due to

---

[1] Chartered Institute of Building (CIOB), formerly the Builders Society, 1834 and The Royal Institution of Chartered Surveyors (RICS) (formerly the 'Surveyors Club', 1792, then the 'Institution of Surveyors' 1862).

[2] Institution of Civil Engineers (ICE), 1828.

[3] Royal Institute of British Architects RIBA 1834 (formerly the 'Institute of British Architects').

structural failure (Lewis & Reynolds, 2002). Decoupling increased as more instructional time became required within the academic institution (Plimmer, 2003). Nevertheless, much of the pioneering engineering education was designed and delivered by practising engineers who divided their time between site and academia (akin to adjunct professors) (Forster et al., 2017). Faculty composition of the academic base was therefore historically a mix of individuals running practices, and career academics (Buchanan, 1985).

Arguably, the significant break in the Vitruvian equilibrium of experience / theory occurred in 1832 with the first full-time academic course in Civil Engineering at University College London (Ferguson & Chrimes, 2011). This signalled a fundamental break from the historically rooted experiential model, and was significant, as for the first time, workplace experience was attained post-academic qualification (Tennant et al., 2015). This arguably set the foundations for future problems of decontextualized teaching and learning, and was not universally welcomed by the profession. Indeed, there was resistance from prominent engineering figures such as Colburn and Sturge (Buchanan, 1985). However, such individuals acknowledged that enhanced theoretical instruction was necessary in light of the Tay bridge disaster. With this new educational framework, however, the 'knowing that' was only possible after the 'knowing how' had been learned (compare Ryle, 1945), rather than both being learned and acquired simultaneously.

Most engineering professionals undertook this mode of delivery by the 1950s (Forster et al., 2017). Other professions followed suit, with universities offering full time RICS (Royal Institution of Chartered Surveyors) accredited degrees by the 1960s (Plimmer, 2003). The drive to attain degree level qualifications within built environment education was to enhance the status and image of the professions that had been publicly viewed as being 'unscrupulous' (Bowyer, 1993; Craig et al., 2020). Indeed, having a degree level qualification was seen as key in professionalising a sector that aspired to be regarded on a parity with lawyers and other similar professions who had been educated on a decoupled basis much earlier (Bowyer, 1993). Decoupling was thus arguably seen as enhancing professional standing. Moreover, staff compositional bases had commonly always had a combination of academics with theoretical and practical backgrounds (Forster et al., 2017). Consequently, whilst on the surface there remained a balance of Vitruvian equilibrium, the institutional parameters had been altered, and this subsequently allowed HEIs to prioritize theory over experience.

The Gaining Employment Traction of the Career Academic and the Dominance of Research

The staffing composition of academic programmes has always been characterised by diversity, with some staff being characterised as more theoretically orientated, and others perceived as having more pragmatic, experiential outlooks (Buchannan, 1985; Forster et al., 2017). Arguably, a significant break in this diversity occurred in the UK with the introduction of the Research Assessment Exercise (RAE) in 1986 (Russell & Russell, 2006), subsequently reimagined as the Research Excellence Framework (REF) from 2008 onwards (Torrance, 2020). With the RAE and REF, and in line with elsewhere in the world, the UK Government endeavoured to evaluate institutional research performance using metrics such as: proportion of staff with PhD level qualifications, volume and quality of journal papers (outputs) published, number of PhD students graduated, and research grant income attained. Inevitably, academics with formal research education, training, and experience, ostensibly attained through a PhD, were now better positioned to attain the desired metrics and rewards from government research block funding for the Research Excellence Framework (REF) than those, such as pracademics, who commonly had little experience in this area (Tennant et al., 2015).

HEIs followed government policy and shifted focus towards research income generation whereby a PhD became increasingly seen as 'essential' for appointment, whilst industrial experience was only a secondary 'desirable' requirement (Pilcher et al., 2020). In short, applicants who were more likely to be professionally chartered, with years of industrial experience, but without a PhD qualification, would be automatically excluded from recruitment processes. This was despite such candidates being previously considered an ideal appointment for delivering an engineering and construction education steeped in the Vitruvian tradition of an equilibrium between theory and practice (Buchannan, 1985). It was during this rapidly changing composition of academic expertise that we witnessed increasingly homogenizing staff bases. Consequently, we have also observed the resultant anxiety for colleagues with limited or no industry experience being required to deliver taught classes to part-time students with significant industry experience. Government acknowledgement of a bias towards research is evidenced by the introduction in 2016 of the Teaching Excellence Framework (TEF). Although no overt metrics are included for the recruitment of pracademics in TEF, it was hoped that the TEF would have resulted in their greater representation in construction and engineering departments, due in part to the known positive benefits in bridging theory and practice (Evans et al., 2015). Although the TEF appears to have had limited initial substantive impact in construction and engineering education recruitment (Pilcher et al., 2020), anecdotal evidence from recent academic job adverts suggests that the trend and institutional bias towards academic staff with research expertise may now be changing.

Although academic faculty has been varied in most HEIs, it remains important to recognise that faculty profile often differed depending on the characterisation of the UK academic institution. For example, staffing at the former polytechnics (now classified as post-1992 universities) were in the past largely composed of pracademics (Barr, 2008). These institutions played a major role in the education of degree-level vocational subjects, including construction and engineering programmes, and had built their reputation on this precise ability to deliver 'industry ready' graduates.

Conversely, the Russell Group, 1994, and plate glass institutions[4] (generally associated with the upper third of universities in the UK league tables) had built reputations on both teaching and learning, and research intensity, even before the initiation of RAE/REF (Wyness, 2010). These institutions commonly offered more academic type programmes; reflecting their historic, classical origins, and typically focused on research output, to the extent that 20% of the top ranked institutions have been shown to attain 80% of the UK research grant funding (Guardian, 2014).

Arguably, the post-1992 HEIs, who had built reputations on highly contextualised and vocational education predicated on the employment of pracademics, have attempted to emulate the more established HEIs and reposition themselves in aggressively deployed institutional level research intensification strategies (Forster et al., 2017). This has arguably altered their business model, whereby they are now competing with the Russell Group institutions to attain funding (Scott, 1995), a strategy which has inevitably led to employing career academics at the expense of pracademics (Nuttall et al., 2013). This has notable and adverse implications for construction and engineering teaching quality (Evans et al., 2015).

As highlighted previously, we are not arguing for a return to antiquated practices, nor to abandon research-focused appointments. Rather, we emphasise that research, and the creation of new knowledge, is a fundamental value of all universities. This is vitally important for institutional status, reputation, ranking, and prestige, all of which positively aid the promotion of the university and can be practically mobilised in student recruitment, marketing strategies, and potential partnerships with industry. It is clearly a powerful motivation for a learner to aspire to attend an institution with a lineage of world-changing discovery via research and, in selective cases, Nobel Prize winners (see, for example, Oxford, Cambridge, Edinburgh, Manchester, and Glasgow). Indeed, many institutions frame their teaching as being 'research-led' and at the vanguard of cutting-edge knowledge imparted to the students. This is clearly illustrated in marketing materials and university recruitment events that attempt to capitalise and create competitive programme advantage over other institutions in an often overcrowded education sector. The logic is that learners will benefit from cutting-edge research being embedded into syllabus content. Whilst this may occur, and students may very well be taught on occasion by leading thinkers in certain fields, how much this features in reality is contested (Brew, 2010).

In practice, research-intensive universities are full of scientific staff with diverse backgrounds, but most staff do not have industry perspectives nor have they been engineering practitioners (Kamp, 2020). Reflecting this, academic staff increasingly lack the practical, integrated core skills associated with those attained via

---

[4] The Russell Group are a self-selected group of the top 24 UK universities and include Oxford and Cambridge and focus on research; the 1994 group were also a prestigious group of universities that focused on research and included 11 universities such as Leicester and Loughborough; plate glass institutions are universities that were established in the 1960s and tend to focus on engineering and technology with originally 7 institutions including Warwick and Kent. This number has now expanded, especially with the disbanding of the 1994 group and now includes, for example, Loughborough.

chartership training requirements of professional bodies such as: systems engineering and project approaches, transferable professional skills, conflict management and negotiation, and ethics (Tennant et al., 2015; Murray et al., 2017; Collins & Collins, 2019). This characterisation decouples the worlds of academic and engineering practice; a development which represents a growing challenge at research-intensive universities. While senior faculty staff control appointments and promotions, it has been suggested that, if there is to be any change, it will not come from within, and thus the templates for recruiting academic staff are becoming narrower. This reduces the opportunity for people with a non-academic background to enter the classroom and thereby bring their experience, tacit knowledge, role models, empathy, and creativity in construction and engineering practice to learners.

Comparatively, the unique selling point (USP) of the former polytechnics, as noted above, was that they produced employable, 'industry ready' graduates due to the delivery of highly contextualised teaching. Understandably, the UK Government is striving to re-establish this, and its efforts to do so can be seen in initiatives such as the Higher Education Apprenticeships. Of importance, these Higher Education Apprenticeships are intended to "benefit the Scottish economy" (SDS, 2017, p. 4) through having individuals studying and working at the same time, ostensibly to directly apply theory into practice. However, the theory-practice nexus has been a contentious issue since the mid-nineteenth century, and many areas of the debate remain unresolved. Indeed, more recently, and particularly within the former polytechnics, the introduction of sandwich courses in the UK from the 1950s to the present day attests to this.

Recoupling Theory and Practice – The Rebalance Driven via the Teaching Excellence Framework

The Teaching Excellence Framework (TEF) was introduced to 'counterbalance' the unintended consequence of perceived institutional research bias (BIS, 2016; Hubble, 2017). Whilst no direct block grant is associated with institutional TEF scores, the awarding of Gold, Silver or Bronze status creates a mechanism for marketing the institution to prospective students (McNay, 2021). Research suggests that pracademics are best placed to attain good teaching feedback within vocational oriented programmes due to their professional background and ability to contextualise teaching and learning (Evans et al., 2015; Murray et al., 2017). Such an ability may improve student retention, engagement, satisfaction, and by extension, university TEF scores.

It is surmised that TEF's influence will increase within a context of difficult research funding streams and the increasing importance of teaching income to all academic institutions. There is a growing recognition that whilst research remains an important income stream, teaching and learning activities are the primary money-generating activities for the majority of HEIs (Olive, 2017). The situation will be exacerbated as the research funding landscape is currently in a transitionary state with the UK Government reducing classical funding streams (such as potential loss of EU Horizon grants and proposed changes to research council structures) and signalling growth in 'industry led research partnerships' (see Innovate UK, Built Environment – Smarter Transformation (BE-ST)). The Government's aspiration to increase industry-led research partnerships (see Knowledge Exchange Framework and Knowledge Transfer Partnerships) is arguably aided by pracademics who may act as an interface between industry and academic research skills.

Moreover, the TEF is focused specifically on pedagogy, rather than on professional and industrial experience. It thus focuses on more holistic and generic teaching qualities that almost any individual, regardless of their industrial experience, could have. Indeed, despite the introduction of the TEF and the desire to rebalance the research / teaching nexus, the TEF had negligible initial impact on recruitment adverts' weighting towards industrial experience (Pilcher et al., 2020). Nevertheless, the TEF is not the only initiative aimed to promote closer alignment between academia and industry; as there are also industry advisory panels that inform syllabus design.

Returning to Classical Experiential Models – The Growth of a New Voluntary Dual System and the Key Role of Pracademics in Its Success

Whilst current research does not indicate that academic appointments are moving away from research, anecdotal evidence suggests a recent increase in the number of teaching and scholarship appointments since our data from 2016–2018 was collected (Pilcher et al., 2020). Potentially driving this change is the relatively new funding stream associated with the Higher Education Apprenticeships. These are increasingly seen as important supplementary income streams over and above traditional full-time modes of delivery and research, with government funding provided in the majority of cases. The introduction of the Higher Education Apprenticeships signals a quasi-return to training frameworks more akin to the nineteenth century and may be interpreted as modernisation of the 'voluntary dual system' (compare Tennant et al., 2015). However, we should qualify that 'voluntary dual' has never really disappeared, with many part time students employed by engineering and construction companies studying at university on day-release / part-time programmes. Yet, the difference between Higher Education Apprenticeships and traditional craft apprenticeships is that with craft apprenticeships the syllabus at the academic institution was never directly contextualised to the workplace, nor was there an expectation of the need to evidence work-based learning. The theory was taught over many years, and the extended period of the apprenticeship meant that eventually learners would encounter most areas of practice, and they would need to personally reflect on their experience to facilitate the coupling of theory and practice.

Students learning via these experiential modes are arguably highly-motivated as they are being financially remunerated by employers, with breach penalties often included in contracts for underperformance and absenteeism (both in the workplace and in their academic studies). Nevertheless, as noted earlier, our own experiences suggest that education of these groups of engineering and construction students is not without its issues for universities that are largely populated by career academics with commonly less workplace experience than those they teach. This is not necessarily a problem if subjects are largely theoretical, but the issue quickly becomes pronounced if the syllabus is practical in focus. Arguably, this causes anxiety for those academics who are not from an industrial background and gives advantage to pracademics who are able to bridge the two worlds more effectively. In a desire to better understand the engineering and construction discipline, these students require and request both the 'knowing how' and the 'knowing that' (Ryle, 1945).

The pedagogical benefits of a well-structured Higher Education Apprenticeship, delivered by a combination of pracademics and career academics is justified. Whilst having practical experience is no guarantee to good teaching delivery, the pracademic can arguably more readily integrate and suggest the important site-based activities, and connect the workplace and academic institution effectively as they understand both realms. It appears an oddity that both career academics and pracademics may experience notions of imposter syndrome whilst working in the same sector, faculty, and institution. This may be exacerbated by the nature of the academic organisation and the terms and conditions of their contractual relationship (Teaching & Scholarship or Teaching & Research[5]). Russell Group institutions, with their expected emphasis upon research delivery may create unease for pracademics trying to integrate, whilst career academics may well experience anxiety if they are allocated practical subjects that are grounded in the everyday realities of engineering and construction practice (Pilcher et al., 2017).

Conclusion

In this chapter, we have outlined the history of how engineering and construction education has evolved. We have described how, up until the last half century, this education had been delivered in a positive Vitruvian equilibrium that inculcated learners with a balance of theory and practice. Even when theory and practice became decoupled, the provision remained healthy, as it was delivered by staff who often had experience of the industry themselves. Such staff implicitly

---

[5] In the UK, academic 'career paths' are often 'Teaching and Research', whereby the academic is expected to lecture and undertake research, applying for grants and publishing journal articles, or 'Teaching and Scholarship' whereby the academic is expected to teach and undertake work to improve the pedagogical delivery of their subject.

contextualise their professional and practical experience to theory in the classroom. This is extremely powerful as it brings to life what can be considered 'dry subjects' such as contract law, or maths and science for engineers. For example, calculations can be contextualised in practical examples of design, and may help answer the time-honoured question from learners, 'when is this used in reality?'. In this regard, Chartered staff have years of experience to draw upon. These examples give insights to learners around the essential interplay of design and theory. However, this balance became disrupted with a government HE policy focus on research. This led to a decoupling so severe that learners were often being taught by academic staff with PhDs and research experience, but little or no practical knowledge of the workplace. Such an entrenched decoupling had an adverse impact on the quality of the vocational education delivered. The UK Government has attempted to improve the balance towards pedagogy through the introduction of the TEF. Whilst it could feasibly be hoped this would improve institutional focus on recruiting pracademics and aid recoupling in engineering and construction, the TEF has had negligible impact on recruitment strategies to date in terms of hiring more pracademics.

It is recognised that anecdotal evidence suggests an increase in teaching and scholarship appointments, and this is also borne out also by recent statistics (Baker, 2021). Whilst this should arguably also mean a greater focus on applicants having significant industrial experience and professional chartered status, more research would be required in this area to attain a better understanding. Importantly, the introduction of Higher Education Apprenticeships, whilst underpinned by sound reasoning, apparently fails to effectively recouple the workplace and the taught theory, and is vulnerable in delivery if all parties are not fully engaged in the process (academics and work-based mentors).

In the future, we see a necessary move being to recalibrate the Higher Education Apprenticeships, and to ensure that pracademics do not feel that they are imposters but understand and recognise that they have an increasingly important role in creating linkages between academia and industry. One way in which this could be aided is through giving greater weight to the industrial advisory panels, despite previous criticism that was directed at them for being largely symbolic (Barr, 2008) or unrealistic in their expectations of pedagogical delivery change in a financially constrained and understaffed university sector. More opportunities for industry secondments could be introduced to give staff the opportunity to work in industry. We emphasize though, that any initiative would need to be fully supported by institutional and government policy. A restorative balance between theory and practice is to be welcomed given that too much of one thing, whether it be theory or practice, at the expense of the other, is never a positive outcome for educating learners in vocational built environment contexts and for enhancing employability. This work endeavours to articulate and frame the importance of the pracademic in the delivery of industrially coupled engineering and construction education and assert their sense of heritage and belonging that goes back centuries following the 'Vitruvian' tradition and essential knowledge constructs espoused by Ryle (1945).

Points for Reflection

- Within this chapter, the authors set out the historical trajectory of decoupling that has been taken by Construction and Engineering education. To what extent does this reflect the development of your own subject area, and if so, how may it have affected the delivery of vocational student learning?
- The authors advocate for a good balance of pracademics and career academics. Consider the composition of teaching staff within your institution, and potential opportunities for establishing more of an equilibrium.
- Throughout this chapter, the authors highlight how a lack of industry experience can impact career academics. How could HEIs support those career academics who may wish to gain more industry experience?
- The authors note the emphasis that the HE sector places on research. What benefits could there be for engaging pracademics in the development of research proposals, especially those that result in the transfer of industrial knowledge?

References

Andrew, N., Lopes, A., Pereira, F., & Lima, I. (2014). Building communities in higher education: The case of nursing. *Teaching in Higher Education, 19*(1), 72–77. https://doi.org/10.108 0/13562517.2013.859850

Baker, S. (2021, April 26). *Some UK universities saw teaching contract jump as REF loomed*. The Times Higher Education. https://www.timeshighereducation.com/news/ some-uk-universities-saw-teaching-contract-jump-ref-loomed

Barr, B. (2008). UK civil engineering education in the twenty-first century. *Proceedings of the ICE – Management, Procurement and Law, 161*, 17–23. https://doi.org/10.1680/mpal.2008.161.1.17

BIS. (2016). *Success as a knowledge economy: Teaching excellence, social mobility and student choice*. Department for Business, Innovation & Skills. https://assets.publishing.service.gov.uk/ government/uploads/system/uploads/attachment_data/file/523396/bis-16-265-success-as-a- knowledge-economy.pdf

Borg, J., & Scott-Young, C. M. (2020). Employers' perspectives on work readiness in construction: Are project management graduates hitting the ground running? *International Journal of Managing Projects in Business, 13*(6), 1363–1379. https://doi.org/10.1108/ IJMPB-10-2019-0238

Bowyer, J. (1993). *History of building* (2nd ed.). Attic Books.

Braga, A. A. (2016). The value of 'pracademics' in enhancing crime analysis in police departments. *Policing: A Journal of Policy and Practice, 10*(3), 308–314. https://doi.org/10.1093/ police/paw032

Brew, A. (2010). Imperatives and challenges in integrating teaching and research. *Higher Education Research & Development, 29*(2), 139–150. https://doi.org/10.1080/ 07294360903552451

Buchanan, R. A. (1985). *The rise of scientific engineering in Britain British society for the history of science*. Cambridge University Press.

Collins, L., & Collins, D. (2019). The role of 'pracademics' in education and development of adventure sport professionals. *Journal of Adventure Education and Outdoor Learning, 19*(1), 1–11. https://doi.org/10.1080/14729679.2018.1483253

Craig, N., Tennant, S., Murray, M., Forster, A., & Pilcher, N. (2016). The role of experienced practitioners in engineering education: The end of an era? In *6th international symposium for engineering education* (pp. 271–278). The University of Sheffield.

Craig, N., Pilcher, N., MacKenzie, R., & Boothman, C. (2020). The UK private housebuilding sector: Social media perspectives. *International Journal of Housing Markets and Analysis, 14*(3), 538–554. https://doi.org/10.1108/IJHMA-05-2020-0051

Dalrymple, R., Macrae, A., Pal, M., & Shipman, S. (2021). *Employability: A review of the literature 2016–2021.* Advance HE. https://www.advance-he.ac.uk/knowledge-hub/employability-review-literature-2016-2021

Evans, C., Muijs, D., & Tomlinson, M. (2015). *Engaged student learning: High-impact strategies to enhance student achievement.* Higher Education Academy. https://www.advance-he.ac.uk/knowledge-hub/engaged-student-learning-high-impact-strategies-enhance-student-achievement-0

Ferguson, E. S. (1992). *Engineering and the Mind's eye.* The MIT Press.

Ferguson, H., & Chrimes, M. (2011). *The civil engineers: The story of the institution of civil engineers and the people who made it.* ICE Publishing.

Forster, A. M., Pilcher, N., Tennant, S., Murray, M., Craig, N., & Copping, A. (2017). The fall and rise of experiential construction and engineering education: Decoupling and recoupling practice and theory. *Higher Education Pedagogies, 2*(1), 79–100. https://doi.org/10.1080/23752696.2017.1338530

Gimpel, J. (1961). *The cathedral builders.* Profile Books.

Guardian. (2014, December 18). *University research excellence framework 2014—The full rankings.* https://www.theguardian.com/news/datablog/ng-interactive/2014/dec/18/university-research-excellence-framework-2014-full-rankings

Hewett, C. A. (1980). *English historic carpentry.* Phillimore.

Hubble, S. (2017). *The teaching excellence framework (TEF).* House of Commons Briefing Paper Number 07484. June 22. https://researchbriefings.files.parliament.uk/documents/CBP-7848/CBP-7848.pdf

Kamp, A. (2020). *Navigating the landscape of higher engineering education: Coping with decades of accelerating change ahead.* Delft University of Technology.

Kant, I., Meiklejohn, J. M. D., & Kant, I. (2018). *The critique of pure reason.* Strelbytskyy Multimedia Publishing, [original 1781].

Lewis, P. M. R., & Reynolds, K. (2002). Forensic engineering: A reappraisal of the Tay bridge disaster. *Interdisciplinary Science Reviews, 27*(4), 287–298. https://doi.org/10.1179/030801802225005725

McNay, I. (2021). Academic capitalism, competition and competence: The impact on student recruitment and research assessment. *Journal of Further and Higher Education, 46*(6), 1–13. https://doi.org/10.1080/0309877X.2021.2003307

Murray, M., Tennant, S., Forster, A., Craig, N., Copping, A., & Pilcher, N. (2017). Talk the talk and walk the walk: Are career academics gatekeepers to my tacit knowledge? *Journal of perspectives in applied academic. Practice, 5*(2), 112–114. https://doi.org/10.14297/jpaap.v5i2.268

Norton, A. (2013, July 21). *Taking university teaching seriously.* Grattan Institute. https://grattan.edu.au/report/taking-university-teaching-seriously/

Nuttall, J., Brennan, M., Zipin, L., Tuinamuana, K., & Cameron, L. (2013). Lost in production: The erasure of the teacher educator in Australian university job advertisements. *Journal of Education for Teaching, 39*(3), 329–343. https://doi.org/10.1080/02607476.2013.799849

Olive, V. (2017). *How much is too much? Cross-subsidies from teaching to research in British universities.* Higher Education Policy Institute. https://www.hepi.ac.uk/2017/11/09/much-much-cross-subsidies-teaching-research-british-universities/

Parkman, A. (2016). The imposter phenomenon in higher education: Incidence and impact. *Journal of Higher Education Theory and Practice, 16*(1), 51.

Pilcher, N., Forster, A., Tennant, S., Murray, M., & Craig, N. (2017). Problematizing the 'Career Academic' in UK construction and engineering education: Does the system want what the system gets? *European Journal of Engineering Education, 42*(6), 1477–1495. https://doi.org/1 0.1080/03043797.2017.1306487

Pilcher, N., Galbrun, L., Craig, N., Murray, M., Forster, A. M., & Tennant, S. (2020). Role requirements in academic recruitment for construction and engineering. *European Journal of Engineering Education, 46*(2), 247–265. https://doi.org/10.1080/03043797.2020.1725451

Plimmer, F. (2003). Education for surveyors: An RICS perspective. *FIG regional conference* Marrakech, Morocco, December 2–5.

Russell, J. L., & Russell, L. (2006). *Change basics*. American Society for Training and Development.

Ryle, G. (1945, January). Knowing how and knowing that: The presidential address. In *Proceedings of the Aristotelian society* (Vol. 46, pp. 1–16). Wiley.

Schuster, J. H., & Finkelstein, M. J. (2006). *The American faculty: The restructuring of academic work and careers*. The Johns Hopkins University Press.

Scott, P. (1995). *The meanings of mass higher education*. SRHE and Open University Press.

Skills Development Scotland (SDS). (2017). *Graduate apprenticeships framework document for civil engineering at SCQF level 10*. Skills Development Scotland. https://www.skillsde-velopmentscotland.co.uk/media/43672/civil-framework-level-10-final-higher-apprenticeship-additions.pdf

Snell, K. D. M. (1996). The apprenticeship system in British history: The fragmentation of a cultural institution. *History of Education, 25*, 303–321. https://doi.org/10.1080/0046760960250401

Summerson, J. (1983). *Architecture in Britain, 1530 to 1830* (7th ed.).

Tennant, S., Murray, M., Forster, A., & Pilcher, N. (2015). Hunt the shadow not the substance: The rise of the career academic in construction education. *Teaching in Higher Education, 20*(7), 723–737. https://doi.org/10.1080/13562517.2015.1070342

Thompson, F. M. L. (1968). *Chartered surveyors the growth of a profession*. Westerham Press Limited.

Torrance, H. (2020). The research excellence framework in the United Kingdom: Processes, consequences, and incentives to engage. *Qualitative Inquiry, 26*(7), 771–779. https://doi.org/10.1177/1077800419878748

Warland, E. G. (2015). *Modern practical masonry*. Routledge.

Wyness, G. (2010). *Policy Changes in UK Higher Education Funding, 1963–2009*. DoQSS Working Papers 10–15, Quantitative Social Science – UCL Social Research Institute, University College London.

Zaheer, M. I., Ajayi, S. O., Zulu, S. L., Oyegoke, A., & Kazemi, H. (2020). Understanding the key competencies of market-ready building surveying graduates from employers' perspectives. *Journal of Engineering, Design and Technology, 19*(1), 291–394.

Zaitseva, E., & Finn, C. (2022). Mining employability narrative: From semantic analysis to institutional strategy. In E. Zaitseva, B. Tucker, & E. Santhanam (Eds.), *Analysing student feedback in higher education: Using text-mining to interpret the student voice* (pp. 133–148). Routledge.

Dr Alan M. Forster is an Associate Professor in the School of Energy, Geoscience, Infrastructure and Society at Heriot-Watt University. His research investigates building conservation & HBIM, architectural technology, low-carbon materials & design, and construction & engineering education. He has published extensively and has attained research grants from major funding councils, including, EPSRC, AHRC, RAE, RSE & Innovate UK. Professionally, he is a Fellow of the Chartered Institute of Builders (FCIOB), the Higher Education Academy (FHEA), and a member of the Institute of Historic Building Conservation (IHBC). He has won several teaching prizes, including the Heriot-Watt University Graduate's Teaching Award in 2010.

Dr Nick Pilcher is a lecturer in The Business School at Edinburgh Napier University. He is the Programme leader for the M.Sc. in intercultural Business Communication and teaches academic writing in subjects. His research interests centre around education, language and qualitative research methods. He has published and contributed to work published in journals such as Qualitative Research, Psychology of Music, the International Journal of Qualitative Studies in Education and the International Journal of Shipping and Transport Logistics. He was voted best research supervisor in 2021, and best lecturer in the School of Marketing, Tourism and Languages in 2022.

Dr Mike Murray is a Senior Teaching Fellow in the Department of Civil & Environmental Engineering at the University of Strathclyde. Mike is a Senior Fellow of the Higher Education Academy (SFHEA) and was awarded best Teacher in the Faculty of Engineering (2014); Most Innovative University Teacher (2018) at the University Teaching Excellence awards; Winner (2021) Faculty of Engineering Excellence in Teaching Awards-Excellence in Supporting Students during the 2020-21 academic year. He has contributed to work in journals such as Teaching in Higher Education, Higher Education Pedagogies, and European Journal of Engineering Education.

Dr Stuart Tennant is a lecturer in the School of Computing, Engineering and Physical Sciences at the University of the West of Scotland. He is a member of the Chartered Institute of Building (MCIOB) and Senior Fellow of the Higher Education Academy (SFHEA) Teaching interests include, project management, construction management, construction technology and industrial workplace learning. Research interests focus on construction supply chain management, procurement, team working in the built environment and educational studies. Stuart has published in journals such as Building Research & Information (BRI), Construction Management and Economics (CME) and Teaching in Higher Education.

Dr Nigel Craig is a Senior Lecturer and Programme Leader in Construction Management in the School of Engineering and Built Environment at Glasgow Caledonian University. Teaching interests include construction technology, construction process management, construction engineering and research methodology. Research interests focus on quality, cost/ finance, IT, plagiarism and building surveying. He has published in journals such as Structural Survey: Building Pathology, International Journal of Housing Markets and Analysis and Records Management.

Dr Laurent Galbrun is an Assistant Professor in Acoustics in the School of Energy, Geoscience, Infrastructure and Society, Heriot-Watt University, Edinburgh (UK). His expertise covers the fields of building acoustics, environmental noise and soundscapes. He is Programme Director for the Graduate Apprenticeship in Civil Engineering at Heriot-Watt University. Professionally, he is a Member of the Institute of Acoustics (MIOA) and of the Acoustical Society of America (MASA), as well as a Fellow of the Higher Education Academy (FHEA). He has won several teaching and learning prizes, including the Heriot-Wat University Graduate's Teaching Award in 2013 and 2017.

Chapter 16
More than Mere Context: The Role of Former Practitioners in Surveying Education

Emily Walsh

Abstract The inclusion of former practitioners in Higher Education is not unusual, particularly in 'vocational' subjects such as law, medicine, journalism, and social work. In some instances, these former practitioners are training students to enter the professional world that they have vacated, taking on similar roles. In others, former practitioners from a range of disciplines, come together within a department to teach different aspects of the curriculum. In this chapter, I consider how my experience as a commercial real estate solicitor impacted my approach to teaching and assessing students studying undergraduate surveying degrees. In so doing, I place my approach to teaching within the context of the broader literature on interdisciplinary pedagogy. I further consider how the lens of my professional practice, and that of other former practitioners from a range of disciplines, combine to contextualise learning. I examine the extent to which the values and skills intrinsic to those from a practitioner background not only situate the curriculum within the 'real world' but introduce additional elements to it.

Keywords Legal practice · Clinical legal education · Autonomy · Values · Ethical practice · Applied learning · Authentic assessment · Practice-informed teaching · Dignity · Paternalism · Lawyers

E. Walsh (✉)
School of Law, University of Portsmouth, Portsmouth, UK
e-mail: emily.walsh@port.ac.uk

© The Author(s), under exclusive license to Springer Nature
Switzerland AG 2023
J. Dickinson, T.-L. Griffiths (eds.), *Professional Development for Practitioners in Academia*, Knowledge Studies in Higher Education 13,
https://doi.org/10.1007/978-3-031-33746-8_16

At a Glance
- Identifies how former practitioners or pracademics are commonly part of the teaching staff in 'vocational' subjects such as law and medicine.
- Notes that, in some subjects, such as surveying, pracademics come from a variety of disciplines to create an interdisciplinary approach.
- Written from the experience of a former solicitor teaching in a real estate department, considers how one practitioner's professional expertise shaped the way in which she taught law to surveying students.
- Concludes that curriculum must be intentionally designed in order to create a fully interdisciplinary experience.

Introduction

Vocational Degrees

With the growth in the number of university places in the United Kingdom (UK) (Bolton, 2022), the debate surrounding the purpose of Higher Education (HE) has gained momentum. In England, the cost of university fees is funded by student loans. The UK Government anticipates that only 25% of full-time undergraduates will repay their student loans in full (Bolton, 2021). This fact has led to perceptions that degrees which are most likely to result in students obtaining well-paid graduate-level employment are valued more highly. Concerns regarding the extent to which the UK Government will use graduate employment data to determine funding have been widely reported (Morgan, 2021). The likelihood of securing a high salary is also valued by applicants, and employment outcomes data presented in university league tables enables applicants to choose courses and universities that score well on these matrices. Research published by the Higher Education Funding Council for England (HEFCE, 2018), and reported in the national press (Adams, 2018), shows that 'vocational' degrees such as medicine, nursing, and engineering result in employment in skilled and well-paid roles.

Practitioners in Higher Education

Degrees such as law or surveying are often marketed as leading to employment in the relevant field. Where this is the case, ex-practitioners are likely to be considered as adding value to degree programmes. Indeed, law schools have always contained a combination of former practitioners and academics. When I was an undergraduate, the balance leaned towards practitioners, with a relatively small percentage of my lecturers having PhDs. This has undoubtedly changed, and although I have not conducted extensive research into the matter, I think it is safe to say that many lecturers in law schools across the UK now hold a PhD, and that a contribution to research is increasingly a requirement of the job. Many law schools also employ teaching fellows who are likely to have a higher teaching workload and may be expected to participate in scholarship[1] rather than research. Similarly, surveying education has tended to employ lecturers from professional backgrounds rather than research-focused academics.

For the seven years that I spent in what became the School of Civil Engineering and Surveying, I was the 'lawyer in the real estate school' rather than 'the real estate lawyer in the law school', and I felt very much at home. In professional practice, my work involved residential and commercial development and commercial landlord and tenant. Teaching surveying students enabled me to teach landlord and tenant law, and land law. Law students do not have to study landlord and tenant law, and it is rarely offered as an optional module on undergraduate degrees. In practice, I had frequently worked with surveyors as they were my main referrers of work. I felt at home with colleagues who had this background and students who were hoping to go into this profession. Many of my colleagues were also from professional practice. I worked with an economist, architect, town planner, quantity surveyor, building surveyor, valuer, and estate manager. None of these colleagues had PhDs or undertook research. Instead, they continued to engage with their professional communities by delivering continuing professional development (CPD) courses and writing for practitioner journals and textbooks. Likewise, my first published article was for one of the Royal Institution of Chartered Surveyors (RICS) journals (Walsh, 2012). Between 2015 and 2017, I delivered seven RICS-accredited CPD courses, four of which I co-presented with specialist surveyors.

Key Themes

Disciplinary Boundaries

As I have stated, whilst some of my colleagues teaching surveying students were surveyors themselves, many were not. These pracademics came from diverse professional backgrounds and what could be described as different academic disciplines. They had undergraduate or postgraduate degrees in economics, architecture, and town planning. The School also included academics from geography and history. This variety raises questions about the nature of disciplines within the academy, the extent to which the boundaries of disciplines are fixed, and whether and how disciplines can collide to create interdisciplines or new disciplines.

---

[1] Scholarship is typically activity with focusses on professionals updating their knowledge and/or skills.

What Is a Discipline?

Law has long been acknowledged as a discipline, and according to Davies and Devlin (2007), it was one of the original four disciplines that were studied at universities, along with medicine, philosophy, and theology. The extent to which surveying is a discipline or an interdiscipline will be considered further below. First, it is necessary to consider what a discipline means, and the extent to which the concept matters to students and academics. It is outside the scope of this chapter to delve too deeply into the literature surrounding academic disciplines. However, according to Barnett:

> Disciplines can be considered vocations. They can exert a life-long claim on the individuals' attention, they call for skills of a high order; they contain their own standards to which academics have to give their allegiance, and they call for devotion in the real sense of the word (1994, p. 123).

This definition resonates with me. Between 1996 and 2004, I ceased being a practising lawyer. I lived abroad and taught English, gaining an undergraduate degree in English Literature and a Master's degree in Education with Applied Linguistics. However, during this hiatus in my legal career, I never really stopped being a lawyer. My worldview had shifted, and it was never going to shift back. It was not that I was unable to be other things as well. I was certainly a teacher; it was just that the notion 'once a lawyer, always a lawyer' very much applied to me. The metaphor of tribes and territories has been applied to academics and their disciplines. The metaphor originates with Becher (Becher, 1989) but has been widely discussed within HE. Tight (2015) found that over 4000 academic publications used the exact phrase 'tribes and territories.' The tribes and territories metaphor, and Barnett's definition, create a view of academic disciplines as hard-edged and exclusive. If the boundaries of disciplines are impermeable, it may be challenging to create space for students and academics to enjoy interdisciplinary experiences. Other scholars have acknowledged that the tribes' metaphor is unhelpful or unrepresentative and have searched for different ways to view disciplines. Donald (2008) uses the metaphor of 'home' to suggest a place where academics gain safety but are free to leave. In this way, academics benefit from their membership of a discipline but are not restricted by it. Others have used metaphors such as "sliding doors" or "shifting sands" (Bamber, 2012, p. 105) or even "oceans of knowledge" (Manathunga & Brew, 2012, p. 52).

It is important to note that academics experience their discipline in the context of both teaching and research, and pracademics experience their discipline, their teaching, and any research undertaken, through the lens of prior professional experience. I would argue that this lens has quite a powerful impact on the notion of discipline. As a lawyer with a strong identity as such, my first experience of the academy was teaching law modules to surveying students in the School of Environmental Design and Management at the University of Portsmouth. No sooner had I joined this department than it merged with Civil Engineering to become the School of Civil Engineering and Surveying (SCES). My professional identity sat comfortably with my students. Real estate law was required for their chosen degree, and this needed to be taught by a lawyer. Furthermore, the School felt strongly that law must be taught by someone with the experience in the practical application of the subjet. When the students questioned the usefulness of legal concepts to them as surveyors, I could reassure them that, from my professional experience, these concepts were essential to their ability to work with, and advise, their clients, and to communicate with lawyers. With regard to research, however, the experience was a little different. My department now comprised academics teaching and researching in disciplines with very different approaches to my own. I was encouraged to undertake my PhD within the SCES rather than the Law School, but my socio-legal methodology was out of place in a school where most of the research undertaken was technical in nature. Some colleagues perceived law as a fixed set of rules and were surprised that it was even possible to undertake research in law. I had to explain that, unlike Engineering, the credibility of legal journals was not based on impact factor. I also found myself forced to defend my preferred methodology. For me, the disciplinary boundaries were being articulated for the first time.

Teaching Law to Surveying Students

For students, disciplinary identity can also be important. It shapes what they are taught, the standards they are expected to attain, and, as I have suggested, it also shapes their identity. Where students, such as those studying surveying degrees are taught by lecturers with different disciplinary backgrounds to their own, questions arise as to whether the degrees themselves align with a single discipline or whether they are more interdisciplinary in nature. There are a number of ways in which undergraduate students can get an interdisciplinary experience. The most obvious of these is a joint honours degree where students typically take two-thirds of their modules in one discipline and a third in another. The two disciplines can be complementary or disparate. As well as being coupled with quite obvious partners such as business, law can be teamed with psychology, social anthropology, and even English literature. In this case, the student's disciplinary identity is likely to be aligned with their home school. They may feel like they are outsiders in their 'other' discipline where the rules seem very different. Indeed, this has been my experience of teaching those studying Law with Criminology degrees where social scientific approaches to analysis and different systems of research and referencing have caused law students to struggle. Issues of interdisciplinarity do not arise as the student is simply taking a degree that has two unequal parts comprising two different disciplines.

Law is also taught as a single module on a number of different degrees. Where law is taught to students in another subject area, it is sometimes referred to as a "service subject" (Yang, 2009, p. 598). In these instances, the law module is designed and taught by lecturers in the law school who may have limited involvement with the department in which the module is delivered. Often these 'service' law modules are hard work for students and lecturers alike, with students struggling with the amount of reading required and the strange lexicon, and ultimately performing poorly in the assessments. Consequently, teaching law to non-law students has been "characterised as being both secondary and inferior to that teaching and those students that are found within the law school" (Bradney, 1998, p. 81). Resultantly, a number of legal academics have made recommendations about how the delivery of individual service modules can be improved to better meet the needs of students from non-law disciplines (Allen, 2007; Byles & Soetendorp, 2002; Endeshaw, 2002). One of the suggestions is to adopt the contextual environmental approach, in which the students' own subject area forms the context within which law is delivered (Byles & Soetendorp, 2002). Designing a law module for non-law students, that is based on context rather than a diluted version of the law school equivalent, can be challenging for module leaders whose professional backgrounds are specialist legal academics. As I have discussed above, lawyers, like members of other disciplines, are part of a community with rules and approaches to knowledge that may differ considerably from those within the department where the service module is delivered. The time allocated to designing the service module may be the same as for a module within their own department even though there may be different and novel considerations to consider. Byles and Soetendorp suggest that in designing a module for non-law students, it is important to understand the nature of the students' own discipline and to work with colleagues within that field to better recognise the needs of the students (2002).

Unlike lawyers in some surveying subject groups or departments at other universities, I was situated within the surveying school. At Portsmouth, the department responsible for surveying education had always had its own lawyer and this was considered important for students. The job description for the role involved a professional legal qualification and experience working in real estate. This gave me an advantage over my colleagues in the law school who taught law to business students. These colleagues were situated in the law school and were not necessarily former commercial lawyers.

When I started teaching law to surveyors, I had never taught before. Fresh out of practice, my focus was on what would be useful to future built environment professionals. I had considerable autonomy in the design, teaching, and assessment of my modules. Whilst the teaching of law is required by both the professional body that accredits the degrees (the RICS) and the Quality Assurance Agency (QAA), the amount, or indeed content, of the law taught is not prescribed. The QAA for Land, Construction, Real Estate and Surveying (2019) lists law as one of seven broad areas in the curriculum. However, there is considerable flexibility about exactly what is taught. My practice background helped me to provide context. I had experience as a solicitor of translating law to clients and surveyors who were non-lawyers but who were often built environment experts. As well as speaking the language of law, I was conversant in a lexicon derived from an applied legal context that included terminology from business and construction. Both my experience in practice and my lack of experience as a lecturer to law students, helped me to teach law in a way that better aligned with my surveying students. Teaching land law to surveying students should be quite different from teaching land law to law students. Traditional land law textbooks focus on appeal court decisions that are alien to the solution-focused surveying students whom I encountered. To surveyors, and indeed commercial real estate clients, the law is often about weighing the risks and reaching a commercial decision. Law is part, but not all, of the picture. In designing my module, I therefore, focused on this commercial approach, acknowledging that when land is purchased for development, the motive is profit. There are a plethora of legal issues from land law (as well as planning law) that can restrict and inhibit this goal. I am inclined to agree with Bennett when he explains that non-law students should be introduced to law as "a framework that subtly (and fundamentally) shapes commercial and professional behaviour - and that disputes comparatively rarely (compared to the focus on senior court cases by traditional legal education) ever reach the courts" (2009, p. 107).

Interdisciplinarity

I have considered the challenges faced in teaching law to non-lawyers and the advantage that a practice background might provide in addressing some of these challenges at a module delivery level. It is necessary to move beyond the teaching of law at a unit or module level to consider the bigger picture. As I have explained, law is one of several disciplines that come together within built environment programmes. How these different disciplines interact within the curriculum will be significant in determining both student experience and student success.

Surveying does not sit neatly in a particular disciplinary paradigm. It is neither a science nor an art, and it is neither fully applied nor pure in its approach. Becher identifies four basic sets of properties: hard/soft and pure/applied in the cognitive realm (1989). Hard disciplines such as physics operate within an agreed paradigm, and knowledge within the discipline is cumulative. Soft disciplines such as sociology are more contested and less cumulative. Pure disciplines are directed towards understanding, and applied disciplines focused on solving practical problems. So, for example, chemistry is a pure discipline whilst law is applied (Tight, 2015). Neuman et al. (2002) categorise academic disciplines into four groups that they refer to as: "hard pure, soft pure, hard applied, and soft applied" (p. 405). Biglan created a disciplinary model that placed academic disciplines within these four groups but also acknowledged the variance between the extent to which each discipline encompassed each property. So, for example, Biglan identifies Geography as a pure discipline but places it on the line between hard and soft. He places Economics within the pure disciplines but closer to the line between applied and pure than the Natural Sciences.

Chynoweth (2009) maps the elements of built environment courses onto Biglan's disciplinary model to illustrate that there are elements that are situated in three of the four quartiles (hard applied, hard pure, and soft applied). If surveying is not a discipline then arguably it is interdisciplinary. However, Chynoweth argues that in order to be truly interdisciplinary, rather than multidisciplinary, a course must have its own identity rather than comprising a collection of disciplines with their own individual characters (multidisciplinary) or adopting the identity of the dominant discipline (cross-disciplinary). Petrie describes multidisciplinary as "everyone [does] his or her things with little or no necessity for any one participant to be aware of any other participant's work" (1976, p. 9). Cross-disciplinarity occurs where a subject normally outside a discipline is investigated without any input from those involved in the outside discipline (Davies and Devlin, 2010). Where communication between disciplines is encouraged but not coordinated, the disciplines may be pluridisciplinary.

The impact of disciplinary differences on teaching style has not been settled within the literature. Some studies suggest that teachers in 'hard' disciplines are more likely to adopt a teacher-focused approach to teaching than those teaching in 'soft' disciplines (Lueddeke, 2003; Trigwell, 2002; Lindblom-Ylanne et al., 2006). Research suggests that it is not only the disciplinary paradigm but also the amount of pedagogical training that has been undertaken by the lecturer that impacts the extent to which the approach is teacher-centred or student-centred (Postareff et al., 2007). Parker (2002) argues that there is much to be gained from distinctive disciplinary knowledge that situates a student within the disciplinary community versus a model of transmission of subject knowledge and skills. Parker's approach resonates at a time when universities are under pressure to demonstrate the monetary value of their degrees by demonstrating that students have met certain levels of knowledge acquisition. Instead of focusing on the formulation that an academic subject is the sum of subject knowledge plus skills, she suggests situating disciplinary knowledge within the discipline communities' activities to produce, rather than acquire, distinctive disciplinary knowledge. Taking this approach to the discipline of law might involve a reduced focus on assessment of the legal rules, and increased consideration of the approaches to interpretation and application of legal rules, besides creating space for considering the impact of law on society and a critical appreciation of the role that law plays in regulating society. Reflection on the meaning of discipline is important for academics who are trained in one discipline and who are teaching students who are being educated in another.

Interdisciplinarity has been said to involve "the emergence of insight and understanding of a problem domain through the integration or derivation of different concepts, methods, and epistemologies from different disciplines in a novel way" (Rogers et al., 2005, p. 3). This suggests a considerable shift from a curriculum in which industry experts create syllabi for their own individual areas of expertise. These disciplinary distinctions are therefore important in considering the extent to which the individual pracademics engaged in teaching coordinate the curriculum to create a true interdiscipline. Where the different disciplines represented in surveying degrees are not integrated into an interdiscipline, and the course remains multidisciplinary, it is likely that students will experience what Klein has described as a "cafeteria-style" educational experience (1990, p. 196).

Pracademics and Interdisciplinary Curriculum Design

There is no consensus as to the meaning of curriculum within HE. Indeed, Barnett and Coate (2005) argue that the term, or indeed even the notion, of curriculum is absent from the narrative surrounding the aims of HE in the UK. They argue that the dominant narrative is skills acquisition. Research undertaken in an Australian university by Fraser and Bosanquet (2006) demonstrates a large divergence of opinion between academics on the meaning of the term. Their data revealed that the term was sometimes understood as relating to the structure and content of an individual unit whilst some took a broader view to include the entire programme. Some academics moved away from this product-focussed conception to include students' experiences of learning and others included both teaching and learning within their conception of curriculum. Walker (1990) explains that whilst academics are experts in a particular discipline, they are not experts in education and do not necessarily engage with educational research and curriculum theory. As a result, the curriculum is merely the syllabus for many academics (Stark & Lattuca, 1997).

Barnett and Coate (2005) develop a discussion of curriculum around three building blocks: Knowing, Acting, and Being. 'Knowing' is not merely the passive acquisition of knowledge but a dynamic process that requires engagement from the student. 'Acting' may include obvious work or community-related activities but can also include activity that occurs within the classroom. This action, or engagement in activity builds the skills that are so frequently the focus of the HE 'value for money' narrative in England. Finally, 'Being' requires the student to absorb information as knowledge and develop skills and also evolve a sense of self such that they are able to operate in a world where the knowledge and skills necessary to succeed are not fixed but are constantly evolving (p. 63). What is interesting, from an interdisciplinary perspective, is that the various disciplines place a different emphasis on these building blocks. From their empirical research, Barnett and Coate created a schema that demonstrates the relationship between the three building blocks in three different groups of disciplines: arts and humanities, science and technology, and professional subjects. Looking at the curriculum in arts and humanities, subject knowledge predominated but was linked to an important element of 'Being'. It may be that, within the curriculum, the 'Knowing' in some modules remained fixed and was delivered over many years with little change. Whilst there was variation between institutions in the domain of action, there was a tendency for practical skills to be less dominant within the curriculum than knowledge. In science and technology subjects, 'Knowing' also dominated but 'Being' was less dominant than in the arts and humanities and was also less integrated with knowledge. In professional subjects such as nursing, 'Acting' dominated and was integrated with the other two domains so that all three areas overlapped in places.

   This analysis of the curriculum is interesting in considering intentional, interdisciplinary design in built environment curricula. As Chynoweth (2009) acknowledges, built environment curricula include elements of several disciplinary areas and will therefore share similarities with the knowledge/action focus of science and technology courses but may also include the kind of analytical elements found within professional subjects. The different emphasis placed on these domains, and indeed the difference in teaching delivery and assessment between different disciplines, may result in challenges around creating an intentional interdisciplinary curriculum. Students who are used to an active approach in learning subjects, such as valuation, may struggle if knowledge predominates in their law modules. This challenge is not unique to built environment curricula but will also be experienced by academics in the design of other interdisciplinary courses.

Conclusion

In this chapter, I have examined my experience of teaching in a school with pracademics from a range of other disciplines. My experience as a former legal practitioner, situated within the real estate school, enabled me to teach law in a way that provided a more useful and engaging experience for students than they might have acquired from a series of serviced modules delivered by the law school. However, in order to provide a truly interdisciplinary experience, a more intentional curriculum design is required. This may involve the creation of modules that engage more than one discipline to solve a practical problem. Too frequently as university lecturers, the cyclical pressures of teaching prevent us from taking a step back and examining both what we teach and how we teach it. This is an area in which further research would be welcomed.

Points for Reflection
- In this chapter, Walsh provides examples of both 'hard' and 'soft' disciplines. Which one of these types does your work most align with? To what extent does that classification impact on how students have traditionally been taught within your area? Could there be any opportunities for drawing on pedagogic approaches from other disciplines?
- Walsh identifies a number of advantages in adopting an interdisciplinary approach. To what extent could there be scope for your School or Department to collaborate with colleagues and students from other areas, and what benefits could that bring, and for whom?
- This chapter has discussed how institutional organisation can foster openings for developing interdisciplinarity. To what extent could there be opportunities for wider groups of academics and students to work across disciplines within your own institution? What role(s) could pracademics play within them?

References

Adams, R. (2018, February 9). Vocational degrees are best route to highly skilled jobs, study finds. *The Guardian*. https://www.theguardian.com/education/2018/feb/09/vocational-degrees-best-highly-skilled-jobs-study

Allen, V. (2007). A critical reflection on the methodology of teaching law to non-law students. *Web Journal of Current Legal Issues* (4), 1360–1326. http://www.bailii.org/uk/other/journals/WebJCLI/2007/issue4/allen4.html

Bamber, V. (2012). Learning and teaching in the disciplines: Challenging knowledge, ubiquitous change. In P. Trowler, M. Saunders, & V. Bamber (Eds.), *Tribes and territories in the 21st century: Rethinking the significance of disciplines in higher education* (pp. 99–106). Routledge.

Barnett, R. (1994). *The limits of competence: Knowledge, higher education and society*. SRHE and the Open University Press.

Barnett, R., & Coate, K. (2005). *Engaging the curriculum in higher education*. Open University Press.

Becher, T. (1989). *Academic tribes and territories: Intellectual enquiry and the cultures of disciplines*. Open University Press.

Bennett, L. (2009). Why, what, and how? Case study on law, risk, and decision making as necessary themes in built environment teaching. *Journal of Legal Affairs and Dispute Resolution in Engineering and Construction, 1*(2), 105–112.

Biglan, A. (1973). The characteristics of subject matters in different academic areas. *Journal of Applied Psychology, 57*(3), 195–203.

Bolton, P. (2021, December 1). *Student loan statistics*. House of Commons Library. https://commonslibrary.parliament.uk/research-briefings/sn01079/#:~:text=The%20Government%20expects%20that%2025,the%20costs%20of%20higher%20education

Bolton, P. (2022, July 8). *Higher education student numbers*. House of Commons Library. https://researchbriefings.files.parliament.uk/documents/CBP-7857/CBP-7857.pdf

Bradney, A. (1998). Law as a parasitic discipline. *Journal of Law and Society, 25*(1), 71–84.

Byles, L., & Soetendorp, R. (2002). Law teaching for other programmes. In R. Burridge, K. Hinett, A. Paliwala, & T. Varnava (Eds.), *Effective learning and teaching in law* (pp. 144–163). Kogan Page.

Chynoweth, P. (2009). The built environment interdiscipline a theoretical model for decision makers in research and teaching. *Structural Survey, 27*(4), 301–310.

Davies, M., & Devlin, M. (2007). Interdisciplinary higher education: Implications for teaching and learning.. Centre for the Study of Higher Education.

Davies, M., & Devlin, M. (2010). Chapter 1 – Interdisciplinary higher education. In M. Davies, M. Devlin, & M. Tight (Eds.), *Interdisciplinary higher education: Perspectives and practicalities* (International Perspectives on Higher Education Research, Vol. 5, pp. 3–28). Emerald Group Publishing Limited.

Donald, J. (2008). The commons: Disciplinary and interdisciplinary encounters. In C. Kreber (Ed.), *The university and its disciplines: Teaching and learning within and beyond disciplinary boundaries* (pp. 35–49). Taylor & Francis Group.

Endeshaw, A. (2002). Teaching law to business students: An inquiry into curriculum and methodology. *The Law Teacher, 36*(1), 24–43.

Fraser, S. P., & Bosanquet, A. M. (2006). The curriculum? That's just a unit outline, isn't it? *Studies in Higher Education, 31*(3), 269–284.

Higher Education Funding Council for England. (2018). *Vocational degrees and employment outcomes*. Higher Education Funding Council for England. https://webarchive.nationalarchives.gov.uk/ukgwa/20180319114826/http:/www.hefce.ac.uk/pubs/year/2018/201801/

Klein, J. (1990). *Interdisciplinarity*. Wayne State University Press.

Lindblom-Ylänne, S., Strigwell, K., Nevgi, A., & Ashwin, P. (2006). How approaches to teaching are affected by discipline and teaching context. *Studies in Higher Education, 31*(3), 285–298.

Lueddeke, G. (2003). Professionalising teaching practice in higher education: A study of disciplinary variation and 'teaching-scholarship'. *Studies in Higher Education, 28*(2), 213–228.

Manathunga, C., & Brew, A. (2012). Beyond tribes and territories: New metaphors for new times. In P. Trowler, M. Saunders, & V. Bamber (Eds.), *Tribes and territories in the 21st century: Rethinking the significance of disciplines in higher education* (pp. 44–56). Routledge.

Morgan, J. (2021, November 18). Should graduate employment data be used to decide course funding? *Times higher education.* https://www.timeshighereducation.com/depth/should-graduate-employment-data-be-used-decide-course-funding

Neuman, R., Parry, S., & Becher, T. (2002). Teaching and learning in their disciplinary contexts: A conceptual analysis. *Studies in Higher Education, 27*(4), 405–417.

Parker, J. (2002). A new disciplinarity: Communities of knowledge, learning and practice. *Teaching in Higher Education, 7*(4), 373–386.

Petrie, H. G. (1976). Do you see what I see? The epistemology of interdisciplinary inquiry. *The Journal of Aesthetic Education, 10*(1), 29–43.

Postareff, L., Lindblom-Ylänne, S., & Nevgi, A. (2007). The effect of pedagogical training on teaching in higher education. *Teaching and Teacher Education, 23*(5), 557–571.

Quality Assurance Agency for Higher Education. (2019, October). *Subject benchmark statement for land, construction, real estate and surveying.* https://www.qaa.ac.uk/docs/qaa/subject-benchmark-statements/subject-benchmark-statement-land-construction-real-estate-and-surveying.pdf?sfvrsn=f9f3c881_4

Rogers, Y., Scaife, M., & Rizzo, A. (2005). Interdisciplinarity: An emergent or engineered process? In S. J. Derry, C. D. Schunn, & M. A. Gernsbacher (Eds.), *Interdisciplinary collaboration* (pp. 265–285). Psychology Press.

Stark, J., & Lattuca, L. (1997). *Shaping the college curriculum.* Allyn & Bacon.

Tight, M. (2015). Theory development and application in higher education research: Tribes and territories. *Higher Education Policy, 28*, 277–293.

Trigwell, K. (2002). Approaches to teaching design subjects: A quantitative analysis. *Art, Design and Communication in Higher Education, 1*(2), 69–80.

Walker, D. (1990). *Fundamentals of curriculum.* Harcourt Brace.

Walsh, E. (2012). The monster in the mirror. *RICS Land Journal*, November–December, 20–21.

Yang, M. (2009). Making interdisciplinary subjects relevant to students: An interdisciplinary approach. *Teaching in Higher Education, 14*(6), 597–606.

Dr Emily Walsh is a Principal Lecturer at the University of Portsmouth. During her ten years at the University, she has taught land and landlord and tenant law to both law and surveying students as well as contributing to a Continuing Professional Development for qualified surveyors. Prior to joining the University, Emily worked as a commercial real estate solicitor acting for both developers and commercial landlords and tenants. This practical experience as a solicitor informed her PhD on obsolete restrictive covenants. Emily is a socio-legal researcher with an interest in the impact of the law on individuals. Emily has published a textbook and a number of publications on landlord and tenant and housing law. Her current research concerns private residential renting and the purpose-built student accommodation sector.

Chapter 17
Exploring the Value of Autonomy in Clinical Legal Education

Laura Bradley and Omar Madhloom

Abstract Framed around the example of law clinics and clinical legal education, which are now mainstream in law schools in England and Wales, the concept of autonomy will be explored through existing pedagogical literature and applied to student supervision and client care. It will be argued that autonomy allows students to develop their reflective practice while simultaneously ensuring that clients are involved in decision-making procedures.

Autonomy promotes students' independent learning and assists in their continued professional development. In relation to client care, many professional codes of conduct encourage professionals to act in the best interest of service users, emphasising the need for further guidance. An advantage of using autonomy as a teaching tool is its association with related concepts such as consent, freedom, and choice. Teaching autonomy, therefore, allows students to not only promote their client's interests but to also their build awareness of policy which may hinder client autonomy and their ability to participate in reform.

The chapter will conclude that a conception of autonomy which focuses on the dignity of the client is a valuable pedagogic tool in law and other disciplines that employ experiential/clinic learning such as medicine, nursing, and social care.

Keywords Business schools · Pracademics · Boundary spanners · Context-specific reflection · Student experience · Leadership · Leadership development · Industry insight · University industry collaboration

L. Bradley
University of Law (Birmingham Campus), Birmingham, UK
e-mail: omar.madhloom@bristol.ac.uk

O. Madhloom (✉)
University of Bristol Law School, University of Bristol, Bristol, UK

J. Dickinson, T.-L. Griffiths (eds.), *Professional Development for Practitioners in Academia*, Knowledge Studies in Higher Education 13,
https://doi.org/10.1007/978-3-031-33746-8_17

At a Glance
- Reflecting on legal education in England and Wales, the authors consider how Clinical Legal Education (CLE) can assist practitioners in bridging the theory-practice divide.
- Examines the value of autonomy in CLE and how this concept, which also has broader application, can develop students' ethical responsibilities towards their clients, third parties, and the environment.
- Using a hypothetical example, as well as case law, the authors reflect on how CLE can assist practitioners in promoting moral education that is underpinned by the concept of autonomy.

Introduction

We will demonstrate the value of autonomy and the related concept of human dignity to legal education in England and Wales. It will be argued that autonomy can be a useful concept to pracademics teaching Clinical Legal Education (CLE), because it promotes students' reflection and analysis of issues such as client care, law reform, and the impact of the law on persons and the environment. We argue that CLE is an optimal methodology (Wizner, 2012) for exploring the benefits of autonomy to legal education and training. Although the focus of this chapter is on the application of autonomy in CLE, autonomy can also be of relevance to non-law pracademics because it underpins professional education and training in other disciplines such as medicine (Williams & Deci, 1998), education (Manzano Vázquez, 2018), and social work (Johnson & Hull, 1992). Therefore, the model for autonomy explored in this chapter may have relevance to pracademics in other disciplines.

The term 'pracademics' is said to "encompass both former and/or current practitioners who are now academics within HE [Higher Education] (as opposed to compulsory or further education)" (Dickinson et al., 2020, p. 291). Within England and Wales, pracademics in law schools tend to be members or former members of the two main branches of the legal profession: solicitors and barristers.[1] At the time of writing, to qualify as either a barrister or solicitor, one must have completed the following stages: (1) the academic stage: a law degree or a one-year conversion course (the Graduate Diploma in Law); (2) the vocational stage which comprises both: the Legal Practice Course for solicitors or the Bar Course for barristers, and a period of recognised training comprising one year for barristers and two years for trainee

---

[1] Historically, barristers were considered experts in advocacy, while solicitors managed the case from initial instruction to its resolution. Solicitors also instructed barristers on behalf of their clients for advice about the law and court/tribunal advocacy. However, this distinction is now less demarcated with barristers authorised to take instructions directly from clients, and solicitors, practising as Solicitor Advocates, have rights of audience in the Senior civil or criminal courts in England and Wales.

solicitors. In November 2021, the Solicitors Regulation Authority, a statutory body that regulates solicitors in England and Wales, introduced a new route to qualifying as a solicitor, the Solicitors Qualifying Exam (SQE). The SQE is a centralised assessment and is outside the scope of this chapter. The focus, however, of this discussion is on CLE in Higher Education (HE).

Due to the distinction between the academic and vocational stages of legal education, undergraduate modules predominantly use appellate court decisions and academic opinions to teach students about the development and application of legal rules and principles. This theoretical approach not only neglects the judgments of the lower courts but also the collection of evidence for, and the procedure involved in, the preparation of a case for trial. Appellate judgments, on their own, "cannot provide a comprehensive account of how or why that decision was reached" (Weait, 2012, p. 163). However, it is acknowledged that in today's law schools, other pedagogic approaches, besides the study of appellate decisions, are used, such as CLE, critical legal studies, feminist jurisprudence, and socio-legal studies. Pracademics "with deep exposure to both theory and practice" (Posner, 2009, p. 17) are ideally positioned to bridge the theory-practice divide in legal education and training. One method through which pracademics can achieve this pedagogic goal is through CLE, which engages students with not only appellate decisions, but also cases in the trial courts and tribunals and Alternative Dispute Resolution (ADR). CLE is also an appropriate methodology for moral education (Nicolson, 2008). Moral education is defined as the acquisition of "a set of beliefs and values regarding what is right and wrong. This set of beliefs guides [students'] intentions, attitudes and behaviours towards others and their environment" (Halstead, 2010, p. 630). This chapter will examine how the concept of autonomy can enhance CLE by providing students with a frame of reference through which they can reflect on, and engage in, client care, law reform, and moral discourse. Reference to clients in this chapter is in relation to persons with mental capacity and legal persons such as corporations.

Key Themes

Clinical Legal Education

McAllister et al. (1997, p. 3) define clinical practice as:

> [A] teaching and learning process which is student-focused and may be student-led, which occurs in the context of client care. It involves the translation of theory into the development of clinical knowledge and practical skills, with the incorporation of the affective domain needed for sensitive and ethical client care. Clinical education occurs in an environment supportive of the development of clinical reasoning skills, professional socializing and life-long learning.

This definition, which is primarily aimed at preparing students for work in the health, education, and welfare sectors, involves the acquisition of skills and attributes that are appropriate in a professional setting. Our definition serves to highlight how clinical education can prepare students for work in various sectors. It is submitted that McAllister et al.'s definition can be extended to CLE. However, the development of moral and ethical positions is equally relevant. With regards to CLE, Dunn (2016) identifies the following types of models: problem-based learning, Street Law, simulations, advice only clinics, externships, and live client clinics. Although live client clinics are the most realistic portrayal of practice, the pedagogic approach that we are advocating in this chapter can be applied to any of the CLE models identified by Dunn, as well as essay and problem questions.

In addition to the acquisition of negotiation and counselling skills, Askin (1998) identifies four contributions of law school clinics to legal education and the legal process. First, clinics provide a practical vision of law as a tool for social justice. Second, they provide an opportunity for students to have a social impact and to engage in law reform. Thus, CLE allows students to discuss normative questions such as 'what is good law?'. Third, it exposes students, under supervised conditions, to the complexities and uncertainties of the law and legal practice. Fourth, clinics can act as a platform for engaging in reflective and ethical lawyering. CLE is, therefore, an optimal methodology for bridging the conceptual gap between theory and practice, and equipping students with the ability to foster improved client relationships during their formative years of legal training.

The Regulation of Law Clinics

In relation to live client clinics, students are involved in providing pro bono legal assistance, under the supervision of legal pracademics. However, there is a limit on the type of legal assistance which students, in unregulated university law clinics, are able to engage in. The relevant statute regarding the provision of legal services in England and Wales is the Legal Services Act 2007 (LSA 2007). Section 12 of the LSA 2007 sets out six specific legal activities that only those who are authorised, such as solicitors and barristers, or who are exempt (Schedule 3 of the LSA 2007), can carry out. These are termed 'reserved legal activities' which unregulated clinics cannot engage in. However, anyone in England and Wales is permitted to offer legal advice provided they do not 'hold' themselves out to be a solicitor, which is a criminal offence (Section 21, Solicitors Act 1974).

The significance of reserved legal activities in relation to CLE is that students are unable to engage in activities such as the conduct of litigation. Thus, students may be unable to gain valuable experience of engaging with the practical aspects of criminal cases. Some clinics elect to partner with law firms in order to provide opportunities for their students to engage in reserved legal activities such as criminal litigation. However, due to law school resources, this option may not be available to some clinics. We therefore suggest using court judgments which contain transcripts, such as *R v Konzani* (2005) 2 Cr. App. R. 14 (this will be discussed in

2.4.2), as case studies to demonstrate how autonomy can promote student engagement in client care and law reform.

Legal Education

Currently, there are two main methods of assessment in legal education (Goold, 2022, p. 370): problem-based questions and essay questions. The former requires students to analyse a fictitious scenario from the perspective of one or all of the parties and apply the relevant law to the facts presented. Problem-based questions present a picture of the law as an autonomous system free from extra-legal considerations. This form of legal reasoning falls under legal formalism, which is a method of legal justification that can be contrasted with the "open-ended disputes about the basic terms of social life, disputes that people call ideological, philosophical or visionary" (Unger, 1983, p. 564). In other words, a formalist approach in legal education involves students identifying the relevant legal principles, applying them to the facts of the problem-question, and deducing a rule that will inform the resolution of the dispute. The advantage of applying formalism is that students are taught that the state and citizens are bound by rules which are fixed and promogulated in advance. Thus, persons can foresee with a degree of certainty how the rules may be applied to them (Healey & Hillier, 2008). Although legal certainty (per Lord Mansfield in *Vallejo v Wheeler* (1774) 1 Cowp 143, p. 153) is an essential element of a legal system, teaching students to focus on precedent omits the fact that legal practice involves the application of rules other than the decisions of appellate courts. Lawyers also apply evidence and extra-legal considerations. When preparing a case for trial, a lawyer constructs their 'case theory', which comprises legal theories and factual theories (Thomas, 2008). Similarly, lawyers may be required to support their case with extra-legal factors such as where there is ambiguity in relation to the meaning of terms such as 'deception' or 'consent'. Consequently, formalism, on its own, is insufficient for the purposes of CLE, such as live-client clinics, where students are predominantly dealing with ADR and with cases in the trial courts and tribunals. A problem question risks teaching law students to focus on the application of settled law and omits important normative considerations such as what the law ought to be.

A normative approach can be introduced into legal education through essay-based questions. Unlike problem questions, "the essay question is broader, more abstract, and discursive in nature. The essay question does not ask the student to assume a role, but instead encourages the student to express their own reasoned opinion on a given issue" (Goold, 2022, p. 371). An advantage that essay questions have over problem questions is that law teachers have discretion when selecting the type of legal issue for students to consider. According to Goold (2022), essay questions can range from the doctrinal (for example, 'To what extent have the courts in England and Wales formulated a test for dishonesty?'); the conceptual (for example, 'The court's approach to what amounts to appropriation has left the issue of culpability far too reliant on dishonesty'); and the normative (for example, 'Should the law of sexual offences protect persons from all types of deception?'). Another advantage of using an essay question is that it provides an opportunity for students to support their argument using secondary sources of law, including academic commentary, and other approaches such as feminist jurisprudence and socio-legal studies. However, despite its advantages, an essay question omits the realities of legal practice, namely advising clients at the initial stages of the dispute and during the trial process. To consider how to equip students with the knowledge and skills needed for dealing with the complexities and uncertainties of legal practice, it is instructive to briefly examine a school of jurisprudence known as American Legal Realism.

A group of American realists, known as fact-sceptics, were primarily concerned with the trial aspects of cases. For Frank (1973), a leading proponent of fact-scepticism, a preoccupation with appellate courts omits an important aspect of unpredictability in the judicial process; namely, the elusiveness of facts. By focusing on statutes and appellate court decisions, students are given the false impression that law consists only of rules that are knowable in advance. However, when a legal dispute arises, it may end up either in a court/tribunal or the parties may engage in ADR. In relation to courts and tribunals, facts are determined by evidence that is heard by a judge or jury (a 'bench' in the case of a tribunal hearing). The court then applies the law to the facts and reaches a decision. However, factors such as potential prejudices of judges and jurors often affect the outcome of a case (Frank, 1930). Frank's jurisprudential critique of the meaning of law led him to advocate for legal clinics in law schools (1933, 1947). For Frank, a clinic provides a learning environment where "[t]heory and practice would...constantly interlace" and "students would learn to observe the true relation between the contents of upper-court opinions and the work of practising lawyers and courts" (1947, p. 1317). CLE, as a form of experiential learning, can be used to bridge the theory-practice divide and the notion of autonomy can be incorporated into CLE to achieve this.

Autonomy

For present purposes, we contend that personal autonomy, as opposed to moral autonomy, is relevant to both client care and law reform. This concept is relevant to various disciplines such medical ethics, law, legal ethics, philosophy, education, and nursing. The term is derived from the Greek 'autos', meaning self, and 'nomos' denoting law. For Raz (1988), an autonomous person is one who can shape their life and have control over its course, while maintaining their dignity and self respect.

Dworkin (2006, p. 37) identifies two dimensions of human dignity. The first, which he calls "the principle of intrinsic value" concerns the objective value of human life. The second, "the principle of personal responsibility", provides that each person has a special responsibility for making decisions about what kind of life would be successful for them. Together these two principles "define the basis and conditions for human dignity" (Dworkin, 2006, p. 10). In the context of CLE, students ought to be taught to respect their clients' decisions to maintain and promote their clients' autonomy. Law clinic students and lawyers should assist clients with taking control over their own lives, not simply because persons are self-ruling, but because the law ought to promote human dignity (Shaffer & Cochran, 2009). Thus, autonomy can inform legal practice in two ways: client care and law reform.

Autonomy and the Lawyer-Client Relationship

Client care, which has client autonomy as its aim, is also referred to as "client-centered" counselling (Shaffer & Cochran, 2009, p. 17). As stated in the previous section, linked to autonomy is the concept of human dignity. According to Freedman (1990, p. 57):

> One of the essential values of a just society is respect for the dignity of each member of that society. Essential to each individual's dignity is the free exercise of his autonomy. To that end, each person is entitled to know their rights with respect to society and other individuals, and to decide whether to seek fulfilment of those rights through the due process of law.

Under this view, the lawyer's task is to assist the client in pursuing their legal rights. This approach, however, omits consideration of the potential harm that the client's decision might have on others. It also neglects the lawyer's autonomy and moral decision-making. However, there is a debate in legal ethics regarding the place of the lawyer's conscience. Freedman (1990) argues that the place for the lawyer's conscience should be at the beginning, while Fried (1976) suggests that the lawyer's conscience should occur in the middle and, therefore, a discussion surrounding any moral issues should be part of the decision-making process. Whereas for Binder et al. (2004), conscientious objection should take place at the end and lawyers should challenge their client's decision, if they believe it to be wrong, and terminate the retainer if the client does not alter their decision. These three approaches need not be mutually exclusive and should inform the lawyer's decision-making throughout the duration of their engagement. This promotes a more holistic approach to client-centred lawyering. It also requires lawyers to be cognizant of the potential consequences of their client's decision on third parties and the environment.

The tension between client autonomy and a lawyer's conscience is illustrated by the recent debate in legal ethics surrounding the issue of representing fossil fuel companies (Slingo, 2021). Proponents of the autonomy-centric approach argue that due to client autonomy being of vital importance, a lawyer's role is to ensure that decisions are made based on what choice is likely to provide a client with maximum satisfaction (Binder et al., 2004). A client-centred approach entails acting for fossil fuel companies despite the harm caused to third parties and the environment. Binder and Price (1977) argue that lawyers and their clients should consider the 'social consequences' of decisions. However, the consequences, which Binder and Price have in mind, are in relation to the client and not on third parties or the environment. By acting as a neutral counsellor whose role is to realise the client's instructions within the limits of the law, a lawyer fails to recognise the moral relationship that exists between them and their client is "one in which the parties influence one another for good and for ill" (Shaffer & Cochran, 2009, p. 22). A holistic approach, on the other hand, entails examining the potential impact of the client's decision on third parties and the environment. A neutral approach to client care also fails to recognise the lawyer's moral values. In relation to fossil fuel companies and the lawyer's morality, Slingo (2021) quotes Professor Paul Watchman, who argues that, "[l]aw firms can say they expect their clients to have certain values – because clients are saying it to the law firms now". In other words, some firms are currently dictated by their clients' values. Despite acknowledging that firms such as Linklaters and Clifford Chance are actively working with their clients to reduce their carbon footprint, Watchman suggests that lawyers may need to start choosing their clients in order to achieve this aim. While we do not advocate denying any client access to legal advice and assistance based on the lawyer's moral values, we are proposing a holistic approach to legal advice. This type of legal counselling involves taking into consideration the client's values and the lawyer's morality when advising clients. Our model entails outlining to the client the potential harm to the public and the environment.

Mill's (1859, p. 22) 'harm principle' states that "[t]he only purpose for which power can be rightfully exercised over any member of a civilised community, against his will, is to prevent harm to others". The harm principle can be a useful concept in the lawyering process as it provides an opportunity to reflect on the potential harm of the client's decision on others and the environment. However, we are not advocating for a paternalistic approach to lawyering. Paternalism is defined as "the interference with a person's liberty of action justified by reasons referring exclusively to the welfare, good, happiness, needs or values of the person being coerced" (Dworkin, 1972, p. 65). In other words, paternalism involves interference with a client's autonomy for their own good. In the fossil fuel scenario, paternalism might occur where the lawyer places themselves as the primary decision-maker to avoid 'social consequences', such as adverse publicity or financial liability.

Our model of autonomy is one that adopts a 'middle ground' approach. It considers the consequences on others as well as the environment while simultaneously avoiding lawyer paternalism by placing an emphasis on client autonomy and dignity. This middle ground view recognises that lawyers ought to engage in a moral discourse with their clients in relation to any potential consequences on the client, third parties, and the environment. This moral dialogue draws on Kohlberg's work regarding moral development (1981). For Kohlberg, morality involves protecting the rights of others. He identifies three stages of moral development: the preconventional level, conventional morality, and postconventional level. The application of Kohlberg's three stages is best illustrated with reference to a hypothetical example involving a lawyer acting for a fossil fuel company.

At the preconventional level, a person's morality serves their own self-interest (ethical egoism) and their moral decisions are shaped by seeking to avoid punishment in pursuance of their own interest. A client company engaged in fossil fuels would operate at the pre-conventional level by changing its business model to less environmentally harmful business practices only if it appeared that such prohibitions were required by law. The client might choose to either change its business model or mitigate the effects of fossil fuels because of the law or social conventions, such as Corporate Social Responsibility (CSR) initiatives. At the pre-conventional level, the lawyer can outline to their client the potential costs incurred in relation to breaching any legislation and/or impact on shareholders as a result of adverse publicity. Conventional morality is the second stage and is characterised by acceptance of social rules pertaining to right and wrong. At this level, a lawyer can inform their corporate client about its moral obligations and the risks its actions might have on its relationships with stakeholders, the wider community, and the environment.

The post-conventional level is characterised by universal ethical principles. In other words, a person upholds basic rights and values, even where they conflict with the rules found in the lower levels. Regarding the issue of universal ethical principles, Antonopoulos and Madhloom advocate incorporating the Universal Declaration of Human Rights (UDHR) into CLE to promote reflective practice (Antonopoulos & Madhloom, 2021) and to facilitate transnational law clinic collaborations (Madhloom & Antonopoulos, 2021). A client company operating at the postconventional level might elect to change its business practice regardless of whether or not the law required it to do so. The client's moral motivation in this case is to uphold the rights of individuals. By adopting Kohlberg's framework, lawyers can engage with their clients at any of the three levels of moral reasoning.

Lawyers tend to operate within Kohlberg's first two levels (Shaffer & Cochran, 2009). However, our model, which respects client autonomy and the dignity of persons, provides for a more holistic approach to client care. This approach has the advantage of taking into consideration the potential harm of the client's decision on third parties and the environment. The proposed model, which respects client autonomy without sacrificing the lawyer's values, can also be applied more widely to pracademics. Dickinson et al. (2020) report that practitioners not only held on to their values post-transition into HE, but that their values as practitioners underpinned their approach to teaching. Pracademics are, therefore, in a unique position of conveying strong professional values while encouraging students to critique their particular field and their profession's norms.

Autonomy and Law Reform

Curran (2007, p. 105) writes that CLE programmes can enable students to engage in "identifying systemic issues in their case work which can be used to inform work on law reform issues". This observation can also be applied to clinical education in other disciplines such as medicine, nursing, and education. CLE programmes can also incorporate the teaching of socio-legal issues that arise in relation to a client's case. The advantage of incorporating this approach into CLE is that it not only allows students to engage in policy reform (Dunn et al., 2020), but also to gain a deeper understanding of the impact of the law on clients and third parties. One method of achieving this is by engaging with the concept of autonomy. To illustrate how this can applied in CLE, we refer to the Court of Appeal's decision in *Konzani*. The Court's judgment contains a transcript of the trial that is beneficial for present purposes because it allows for the analysis of the Court's decision and the cross-examination during the trial.

The brief facts of the case involve the appellant, Feston Konzani, who appealed against his conviction of inflicting grievous bodily harm (GBH) on three women contrary to s. 20 of the Offences Against the Person Act 1861. Konzani, who was HIV positive, had unprotected sexual intercourse with the complainants, without disclosing his HIV status. The complainants contracted the HIV virus. At his trial, Konzani submitted that as infection with the HIV virus might be one possible consequence of unprotected sexual intercourse, the complainants had consented to the risk of contracting the HIV virus from him. He also submitted that he had an honest, even if unreasonable, belief that the complainants had consented to the risk. The trial judge had directed the jury that the complainant in each case 'did not willingly consent to the risk of suffering that infection' and emphasised that 'willingly' meant 'consciously', and declined to leave to the jury the issue of reasonable belief. Konzani was convicted and sentenced to a total of 10 years' imprisonment and appealed against his conviction on the ground that the trial judge had misdirected the jury as to the proper meaning of consent. The Court of Appeal upheld his conviction. In relation to autonomy, the Court stated [42]:

> If an individual who knows that he is suffering from the HIV virus conceals this stark fact from his sexual partner, the principle of her personal autonomy is not enhanced if he is exculpated when he recklessly transmits the HIV virus to her through consensual sexual intercourse.

The Court's judgment has been criticised for "imposing criminal liability via the denial of a defence based on honest belief in consent" (Weait, 2005, p. 768). Alternatively, it could be argued that by failing to disclose his HIV status, the appellant denied the complainants the opportunity to make an informed decision in relation to the risk of HIV. Autonomy, which signifies the absence of unwanted interference, can be said to be violated where a person conceals a material fact from the complainant (Madhloom, 2019). The pedagogic advantages of using *Konzani* is that it reinforces the point that appeal cases have their origin in the trial courts, an element that is absent in both problem and essay questions. According to Weait "[a]ll legal principles developed by the appellate courts have their origins in things that have happened to and between real people living in the real world" (2012, p. 180). The trial transcript provides students with an opportunity to gain an insight into the lived experience of the parties, which can be analysed with reference to the autonomy and dignity of the parties.

Conclusion

Due to the separation of the academic and vocational stages of legal education and training in England and Wales, students are not fully exposed to the complexities and uncertainties of legal practice unless they take part in CLE. Although the two main forms of assessment, namely essay questions and problem questions, allow students to apply the law to hypothetical scenarios and to reflect on normative questions such as 'what is good law?', these assessments focus on the application of primary and secondary sources of law while ignoring or minimising the role of extra-legal factors, the trial courts, and ADR. Pracademics can contribute to addressing these limitations by encouraging students to reflect on what they would do in particular situations from practice. Pracademics are also in a unique position to promote moral education. One method of achieving these aims is to adopt a holistic approach through CLE. This involves teaching students to reflect on the consequences of their actions, and the impact of the law on their clients, society, as well as the environment. This can be achieved by using the concept of autonomy to analyse the law and legal principles as well as engaging in a moral discourse with clients. The notion of autonomy considered in this chapter discourages lawyer paternalism and applies Mill's harm principle as a moral constraint on the client's intended course of action, particularly where consequences of the client's instructions are likely to cause harm to third parties and/or the environment. This pedagogic approach not only facilitates the application and critique of law and legal principles but also allows for the incorporation of values into legal education (Cownie, 2003).

Given that autonomy is used in vocational programmes such medicine, social work, and education, to name but a few, the argument presented in this chapter can be adopted by pracademics in other disciplines. Many of these overlap, for example social work and law, and by considering the consequences of actions and the law on the parties, students will begin to make connections between these disciplines and develop creative solutions that are not confined to that particular domain and can therefore have a greater impact on the individuals concerned. It may also create a universal language between professions to increase collaboration and reduce difficulties in communication, diminishing the risk of failing to help their clients when they most need it.

The value of autonomy to pracademics is that it can be used as a conceptual tool to promote practice-informed teaching and to develop students' professional identity. Focusing on autonomy in CLE, whether through essay-based questions, analysis of trial transcripts, or live-client clinics, can enhance legal education by allowing students to reflect on the complexities and uncertainties of professional practice.

Points for Reflection
- Do you agree with some of the benefits of practical assessment methods outlined by Bradley and Madhloom? Could you consider how you could increase autonomy for your students?
- The authors suggest that autonomy may support interdisciplinary working and professional collaboration. Do you agree? How can you relate the concepts of autonomy to your own field/profession?

References

Antonopoulos, I., & Madhloom, O. (2021). Promoting international human rights values through reflective practice in clinical legal education: A perspective from England and Wales. In E. Sengupta & P. Blessinger (Eds.), *International perspectives in social justice programs at the institutional and community levels* (Vol. 37, pp. 109–127). Emerald Publishing Limited. https://doi.org/10.1108/S2055-364120210000037008

Askin, F. (1998). A law school where students don't just learn the law; they help make the law symposium. *Rutgers Law Review, 51*(4), 855–874.

Binder, D. A., & Price, S. C. (1977). *Legal interviewing and counseling: A client-centered approach*. West Publishing Company.

Binder, D. A., Paul, B. B., Susan C. P., & Tremblay, P. R. (2004). *Lawyers as counselors: A client-centered approach*. Thomson/West.

Cownie, F. (2003). Alternative values in legal education. *Legal Ethics, 6*(2), 159–174. https://doi.org/10.1080/1460728X.2003.11424188

Curran, L. (2007). University law clinics and their value in undertaking client-centred law reform to provide a voice for clients' experiences. *International Journal of Clinical Legal Education, 12*, 105–130. https://doi.org/10.19164/ijcle.v12i0.73

Dickinson, J., Fowler, A., & Griffiths, T.-L. (2020). Pracademics? Exploring transitions and professional identities in higher education. *Studies in Higher Education, 47*(2), 290–304. https://doi.org/10.1080/03075079.2020.1744123

Dunn, R. A. (2016). The taxonomy of clinics: The realities and risks of all forms of clinical legal education. *Asian Journal of Legal Education, 3*(2), 174–187. https://doi.org/10.1177/2322005816640339

Dunn, R., Bengtsson, L., & McConnell, S. (2020). The policy clinic at northumbria university: Influencing policy/law reform as an effective educational tool for students. *International Journal of Clinical Legal Education, 27*(2), 68–102. https://doi.org/10.19164/ijcle.v27i2.960

Dworkin, G. (1972). Paternalism. *The Monist, 56*(1), 64–84. https://doi.org/10.5840/monist197256119

Dworkin, R. (2006). *Is democracy possible here?: Principles for a new political debate*. Princeton University Press.

Frank, J. (1930). *Law and the modern mind*. Routledge & CRC Press.

Frank, J. (1933). Why not a clinical lawyer-school? *University of Pennsylvania Law Review and American Law Register, 81*(8), 907. https://doi.org/10.2307/3308391

Frank, J. (1947). A plea for lawyer-schools. *The Yale Law Journal, 56*(8), 1303–1344. https://doi.org/10.2307/793068

Frank, J. (1973). *Courts on trial: Myth and reality in American justice*. Princeton University Press.

Freedman, M. H. (1990). *Understanding lawyers' ethics*. M. Bender.

Fried, C. (1976). The lawyer as friend: The moral foundations of the lawyer-client relation. *Yale Law Journal, 85*, 1060–1089. https://dash.harvard.edu/handle/1/23903316

Goold, P. R. (2022). The legal judgment: A novel twist on the classic law school problem question. *The Law Teacher, 56*(3), 368–383.

Halstead, J. M. (2010). Moral education. In C. S. Clauss-Ehlers (Ed.), *Encyclopedia of cross-cultural school psychology* (pp. 630–631). Springer. https://doi.org/10.1007/978-0-387-71799-9_260

Healey, P. & Hillier, J. (2008). Hayek, F.A. (1944). Planning and democracy. In F. A Hayek (Ed.), *The road to serfdom* (pp. 42–53). Routledge & Kegan Paul. In Healey, P. & Hillier (Eds.), J. *Foundations of the planning enterprise* (pp. 42–53). Routledge.

Johnson, H. W., & Hull, G. H. (1992). Autonomy and visibility in undergraduate social work education. *Journal of Social Work Education, 28*(3), 312–321.

Kohlberg, L. (1981). *Essays on moral development: The psychology of moral development.* Harper & Row.

Madhloom, O. (2019). Deception, mistake and non-disclosure: Challenging the current approach to protecting sexual autonomy. *Northern Ireland Legal Quarterly, 70*(2), 203–219. https://doi.org/10.53386/nilq.v70i2.261

Madhloom, O., & Antonopoulos, I. (2021). Clinical legal education and human rights values: A universal pro forma for law clinics. *Asian Journal of Legal Education, 9*(1), 23–35. https://doi.org/10.1177/23220058211051031

Manzano Vázquez, B. (2018). Teacher development for autonomy: An exploratory review of language teacher education for learner and teacher autonomy. *Innovation in Language Learning and Teaching, 12*(4), 387–398. https://doi.org/10.1080/17501229.2016.1235171

McAllister, L., Lincoln, M., McLeod, S., & Maloney, D. (1997). *Facilitating learning in clinical settings.* Nelson Thornes.

Mill, J. S. (1859). *On liberty.* J. W. Parker and Son.

Nicolson, D. (2008). 'Education, education, education': Legal, moral and clinical. *The Law Teacher, 42*(2), 145–172. https://doi.org/10.1080/03069400.2008.9959773

Posner, P. L. (2009). The pracademic: An agenda for re-engaging practitioners and academics. *Public Budgeting & Finance, 29*(1), 12–26. https://doi.org/10.1111/j.1540-5850.2009.00921.x

Raz, J. (1988). *The morality of freedom.* Oxford University Press. http://ebookcentral.proquest.com/lib/bristol/detail.action?docID=3053254

Shaffer, T. L., & Cochran, R. F. (2009). *Lawyers, clients, and moral responsibility.* Thomson/West.

Slingo, J. (2021, August 27). *In focus: Should city firms cut ties with fossil fuel giants?* Law Gazette. https://www.lawgazette.co.uk/news-focus/in-focus-should-city-firms-cut-ties-with-fossil-fuel-giants/5109612.article

Thomas, K. A. (2008). Sentencing: Where case theory and the client meet. *Clinical Law review, 15*(1), 187–210.

Unger, R. M. (1983). The critical legal studies movement. *Harvard Law Review, 96*, 561–675.

Weait, M. (2005). Knowledge, autonomy and consent. In R. v. Konzani (Ed.), *Criminal law review* (pp. 763–772).

Weait, M. (2012). Criminal law: Thinking about criminal law from a trial perspective. In C. Hunter (Ed.), *Integrating socio-legal studies into the law curriculum* (pp. 161–183). Springer.

Williams, G. C., & Deci, E. L. (1998). The importance of supporting autonomy in medical education. *Annals of Internal Medicine, 129*(4), 303–308. https://doi.org/10.7326/0003-4819-129-4-199808150-00007

Wizner, S. (2012). Is social justice still relevant? *Boston College Journal of Law & Social Justice, 32*(2), 345–355.

Laura Bradley is a Senior Tutor and Head of Tutors at the University of Law (Birmingham Campus, UK). Laura has a MA in Countryside and Environment Management from the University of Aberdeen and a LL.B (Hons) from the University of Wales, Aberystwyth. She qualified as a solicitor in 2004 and worked at Legal 500 firms specialising in Private Client until she moved to legal education. Laura teaches EU Law, Mental Health and Capacity Law, and Real Estate on undergraduate and postgraduate law courses. She has published on EU Law matters in the Journal of Criminal Law and also, in the area of Clinical Legal Education. She is a Senior Fellow of the Higher Education Academy. Laura's research focuses on the education and training of solicitors and barristers in England and Wales.

Dr Omar Madhloom is a Senior Lecturer at the University of Bristol. He is also a supervising solicitor at the University of Bristol Law Clinic. Omar's research focuses on applied legal ethics and exploring the philosophical foundations of clinical legal education. He is the co-editor of Thinking About Clinical Legal Education: Philosophical and Theoretical Perspectives (Routledge 2021). Omar is the Co-Chair of the Bristol Pro Bono Group, a member of the board of trustees of CLEO (Clinical Legal Education Organisation), and a member of the editorial board of the Asian Journal of Legal Education (Sage).

Chapter 18
Developing Leaders in Business Schools: Academics as "Boundary Spanners"

Abinash Panda

Abstract Management and organizational theories are not as universal as they are claimed to be. Most of the existing management and organisational theories have been developed in the Western Anglo-Saxon socio-cultural context. Given that management and organisational theories cannot have universal applicability, these theories need to be tweaked judiciously to make them relevant for one's own circumstance. There is a need for context-sensitive reflection.

The role of academics is salient in the process, as enablers and stimulators. As stimulators, academics need to guide learners to reflect on academic and personal experiences. They need to be boundary spanners – crossing the boundaries of academic and corporate worlds. They must share their insights gained as teachers, trainers, consultants, and field researchers about the corporate world with regard to their domains of expertise and interest; help participants to reflect on their experiences; and create learning zones in and outside the classrooms.

This chapter deals with the disconnect between the world of academia and practice with a specific reference to leadership development. After working with various business organizations as a learning and development specialist, and working with business schools as a teacher, trainer, researcher, and consultant, the author realised that leadership development is more salient than leader development. Though leadership development, interventions are designed to develop the process of leadership, they are essentially focused on cultivating people as leaders. Business schools must take up the responsibilities of developing leaders who can exercise leadership in the corporate world. The author offers a framework of leadership development for business schools to consider.

A. Panda (✉)
Organizational Behaviour and Human Resource Management Area, Management Development Institute, Gurgaon, India
e-mail: abinash.panda@mdi.ac.in

J. Dickinson, T.-L. Griffiths (eds.), *Professional Development for Practitioners in Academia*, Knowledge Studies in Higher Education 13,
https://doi.org/10.1007/978-3-031-33746-8_18

Keywords Business schools · Pracademics · Boundary spanners · Context-specific reflection · Student experience · Leadership · Leadership development · Industry insight · University industry collaboration

At a Glance
- Reflecting on their journey to becoming a pracademic, the author meditates upon their professional journey in the scholastic and practice domains of leadership development.
- Presenting differences between leadership development and leader development, with suggestions of how business schools can support students to learn leadership.
- Articulates the process of becoming a leader and learning to lead and champions academics, but particularly pracademics, both as boundary-spanners and stimulators to help learners to develop personal abilities.
- Offers suggestions for how pracademics may be cultivated in business schools.

Introduction

Management and organisational theories are not as universal as they are claimed to be. Most of the existing management and organisational theories have been developed in the Western Anglo-Saxon socio-cultural context. These theories seem to have failed to consider the contextual peculiarities of non- Anglo-Saxon economies (e.g. Lammers, 1990; Gopinath, 1998). Scholars including Hofstede (1983) and Rosenzweig (1994) have questioned the universal applicability of Western management models and frameworks in other social contexts, particularly in developing countries, where the socio-cultural contexts are distinctly different from those of developed countries. Scholars such as Rousseau and Fried (2001) and Schneider (1985) have argued for contextualisation with the aim of rendering management models and frameworks more accurate, and interpretation of results more robust. Academic scholars in India, for instance, have primarily focused on validation of organisation and management theories developed in the West, in the Indian context. However, I contend that they have failed to understand the socio-cultural context of India and develop culturally-relevant management and organisational theories (Panda & Gupta, 2007).

Consequently, most of the academic studies were found to lack 'India-ness', and hence, relevance for corporate executives in India. Gupta (1991) has urged academic scholars in India to understand and conceptualise an Indian approach to management and move beyond American and Japanese models of management.

Corresponding with the international context, stories are aplenty when it comes to disillusionment of corporate India with respect to the preparedness of business school graduates to take up leadership positions. A human resources (HR) head of an Indian conglomerate is quoted as stating, "[Business school graduates] are divorced from reality. They want to become CXO in their next promotion but have never worked in the trenches" (Sengupta, 2022, p. 1).

Given that management and organisational theories cannot have universal applicability, these theories need to be tweaked judiciously to make them relevant for one's own circumstance, which can be achieved through contextual reflection. The role of academics is salient in the process, they must act as enablers and stimulators. As enablers, academics need to create a psychologically safe learning zone, where participant-learners[1] do not feel inhibited to reflect and develop new insights. As stimulators, academics need to nudge learners to reflect on academic and personal experiences. They need to ask probing questions that will help learners to seek answers to the questions or dilemmas with which they are grappling. Moreover, in order to be effective as stimulators, academics need to be boundary spanners[2] (e.g. Walker, 2010, as cited in Hollweck et al., 2020, 2022; Posner & Cvitanovic, 2019) – transcending the boundaries of academic and corporate worlds in their roles as field researchers and corporate consultants. They must: share their insights gained as teachers, trainers, consultants, and field researchers about the corporate worlds with regard to their domains of expertise and interest; help participants to reflect on their experiences; and create learning zones in and outside the classrooms.

What I have observed and experienced is the real disconnect between the world of academia and practice regarding the way leadership development is understood and the process executed. Leadership development is different from leader development (Hart et al., 2008). Leader development is focused on expanding an individual leader's capacity to lead (McCauley & Van Velsor, 2004), whereas leadership development entails interactions between individual leaders and the social-cultural environment in which they operate (Ardichvili & Manderscheid, 2008). After working with various business organisations as a learning and development specialist, and being associated with business schools as a teacher, trainer, researcher, and consultant, I realised that leadership development is more salient than leader development. Though leadership development interventions are designed to develop the *process* of leadership, these interventions are essentially focused on cultivating *people* as leaders.

Though leadership courses are now a part of nearly every major business school's curriculum across the globe, business schools tend to focus more on leader development rather than leadership development. Studies on leadership have revealed that

---

[1] I make a subtle distinction between participant-learner and learner. Learners may be passive, whereas participant- learners actively participate and engage in the learning process via debate, discussion, and dialogue. Learner and participant-learner are used interchangeably and both means a learner who actively participates in the learning process.

[2] Taking cues proffered by Søderberg and Romani (2017) and Bordogna (2019), boundary-spanner, here is understood to be a "broker," who provides the exchange and sharing of insights and knowledge among consulting, training, corporate, and teaching domains.

executives learn to lead through experiences (McCall, 2010; Panda, 2017; Van Velsor et al., 2013). It is an on-going process of reflection on those experiences to distil insights that inform future practice. Business schools need to share the responsibilities with the corporate world of developing leaders who can exercise leadership in the corporate world.

Exercising leadership is different from being an effective leader. The former is a process, a means to achieve a goal. The effectiveness of the process is bound by cultural context and psychological makeup of the team members. Hence, the process of exercising leadership is situational. Though the proposed leadership development framework is conceptualised on the basis of my experience in an Indian context, the process of becoming a leader is generic and hence can be applied in any context.

Key Themes

Evolving to Become a Pracademic: Reflecting Back and Looking Forward

Becoming a Pracademic in the Field of Leadership Development

I have been fortunate to have worked in both corporate executive and career academic roles in various capacities to become a sort of pracademic in the field of leadership development. Pracademics may be narrowly described as persons who are dually recognised experts in both academic and professional practice (Panda, 2014). For Volpe and Chandler (2001), pracademics are "faculty who are both scholars … as well as practitioners…" (p. 245). Owens' (2016) understanding of pracademic is broader- a blend of the practical with the academic. McDonald and Mooney (2011) describe "pracademic" as a teaching style that focuses on the practical application of academic theory and knowledge.

The term pracademic is considered synonymous with that of "scholar practitioner". Kormanik et al. (2009) used the term "scholar practitioner" to describe "someone who is dedicated to generating new knowledge that is useful to practitioners … scholar practitioners are interpreters, speaking the languages of research, academic and practice" (Kormanik et al., 2009, p. 488).

My understanding of pracademic is a scholar who understands the nuances of both academic and corporate worlds and believes in co-creating organisationally relevant insights in the 'world of science' for the 'world of practice'. Pracademics, or academics with a pracademic mindset, are assets to any business school as all business schools operate in a shared space, where both the worlds of scholarship and practice merge. Business schools are mandated to develop leaders who will potentially lead business entities. Having worked in both spaces of scholarship and practice, I consider myself to be a pracademic.

My Professional Journey

After graduating from a doctoral research program at a business school in India, I joined another business school in India as an assistant professor. After eighteen months, I landed in the corporate world as a learning and development professional, where I got involved in leadership development research, designing, and deploying learning and development interventions to enhance people capabilities.

During my initial days as a corporate executive, I experienced a lot of discomfort and went through a series of anxious moments. Many of my senior colleagues from the corporate world then gave me a lot of advice (at times unsolicited) as to how to acclimatise oneself to the idiosyncrasies of the corporate world. Some of which, still fresh in my mind, are the following:

- Do not think like a professor…
- Don't do serious academic research, we need some quick and dirty research….
- We pay for the outcome, not for thinking….
- Please do not use academic jargon, it is too complicated for us to understand and appreciate….
- Please think of some research that would help managers solve some of the pressing problems that our organisations are facing today….
- Go to the field, talk to business leaders and help them solve problems…

After a tenure of around 10 years in the corporate world, I returned to academia as a pracademic. During these ten years, I worked with three different business organisations in various roles, which offered me significant insights about the world of practice (refer to Fig. 18.1: My professional journey below).

Insights Gained on Effective Leaders and Leadership Development

The topic of my doctoral thesis was effective leadership in retail branches of a public sector bank in India; more specifically, whether the effectiveness of a leadership style is influenced by the cultural context. Given the cultural diversity within India,

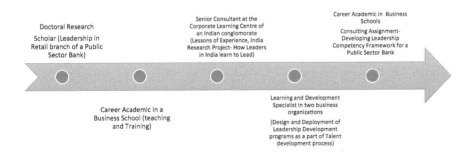

Fig. 18.1 My professional journey

the study examined the effectiveness of six leadership styles in two distinctly different cultural contexts within India. I found that effectiveness of leadership style is
shaped by the expectations of the followers, which are influenced by the way they
are socialised in their cultural preferences as well the organisational context. The
same leader may be effective with one group of followers or/and in one organisation
and may not succeed in another set of followers and/or organisational context.

Moving on, my next research project, as a senior research consultant with one
Indian multinational, considered how leaders in India learn to lead (Lessons of
Experience Study, India), jointly conducted by the Tata Group and the US-based,
the Center for Creative Leadership (CCL). The key insight of this study was that
most leaders in India learned to lead from two key learning opportunities- challenging assignments on the job and via other people through mentoring and coaching.
They acknowledged that classroom sessions were not good enough for the individuals to learn leadership. These leaders acknowledged that one can learn most from
personal and professional experiences, provided that one reflects on these experiences. One needs a mentor or/and a coach who guides them to reflect on these
experiences to draw on leadership insights.

Another research project that I co-led, as senior research consultant, was a leadership gap study, where the purpose was to identify leadership capability gaps
(organisational leadership capability refers to what the organisation already "has"
and "what is required" to achieve the organisational goals) at the organisational
level and develop a roadmap to bridge the capability gap. The developmental roadmap for each key individual leader was the basis for the targeted leadership developmental plan. The learning from this research project was how to diagnose
capability gaps and bridge the same through an appropriate suite of developmental
opportunities. These insights helped me in designing leadership development programs in my next role as a learning and development specialist in another Indian
conglomerate.

As a learning and development specialist, I got involved in designing and deploying many leadership development programs. What I found very disturbing was that
although organisations used to invest financial and intellectual resources to develop
leaders from within, these organisations in many cases hired executives from outside for key leadership positions. Secondly, despite the access to significant insights
and understanding on leadership and leadership development in the world of schol-
arships, and availability of resources for cultivating leaders, organisations do experience the brunt of leadership deficit, which is acknowledged by many academic
scholars including Hou (2010), Panda (2017), and Shyamsunder et al. (2011).
Thirdly, many leaders having required qualities to be 'effective' are found wanting
when it comes to achieving results. It was a puzzle for me.

I found an answer to my puzzle when I came across the scholarly work of Heifetz
(see, for example, Heifetz, 1994; Heifetz & Linksy, 2002; Heifetz et al., 2009)
which assisted in my understanding of the essence of leadership. Often, individuals
with relevant qualities fail to exercise leadership. Heifetz defines leadership as an
activity, *not* as a set of personality characteristics. Leadership development should
focus on developing people's capacity to perform "leadership", which is about the

mobilisation of the resources of people or of an organisation to make progress on difficult problems.

Interestingly, organisations mostly focus on developing leaders rather the developing leadership. Day (2001) has distinguished between developing leaders and developing leadership. Leader development focusses on developing individual leaders, whereas leadership development focusses on a process of development that inherently involves multiple individuals (for example, leaders and followers, or peers in a self-managed work team). On the whole, my view is that the corporate world needs competent leaders who are adept in exercising leadership.

Finally, I moved back to academia in a career academic role, where I engaged myself in teaching, training, researching, and consulting, primarily in the domain of leadership development. During one consultation assignment, I developed a leadership competency framework for an Indian public sector bank. Later, I also got an opportunity to articulate my thoughts on leadership development and proposed an integrated approach.

My Take on Leadership Development and What Business Schools Need to Do

The corporate world today needs competent leaders who exercise leadership and help organizations deal with adaptive challenges. These leaders need to mobilise resources at one's disposal to help their organisation to confront the new realities and succeed against competition. The challenges of today are unique and different from the past. Leaders may not always have answers to these challenges. Their expertise may not be enough. They need to rely on the collective intelligence of the group to face the new reality. Having desirable leadership skills, such as the ability to visualise, persuasively communicate, and motivate the team, may not be enough. Individuals in leadership positions need to use these skills to mobilise followers and organisational members to solve collective problems. The leaders need to be emotionally intelligent, besides having job competence. We need leaders who can mobilise their groups and teams, by applying leadership skills to achieve a collective goal.

Leader development is a necessary but not sufficient condition for leadership because leadership requires that individual development is integrated and understood in the context of others, social systems, organisational strategies, missions, and goals (Olivares et al., 2007). Therefore, the approach to leadership development should ideally be different from developing leaders. It is mostly believed that leadership can be taught, though this approach is complex, because exercising or practising leadership has both explicit and tacit components. One can impart explicit knowledge, which includes knowledge on the qualities and competencies of effective leaders in a given context. However, one develops one's own unique ways of exercising leadership.

With the help of conceptual frameworks that enable them to make sense of their experiences, and supportive, diverse communities that assist them in examining those experiences from new and different angles, individuals may learn more in a business school than they would in the workplace. They may also gain access to opportunities to lead that they would not have otherwise.

The current approach to teaching leadership in business schools is primarily confined to imparting cognitive or informational knowledge to participants, leaving them mostly ill-equipped to teach leadership. The world of practice serves as the centre point of the academic compass for most professional programs. Many recruiters have rightly expressed their concerns about the dearth of competent faculty, which focusses too much on theory and, in the process, often crowds out practice. One of them suggested that, "the directors move from one B[usiness]-school to another, teachers have theoretical knowledge, but more case studies need to be taught." He added further that "when a case study is taught, then either representatives of the company or those who were part of it, or tracked the case closely, are invited to talk to students. It makes all the difference" (Sengupta, 2022, p. 1). Sengupta also rightly concludes, "roaring placements at India's premier B-schools, it seems, are no indication of how good India Inc's leadership pipeline is" (p. 1).

On the other hand, advocates of business schools argue that there is immense value in business education as a platform for leadership learning, because on-the-job assignments do not always offer optimal conditions for individuals to draw meaningful lessons from. In performance-obsessed organisations, learning takes the back seat.

What is needed therefore is helping students, the future leaders, to be sensitive to the contextual realities and to develop personal insights on exercising leadership. Although business schools have a critical role to play in developing the kind of leaders that today's corporate world needs, we should also keep in mind the fact that leaders are not the finished product of any single business school (Panda, 2019). Learning for leadership lasts a lifetime.

The failure of business schools to develop leaders for the corporate world may have undesirable consequences. First, it may prompt other providers (for example, a leadership development service provider such as the aforementioned CCL) to emerge. Secondly, it may lead to the eclipse and ultimate decline in the ability of professional academic programs to thrive or even survive over the longer-term. Teaching leadership, in fact requires a different approach. Let us consider a way forward.

Helping Participant-Learners to Learn Leadership in Business Schools

Can business schools create a learning ecosystem that may help their participants learn leadership? They can, but it calls for a shift in approach. Participant-learners, besides acquiring relevant leadership knowledge need to develop learning agility. They must reflect on their everyday personal and professional experiences to draw leadership insights. Business schools should help them by creating an ecosystem where participant-learners receive time and space to engage themselves in both solo- and group reflection. The teachers should act as mentors to equip participant-learners with skills to reflect on experiences. Participants, in the process become lifelong learners, which help them to learn to lead in various socio-cultural contexts. The idea of context sensitisation was developed by Schön. These participants, as practitioners, will be confronted with a plethora of challenges and surprises. They need to view each situation as a learning opportunity to develop new insights. As Schön (1983) explains:

> The practitioner allows himself to experience surprise, puzzlement, or confusion in a situation which he finds uncertain or unique. He reflects on the phenomenon before him, and on the prior understandings which have been implicit in his behaviour. He carries out an experiment which serves to generate both a new understanding of the phenomenon and a change in the situation. (p. 68)

Secondly, given that socio-cultural contexts vary within and across nations, participant-learners should be sensitised about the contextual (including organisational) realities. One should examine generalised 'theories' in terms of their effectiveness in a given context assuming that every situation is unique. One should not follow theories blindly. Learners may need to tweak these theories to make them contextually relevant. For instance, it has been proven that given the resource crunch situation in the Indian context, achievement motivation theory, as conceptualised by McClelland (1961), is of limited help to understand the behaviour of employees in organisations in India (Sinha, 1968). Pracademics and corporate executives, armed with field insights, may contribute significantly to this process of contextual sensitisation through the dialoguing process. They can provide leads from their own experiences of corporate, consulting, and training to develop skills to make sense of the situations to tweak their leadership and managerial styles and approaches.

Thirdly, individuals learn when they introspect and critically reflect on their experiences with an open mind. Students in business schools go through different experiences, both academic and personal. They are part of academic teams engaged in group assignments. They organise and participate in many events while they study. They can learn salient leadership lessons outside the classroom by participating in various competitions, being part of various governance committees and organising events, and so on. Each of these experiences are enriched with learning opportunities, which need to be leveraged for inculcating leadership insights.

Finally, academics at business schools have important roles to play in the leadership development process. They should encourage their student-participants to reflect on their experiences and learn. Currently, the focus tends to be on developing analytical skills to become better problem-solvers and decision makers. This approach rarely focuses on reflective learning. Hence, there is a need to shift the teaching-learning focus towards helping learners to reflect on experiences. Moreover, students should also be encouraged and given opportunities to exchange experiences and perspectives through authentic and meaningful debate and dialogue with others having similar or different experiences. Such an approach is key to developing awareness of self and others. Time spent inside the classroom could be better utilised by conducting interaction, and debate: the Socratic foundation of powerful learning. Possessing knowledge is not enough, participants must know how to apply that knowledge to achieve results. I generally present real-life leadership and organisational situations from my corporate and consulting experiences to initiate debate and discussion on the applicability of generalised theories in that situation. I push them further to discuss: why the theory may not be as effective as it is claimed to be; what should be done about it; and what are the leadership learning philosophies. I act as devil's advocate to push them beyond their comfort zone into a learning zone. Such constructive debate, discussion, and deliberation are salient in helping participants to learn leadership.

Individuals prefer a psychologically safe environment to reflect on their experiences to draw meaningful insights (Edmondson, 1999, 2019). In a business school context, academics should mentor participants by creating an enabling environment, where participants feel psychologically safe to confide in their respective mentors. Academics need to act as enablers to help participants to reflect and introspect on their experiences. Academics can act as stimulators by asking apt questions, and thereby guiding students to reflect on such experiences to help them learn leadership lessons. While encouraging students to learn leadership in business schools, the facilitator must leverage classroom as a leadership laboratory. The facilitator should simulate real life organisational situations in the classroom. This can be achieved by judiciously selecting an appropriate teaching case. The participants should be encouraged to think as protagonists, as if they are actors in real situations. They should be encouraged to engage themselves in debates and discussions, besides offering and seeking feedback from other participants.

Learning to Lead: The Process

Learning happens when one reflects on experiences. Reflection is a process of exploring and examining one's own perspectives, attributes, experiences, and actions and interactions. It helps to gain insight and see how to move forward (Schön, 1983). Schön (1973) has also pointed out that a business organisation is a learning system at its core. Hence, context sensitive reflection is key to the effectiveness of any corporate executive. Business education, by implication, must go beyond imparting theoretical knowledge, to help learners in business schools to develop personal abilities to reflect. Moreover, given that management of organisation is an applied discipline, participants must understand the situation from multi-disciplinary perspectives. Learners can reflect while going through an experience and after going through the same (Schön, 1983), which is feasible with a tutor's help and assistance (Schön, 1983). This happens through dialogue between the learners and tutors (Argyris & Schön, 1978). Academic staff, hence, are key to this learning process.

Academics could be career academics focussed on theoretical concepts, pracademics with a dual mindset, or fully-fledged practitioners (as adjunct faculty/

associate lecturers). Though pracademics may be better equipped to sensitise students about corporate realities from the outset, career academics can collaborate with practitioners to jointly bring academic insights and field insights respectively to the class for meaningful discussions. Figure 18.2 captures this process; namely, how students can leverage various experiences to learn leadership with the support and guidance of academics.

Students in business schools are likely to learn to lead when they go through the virtuous cycle of reflection and context sensitisation (refer to Fig. 18.3). Academics in business schools guide these students to reflect on their experiences and sensitise them with their own insights (from training, consulting, teaching, and research) about what works, what may not work, and how to adapt with creativity.

Academics should provide support and guide learners by ensuring genuine and relevant feedback available in a timely manner (Day, 2010), which helps to track progress in specific development dimensions over time (McCall, 2010). Developmental feedback offered in a psychologically safe environment is more likely to trigger reflection and introspection. Such guided reflection and introspection may help learners to become self-aware, assess their self-worth, and become more confident. It also helps executives to learn desired lessons from experiences

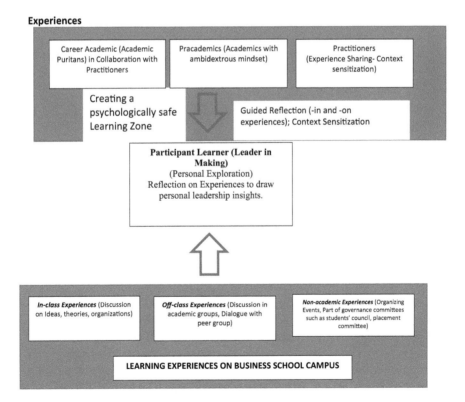

Fig. 18.2 Learning to lead from business school experiences

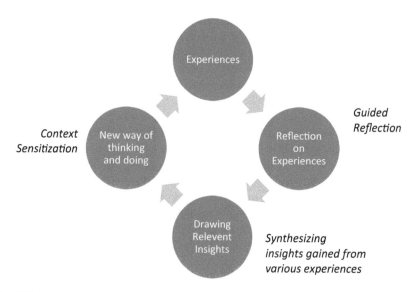

Fig. 18.3 Virtuous cycle of reflection and context sensitisation

(Shamir & Eilam, 2005). Reflective questions (Daudelin, 1996) may also help learners to find answers to their questions and unresolved dilemmas. Students, while reflecting on various experiences tend to develop novel leadership insights, which ultimately may influence their thought process and the way they lead.

The Role of Academics

Academics as Traditional Academics, Practitioners and Pracademics

Academics as boundary spanners can play a significant role in sensitising participant learners about the realities of the corporate world, which they have gained as consultants, researchers, trainers, and even as corporate executives. Insights gained from these roles can help academics to act as a stimulator. In this role, academics generally nudge participants to move beyond their comfort zone and help them to learn to lead. Without such encouragement, participants may interpret their experiences to reinforce their current thinking and worldviews. My submission here is that varieties of experiences in multiple roles (teaching, training, consulting, field research) should equip academics to be effective in the role of stimulator. By implication, one needs to have a pracademic mindset (refer to Fig. 18.4).

A pracademic is both an academic and an active practitioner in their subject area. They span both the enigmatic world of academia as a scholar and the pragmatic world of practice. They are a rare breed of individuals who are boundary spanners.

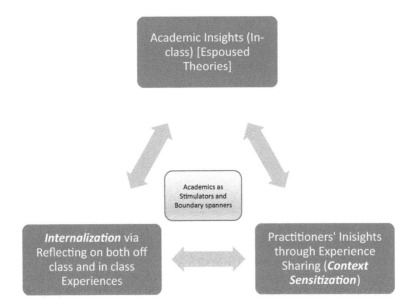

Fig. 18.4 Academics as boundary spanners

They possess the mindset of both practitioner and academic scholar, though exclusively belong to neither (Bartoli et al., 2012). The twin objectives of guided reflection and context sensitisation can effectively be achieved by academics with a pracademic mindset, and there is a need to expand the pool of pracademics. Pracademics constitute a rare tribe of boundary spanners; being active knowledge creators and disseminators in academia as well as active knowledge consumers in the world of practice.

Cultivating Pracademics in Business Schools

Practitioners can be nurtured to become pracademics by accessing existing theories through continuing education and guidance (through mentoring and coaching) by an academic scholar. Practitioners have rich and varied field insights. However, they need to explore, understand, and examine the science underlying these practices, knowledge which can be gained through academic research. Practitioners can develop researching skills by joining doctoral research programmes and being mentored by academics.

Conversely, academic scholars can be developed to be boundary spanners through understanding how an organisation functions. This may include various mechanisms such as interaction with corporate leaders and executives, taking up corporate assignments, and so on, with the aim of understanding the interrelationships between academic theories and organisational practices. A stint with industry after a doctoral research programme, for example, would help support this aim, or a scholar might be encouraged to put their theories into practice in the field. Such industry experience can help to develop the skills and acumen of a practitioner, with the corporate assignment viewed as a learning factory.

In lieu of above-mentioned routes, career academics may take up field research to understand organisations or write cases for teaching. Both of these activities may help career academics to develop their understanding about how organisations are managed and led.

Conclusion

Exercising leadership is essentially a social behaviour, which requires an individual to be self-aware alongside understanding and relating to followers in a meaningful way. It requires contextual intelligence and an appreciation of the challenges on hand. As I have put forward in this chapter, leadership development is different from leader development. Pracademics can play a significant role in helping business school students to become managers who can exercise their leadership qualities intelligently to get things done. It is heartening to note that pracademics have made significant and substantive contributions to various disciplines, including public administration (Posner, 2009), practice management (Walker, 2010), political science (Murphy & Fulda, 2011), sustainable tourism (Dredge & Wray, 2012), conflict resolution (Susskind, 2013), and social work (Owens, 2016).

Handy (2015) has rightfully pointed out that there are limits to how much one can teach about the practice of management in the classroom. Thomas et al. (2014) feel that business schools are doing irrelevant and impractical academic research and a poor job at preparing students for management careers. Johnson (2015), while attempting to address this aspect, has urged academic institutions to focus more on student employability rather than rewarding teaching excellence. The emphasis should ideally be on developing critical, reflective abilities, with a view to empowering and enabling the learner. All of these require a paradigmatic shift towards understanding the practice of business away from analysis of business. The focus should be on both context and the content, rather than purely on content. As Hutchins (1970, p. 133) has mentioned in the context of ancient Athens:

> [...] education [in Athens] was not a segregated activity, conducted for certain hours, in certain places, at a certain time of life. It was the aim of the society. The city educated the man. The Athenian was educated by culture, by *paideia*. (Hutchins, 1970, p. 133)

McQuillan and McQuillan (2016) have proposed a pracademic approach to enrich the learning experience context in business schools. The leadership development process, supported by the pracademic mindset, will get the much-needed impetus, provided business schools leverage their expertise and understanding through the cultivation of pracademics.

Points for Reflection

- Panda shares insights for how academics of all backgrounds could act as boundary spanners. Regardless of your own journey to academia, consider how you could develop a pracademic mindset.
- Although the chapter focusses on the business school context, the teaching concepts that have been explored could be applied in many disciplines. Consider how could you help students reflect and learn from their experiences.
- One of the key messages of this chapter is the importance of leader development. Consider how you might guide the "leaders in making" to reflect and contextualise the corporate realities.

References

Ardichvili, A., & Manderscheid, S. V. (2008). Emerging practices in leadership development: An introduction. *Advances in Developing Human Resources, 10*(5), 619–631.

Argyris, C., & Schön, D. (1978). *Organizational learning: A theory of action perspective.* Addison Wesley.

Bartoli, A., Manojlovic, B., & Geiff, J. (2012, April 19–21). *Practice and practices: Experimenting with peacemaking at S-CAR* [Conference paper]. School for Conflict Analysis' Conference on Conflict Resolution Practice. George Mason University, Arlington, VA.

Bordogna, C. M. (2019). The effects of boundary-spanning on the development of social capital between faculty members operating transnational higher education partnerships. *Studies in Higher Education, 44*(1), 217–229.

Daudelin, M. W. (1996). Learning from experience through reflection. *Organizational Dynamics, 24*(3), 36–48.

Day, D. V. (2001). Leadership development: A review in context. *Leadership Quarterly, 11*(4), 581–613.

Day, D. (2010). The difficulties of learning from experience and the need for deliberate practice. *Industrial and Organizational Psychology, 3*(1), 41–44. https://doi.org/10.1111/j.1754-9434.2009.01195.x

Dredge, D., & Wray, M. (2012). Exploring the boundary spanning leadership of 'pracademics': The teaching-research-service nexus in sustainable tourism. In C. Schott & M. Fesenmaier (Eds.), *Tourism Education Future Institute 6th meeting* (pp. 23–141). Tourism Education Futures Institute.

Edmondson, A. (1999). Psychological safety and learning behaviour in work teams. *Administrative Science Quarterly, 44*(2), 350–383.

Edmondson, A. (2019). *The fearless organization.* Wiley.

Gopinath, C. (1998). Alternative approach to indigenous Management in India. *Management International Review, 38*(3), 257–275.

Gupta, R. K. (1991). Employees and organizations in India. *Economic and Political Weekly, 26*(21), M68–M76.

Handy, C. (2015). The past is not the future. *EFDM Global Focus, 9*(3), 15–18.

Hart, R. K., Conklin, T. A., & Allen, S. J. (2008). Individual leader development: An appreciative inquiry approach. *Advances in Developing Human Resources, 10*(5), 632–650.

Heifetz, R. (1994). *Leadership without easy answers.* HUP.

Heifetz, R., & Linksy, M. (2002). *Leadership on the line: Staying alive through the dangers of leading.* HUP.

Heifetz, R., Grashow, A., & Linsky, M. (2009). *The practice of adaptive leadership*. HUP.

Hofstede, G. (1983). The cultural relativity of organizational practices and theories. *Journal of International Business Studies, 14*, 75–89.

Hollweck, T., Netolicky, D., Campbell, P., & Schnellert, L. (2020). *Pracademics: Exploring the tensions and opportunities of boundary-spanners who straddle the worlds of academia and practice* [Symposium presentation]. International Congress of School Effectiveness and Improvement (ICSEI), Marrakesh, Morocco.

Hollweck, T., Netolicky, D. M., & Campbell, P. (2022). Guest editorial: Pracademia: Exploring the possibilities, power and politics of boundary-spanners straddling the worlds of practice and scholarship. *Journal of Professional Capital and Community, 7*, 1–5.

Hou, W. C. (2010). Developing Asia's corporate leadership: Challenges and moving forward. In D. Ulrich (Ed.), *Leadership in Asia* (pp. 40–52). McGraw Hill.

Hutchins, R. M. (1970). *The learning society*. Penguin.

Johnson, K. (2015). Behavioral education in the 21st century. *Journal of Organizational Behavior Management, 35*, 135–150.

Kormanik, M. B., Lehner, R. D., & Winnick, T. A. (2009). General competencies for the HRD scholar practitioner: Perspectives from across the profession. *Advances in Developing Human Resources, 11*(4), 486–506.

Lammers, C. J. (1990). Sociology of organisations around the globe: Similarities and differences between American, British, French, German and Dutch brands. *Organisation Studies, 11*(2), 179–205.

McCall, M. W., Jr. (2010). Recasting leadership development. *Industrial and Organizational Psychology, 3*(1), 3–19.

McCauley, C. D., & Van Velsor, E. (2004). Introduction: Our view of leadership development. In C. D. McCauley & E. Van Velsor (Eds.), *The center for creative leadership handbook of leadership development* (pp. 1–22). Jossey Bass.

McClelland, D. C. (1961). *The achieving society*. Van Nostrand.

McDonald, M. P., & Mooney, C. Z. (2011). "Pracademics". Mixing an academic career with practical politics. *PS: Political Science and Politics, 44*(2), 251–253.

McQuillan, N., & McQuillan, M. (2016, April 26–27). *A 'pracademic' approach to enrich the student experience in business management teaching* [Conference presentation]. Association of Business Schools – Learning, Teaching and Student Experience Conference Aston Business School –Birmingham.

Murphy, A., & Fulda, A. (2011). Bridging the gap: Pracademics in foreign policy. *PS: Political Science and Politics, 44*(2), 279–283.

Olivares, O. J., Peterson, G., & Hess, K. P. (2007). An existential-phenomenological framework for understanding leadership development experiences. *Leadership & Organization Development Journal, 28*(1), 76–91.

Owens, L. W. (2016). Reflections of a pracademic: A journey from social work practitioner to academic. *Reflections: Narratives of Professional Helping, 22*(1), 37–43.

Panda, A. (2014). Bringing academic and corporate worlds closer: We need pracademics. *Management and Labour Studies, 39*(2), 140–159.

Panda, A. (2017). Experience-centric leadership development process: Challenges and way forward for organizations in India. *International Journal of Indian Culture and Business Management, 16*(1), 99–116.

Panda, A. (2019). A role to play. *Indian Management, 58*(12), 43–45.

Panda, A., & Gupta, R. K. (2007). Call for developing indigenous organisational theories in India: Setting agenda for future. *International Journal of Indian Culture and Business Management, 1*(1–2), 205–243.

Posner, P. L. (2009). The pracademic: An agenda for re-engaging practitioners and academics. *Public Budgeting and Finance, 29*(1), 12–26.

Posner, S., & Cvitanovic, C. (2019). Evaluating the impacts of boundary-spanning activities at the interface of environmental science and policy: A review of progress and future research needs. *Environmental Science & Policy, 92*, 141–151.

Rosenzweig, P. M. (1994). *National culture and management.* Harvard Business School Publishing.

Rousseau, D. M., & Fried, Y. (2001). Editorial: Location, location, location: Contextualizing organizational research. *Journal of Organizational Behavior, 22*(1), 1–13.

Schneider, J. W. (1985). Social problems theory: The constructionist view. *Annual Review of Psychology, 11*, 209–229.

Schön, D. A. (1973). *Beyond the stable state. Public and private learning in a changing society.* Penguin.

Schön, D. (1983). *The reflective practitioner. How professionals think in action.* Temple Smith.

Sengupta, D. (2022, June 9). *India Inc's dissonance over top B-school recruitment.* Mint. https://www.livemint.com/opinion/columns/india-inc-s-dissonance-over-top-b-school-recruitment-11654793252410.html

Shamir, B., & Eilam, G. (2005). What's your story? A life-stories approach to authentic leadership development. *The Leadership Quarterly, 16*(3), 395–417.

Shyamsunder, A., Anand, S., Punj, A., & Shatdal, A. (2011). Leadership development in organizations in India: The why and how of it (Part I and II). *Vikalpa, 36*(3–4), 61–132.

Sinha, J. B. P. (1968). The n-ach/n-cooperation under limited/unlimited resource conditions. *Journal of Experimental Social Psychology, 4*(2), 233–246.

Søderberg, A. M., & Romani, L. (2017). Boundary-spanners in global partnerships: A case study of an Indian vendor's collaboration with western clients. *Group and Organization Management, 42*(2), 237–278.

Susskind, L. (2013). Confessions of a pracademic: Searching for a virtuous cycle of theory building, teaching, and action research. *Negotiation Journal, 29*(2), 225–237.

Thomas, H., Lee, M., Thomas, L., & Wilson, A. (2014). *Securing the future of management education: Competitive destruction or constructive innovation?* (Vol. 33, pp. 503–519). Emerald Group.

Van Velsor, E., Wilson, M., Criswell, C., & Chandrasekar, A. (2013). Learning to lead: A comparison of developmental events and learning among managers in China, India and the United States. *Asian Business & Management, 12*, 455–476. https://doi.org/10.1057/abm.2013.9

Volpe, M., & Chandler, D. (2001). Resolving and managing conflicts in academic communities: The emerging role of the "Pracademic". *Negotiation Journal, 17*(3), 245–255. https://doi.org/10.1111/j.1571-9979.2001.tb00239.x

Walker, D. H. T. (2010, October 10–13). Being a pracademic – Combining reflective practice with scholarship. *Keynote address AIPM Conference in Darwin.* Accessed through https://www.researchgate.net/profile/Derek-Walker-2/publication/267995102_Being_a_Pracademic_-_Combining_Reflective_Practice_with_Scholarship/links/54727e350cf2d67fc035c772/Being-a-Pracademic-Combining-Reflective-Practice-with-Scholarship.pdf. Accessed 21 May 2023.

Abinash Panda is currently an Associate Professor in the area of Organizational Behaviour and Human Resource Management at the Management Development Institute (MDI), Gurgaon, India. He has a rich and varied experience of more than twenty-five years in corporate, academic, and research roles. Prior to joining MDI, Gurgaon, he worked with: the Indian Institute of Management, Kashipur; the XLRI School of Management, Jamshedpur; and also as a visiting faculty with the Indian Institutes of Management, Indore and Lucknow. He is a graduate from the International University of Japan (IUJ), Japan, specializing in Comparative Business and Management and is a Fellow of Management (MDI). He has published more than 55 research papers in various international and national journals, including Journal of Business Research, Business Strategy and the Environment, International Journal of Productivity and Performance Management, Telematics and Informatics, International Journal of Energy Sector Management, and Review of Behavioural Finance. He has also presented a number of papers in various national and international conferences, including the Academy of Management.

Part IV
Conclusion

Chapter 19
Pracademia: Past, Present, and Where Next?

Jill Dickinson and **Teri-Lisa Griffiths**

This collection has convened a range of contributors from different countries, assorted disciplines, and at varying stages of their pracademic journeys. It has illuminated the diversity and value of knowledge and insights that pracademics can bring with them from practice into academia. The contributors come from a variety of professional backgrounds, including construction and engineering, nursing, accountancy, careers guidance, law, psychology, education, and housing, to name a few. Whilst such disciplines may be diverse, this collection has revealed clear evidence of pracademics' shared beliefs around the value of drawing on their practitioner skills and experience for the benefit of the academy, the students whom they teach (as the potential practitioners of the future), and their peers who may be looking to make similar career transitions. The importance of maintaining links between practice and theory, and connections with practice to sustain research relevance, is also in evidence.

The contributions have re-emphasised the need for Higher Education (HE) to recognise the value of recruiting and providing tailored induction and development opportunities for pracademics. The benefits from the provision of improved transitional support for pracademics, as part of a diverse and responsive academy, can extend to those in leadership and management, traditional career academics, and students. Also, we should not forget the potential advantages for the pracademics themselves who may need reminding of their professional contribution as they navigate their career transitions from practice into academia and engage in continuing

J. Dickinson (✉)
School of Law, University of Leeds, Leeds, UK
e-mail: j.dickinson1@leeds.ac.uk

T.-L. Griffiths
Department of Law & Criminology, Sheffield Hallam University, Sheffield, UK
e-mail: teri-lisa.griffiths@shu.ac.uk

© The Author(s), under exclusive license to Springer Nature
Switzerland AG 2023
J. Dickinson, T.-L. Griffiths (eds.), *Professional Development for Practitioners in Academia*, Knowledge Studies in Higher Education 13,
https://doi.org/10.1007/978-3-031-33746-8_19

professional development. Throughout this concluding section, we will be reflecting on, and drawing together, some of the key themes arising from the collection, and illustrating various points with specific reference to some of the chapters included.

Mirroring the use of multiple terms and/or definitions within extant literature to refer to those who have both practitioner and academic experience, this collection has included an array of designations including "academics with industrial experience" (Forster et al., Chap. 15), "lecturer[s] with first-hand practitioner experience" (Stirk, Chap. 4), and individuals who are "both an academic and an active practitioner" (Wilkinson and Wilkinson, Chap. 5). There are synergies here with our previous research that suggests how pracademics may adopt chameleonic strategies when introducing themselves; tailoring their approach according to their audience (Dickinson et al., 2022). In a similar vein, this collection has also used particular phrases to distinguish pracademics as a group from other academics. For example, Forster et al. refer to 'career academics' as those "with largely theoretical experience and knowledge alone". Conversely, Wilkinson and Wilkinson prefer to refer to themselves as 'accidental academics' rather than 'career academic[s]', suggesting that this is because of the less formally-planned approach that they have taken to career development. They also coin a new phrase, the 'non-pracademic', referring to those academics in disciplines with an applied tradition that have a predominantly pracademic faculty. This presents a challenge to the idea that only pracademics experience insecurity, as a result of their differential career journeys, but we think that this reflects the diversity of experiences for academics and pracademics across different disciplines.

As editors, we perceive this variety of terms as positive, not least because it reveals how individuals are reflecting on their own and others' roles, and the potential for connections between them. It also demonstrates the importance of self-perception across the wide breadth of potential routes, positions, and professional and career development paths that may be taken by current or former practitioners working in the HE sector. Some pracademics, like ourselves, made a formal role transition from practice into academia; one from law and the other from careers guidance. Others hold concurrent positions in practice and academia; for example, one of our contributors (Skea, Chap. 13) is an academic and works in event management. Regardless of the extent of this hybridity, this collection demonstrates how the recruitment of pracademics can support the development of multi-beneficial opportunities. These include, for example, building connections between practice and theory (Johnson and Ellis, Chap. 12; Madhloom and Bradley, Chap. 17; Walsh, Chap. 16; Forster et al., Chap. 15), developing employability (Skea, Chap. 13; Panda, Chap. 18), and cultivating networks (Cadet, Chap. 14; Gurung, Chap. 11; Hodgson, Chap. 3).

Against that backdrop, we should reiterate our view, that pracademics cannot be perceived as a panacea (Eacott, 2022) to the complexities of a HE sector under significant pressure. Whilst they have the potential to play an integral role, it is important to remember that they represent one part within the much larger context that is presented by both their respective institutions and the HE sector as a whole. To make the most of pracademics' skills, experience, knowledge, and insights, HE organisational cultures, structures, and processes do need to support pracademics, career academics, and non-pracademics, to work together in complementary, rather than separate, ways. Opportunities for bringing together these groups as a community, and encouraging them to share experiences and develop common understandings around the value that each brings could form an important part of that.

Within this collection, Kitchener identifies the need to consider the various professional and career pathways that pracademics may choose once they are in their academic roles and the importance of ongoing support. Such opportunities may include, for example, pursuing leadership and/or management, and within either a teaching and learning, or research pathway, or indeed a combination of both. As Obembe recommends, some pracademics may have reached the decision to move into academia some time before they actually make the transition. This may give them valuable time and space for developing additional insights around career planning and progression. The editors recall moving into HE and quickly being faced with multiple expectations around professional development; for example, through completion of a teaching qualification, achievement of recognition through Fellowship of Advance HE,[1] and alongside preparation of teaching and learning materials. These challenges could seem equally daunting and exciting for the novice pracademic as they look to establish themselves in their new role. Another contributor, Taylor, explores how the benefits of building external networks can help the pracademic to face such challenges.

As contributors Hunter and Carr note, universities are also increasingly requiring prospective candidates to hold a doctorate. Whilst this is something that was traditionally required by research-intensive institutions (forming part of the Russell Group),[2] Hunter and Carr discuss how it is becoming the norm for teaching-focused and applied, post-1992 institutions[3] despite changes in external funding, regulations, and university structures that have resulted in rising numbers of teaching-only posts. We have also seen increasing instances of institutions marketing themselves as both research and teaching organisations; for example, by offering to provide "research-intensive learning and teaching" (University of Birmingham, 2017) or "research informed teaching" (University of Plymouth, n.d.). Indeed, contributors Forster et al. explore how practitioners were traditionally appointed to roles within post-1992 institutions, and the editors have, anecdotally, seen an increase in pracademics being recruited to Russell Group universities. This all points to a blurring of

---

[1] 'Advance HE is a member-led, sector owned charity that works with institutions and higher education across the world to improve higher education for staff, students and society.' It awards fellowship in recognition of professionalism. (Advance HE, 2020)

[2] The Russell Group comprises 24 universities across the UK who collectively market themselves as 'world-class and research-intensive universities' based on their research, teaching and learning experience, and HE-industry links. (Russell Group, n.d.).

[3] Post-1992 refers to HEIs in the UK who were granted university status through the Further and Higher Education Act 1992. This can include both former polytechnic colleges and institutions that have been created since 1992.

boundaries between different types of institutions and the potential for both increased opportunities and barriers for pracademics who have may have practitioner, teaching, and research experience, but who may not have the support to complete a PhD whilst still in practice.

In terms of professional development more generally, this collection has highlighted the benefits for pracademics in adopting a combined reflective and reflexive approach. As we note in our chapter, one possible method for supporting individuals' self-development and professional growth is through identifying, and focusing on, objects that hold particular meaning for them. Another contributor, Gurung, discusses how pracademics may develop specific strategies around reflection whilst they are in practice and then bring these with them into academia, for example as they engage with research. In a similar vein, Hodgson identifies the importance of reflection for building networks, particularly to support completion of doctoral studies.

Drawing these themes together, this collection has highlighted how pracademics from varied disciplinary backgrounds share common values. The contributions collectively demonstrate the potential for pracademics to play a key role in HE as part of a diverse and collaborative academy. By promoting the value of pracademia through this collection, we hope that it helps to push the creation of tailored induction and continuing professional development opportunities higher up institutional agendas.

Looking to the future, we would like to encourage more people to become involved in the ongoing dialogue around pracademia to help bring about evidence-informed sector, institutional, and local change. Key focal points include:

- the potentially diverse roles that pracademics can play within HE;
- the need for increased recognition of the value that this group can bring; and
- the necessity to move towards a more inclusive outlook that recognises the pracademic role as integral, but just one of many elements that are needed, to help ensure that the HE sector meets societal and individual needs.

References

Advance HE. (2020). *Helping HE shape its future*. Available from: https://www.advance-he.ac.uk/about-us

Dickinson, J., Fowler, A., & Griffiths, T. (2022). Pracademics? Exploring transitions and professional identities in higher education. *Studies in Higher Education, 47*(2), 290–304. https://doi.org/10.1080/03075079.2020.174412

Eacott, S. (2022). Pracademia: An answer but not the answer to an enduring question. *Journal of Professional Capital and Community, 7*(1), 57–70. https://doi.org/10.1108/JPCC-12-2020-0100

Russell Group. (n.d.). *Our universities*. https://russellgroup.ac.uk/about/our-universities/

University of Birmingham. (2017). *MicroCPD: Defining and delivering 'research-intensive learning and teaching' at the University of Birmingham*. https://www.birmingham.ac.uk/news/2017/microcpd-defining-and-delivering-research-intensive-learning-and-teaching-at-the-university-of-birmingham

University of Plymouth. (n.d.). *Research-informed teaching*. https://www.plymouth.ac.uk/about-us/teaching-and-learning/guidance-and-resources/research-informed-teaching

Dr Jill Dickinson is an Associate Professor in Law at the University of Leeds. A former Solicitor specialising in Real Estate, Jill's research interests encompass place-making, learning landscapes, and professional development. As an SFHEA, Jill was selected to review the Advance HE Global Teaching Excellence Awards and her approach to research has been recognized through the Emerald Literati Awards.

Teri-Lisa Griffiths is a Senior Lecturer in Criminology at Sheffield Hallam University. Her teaching is focused on the development of student employability and academic skills, working with external partners to provide relevant and high-quality experiences for students. Her research interests are student engagement and professional development. As a former careers adviser, Teri-Lisa is interested in how education and professional identity can influence career and development choices. She is a co-founder of the pracademia community of practice.

Index

Milton Keynes UK
Ingram Content Group UK Ltd.
UKHW020604130923
428585UK00001B/11